"The masses of Italian immigrants who arrived in New York City in the late nineteenth and early twentieth centuries found Irish Americans everywhere in charge: as cops and robbers, saints and sinners, and wary gatekeepers of nearly all the occupations the newcomers hoped to pursue. By Paul Moses's delightfully insightful, warm, and witty account, ethnic tribalism proved no match for enterprising immigrants who saw their opportunities and took them."
—James T. Fisher, author of *On the Irish Waterfront: The Crusader, the Movie, and the Soul of the Port of New York*

"*An Unlikely Union* is an unlikely success. . . . It is a vivid history of conflict . . . and then it turns into a romance mediated by food, religion, and burning proximity. It is a Shakespearean tale, with occasional episodes of *Romeo and Juliet* but the overarching plot of *Much Ado about Nothing*, where the intense mutual distaste of the hero and heroine turns into an equally intense and enduring bond."
—Robert Viscusi, general editor of the American edition of *Italoamericana: The Literature of the Great Migration, 1880–1943*

An Unlikely Union

An Unlikely Union

The Love-Hate Story
of New York's Irish and Italians

Paul Moses

NEW YORK UNIVERSITY PRESS
New York and London

NEW YORK UNIVERSITY PRESS
New York and London
www.nyupress.org

References to Internet websites (URLs) were accurate at the time of writing.
Neither the author nor New York University Press is responsible for URLs that
may have expired or changed since the manuscript was prepared.

Library of Congress Cataloging-in-Publication Data
Moses, Paul An unlikely union : the love-hate story of
New York's Irish and Italians / Paul Moses.
pages cm   Includes bibliographical references and index.
ISBN 978-1-4798-7130-8 (cl : alk. paper)
1. Italian Americans—New York (State)—New York—History.
2. Irish Americans—New York (State)—New York—History.
3. Italian Americans—New York (State)—New York—Ethnic identity.
4. Irish Americans—New York (State)—New York—Ethnic identity.
5. New York (N.Y.)—Ethnic relations. I. Title.
F128.9.I8M67 2015
973'.0451—dc23   2015000490

New York University Press books are printed on acid-free paper,
and their binding materials are chosen for strength and durability.
We strive to use environmentally responsible suppliers and materials
to the greatest extent possible in publishing our books.

Manufactured in the United States of America

Also available as an ebook

To Maureen; to Matthew and Caitlin, our Irish-Italian kids;

and to Frank and Marie Bradley.

Go raibh maith agaibh.

Grazie mille.

CONTENTS

PART III. SHARING THE STAGE:
Politics and Entertainment

PART IV. AT THE ALTAR:
Becoming Family

ACKNOWLEDGMENTS

Sometimes a story just takes hold of a writer and demands of him that it be told. This book would never have resulted without the help of many people. I thank them, starting with the literary agent Steve Hanselman, a steadfast supporter of this off-the-beaten-path idea from the start. Julia Serebrinsky offered excellent advice on the proposal. My editor at New York University Press, Jennifer Hammer, grasped immediately what I was trying to do and made very wise suggestions on the manuscript. Thanks also go to Adam Bohannon for his creative cover design and to Constance Grady and Rosalie Morales Kearns for their important assistance.

I am grateful to Brooklyn College and the City University of New York for a sabbatical that gave me time to immerse myself in research. My colleague Ken Estey provided crucial help, and a writing group with Jocelyn Wills and Martha Nadell was helpful. Fabio Girelli-Carasi made it fun to study Italian. Fellow members of the college's Presidential Advisory Committee on Italian American Affairs, especially Robert Viscusi, encouraged me along the way.

The New York Public Library's research collections were essential to this book, as were the archives of the Center for Migration Studies and the help of the center's archivist, Mary Elizabeth Brown. Dr. Brown's writings on the Catholic Church and immigrants were also of great value. I am indebted to the staff of the

Brooklyn College Library for tracking down many hard-to-find sources and to the Archives of the Archdiocese of New York. I am also grateful for the opportunity to do research in the Tamiment Library and Robert F. Wagner Labor Archives at New York University; the Criminal Trial Transcripts Collection of the Lloyd Sealy Library at John Jay College; and the New York City Municipal Archive and City Hall Library. Online databases such as Ancestry.com, the Brooklyn Public Library's *Brooklyn Eagle* archive, the Old Fulton Postcards website for New York State newspaper articles, the Unz.org site for magazines, Archive.org, Google Books, the Italian Genealogical Group, and the Library of Congress's *Chronicling America* were important research tools. I am indebted to all those who made these resources available.

Two anonymous reviewers at New York University Press provided expert readings of the manuscript and many important suggestions. Anne O'Connor helped me to understand how the Risorgimento was viewed in Ireland. I'm grateful to Jim Bradley, Marie Bradley, Susan Burke, Linda Cronin-Gross, Tony De-Marco, Mary Macchiarola, and John O'Beirne Ranelagh for telling me the family stories that appear in this book. Many, many other people shared their Irish-Italian stories with me, including Susan Healy, Anna Hunt, Patrick McNamara, Jim Mulvaney, Aldo Orlando, Sherry Pacelli Haddox, a descendant of the labor leader Tito Pacelli, and Maureen Viani. My thanks also go to the late Michael and Helen Alba, Sister Maryellen Blumlein and the Sisters of Charity of New York, Joe Calderone, Father Jim Collins, Michael Collins, Regina Collins, Frank DeRosa, Kate Donovan, Jim Dwyer, Kate Feighery, James T. Fisher, Sister Maureen Foy, Joe Giordano, Tim Healy, Melinda Henneberger, Father Brian Jordan, Bill McGarvey, Anthony Mancini, James Moses, Len Muscato, the late Nunzio Pernicone, John Power, Peter Powers, Betty Smith, and Bernadette Walter. So many other people encouraged me along the way.

My father, Bernard L. Moses, was an inspiration to me as I worked on this book, both before and after his death on April 27,

2012. My mother, Anne Moses, offered family stories I'd never heard before and helped make the New York of distant decades come alive.

Writers often complete their work by acknowledging that they never could have done it without their spouse and children. That's literally true for me. I never would have conceived of this book had it not been for my happy Irish-Italian marriage with the former Maureen Collins and the pride we take in the children of that union, Matthew and Caitlin. For that reason, I've dedicated this book to them, and to my earliest model of an Irish-Italian marriage, Marie and Frank Bradley.

*   *   *

Grateful acknowledgment is made for permission to quote from the following works:

Center for Migration Studies: *For the Love of Immigrants: Migration Writings and Letters of Bishop John Baptist Scalabrini, 1839–1905.*
Tamiment Library: Elizabeth Gurley Flynn Papers.
International Publishers: *The Rebel Girl: An Autobiography, My First Life, 1906–1926.*

Introduction

O n those chilly March days when I walked home with the other boys from Mary Queen of Heaven School in the Flatlands section of Brooklyn in the mid-1960s, someone would occasionally shout, "Rumble!" This shout would go out in March because it was the month of Saint Patrick's Day, and his sainthood naturally needed to be celebrated with a street fight between the Irish kids and the Italian kids. I cast my lot with the Italian kids, for my ancestry is Italian on my mother's side of the family. There was no percentage, in choosing sides for a scuffle among Catholic schoolboys, in acknowledging that two of my grandparents were Jewish. I kept this fact a secret (rather awkwardly, my last name being Moses).

Nothing ever came of the calls for an Irish-Italian rumble, and all was quickly forgotten as we boys went on our way. What I realize now, however, is that the challenge to duke it out on East Fifty-Seventh Street recalled our collective history in much the same way that we pretended to shoot Germans and "Japs" in World War II combat. It faintly echoed the days when the Irish and Italians of New York rumbled for real—when they fought over jobs or turf, and when they jockeyed for power in the church, in politics, in unions, and in the civil service.

Those battles were mostly forgotten—although not entirely, and by some, not at all—by the time I was growing up in the 1960s.

Intermarriage between Americans of Irish and Italian ancestry in the years after World War II had changed everything.

The story of this unlikely union—how New York's Irish and Italians learned to love each other after decades of hostility and ethnic rivalry—is told in this book. For me, it is a personal story, since I benefited from its legacy. When I walked down the aisle from the altar of St. Vincent de Paul Roman Catholic Church in Elmont, New York, on August 7, 1976, with the former Maureen Collins at my side in her bridal gown, there was no trace of regret to be discerned from my family that I had married someone who, with her red hair, her lovely freckles, and her name, so clearly had her roots in Ireland. Nor was there any objection from the Collins side of the aisle that the darkly tanned, unemployed student their pretty, twenty-three-year-old registered nurse had just married had his roots in southern Italy and German Jewry. That's unremarkable, of course, but not so many decades before, a union such as ours could well have provoked anger and hostility in our respective tribes.

To sociologists, this changed attitude is the result of assimilation: the children, grandchildren, or (in Maureen's case) great-grandchildren of immigrants from once-warring ethnic groups were increasingly likely to intermarry as the new generations lost their attachment to the Old World and Americanized. This was true enough in our case and many others'. But to describe that process solely in such dry terms would miss the human drama of what happens when two peoples learn to put aside ingrained resentment, mingle, blur their social boundaries, and become one.

This book tells that story. Not my story, but the story of millions of people of Irish and Italian ancestry who trace their roots to places like Transfiguration Church on Mott Street—once an Irish Catholic parish—or to the docks of Brooklyn, the tenements of Mulberry Street and East Harlem, or the long lines outside the Bowery office of "Big Tim" Sullivan, the Tammany politician who gave out thousands of pairs of free shoes to both the Irish and Italians. It is a story about people: of Giuseppe Garibaldi, who left his exile on Staten Island to liberate Italy, much to the dismay of

Irish New Yorkers offended that the pope's land was confiscated; of Sister Monica McInerney, an Irish American who warned Italian girls in St. Patrick's School that they'd wind up working in garment factories if they didn't study; of Francis L. Corrao, Brooklyn's first Italian American assistant district attorney, who investigated organized crime in Sicily in 1908 only to return and quit with an angry blast at an Irish American boss he believed treated him as an inferior; and of the radicals Elizabeth Gurley Flynn and Carlo Tresca, whose tempestuous Irish-Italian love affair gave the yellow press something to write about. It is a story of saints and sinners. Among these saints, one is canonized: Mother Frances Xavier Cabrini, who refused to return to Italy after the Irish American archbishop of New York, Michael Corrigan, told her to do so the day after her landing. Among the sinners: Al Capone, who was married to an Irish American woman and who tore the heart out of the Irish "White Hand" gang on the Brooklyn waterfront by murdering Richard Lonergan in 1925.

So many people share Irish and Italian ancestry that it is easy to forget the depth of the bitterness that once existed between Irish Americans and Italian Americans. The great Irish American newspaperman Jimmy Breslin put it this way in his 1970 book *The Gang That Couldn't Shoot Straight*: "Among the most overlooked racial problems in the country is the division between Irish and Italians."[1]

The history of this long Irish-Italian wrestling match is plenty colorful, but that story alone would not have been reason enough for me to write this book. What moved me to do so is that in this world of frayed and raw racial and ethnic connections, the Irish and the Italians of New York offer a story of how peace was made. Having spent some two decades in daily journalism in New York and as a lifelong Brooklynite, I'm certainly familiar with the old tribal conflicts that dwell within the shiny steel-and-glass exterior of the city's civic life. Ethnic conflict is part of the urban turf. The news from the Irish and Italians is that it can be overcome.

This peace was achieved through love and intermarriage and because, in the fluid world of American democracy, the Irish and

Italians were so often thrown together, whether or not they liked being near each other. They clashed in parishes, workplaces, neighborhoods, and politics. But over time, these same arenas came to unite them. The Italians had no choice but to deal with the Irish, who were their union leaders, foremen, schoolteachers, cops, and ward heelers. The Irish had to deal with the Italians if they were to raise the status of the Catholic faith in Protestant America.

Glimmers of peace can be glimpsed even in early accounts that note the acrimony between the Irish and Italians. Writing in 1905, the U.S. census official Eliot Lord noted "the jealousy of the Irish at the intrusion and their free-spoken jibes at the 'Dago,'" a slur once used for Spanish immigrants, apparently based on the common name Diego, and now adapted to Italians. But, he added, "There is less clashing between the two nationalities than might be expected," owing to their "good nature." He added that "the common religion is also a bond of union."[2]

Lord's observation about the role of the Catholic Church was an ultimately correct but bravely optimistic statement at the time. The unenthusiastic reception the Irish-run institutional church gave to the Italians when they began arriving in large numbers in the 1880s is reflected in the Reverend John Talbot Smith's official history of the Archdiocese of New York, also published in 1905: "The Italians showed very little interest in religion after their arrival, and acted as if the Catholic Church did not exist in the United States."[3]

Religion plays an important role in the story of the Irish and Italians. They were baptized in the same faith, but clashing senses for the sacred contributed to their conflict. One might expect construction workers to get into brawls to protect their jobs, but an uncivil war of words was also fought between Irish pastors and Italian priests. The construction workers' battles led to the courthouse, an arena that favored the Irish. The priests' battles went all the way to the Vatican, an arena that favored the Italians. Yet, in the years after World War II, the church played a key role in bringing the Irish and Italians together, and to the altar in marriage.

While the church took many decades to unite its Irish and Italian members, there were shrewd leaders in other New York institutions—the underworld and politics—who quickly saw the possibilities. The gang leader Paul Kelly, in particular, mastered the art of Irish-Italian deal making. Born Franco Antonio Paolo Vaccarelli, he had his name legally changed to Paul Kelly. Starting in the 1890s, he headed the Five Points gang, which morphed into a supposed sports club, the Paul Kelly Association. Its main event came on election days, when members earned their drinking money by fixing the vote for the Bowery's powerful boss, "Big Tim" Sullivan. Big Tim protected Kelly's gang from the police, allowing its reign of violence on the streets of lower Manhattan. He also was a master at courting Italian voters, wooing them with his own stories of growing up in poverty and passing legislation that made Columbus Day a New York State holiday.

After a rival thug nearly assassinated Kelly, he put aside his gang activities and began a second career as a respected labor leader, organizing Italian waterfront workers and becoming a vice president of the International Longshoremen's Association. He changed his name back to Vaccarelli. When he died in 1936, his obituary in the *New York Times* made no mention of his criminal past as Paul Kelly.[4] And when Big Tim died under mysterious circumstances in 1913, Italian immigrants were shoulder-to-shoulder with the Irish among the fifty thousand mourners, weeping for their benefactor.

In the same way, the Irish and Italians both wept at the funeral of Lieutenant Joseph Petrosino, a star detective who was assassinated while on a not-so-undercover assignment in Sicily in 1909. Once routinely dubbed "the Dago" when detective bosses called him to crime scenes, the Italian-born detective became the greatest hero in the history of the Irish-dominated New York Police Department after he was slain on his dangerous solo assignment.

But such moments of Irish-Italian reconciliation were not common in those days. The Irish came first. Many arrived in the late eighteenth century. A good number were Protestants from Ulster;

some were Catholics. Then came a huge influx of Catholic Irish in the 1840s and 1850s, fleeing the Great Famine. After struggling for acceptance in New York, the Irish felt they were being invaded when large numbers of Italians began arriving in 1880 to the impoverished Five Points section of lower Manhattan, looking for housing and work. It's natural for sympathy to go to the underdog in such situations, but the Irish were underdogs too—and certainly felt that way. As the *New York Times* declared in 1880 when opposing William R. Grace's winning campaign to become the city's first Irish Catholic mayor, New York was "an American Protestant city"—one that the "average successful Irish Catholic" was not fit to lead.[5] We cannot understand the Irish reaction to the Italians without considering the enormous obstacles Irish Catholics faced in establishing themselves in Protestant America. The Irish spearheaded the battle for Catholic acceptance.

The early Irish in New York mostly lived in severe poverty. They were the ones hit hardest in time of epidemic or food shortage. After building their church, creating a school system, and seizing control of the city's political machinery, the Irish were finally beginning to make it when the Italians arrived, willing to do their jobs for lower pay and longer hours. Resentment and violence followed.

The old tensions sometimes surface nowadays, usually in the form of jokes and teasing banter on March 17 and 19, when the Irish celebrate Saint Patrick's Day and the Italians mark the Feast of Saint Joseph. In my Brooklyn parish, where people are mostly of Italian or Irish ancestry, a single dance is often held to celebrate both dates, with corned beef and cabbage served along with pasta and meatballs. The parish, Saint Columba, was founded in the 1960s by an Irish American pastor with a stentorian voice. It is said that while he named the parish for an Irish saint, he was careful to choose one whose name ended in a vowel, which pleased his Italian parishioners.

In many ways, the Irish and Italians have become family. But, as in a family, the old hurts can persist. As I worked on this book, I received more clear-cut warnings to be fair—from friends of either Irish or Italian ancestry—than I have for any other story I've told in decades of writing about the subjects once considered too controversial to discuss in polite society, politics and religion.

And so in fairness, we must remember that if the Irish of a century ago treated the immigrant Italians as inferior, so too did the rest of society, and in harsher terms. The southern Italians' migration from desperate conditions in their homeland coincided with an era when intellectuals endorsed now-offensive theories about superior races and nationalities. Southern Italians were placed near the bottom of this racist hierarchy. Yet despite many barriers, the Irish and the Italians eventually became two of the most intermarried ethnic groups in America.

Other ethnic and racial groups also contributed to the making of a mighty city, of course. For purposes of this book, I've focused on important groups such as Jews, blacks, and Hispanics only to the extent that they were a factor in the Irish-Italian relationship. As intermarriage continues to become ever more typical in American life, perhaps more books will be written on relationships between specific ethnic and racial groups and the dual ethnicities that have resulted.

The reason often offered for Irish-Italian intermarriage is that New York was a "melting pot," at least for the generations of European immigrants who arrived in the nineteenth and early twentieth centuries. That notion was challenged in the 1963 classic *Beyond the Melting Pot*, in which Nathan Glazer and Daniel Patrick Moynihan, focusing on blacks, Puerto Ricans, Jews, Italians, and Irish in New York, argued that ethnicities retained their individual identities from one generation to the next. Other experts have argued that there was a "triple melting pot" based on religion—Catholics, Protestants, and Jews each marrying within their own religion—or that the real determinant for intermarriage is whether people from different ethnic groups live close to each other. New York's first African American mayor, David N. Dinkins, brought this debate into politics with his multicultural vision of the city. "This city is not a melting pot but a gorgeous mosaic," he often said in his 1989 mayoral campaign.

The "melting pot" metaphor is, as many have noted, an imperfect one. The image—a crucible heated to purify metals—makes it sound as if the process of assimilating and mixing immigrants is much more certain and scientific than it really is. The chemical reaction in a crucible is predetermined by the ingredients added and the heat applied. The "melting pot" metaphor leaves out the unpredictable, unscientific, human element—and it is this very human story of how two peoples mixed that I tell here.

PART I

In the Basement

The Church as a Battleground

"Garibaldi and His Hordes"

Giuseppe Garibaldi would not be the last Italian to learn after arrival in New York that he had to reckon with the power of the Irish.

The future Italian liberator came to the city in the summer of 1850 at the low point in his struggle, fleeing a disastrous military defeat in Rome. Italian nationalists had taken the city from Pope Pius IX, only to lose it again. Garibaldi had fought valiantly on the barricades to hold the city for the nationalists, then fled when it fell as forces from France and Austria rallied to the pope's aid. While evading the Austrian army in a series of hairbreadth escapes, he lost his wife, Anita, to illness. Hurting both emotionally and physically, he was unable to move his right arm because of severe rheumatism that worsened during his thirty-three-day passage from Liverpool.

Still, he was "the world renowned Garibaldi," a man who "will be welcomed by those who know him as becomes his chivalrous character and his services in behalf of Liberty," as the *New York Tribune* put it. Many New Yorkers were eager to greet him as a hero for his fight against Old World despots.

Even so, the *New York Herald* warned, Garibaldi was likely to incur the wrath of Bishop John Hughes, the tough-minded chieftain of the rapidly growing Irish Catholic population, when he arrived. The city's Common Council showed no interest in welcoming Garibaldi. The *Herald* averred that since the Italian revolutionaries had dared to oppose the pope, "the petty politicians, fearing the influence of Bishop Hughes, are silent about their efforts in the cause of freedom."[1]

Were it not for attacks on the pope, it might be expected that a man like John Hughes would have had a soft spot for Garibaldi and his liberation movement. Having grown up in County Tyrone with the legacy of British penal laws, he knew what it was to live under oppressive foreign domination. Those laws resulted in a massive transfer of land and wealth from Irish Catholics to Protestants in the seventeenth and eighteenth centuries, with Catholics barred from acquiring property unless they converted. The rural Irish became tenant farmers, with tiny plots of land and without access to the common grazing pastures they had traditionally used. British landlords profited by selling Irish-grown food to industrializing England. Against that background, the disastrous potato crop failure that began in 1845 turned into a massive, history-transforming catastrophe. By 1851, the Irish population had dropped by about two million. More than a million died of starvation and related diseases, and many more people migrated. The population continued to dwindle for decades. One consequence of the Great Famine was that New York turned increasingly into an Irish Catholic city, despite its powerful anti-Catholic undercurrent. In New York, as in the nearby city of Brooklyn, a quarter of the population was Irish by 1860. Hughes was their leader, and he never forgot the long suffering of the Irish or their humiliation at Protestant hands.[2]

A well-built former day laborer who spoke without the brogue of his native land, Hughes took part in a New York fundraiser for a planned insurrection in Ireland in 1848, ruefully aware that encouraging warfare clashed with his role as a bishop. "My contribution shall be for a shield, not a sword; but you can contribute for what you choose," he said as he donated five hundred dollars. He was embarrassed when the rebellion quickly failed.[3]

Archbishop John Hughes circa 1863, the year before his death. J. B. Forrest Engraving. Library of Congress.

While Hughes was not shy about supporting rebels in Ireland, he condemned the Italian revolt for its attack on the pope. The publisher Horace Greeley, present when Hughes put down his money for the Irish rebellion, needled him for opposing Italian freedom. But to Hughes, an attack on the pope was an attack on the Catholic faith.

So he swung into action, assailing the "sacrilegious invaders" who had dared to drive the pope from Rome. "They wield the stiletto, and sacrifice by assassination the human victims who are to propitiate the goddess of Young Liberty in Italy," Hughes wrote, accusing Greeley of overlooking Italian atrocities against the church.[4]

In a follow-up letter published in the *New York Courier and Enquirer*, Hughes attacked one of the city's most prominent Italians, G. F. Secchi di Casali, who had come to New York from Piacenza in northern Italy six years earlier and founded the newspaper *L'Eco d'Italia*, or *Echo of Italy*, in 1849 to support the Italian cause. The bishop noted that Secchi di Casali "had volunteered his able pen to sustain Mr. Greeley's view of Italian affairs." He continued,

> Mr. Casali is an Italian, and professes to be a Catholic, although the spirit of a decided enemy to Catholic faith breathes through all I have seen from his pen . . . he is mistaken, if he supposes that American Protestants will respect him the more for the infidel sneers which he utters against the Catholic religion, while he has not the Saxon candor and moral courage to disavow the outward profession of it.

Hughes also assailed a small group of Irish Catholic New Yorkers who planned to meet with the aim of raising funds for the Italian revolution. "I have a pretty good idea of what description of Irish Catholics will compose such a meeting—Irish Catholics *à la New York Nation*, who imagine themselves patriotic simply because they are not religious," he wrote in the same letter.[5] The *New York Freeman's Journal*, a paper Hughes started and then sold in 1848 to the aggressively outspoken Episcopalian convert James McMaster, carried on the fight. It denounced the Italians as false patriots, reckless killers, and political quacks.

And so the line of battle was set. From Hughes's point of view, even a great freedom fighter like Giuseppe Garibaldi was on the wrong side of the barricades. The deepest political aspirations of the Irish and the Italians conflicted—they were tied up in diametrically opposed views of the pope. For Italians who dreamed of freeing their native land from the dominance of hated foreign powers such as Austria, the Catholic Church was an obstacle. Pope Pius, after initially raising the nationalists' hopes that he would support their cause, seemed to retreat into the hurtful past when he continued the Vatican's alliances with foreign royalty. Italian nationalists treated this as a betrayal, and realized that to achieve their goals, they had to conquer Rome itself and the surrounding papal states. This meant going to war against the pope and the armies of his formidable allies in Austria, Spain, and France.

At the same time, for the Irish who dreamed of freeing their island from centuries of unjust British rule, Catholicism was fused with national identity. The Catholic Irish had clung to the faith of their fathers even when the crown had tried to subjugate them by outlawing the practice of "popery."[6] And then came the Great Famine, changing the course of Irish history in many ways. One result, beyond prompting a massive migration that filled lower Manhattan with a ragged, impoverished people, was that the Irish would hold ever more fervently to their faith. Defending it meant everything. In 1850 the typical Irish Catholic in New York would be unlikely to know an Italian, since there were so few in the city. But anyone who read a newspaper would know that the Italians had gone to war with the pope, a fact that would color the Irish Catholic view of the Italians in New York from the very beginnings of their relationship.

* * *

There were just 853 Italians living in New York in 1850, while more than a quarter of the city's population of 515,547 was Irish. (Census data don't distinguish between Protestant and Catholic Irish.)[7] From its small numbers, the Italian community produced a committee of prominent men to welcome Garibaldi, including Felice Foresti, a white-haired professor of Italian literature at Columbia College whom the Austrians had imprisoned for eighteen years; General Giuseppe Avezzana, who had defended Rome with

Garibaldi; and the inventor Anthony Meucci, who is often credited with having invented the telephone ahead of Alexander Graham Bell.

Reporters scrutinized the hero: "Garibaldi is not so ferocious in appearance as some engravings have represented him to be; he has fair hair, and a red beard," the *Herald* remarked. "He is of middle stature, and of pleasant countenance, with eagle eyes."

The newspapers heralded plans for Mayor Caleb Woodhull to receive Garibaldi at the Astor House, a leading hotel on lower Broadway. French and German socialists jumped in with their own plans for a parade. But Garibaldi wanted so much to avoid a fuss that when he cleared quarantine on Staten Island on August 4, 1850, he didn't alert anyone. Finding refuge north of the city in Hastings-on-Hudson, he wrote a letter on August 7 in which he begged off from the planned celebration for health reasons. Nor could he foresee a time when he would be well enough for such an event.

Both Bishop Hughes and James McMaster avoided commenting on the presence of the Italian hero in their midst. If the suspicions of the New York papers were right, Hughes was working behind the scenes to discourage any outpouring for Garibaldi. Meanwhile, McMaster continued using his newspaper to assail the Risorgimento, the "resurgence" aimed at unifying Italy politically and recovering its cultural prestige.

In October, Garibaldi moved from Manhattan to Staten Island to live with Meucci in the village of Clifton. Garibaldi wanted to work, and Meucci came up with the idea of opening a sausage factory. When that business failed, Garibaldi worked in a candle factory started by the enterprising Meucci. For recreation, he went fishing with Meucci in a small boat with a sail painted in red, white, and green. He also hunted in the wooded Dongan Hills near Staten Island's eastern shore, south of what would one day be the Staten Island Expressway. This outing led to his arrest for violating a minor town ordinance—a case the magistrate quickly voided when told who Garibaldi was. Garibaldi took walks on

Richmond Terrace on Staten Island's north shore, went to the market in Stapleton, a village on the island's northeast corner, across the harbor from lower Manhattan, and played bocce on New York Avenue, near the shore. His neighbors, though aware of his fame, viewed him as a simple workingman. This quiet period helped Garibaldi to recover from his jarring wartime experiences. In any case, it would have done him little good to spend his days rousing New York's Italians to his cause since their numbers were so small. There were many Irish to oppose him, however, and Garibaldi's low profile in Staten Island allowed him to avoid a useless conflict with them. Instead, he prepared himself for the revolutionary struggles that were still to come.

Giuseppe Garibaldi ultimately returned to fighting in Italy, conquering Sicily and southern Italy in 1860 in a stunning triumph that delighted most Americans, especially the few Italians among them. But it scandalized Irish Catholics, who could see that the Italian nationalists were advancing again toward the pope in Rome.

* * *

While Garibaldi lived with quiet dignity in New York, that wasn't the case for another visiting Italian revolutionary. The turncoat priest Alessandro Gavazzi, known for his fiery orations against the Catholic Church, received a hero's welcome in the New York papers when he arrived on March 20, 1853. He had been invited to America by Protestant organizations campaigning to win over Catholic converts, and his slashing attacks on Pius IX and on core Catholic beliefs contributed to "Know Nothing" sentiment against Catholic immigrants from Ireland and Germany.

Gavazzi was greeted with prolonged applause and a flutter of waving handkerchiefs—"with an enthusiasm we have seldom witnessed," the *Times* said—when introduced at the Broadway Tabernacle, several blocks north of City Hall on Broadway near Worth Street, on the evening of March 23, 1853. Six pillars encircled the space around one of America's most powerful pulpits, and beyond them were 2,400 packed seats. From this, the first of his many lectures, Gavazzi seemed especially interested in provoking the Irish—with the aim, as he put it, of saving them from the pope.

"The Popish religion is the personification of the Monarchical Government," he charged. "In your country, this large Irish emigration is intended to overthrow your American freedom." These were obvious fighting words, hurled in the face of now-Archbishop Hughes—who, organizers later discovered, was present in the audience in disguise. Even so, Hughes did not respond directly.

But Patrick Lynch, editor of the *Irish American*, was disgusted at what he read in the morning papers and sent an earnest letter of protest to the *Times*. Lynch, who had emigrated from Limerick in 1847, said it was clear that Gavazzi had "aimed at exciting and directing the Protestant animosity of Americans against Irish Roman Catholics."

After nearly a month of crowded speaking engagements, Gavazzi decided to provoke the Irish to their faces, running a free event so that the impoverished immigrants would attend. A handsome, tall man with long, dark hair, Gavazzi wore black robes with a red cross emblazoned in the center of his chest. He argued for the superiority of Protestant countries over Catholic ones. "Everywhere, my dear brethren, the Papists are poor, miserable, unclean; and the Protestants, rich and prosperous," he declared, to a storm of hisses from the Irish, many of them Famine survivors.

He recounted his travels in Ireland ten months earlier. In Belfast, he went on, Protestants had established many factories, while the Catholics had little. Wherever he went in Ireland, Gavazzi said, he saw filthy, miserably furnished Catholic cottages side by side with neat, well-furnished Protestant cottages. The Catholics always blamed the English for their poverty, but instead they should "reproach your priests, who oppress and rob you," Gavazzi urged, insisting that the Irish enjoyed liberty under the British. The priest echoed a common British response to the Famine: the Irish were poor because of their own flaws and would not have been starving if they were more disciplined.

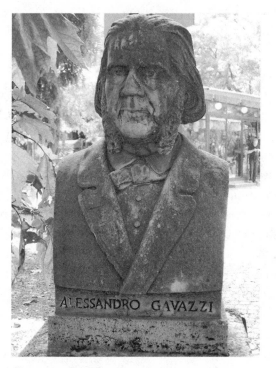

Alessandro Gavazzi is among the heroes of the
Risorgimento memorialized in busts on Rome's
Janiculum Hill, overlooking the Vatican. Paul
Moses photo.

With factions in the crowd battling each other with hisses and
cheers—and with police making arrests in the midst of disorder—
Gavazzi spoke of his visit to St. Patrick's Purgatory, a traditional
pilgrimage location in County Donegal where penitents washed
themselves in the waters of Patrick's well. Gavazzi provoked much
laughter and competing hissing when he observed that he "knew
of no use for St. Patrick's Purgatory, other than to wash Irishmen,
who sometimes never wash themselves in their lives." The lecture
ended with shouts of "Bravo" and loud applause.

Lynch penned yet another letter to the *Times*, saying that Gavazzi "is betrayed by impulse and hot blood into wild, rash and

vehement oratorical flourishes." He added, "I look on it as passing strange, that Father Gavazzi should become a crusader against the Irish in America. They have not (as far as I know) offered him an injury, or done him a wrong."[8] It was indeed "passing strange" that two oppressed peoples who had relatively little to do with each other in the scheme of world affairs should find that their deep aspirations for freedom conflicted so intensely. And it was about to get worse.

In June 1853, Gavazzi lectured in Quebec and then Montreal, leading to riots in both cities. The more serious one occurred in Montreal, where a battle outside a Protestant church between incensed Irish Catholics and armed Protestant attendees led police to open fire. Seven people reportedly died that day, and an equal number died later of wounds. An estimated fifty people were wounded. The "Gavazzi Riots" in Canada, as they became known, showed what could have happened in New York where, as the *Times* reported, "the more excitable classes . . . were restrained by more just and prudent counsels."[9]

*   *   *

In 1860 the conflicting visions of the Irish and Italian people turned into actual warfare. Responding to Pius's call for help, the Irish gathered a brigade of about 1,300 soldiers to fight the Italians on the pope's behalf in Italy. Dublin's Cardinal Paul Cullen, who spurred a Catholic revival in his country, encouraged recruiting throughout Ireland.[10]

To the Irish soldiers, twenty-four of whom arrived to serve in the pope's honor guard at St. Peter's Basilica for the Feast of Saints Peter and Paul on June 29, 1860, it was a sacred mission. One of them, Edward Patrick Naughten, wrote back to the *Catholic Telegraph*, Cullen's paper, to report that he had kissed the pope's foot. With obvious excitement, Naughten wrote that the Irish troops would wear green uniforms and hats with the papal coat of arms and the harp of Erin underneath.

Irish and Italian forces fought in 1860 at the Rocca, a former papal fortress in
Spoleto. Paul Moses photo.

American newspapers and magazines, following the sneering example of their British counterparts, mocked the Irish soldiers, while
in Ireland, the war was celebrated.[11] It was not only a papal crusade
but a chance to march to war as Irishmen—and on the opposite side
from the British, at that, since hundreds of Englishmen had signed
up to fight for the Italian insurgents. The British press idolized
Garibaldi, poets rhapsodized about him, and a popular London
play celebrated his life. "We are all talking and dreaming Garibaldi just now in great anxiety," the poet Elizabeth Barrett Browning
wrote. "Scarcely since the world was a world has there been such a
feat of arms. All modern heroes grow pale before him."[12]

In New York, Hughes anxiously followed the news about Italian
advances into papal territory. Writing on September 9, 1860, to a
priest who had just had an audience with Pius IX, Hughes said he
was pleased to hear that the pope was secure, "notwithstanding the
reported success of Garibaldi and his hordes."[13]

It turned into a short, frustrating campaign for the outnumbered Irish Brigade. Some 145 Irishmen were part of a small force that defended Perugia against a 12,000-strong army. Similarly, a force of about 600 Irish soldiers made its stand in the hilltop castle in Spoleto called the Rocca, a papal fortress since the late Middle Ages. Amid colorful frescoes of papal coats of arms and medieval hunting scenes, they were ridiculously outgunned. At the peak of the fighting, the Italian troops tried to hack their way through the wooden gate to the Rocca as both sides used bayonets and fired shots through holes in the barrier. The Irish force surrendered on September 18, 1860.[14]

The *New York Times* ran dispatches from the *Times* of London that ridiculed the Irish troops. The defeated Irish soldiers were unjustly accused of cowardice.[15] Many of these Irishmen later took part in the American Civil War, taking memories of the Italian conflict with them. Michael J. A. McCaffery, who fought with the Irish Brigade at Spoleto, published a dramatic, book-length poem called *The Siege of Spoleto* through a publishing house on Bleecker Street in 1864. In his telling, an Irishman named Gleeson who had fought in Spoleto and then served in the Union army regaled fellow Northern soldiers around a campfire with stories of Irish heroism in Italy. The poem celebrates the Irish soldiers as modern Crusaders and portrays the Italians as infidels.[16]

Archbishop Hughes died in 1864 at the age of sixty-six, one of the most influential figures in the history of American Catholicism. His vision of the Catholic Church as a holy fortress to be protected against its enemies, forged in a time of fiery anti-Catholicism, continues to affect the American church.[17]

Irish eyes remained on the pope, and Hughes's associate James McMaster used the *Freeman's Journal* to push for American Catholics to send a brigade to aid Pius. His effort was helped along by a frenzy that took hold in the city's Irish community when 140 Catholics from Quebec came to New York in January 1867 en route to Rome to fight for their pope. Archbishop John McCloskey greeted them warmly and celebrated Mass for the young men at St. Peter's

A plaque in Spoleto marks the burial place of fifteen Italian soldiers killed in the assault on the Rocca on September 17, 1860. Paul Moses photo.

Church on Barclay Street, a few blocks from City Hall in lower Manhattan. This inspired at least some Irish Catholics in New York to join the fight; students at local Catholic colleges such as Seton Hall especially "felt the impulse to the Holy War," Father John Talbot Smith wrote in his 1905 history of the archdiocese. In May 1868, Pius sought help from the American bishops, asking them to send troops at their expense. James McMaster used the *Freeman's Journal* to stir up young New York men to take up arms for the pope.

A few of those wealthy enough to afford the trip went to Rome, but American bishops were cool to the pope's request to create and fund a battalion, partly out of concern that it would violate U.S. law and also aware that such an action would stir up anti-Catholic feeling. Instead, a large collection was taken up in 1869 to help Pius IX fight his war. But on September 20, 1870, Rome fell to the Italians, completing Italy's unification. Pius declared himself a "prisoner" in the tiny Vatican state.[18]

New York's Catholic pulpits resounded with denunciations of the Italians for seizing the pope's lands. The Reverend Thomas S. Preston, vicar general of the New York archdiocese, portrayed the Italian King Victor Emmanuel as an outlaw and warned a packed St. Ann's Church in Greenwich Village, "There is no difference of opinion among Catholics on this subject, for we do not allow any difference on such questions."[19]

Italians in New York would celebrate the victory of September 20 annually—"a day cordially hated by the Irish Catholics," the *Tribune* later noted.[20] While the Irish-Italian conflict over Italy's Risorgimento may seem remote today, it clearly colored relations between the two peoples in the nineteenth century, including in New York. Irish priests in New York knew that there was a strong anticlerical streak in the immigrants arriving from Italy. The Irish looked on the Italians' September 20 celebrations as a sacrilege.[21]

This tension was reflected in a dispute that broke out in August 1874 in the city's first Italian parish, St. Anthony of Padua on Sullivan Street. Hughes had scuttled New York's initial Italian chapel after a dispute with the Italian priest who founded it, but after his death the Franciscan order created a new Italian parish in 1866. By the summer of 1874, the parish was ready to consecrate a new parochial school in a former factory on MacDougal Street. The Society of St. Anthony, an Italian fraternal group, wanted to march in the ceremony carrying the tricolored Italian flag. But the pastor, Father Giacomo Titta, refused out of fear that any display of Italian national pride would offend the Irish, who outnumbered the Italians in the parish and provided nearly all its income.

This prompted an angry blast in G. F. Secchi di Casali's newspaper, *L'Eco d'Italia*, which called the decision a "cowardly insult to our nationality." The paper complained that the parish would not have existed without the Italians' contributions, and added that the

KEY

A. The Five Points intersection, Baxter and Worth Streets.
B. Transfiguration Church, 29 Mott Street.
C. St. Anthony of Padua Church, Sullivan and Houston Streets.
D. Most Precious Blood Church, 113 Baxter Street.
E. St. Patrick's Old Cathedral, 263 Mulberry Street.
F. Our Lady of Loreto Church, 309 Elizabeth Street.
G. Joseph Petrosino's apartment, 233 Lafayette Street.
H. Little Naples Cafe, Paul Kelly's saloon, 57 Great Jones Street.
I. Big Tim Sullivan's headquarters, 207 Bowery.
J. Black Hand bomb sites, 240–246 Elizabeth Street.
K. Al Smith's home, 25 Oliver Street.
Based on *Map of New York City, South of 46th St.: Showing New Arrangement of Docks, Piers, and Water Frontage, Also Soundings and Former High Water Line* (M. Dripps, 1877). Courtesy of New York Public Library.

25

first pastor, Father Leone Pacilio, a native of Naples, had always allowed the Italian flag to be displayed more prominently than others. The newspaper mocked the competing flags—the pope's yellow banner, which was "the color of a fried egg," and the Irish standard, with its "discordant Irish harp."[22]

Religion is often a factor in ethnic discord, but the Irish and the Italians in 1870s New York provide an unusual twist to this conflict: They were two peoples divided by the *same* religion, not competing faiths. The profound nationalist ambitions of the Irish and Italians clashed amid the intensity of their feelings for and against the pope. In the quarter century after the Great Famine, the Catholic Irish experienced a religious revival—what historians have called a "devotional revolution," marked by large increases in the number of priests and nuns and more frequent reception of the sacraments.[23] The emigrants brought this austere devotion with them to New York, turning to their faith and their obedience to the pope to define themselves as Irish. At the same time, Italians found a national hero in Giuseppe Garibaldi, who wrote during his exile in New York that Catholicism was "the religion of hell," adding, "the Pope is Lucifer."[24] Men like Garibaldi, who spurred an end to the centuries-long foreign domination of the Italian peninsula, and Archbishop John Hughes, who helped the oppressed Irish attain freedom in America, would have found it hard to sit down at the same dinner table, much less gather around the same altar.

The political and religious dispute that Garibaldi and Hughes exemplify stirred anger, resentment, and even hatred, helping to divide two impoverished rural peoples who would encounter each other, thousands of miles from their homelands, in the crowded churches and narrow streets of lower Manhattan. However passionate these differences were, the fact that there were relatively few Italians in New York in the 1870s kept such matters fairly obscure. But that was about to change with the arrival of many more thousands of immigrants from southern Italy in the 1880s as they fled a poverty that had worsened under Italy's new, unified government. The discord between New York's Italians and Irish had only begun.

2

"The Italian Problem"

When the Reverend Thomas F. Lynch arrived at Transfiguration Church on chaotic Mott Street to become
a pastor for the first time at the age of thirty-three, he entered
a new world. Before that, Lynch had served at New York's most
fashionable Catholic church, St. Ann's on East Twelfth Street.
There, he catered to the carriage crowd from Greenwich Village,
taking up such tasks as directing the parish's Literary Society for
Young Ladies. His pleasant duties included a friendly popularity
contest at the church fair with the Reverend James Hayes, who
led the St. Ann's Literary Union. In a fundraising gimmick that
raised $1,200—the equivalent of more than $26,000 today—the
parishioners voted on who would win white silk, gold-embroidered
vestments. After "a good deal of excitement," as a news report put
it, Lynch won the contest.

If New York was "an American Protestant city," as the *Times*
insisted in 1880, well-to-do St. Ann's was as close to respectable as
a Catholic church could be. Its pastor, Monsignor Thomas Preston,
was a former Anglican cleric and a renowned preacher trained at
the Episcopal Church's General Theological Seminary in nearby
Chelsea.[1]

Lynch's new assignment, Transfiguration Church, was a rock of
tough Manhattan schist located downtown in the midst of the notorious Five Points slums. For decades, the poverty and crime had
been so intense there that well-to-do adventurers such as Charles

Dickens visited to gape at the wreckage, helping to give rise to the term "slumming." The Famine Irish had packed the neighborhood, just north of the area in lower Manhattan where the Brooklyn Bridge would open in 1883. Others crowded into the notorious neighborhood as well, African Americans and German immigrants among them. When Father Lynch arrived in 1881, Chinese immigrants were just beginning to move onto Mott Street across the street from Transfiguration Church, the beginning of what would eventually be called Chinatown.[2] The 1880 census counted 12,223 Italian-born New Yorkers—still a relatively small community—but in the Five Points, Italians already made up nearly a quarter of the population. Squalor was common; a *New York Sun* reporter counted seventeen men living in a basement room that measured fifteen by ten feet.[3]

Father Lynch was about to become one of many Irish American pastors in New York to struggle over how to work with this burgeoning Italian minority. Bishops would soon come to call it the Catholic Church's "Italian problem." For now, it was Father Lynch's problem.

By 1881, enough Italians had moved into the parish for the previous pastor to permit them one Mass each Sunday in the church basement. One might assume that a Catholic parish catering to immigrants from two Catholic countries in Europe would be a safe haven for newcomers, especially given the strong anti-Catholic sentiments in the surrounding city. But the peoples in the pews were rivals for low-level jobs and for housing; they spoke different languages, looked different, ate different foods, and worshipped in different ways. That they shared the same religion seemed only to intensify the rivalry, since it extended their fight over turf into the sanctuary and added the emotions surrounding faith to their disputes.

From the start, religion played a complex role in the relationship between New York's Irish and Italians. Since religion is closely tied with ethnicity—especially among immigrants, since it connects them to their heritage and to each other—it is a factor that needs to be looked at closely as we examine the Irish-Italian relationship in New York as Italian migration began to pick up in the 1880s and 1890s.[4] Although they shared the same religion, the Irish and Italians had very different ideas of what it meant to be religious. Furthermore, as we've seen, history had left them with opposing ways of relating to church authority figures—not only the pope, but also pastors like Father Lynch. There have always been dissenters, but in general, the Irish prized obedience to clerical authority and southern Italian immigrants were known to have an anticlerical streak.

As far as the Irish at Transfiguration were concerned, the parish was theirs. And with the 1880 census showing that 44 percent of New Yorkers were either Irish-born or children of the Irish, they might be forgiven for thinking the city was theirs, too. After all, in 1880 they had elected an Irish Catholic mayor, William R. Grace, the Corkman who overcame anti-Catholic screeds preached from many a Protestant pulpit on the Sunday before the vote. And Tammany Hall's boss, "Honest John" Kelly, was an Irish immigrant—the first of ten Irishmen in a row to head an institution that was both as hierarchical and local as the Catholic Church.[5] Cementing Kelly's status as a sort of secular bishop, he was married to the niece of Cardinal John McCloskey, the archbishop of New York.

As Lynch began his assignment to the ghettos of lower Manhattan in November 1881, he met his tenacious Irish congregation. Many of Transfiguration's elderly members had grown up in intense poverty as tenants on two estates in County Sligo and one in County Kerry before seeking refuge in America.[6] Father Lynch, a ruddy, blue-eyed man, was part of the new Irish middle class trained in the Catholic schools. He had attended La Salle Academy, then received a bachelor's degree from Manhattan College before being ordained in 1872. A son of Irish immigrants, he surely knew that the Irish in his parish resented the Italians because they drove down wages by working for less and forced up housing prices through their willingness to pay more.

"The result of this was to stir up an ill feeling among tenement house occupants against the Italians," the *Sun* reported. Irish toughs, practiced at urban street fighting, intimidated the Italians, who resorted to carrying guns and knives. "The Italians are cowed down by the roughs who are about here, mostly Irish," James E. March, a deputy sheriff and hiring contractor who was one of the few Italians in public office, told the *Sun*. "The Irish hate them because of the competition for the rougher kinds of work."[7]

The constricted streets surrounding Transfiguration Church in the area north and east of City Hall were a battleground. Italian-Irish fights erupted often, and even one Irish judge questioned police about why only Italians were arrested. That was the case after a riot on Mulberry Street between Canal and Hester Streets on March 24, 1884. The battle began when two Irish bootblacks—shoeshiners, one of the first lines of work to fall to Italian competitors—threw stones, mud, and chunks of coal at an Italian with whom they had argued. He ran around the corner, looking for help, and Italian men inside Domenico's beer hall at 113 Mulberry Street responded. When the Irish poured out of their tenements, the combatants filled the street, heaving bricks, rocks, and coal and firing guns as well.

Three cops—Taylor, Kelly, and Mahoney—arrived after ten minutes and sent a messenger to the Elizabeth Street stationhouse for reinforcements. A sergeant named Ryan responded with thirty more officers and, clubs drawn, they dispersed the crowd and arrested nine Italians. Cops were stationed on the street to prevent further fighting, "as the feeling against the Italians is very bitter," the *Times* reported.

When the Italians arrested in the imbroglio were led into court the following day, a reporter observed, "All had scars and gashes on the face, which they said had been inflicted by the missiles thrown by the attacking party." "How was it that you arrested only Italians?" Police Court Magistrate Maurice J. Power, a native of County Cork, asked the police, who were led by detectives named Brennan and Hart. "There must have been some Irishmen at hand." Shrugging his shoulders, one of the Italian defendants told the judge that all the cops were Irish. The answer was obvious.

The rumble on Mulberry Street was not an isolated incident, as the *Sun* noted: "In several tenement districts of the city the crowding of Irish and Italian tenants in neighboring houses has given rise to frequent fights and trouble."[8] Such animosity suggests how difficult it would have been for Father Lynch to merge his Irish and Italian congregations into one parish community (had he tried). He noticed that when an Italian family or two moved into a tenement, the Irish families left. When Italian children entered the parish school, Irish parents began to withdraw theirs; in five years, it went from being entirely Irish to almost completely Italian. Lynch had some sympathy for the Italian immigrants; he appreciated how hard they worked. And he and other Irish American church leaders were well aware that they had a religious duty to come to the aid of fellow Catholics. Above all, they worried that the Protestant enemy would convert the Italians—a fear ingrained in Irish Catholics as a result of Protestant efforts to convert starving Catholics during the Famine.[9] And they also knew that powerful Italian churchmen in the Vatican and even the new Pope Leo XIII, elected to the papacy in 1878, were paying attention to the plight of Italian emigrants. They monitored the situation through the Sacred Congregation for the Propagation of the Faith, or Propaganda Fide, which oversaw church activity in areas considered mission territories. And so, even as his parish became a battleground in the turf war that the Irish and Italians fought in the Five Points, the teachings and politics of the Catholic Church required that Lynch shepherd the Italians, or at least appear to.[10]

Lynch decided it was best to segregate the Irish and Italians; his solution was to seek Italian priests to serve an "annex" congregation in the Transfiguration basement. Like many Irish American bishops and pastors, he didn't want separate Italian parishes, in part because he thought this would slow the process of Americanizing the Italians.[11]

In 1885 Lynch's archbishop asked him to write a report to the Vatican to help the church find a solution to what American bishops called "the Italian problem." In that document, Lynch insisted that it wouldn't work to create a separate Italian church in the neighborhood because the Italians didn't have enough money to support it. The pastor referred only in an obscure way to the fact that his Italian services were held in the church basement.

If Lynch had tried to be diplomatic on this point, New York's archbishop, Michael Corrigan, gave an embarrassingly clear explanation to the Vatican. "For four years now, they have had free use of the basement of Fr. Lynch's church," Corrigan wrote to Archbishop Domenico Jacobini at the Vatican in a cover letter sent with Lynch's report. "Why only the basement? Forgive me, Excellency, if I tell you frankly that these poor devils are not very clean, so that the others do not want to have them in the upstairs church. Otherwise the others move out, and then good-bye the income. In time we hope to remedy these things. But it is necessary to move slowly." The remark raised eyebrows in the Vatican, where the Propaganda Fide was preparing a report for the pope.[12]

In the meantime, Lynch pursued a grievance with the Italian congregation at Transfiguration and its Italian Franciscan priests visiting from St. Anthony of Padua Church on Sullivan Street, a mile and a half to the north. In a letter to Monsignor Thomas Preston, now vicar general of the archdiocese, Lynch complained that the Franciscans were holding five thousand dollars collected over nine years at the Italians' basement Masses in his church. (The Franciscans held the money in hopes the Italians could use it to build their own church.) Transfiguration parish had received no money from the Italians during this period for maintenance and "cleaning," Lynch wrote, underlining *cleaning* twice. He wanted the money back.[13]

Vatican officials were not pleased with what Lynch and Corrigan had written to them. Their 1887 report found that the "religious indifference" Italian immigrants exhibited could well have stemmed from the chilly reception they received in the church in America—and not from poor religious training in Italy. The report praised Corrigan for his zeal on behalf of the Italian immigrants in

New York, but also included scathing criticism based on Corrigan's own letter about the situation in Transfiguration Church:

> It is humiliating to acknowledge that, after the disappearance of the Indians from the United States and the emancipation of the Negroes, the Italian immigrants in large number represent the pariahs of this great American Republic. It is sufficient to point out that they are so despised for their filth and beggary that in New York the Irish granted them free use of the basement of the Church of Transfiguration, so that they could gather for their religious practices, since the Irish did not want to have them in the upstairs church.

The report used Transfiguration as a prime example of American priests' ineffective work with Italian congregations: "The Italians are placed in an inferior position, for many one of real beggary."[14]

One could not blame the Reverend Thomas F. Lynch if he was angered that his effort to bring the faith to the slums of the Five Points had been reviewed amid the finery of the Vatican palaces and found wanting. And in time, he got his side of the story out. The April 1888 issue of the Paulist Fathers' journal *Catholic World* carried an article that aired Lynch's views. His name appeared nowhere in it; the byline went to his twenty-seven-year-old brother, Bernard, eleven years his junior and a journalist who had graduated in 1881 from the Jesuits' College of St. Francis Xavier. But since the article closely tracks remarks in Father Lynch's private correspondence, it is clear he was at least the source, if not the actual author.

The opening pages expressed a certain respect for "these dark-eyed, olive-tinted men and women," but also contended that they had "invaded" the city. "The traditional Irish apple-woman is in every direction giving place to the Italian corner fruit-vender," Lynch—whichever brother—wrote, adding that "a vast army of sinewy and dark-browed men are taking the place of the Irish laborers."

The true point of the article emerged when it turned to "the delicate question of religion" to defend Father Lynch's ministry to the Italians. It is a brief that would echo for decades in the complaints of Irish American pastors. The Italians in Transfiguration "come to America the worst off in religious equipment of, perhaps, any foreign Catholics whatever," the article asserts, reporting that they did not know elementary Catholic doctrines. Lynch had high hopes for the children of Italian immigrants, but not for the immigrants themselves: "They must tag after the Irish." Echoing Archbishop Hughes's battles with Garibaldi supporters three decades earlier, Lynch blamed the "atheistic" Italian government in part. "But, when all other causes have had due weight, the miserable truth is that the people have been neglected by their priests" in southern Italy, he wrote.

In a clear reference to the Italian Franciscans at St. Anthony of Padua Church, Lynch argued that there could not be a true Italian parish with Italian priests because "it begins Italian and it ends Irish—except in the personnel of the clergy—who, like the Normans in Ireland, sometimes become *Hiberniores Hiberniis*," or "more Irish than the Irish." The Italian priests favored the Irish because they donated money, the article maintained, adding that in Transfiguration, two thousand Italian churchgoers a week contributed just forty-five dollars.

Lynch rejected the idea that thousands more Italians would come to a church of their own, then worked his way up to the subject the Vatican had addressed with embarrassing clarity in its report to the pope: his church's basement. "It may be said that the persons among them who object to the basement are not numerous," Lynch insisted, adding the caustic sentence for which the article is chiefly remembered: "The Italians as a body are not humiliated by humiliation." While some northern Italian emigrants such as the Genoese did in fact worship upstairs with the Irish, "the bulk are not like that," Lynch wrote. "The fact is that the Catholic Church in America is to the mass of the Italians almost like a new religion."[15]

These were fighting words for a prominent Italian priest who had been ministering to Italian emigrants in America since 1860. Monsignor Gennaro De Concilio, born in Naples, was a brilliant professor of logic at Seton Hall University and primary author of the first *Baltimore Catechism*, written on orders of a bishops' plenary council in Baltimore in 1884. He wrote a blistering pamphlet, "On the Religious State of the Italians in the United States," and sent it to every bishop and cardinal in Italy. De Concilio lambasted Lynch for permitting the Italians to be ridiculed in the article. "There is no other pastor in New York City who would allow his brother to say this, so disparaging a remark, against 14,000 of his own," he wrote.[16]

The counteroffensive against Father Lynch continued when one of the two Italian priests assigned to his parish, Father Marcellino Moroni, complained to the Vatican that Lynch himself had confided that the archdiocese was not sending more Italian priests to him because he expected any who came to be a servant. This alleged remark became notorious among the Italian priests, judging from a letter the Reverend Francesco Zaboglio sent to his superior in Italy a month later: "Your excellency knows that Fr. Lynch said that here the Italian priests, ours included, must be servants, servants, servants."[17]

A furious De Concilio wrote to his bishop in Italy that "I have proofs at hand—it would make your blood boil—to see how Italian priests have been treated by American pastors."[18]

* * *

The timeworn machinery of the Roman Catholic Church creaked under the pressure of one of history's great mass migrations. From 1880 to 1920, some four million Italians migrated to the United States, mostly through the Port of New York. Many of them stayed in Manhattan: in the 1890s, New York County's Italian-born population shot up from 39,951 to 178,886.[19] The challenges Father Lynch confronted in Transfiguration Church were becoming widespread. As the migration increased, church leaders on both sides of the Atlantic took more deliberate steps to deal with the so-called Italian problem. But the Irish American bishops and the Italian prelates had very different views of the source of the "problem," and blamed each other for the unfriendly reception Italians were receiving in the American church. Two bishops—Archbishop Michael Corrigan in New York and Giovanni Battista Scalabrini of Piacenza in northern Italy—tried to overcome these differences and work together.

Michael Augustine Corrigan, who became coadjutor of the Archdiocese of New York in 1880 and archbishop from 1885 until his death in 1902, was an unlikely successor to Archbishop John Hughes. American-born, he grew up relatively well off in Newark, New Jersey. His father, Thomas, was a grocer who had come to America in the late 1820s from Kells, where the abbey once held the medieval masterpiece called the Book of Kells. His mother, Mary, was from Kingscourt in County Cavan, where her father, who came from a Presbyterian family, had substantial land holdings

Corrigan was low-key, precise, and careful. No newspaper would have depicted Hughes in the way the *Tribune* described Corrigan: "he was a small man without a powerful voice." Corrigan, who was five feet, eight and a half inches tall, had started on a scholarly path with his acceptance into the first class of seminarians at the North American College in Rome. He stopped off in Ireland to visit the family homes of both of his parents on the way.

A clean-shaven man with gray eyes, a straight nose, straight brown hair, and a quiet sense of humor, he excelled in studying church and classical history. Ordained in 1863, he became a professor at Seton Hall University and by 1868 was the school's president at the age of twenty-eight. Though a quiet, mild-mannered man, he became the strong-willed conservative leader of the U.S. Catholic Church.[20]

Corrigan at first had a difficult time coming to terms with the church's changing demographic. He resisted when an influential cardinal in the Vatican, Giovanni Simeoni, urged the American bishops to take up the Italians' plight at their plenary council in

Baltimore in 1884 because he didn't want to single out the newcomers for special attention.

Corrigan wanted the American bishops to go straight to Pope Leo XIII to persuade him to command the Italian bishops to do their most basic job of teaching their people. But it was not politically realistic to think that the upstart missionary church in America would outmaneuver the Italian bishops in Rome.[21] The bishop assigned the task of drafting a letter for the pope, Thomas A. Becker of Wilmington, Delaware, had a hard time finding the right words. "It is a very delicate matter to tell the Sovereign Pontiff how utterly faithless the specimens of his country coming here really are," Becker wrote to Archbishop James Gibbons of Baltimore.[22]

Italian Bishop Scalabrini, born in 1839, traced his concern for Italian emigrants to a walk he took through the Milan train station, where he saw hundreds of impoverished peasants awaiting transport to the port to leave for America and thought of the suffering they would face. Scalabrini, who had gray-streaked brown hair combed neatly back from his high forehead and large, intense brown eyes beneath thick, dark eyebrows, declared that emigration was a God-given right, a form of self-preservation for those forced to search for work.[23]

In an 1887 pamphlet, Scalabrini lamented that with few Italian-speaking priests available, Italians in America were forced "to live a life that is worse than pagan." This concern inspired a long correspondence with Archbishop Corrigan that was often warm but, like the relationship between their peoples, also marked at times by distrust. Corrigan was typically forward in writing to Scalabrini about his pamphlet, noting the shortcomings of Italian priests who had come to New York to that point. The following month, Scalabrini responded cordially, acknowledging the poor religious training of emigrants from southern Italy, and calling the Italian priests who so far had gone to America "nothing more than rejects of Italian dioceses." Scalabrini realized that Corrigan, despite his criticisms of the Italian immigrants and their priests, was serious about providing for the Italians. He addressed him as a cherished friend:

"If I were not quite inferior to Your Excellency in every aspect, I would say that we are old and sincere friends." Corrigan wrote back in kind: "Every day I am worried about our dear Italians."[24]

The tensions among their priests would soon test their friendship. Scalabrini began receiving angry letters from Italian priests in America, including complaints about Father Lynch at Transfiguration Church. Against the background of such squabbles, a concerned Corrigan came to agree with Scalabrini that there should be national parishes for the Italians, staffed by the Italian bishop's missionary priests. Corrigan's worries could only have increased after Pope Leo XIII issued an 1888 encyclical "On Italian Immigrants," addressed to the American bishops. Reflecting Scalabrini's influence, it cited his concern for people "who spring from the same race as ourselves." Leo, born Gioacchino Pecci in a town southeast of Rome, grimly described the fate of the many Italian emigrants who left their homeland in search of a better life. However adept the Irish were as church politicians in America, they had been outflanked in Italy. Scalabrini helped to write the encyclical, and much of his information came from Italian priests in America who were angry with the Irish clergy they encountered.[25]

Archbishop Corrigan's "Italian problem" multiplied when New York newspapers implied that the pope was unhappy with the treatment of Italian emigrants. Dating back to Archbishop Hughes's days, criticism in the press had always riled officials in the New York archdiocese (and would continue to). Church officials did damage control. Monsignor Thomas Preston penned a lengthy letter published in the *Sun*, the *Freeman's Journal*, and the *Catholic Review*, detailing what he said were the zealous efforts by pastors such as Lynch to provide for the Italian immigrants.[26]

*   *   *

One of Bishop Scalabrini's solutions to the "Italian problem" was to send thirty-eight-year-old Mother Frances Cabrini and six of her Missionary Sisters of the Sacred Heart to New York to aid Italian immigrants. After a harrowing journey across the Atlantic, they arrived on March 31, 1889, with illusory expectations. They'd been told there would be a house for them, a school to teach in, and an orphanage to run for Italian girls. In fact, there was nowhere for them to stay; the school was not ready; and Archbishop Corrigan was adamantly against the orphanage, opposing the location on upscale East 59th Street. The fault for this rested mostly with the Italian priests, who were responsible for a string of miscommunications. The sisters found out only when they arrived at the dock that their promised house wasn't actually ready. The Italian priests took them to a dirty, rundown hotel in the Five Points, where they put up in two filthy rooms. The beds were so uncomfortable and the neighborhood so frightening to the sisters that they passed the night without sleep.

The next setback came when a tired Mother Cabrini and the sisters met with Corrigan at his residence near St. Patrick's Cathedral the next morning. The archbishop, appearing ill at ease, told Cabrini there would be no orphanage. Speaking in Italian, he also insisted that the sisters live in one of the Italian neighborhoods. For the time being, then, it seemed the sisters had no place to go. "I see no better solution of this question, Mother, than that you and your sisters return to Italy," Corrigan announced. Mother Cabrini went pale, according to one of the participants in the meeting, as she thought about the frightening storm the sisters had endured on their long passage to New York. "It was an indescribable moment," one of the sisters later recalled. But Cabrini coolly informed the archbishop, "No, not that, Your Excellency. I am here by order of the Holy See, and here I must stay."[27]

At one point in the conversation, "the Archbishop grew red in the face," according to one account.[28] "Very well," Corrigan replied to the formidable mother superior. "Stay here, but give up all thought of the orphanage and think only of the schools." The archbishop then brought Cabrini and her sisters to meet the Sisters of Charity, who welcomed them in their convent.

The sisters caught on quickly to the prejudice against Italians, and decided that Irish influence often stood in their way.[29] One sister wrote home on her third day in New York that the sisters "had heard of the hatred that there is for the Italians." Mother Cabrini quickly wrote home for additional habits and veils for the sisters to have clean clothing always available, "otherwise they will call us 'guinea-pigs' the way they do to the Italians here."[30] The hurtful term "guinea" was just coming into use in the 1890s as a slur for Italians; it was previously aimed at blacks, derived from the gold coin once used in the African slave trade.[31]

Within their first month in America, the sisters recognized that there were factions in the church lined up against the Italians, "even among those who pretend to be our friends." One wrote, "We have to recognize more and more clearly that Italian sisters are not too highly regarded by the Irish and this will cause us difficulties." Of Corrigan, one sister wrote, "He pays too much attention to what the Irish suggest to him against us Italians."[32]

Corrigan ultimately allowed the orphanage, writing to Scalabrini to tell him. Mother Cabrini and her sisters opened the institution at 43 East 59th Street.[33] But Mother Cabrini was frustrated by the archbishop's order that she limit her fundraising to the Italian community, which was mostly impoverished. She tried the superior of the Jesuits, who were beginning their own mission to the Italians, and wrote of that encounter, "But, alas! He was more than Irish, that is to say for nothing was he disposed to help the Italians." Finally, the sisters resorted to begging, door-to-door. They did find some aid from the American Sisters of Charity.[34]

Mother Cabrini recognized Italian shortcomings, too. She found the same problems that Lynch and other Irish American pastors complained about, writing to a cardinal in the Vatican about incompetent Italian priests and the poor religious schooling of Italian immigrants.[35] But through her sisters' visits to their homes, through their orphanages, hospitals, and unending devotion, Mother Cabrini brought the church to the immigrants. Despite their frosty first encounter, she befriended Corrigan and they were able to work closely in the immigrants' service. Before her death on December 22, 1917, at the age of sixty-seven, she founded more than fifty schools, hospitals, orphanages, convents, and other institutions. Among many other works, she took over management of Transfiguration School in 1899. In 1946 she was the first U.S. citizen to be canonized.

* * *

Perhaps it indeed took the patience of a saint to overcome the barriers that divided the Irish and Italians in 1880s and 1890s New York. Pastors such as Father Thomas F. Lynch faced a nearly impossible task of unifying congregations split by intense ethnic rivalry for low-level jobs and housing. Nor were clergymen immune to prejudice against the newcomers, with even church leaders such as Archbishop Corrigan initially adopting a stance that the majority often takes toward a minority group: no special treatment. From bootblacks to bishops, Italians were quick to catch on when the Irish belittled them. For bootblacks, it led to street fights. In the more refined world of the rectory and chancery, it provoked Italian priests to write angry letters to Rome. That's not to say the Irish American church leaders lacked grounds for complaint. They saw that a good number of the early Italian priests were incompetent misfits, and they were also quick to catch on to the anticlerical attitude among the Italian immigrants. They resented the implication coming down from the Vatican to the young American church that the immigrants' difficulties were their fault.

In any case, it was painfully clear that temporary measures such as shooing Italians into church basements for their services were not going to solve the "problem" that their massive migration caused. The "Italian problem" called out for a solution.

3

Tipping Point

In his later years, Monsignor John F. Kearney loved to tell stories about what it was like back in the days when St. Patrick's Old Cathedral in lower Manhattan was an Irish parish. He served as its pastor for forty-three years, and experienced it even longer, for he was baptized in its font. After his ordination in 1866 (after studying in Rome), his first assignment was to the cathedral parish where he had grown up. The seat of the archbishop was moved in 1879 to the gleaming new Gothic-style St. Patrick's Cathedral that opened on Fifth Avenue, but Kearney stayed at the "old cathedral" and became pastor.

At the church's hundredth anniversary celebration in 1909, the aging pastor, a short, bald man with blue eyes and brilliant white hair thick at the temples, entertained a gaggle of younger men—doctors, lawyers, politicians—who had graduated from his school. They celebrated in one of the city's most famous hotels, Brevoort House on Fifth Avenue between Eighth and Ninth Streets. The population of St. Patrick's was almost entirely Italian by then, but for Kearney, a New York-born son of Irish immigrants, the Irish days were alive in memory. He told of how the immigrant Irish parishioners of St. Patrick's would crowd around the latest newcomers near a water pump at Spring and Mulberry Streets after Sunday Mass ended, pressing for the latest gossip from the counties of Ireland. Kearney, known for his salty humor, remembered a teacher known as "Daddy" Walsh who used a strip of leather to keep the students at the parish school in line, "and terrible whalings he used to give us."[1]

There were still plenty of Irish-born New Yorkers in 1909; the census the following year counted 169,321 in New York County, and there were many more American-born descendants of Irish immigrants. But Italian-born New Yorkers outnumbered the Irish-born by a third, and there were even larger numbers of Jewish immigrants from eastern Europe.[2] German immigrants, like the Irish, had also arrived in great numbers earlier in the nineteenth century, and they kept coming. And yet, in their bastions of church and state, the Irish continued to hold enormous power. The Germans, a third of whom were Catholic, often felt stymied by Irish control of the church. The Irish American bishops, not about to let go of that control, overcame an attempt by the German Catholic layman Peter Paul Cahensly to persuade Pope Leo XIII to create bishops for different ethnic groups in the United States in the 1890s.[3]

It was true, as Kearney told the young men at his parish's centennial celebration, that "things have changed mightily in the last sixty years." But even so, Irish American pastors like Kearney and their friends in politics and the police still ruled New York's neighborhoods.[4] The story of Monsignor Kearney and St. Patrick's Old Cathedral provides a window to see how the Irish remained influential for decades after the city's demographics changed with the arrival of so many immigrants from southern and eastern Europe. It shows the difficult challenges Kearney faced—especially from prominent Italian priests who thought he was biased against their people—and how he eventually succeeded in absorbing the Italians into his parish. It also captures the frustrations the Italians experienced as they tried to make a place for themselves in New York's Irish-controlled Catholic Church.

On the streets surrounding the old cathedral, Irish-Italian violence abounded, just as it did downtown in the Five Points section.[5] Italians soon outnumbered the Irish. Neapolitans moved in on one side of the block that bounds St. Patrick's on the east, Mott Street between Prince and Houston Streets. Basilicatans lived across the street from them. Sicilians lived on Prince Street on the south side of the church's brick-walled property, a block where the Hibernian Hall at number 42 had been an important headquarters for Irish activities. Calabrians spilled into the tenements two blocks south on Mott Street between Broome and Grand Streets, and Neapolitans filled Mulberry Street, which bound St. Patrick's on the west.[6]

The Irish saw them as invaders, but the early Italians in the neighborhood felt that they were the ones intruded upon. Dr. Raffaele Asselta, who worked among the area's Italians, recalled what it was like at the corner of Prince and Mott Streets when the Irish kids were released from the parish school. "It used to be simply bedlam let loose when school was dismissed," he told the *Sun*. "Police lined the streets, and were posted on every corner, trying to protect the few Italian children that ventured out." Asselta, who was born in Laurenzana in Basilicata and migrated to New York in 1884 at the age of twenty-eight, recalled that mothers opened their windows to shout encouragement to their children to "kill the dagos." Kearney tried to make peace but "struggle as he might, could not allay the animosity of his people."[7]

In January 1889, Kearney reported to Archbishop Corrigan that half of his fourteen thousand parishioners were Italians, a tipping point. The pastor was seeing the early stage of a vast demographic change. Overall, New York was still heavily Irish; its population of about a million and a half included two hundred thousand born in Ireland and four hundred thousand children of the Irish-born.[8] Hard times in Ireland had brought more Irish emigrants in the 1880s; the city had about seventy thousand Gaelic speakers in 1890. Germans, who had arrived earlier with the Irish, also continued to come in great numbers, with the city's German-born population peaking at 324,224 in 1900.[9] But the public debate was about the Jews from eastern Europe and the southern Italians who arrived in the immigration center at Castle Garden at Manhattan's southern tip, and beginning in 1892, on Ellis Island. So many of them stayed in New York—starting with the Five Points and the Lower East

Official portrait of Nicholas Russo, S.J., president
of Boston College. He gave up academia to start a
parish for Italians amid the slums of lower Manhattan. Courtesy of Boston College.

Side—that most of the city's institutions were under heavy pressure
to keep up with the transformation.

Kearney, taking close note of the change in his own domain,
started a special ministry to the Italians. Then he decided to merge
the Italians into the general congregation. He wrote to Corrigan
that in his parish, "there is no distinction made between Americans and Italians." But to Father Nicholas Russo, a Jesuit scholar
who witnessed the experiences of Italians in the parish, this was far
from true. From the first, Kearney's treatment of the Italians infuriated him. Russo, who was born in Ascoli Satriano in the Puglia
region in southeastern Italy in 1845, tangled with Kearney when he
went to preach a mission at St. Patrick's in 1889 with a fellow Italian Jesuit, Father Philip Cardella.[10]

As pastor of St. Patrick's Old Cathedral in
Manhattan, Monsignor John F. Kearney had to
manage the congregation's transition from Irish to
Italian. Archives of the Archdiocese of New York.

Irish American pastors often looked down on Italian priests.
There was sometimes reason for this, since, as we have seen,
some of the first to arrive were miscreants. The problem was serious enough that in 1890, Pope Leo issued a circular to Italian
and American bishops that expressed sorrow for the immorality of
some Italian priests, especially from the south, and instructed Italian bishops not to let priests transfer unless they had an excellent
record.[11]

But the two Italian Jesuits were exemplary. Cardella, an accomplished missionary, taught at the College of St. Francis Xavier,

located at West 15th Street near Sixth Avenue in Manhattan. His obituary in 1901 headlined him as "Archbishop Corrigan's Confessor and a Pillar of the Society of Jesus." Russo, who emigrated from Italy in 1875 at the age of thirty, was an acclaimed scholar. He taught philosophy at Boston College, serving as its president from 1887 to 1888, then went to Georgetown. The Jesuits of Ireland published a book of Russo's Georgetown lectures on moral philosophy. He later became a professor and trustee at St. Francis Xavier College, and also served in an important post in the archdiocese, which reflected the trust Corrigan had in his judgment. The *Times* called him "the eminent Jesuit theologian."[12]

In short, Russo and Cardella were not priests accustomed to a requirement that they preach in the basement. But this is what happened, according to Russo, who said that "for reasons which a priest should be ashamed to give," Kearney refused to let Cardella and him preach their mission to the Italians in the upper church. In a letter to Corrigan in 1891, Russo did not say what Kearney's reason was, but warned that he would disclose it if necessary: "His words to Fr. Cardella on that occasion are not forgotten; I hope he will never oblige me to repeat them."[13]

Writing in the Jesuit journal the *Woodstock Letters*, Russo described Kearney's ministry to the Italians in Old St. Patrick's as a failure—that after a year, the pastor "was disgusted, asked the archbishop to make other provisions for them, and the basement of his church was consequently closed to the Italians."[14] In contrast, a history of the archdiocese by Father John Talbot Smith, himself the son of Irish immigrants, portrays the decision to close the Italian ministry as Kearney's strategy to help the Italians, not to abandon them: "He abolished the distinction of races, and made Italians and natives join in the same services."[15]

But according to Russo, the Italians at St. Patrick's were "deprived of religious instruction" and reluctant to attend Mass in the upper church because of the then common practice of charging five cents a seat. Those who could not pay were permitted to attend, but had to stand. Neither paying nor gaining free admission only to stand was acceptable to the Italians. "The former attacked their purse, the latter their pride and sensitiveness. They were unwilling to be treated as paupers," wrote Russo, who, as one of the very few priests in New York from southern Italy, had an understanding of the immigrants' sense of dignity that even many of the northern Italian priests lacked.

Russo was well aware of what it meant for him to go from being an esteemed scholar to a priest laboring in the slums, and even so begged both Corrigan and his Jesuit provincial, the Reverend Thomas J. Campbell, to assign him to a new Italian parish. With their permission, Russo and another Italian-born Jesuit, the Reverend Aloysius Romano, rented an old barroom at 192 Elizabeth Street and, doing their own carpentry, painting, and decorating, built an altar and two confessionals to create a small chapel, Our Lady of Loreto, with a big sign outside: "Missione Italiana della Madonna di Loreto."[16]

Russo knew it would be difficult to get the neighborhood's Italian immigrants to come to Mass, so he scheduled the opening service for August 16, 1891, the Feast of Saint Rocco, whom a local aid society honored with a parade, music, and fireworks. As he later wrote, "for many of them it is perhaps the only time of the year when they put their foot in the church." Russo was relieved when fifty men from the Saint Rocco society showed up, accompanied by many more people, and filled "my new Basilica," as he wryly called it.

Russo gradually bonded with his people. Much like the city's Irish American clergy, he had thought that the southern Italians were indifferent to their religion because the church in southern Italy neglected them. But as he got to know them, he often heard people say that the last time they had gone to confession was in their homeland. What he once thought to be ignorance about religion turned out to be in part an inability to articulate what they knew, since the immigrants could speak only in their dialects.

The discord between Russo and Kearney continued. Our Lady of Loreto had no boundaries; it was supposed to attract the Italians who lived within the borders of St. Patrick's parish. "Whatever Fr. Kearney may say to the contrary, he is *not* favorable to anyone else having anything to do in this district," Russo wrote to Corrigan. "I am not a child—nor given to take the phantom for reality . . . my presence here is looked upon as an intrusion." Russo complained that Kearney was continuing to perform far more baptisms and marriages for Italians than he did because the spacious old cathedral was a much grander venue for these sacraments than the 150-person-capacity chapel Russo had built in the former bar, thus taking in donations that Russo needed badly. "He is taking the very bread from us," Russo wrote, explaining that while he did the hard work of getting the Italians to come to church, Kearney was reaping the benefit. Still, Russo told the archbishop that he didn't think money was Kearney's motive: "There is something else at the bottom of all that, which *will have to come out* to light sooner or later."[17]

When Russo had built a regular congregation of five hundred people attending Masses offered in Italian in the chapel each Sunday, he started to look for a larger church. He bought four tenement houses on Elizabeth Street—two front, two back—and turned them into Our Lady of Loreto Church, with the inscription "Madonna di Loreto" on the brownstone portico. The church had three altars, with a carved stone image of the Last Supper on the main altar. The bright interior was painted pink, with gleaming wooden pews and altar rails. Corrigan blessed the new church on September 25, 1892, with Kearney assisting him. "The edifice, which affords seats for 500 persons, was packed during the whole service with worshippers, the swarthy-faced men in all their Sunday glory and decked with strange and gaudy medals and ribbons, and the black-eyed women with their heads covered with picturesque shawls," the *Times* reported.[18]

The drawback of creating national parishes soon emerged. As the Irish moved away, St. Patrick's turned into an Italian church. Then in 1898, Kearney decided to bring back an Italian ministry, much to Russo's consternation. In a letter to Corrigan, he called

Kearney "the opposition" and said it was wrong for him to try to reclaim the Italians after halting his services for them. "All the sacrifices I had to make from the beginning, were made only because he refused to look after the Italians," he wrote, adding, "Excuse me, if I show some feelings in this matter."[19]

But Kearney was a skillful player in church politics. In the later 1880s and into the 1890s, Archbishop Corrigan was facing the political fight of his life, a feud with the charismatic, liberal, nationally prominent Reverend Edward McGlynn. The priest riled his archbishop by supporting Irish nationalists' land reform movement and backing the socialist Henry George for mayor. Their battle was among the biggest controversies in the American Catholic Church in the nineteenth century.[20]

Both Kearney and Father Lynch of Transfiguration Church took important roles in trying to unite fellow priests behind Archbishop Corrigan. Other priests wrote to Corrigan urging that he distance himself from Kearney and Lynch, as well as from the vicar general, Monsignor Preston, portraying them as malicious and vindictive. It could be that Corrigan yielded ground to Kearney and Lynch on the Italian immigrants because he needed their loyalty for his fight with McGlynn.

In any case, Kearney continued to get his way when it came to ministering to the Italians. St. Patrick's Old Cathedral was to become an Italian parish with an Irish American pastor who added Italian priests to his staff. One of them, the Reverend Dominic Epifanio, wrote in 1909, "There is no parish in New York City or elsewhere, in my opinion, where the work for the Italians is so well conducted as in old St. Patrick's."[21] Monsignor Kearney exhibited the same nimbleness as the Irish American ward bosses, who, as we will see, held their grip on power even as Italians and Jews replaced Irish residents in their districts.

*　*　*

For all the acrimony that occurs when a house of worship becomes an ethnic battleground, this discussion would be incomplete without adding that stories passed down in my own family have painted a nostalgic portrait of St. Patrick's Old Cathedral.

My maternal grandfather, Cristoforo Moscato, is said to have arrived in New York on board the SS *Bolivia* on March 29, 1902, at the age of twenty. He had come from Cerasi, an impoverished village of several hundred people in Calabria, near the toe of the Italian boot. According to family lore, he was a stowaway. My maternal grandmother, Rachela Martocci, arrived on May 11, 1906, with her mother and three younger brothers on board the ship *Lombardia* from Naples. They had come from Laurenzana, a hilltop town with an ancient castle and a medieval church named for the Madonna of Mount Carmel. It is in hilly Basilicata, above the boot's instep. The family met Rachela's father, who had migrated to New York in 1902 and lived at 18 Mott Street, across the street from Transfiguration Church.

Cristoforo was a fruit vendor. Rachela held a more prestigious job, working in the office of Browning, King and Company, a well known clothing company. They met at his fruit stand. Rachela's family would not let her marry the fruit vendor, but she refused to eat until her parents relented. This strategy worked, and they were married, first before Alderman James J. Smith at City Hall on November 8, 1909, and then at St. Patrick's Old Cathedral on December 19 with the Reverend Gaetano Arcese presiding.

As we've seen, this was the same year the old cathedral celebrated its centennial. The souvenir program took note of the Italians' arrival in the parish, sounding a note of caution that dated back to the days when Archbishop Hughes took a wary view of Giuseppe Garibaldi and his followers. "Not a few of the fathers of families are imbued with the spirit of liberalism and a consequent contempt and antagonism toward the Church," wrote the thirty-six-year-old Reverend Henry P. Tracy, who was born in Ireland and came to America as an infant.[22] The souvenir journal also sounded a note of hope for the offspring of people like Cristoforo and Rachela Moscato. It pointed out that there were 2,800 children in the parish school, with nine-tenths "of the Italian race, and bright, clever little pupils they are, destined one day to play an important part in the affairs of our country."[23]

One of the children soon to attend the school was the Moscatos' oldest daughter, Giuseppina, born on May 1, 1911. I never knew my Italian grandparents, who died before I was born. But Aunt Josephine, who was my godmother and seventeen years older than my mother, filled their role. Going back to my grade school days, I heard her extol her time as a student at St. Patrick's Old Cathedral school. She often recounted her days in the choir, singing the Pater Noster. The Latin words, the ancient melody, the candles, the incense, the dark crypt beneath the church, the historic cemetery walled off from the bustle of the surrounding streets—she described the mystery of all these in tones of wonder.

When I was a boy, Aunt Josephine also recalled for me the processions in honor of Saint Rocco. As a girl, she saw the parade go right past the various Mott Street tenements where her family lived. Participants would often march with wax models of the parts of the body that needed healing, she said, laughing with the memory. Children would gather on the sidewalk and joke about the various organs on display. Since I was only about ten years old when she told me this story, she didn't specify the parts of the body that induced such amusement, but led me to believe they were usually considered private.

She also used to speak about a Sister Monica and her fellow Sisters of Charity, who ran the parish school. The Sisters of Charity were *strict*. When the students displeased Sister Monica, she would warn them—girls born the same year in which a fire in the Triangle Shirtwaist Factory on Washington Street killed 146 people—"You're going to end up sewing doll's clothing in the factory." Aunt Josephine admired Sister Monica for her tough love, and never forgot her.

Josephine D'Esposito is gone now, but could only have been referring to Sister Monica Maria McInerney, the sole Sister Monica listed in the 1920 census among the twenty sisters living at the parish convent. Sister Monica, born in New York in 1879 as Ellen L.

Sister Monica McInerney taught generations of
Italian children in the parochial school at St.
Patrick's Old Cathedral. Courtesy of the Archives
of the Sisters of Charity of New York.

McInerney, had Irish parents, as did more than half of the sisters living in the convent. (Twenty years earlier, all but one of the
twenty-three sisters were daughters of the Irish.)[24]

Sister Monica had begun teaching at St. Patrick's in 1896, at the
age of seventeen. The school had sixty-five to seventy-five students
in a class. Perhaps five students in a class spoke English on the first
day of school. During this time, Sister Monica would later recall,
the sisters went out to the tenements on Monday afternoons to
visit parents whose children had not attended Sunday Mass. They
understood this transgression better when they saw the families'
poverty, and would return with gifts of coffee or tea. Sister Monica
once visited a family of eight children who attended the school, all
of them clean-looking but obviously poor. The children proudly

welcomed the sister to their two-room apartment, and showed her the bedroom, with one large bed, where all eight slept. When Sister Monica asked how they managed, the children responded that it was fine: the four girls and four boys alternated sleeping on the bed one night, and underneath it the next.

This story tops any of the stories of poverty I heard from my own relatives, but not by all that much. It explains how Sister Monica came to understand and motivate the Italian immigrants and their children, such as my Aunt Josephine. Sister Monica became the principal of St. Patrick's in 1925 and remained so, except for six years when she headed Sacred Heart School in Mount Kisco, until 1946.[25]

It is well documented that the Catholic Church was a battleground for the Irish and Italians during these years, but even so, Sister Monica and many others were planting seeds for better times. The glimmers of Old St. Pat's that I have seen through my family over the years suggest that the pastor, Monsignor John F. Kearney, was sincere when he wrote in a report, "We admit Italian children into the parish school without question. We are anxious to receive them."[26]

*   *   *

On April 11, 1923, Monsignor Kearney called the other priests in the St. Patrick's rectory to his room. Of the four, three were Italians. The eighty-five-year-old pastor gave them his blessing, and died a few minutes later. Ten thousand people attended his funeral, many of them on the street outside. "The company was about equally divided between former parishioners, who include many of the best known Catholics in this vicinity of Irish descent, and the present parishioners, all of whom are Italians," the *Times* reported. "To the latter Mgr. Kearney was known as 'Father Carni.'"

To recognize Kearney's contributions is not to deny the heroism of the Reverend Nicholas Russo, the Italian Jesuit who clashed with him. Russo had died of pneumonia in St. Vincent's Hospital on April 1, 1902. He was fifty-seven. "Some years ago Father Russo put aside all his intellectual work to devote himself to the care of the Italian immigrants," the *Times* commented in his obituary. "At the cost of great privations, and in spite of continual ill-health, he lived in absolute poverty in a part of the tenement house which he had converted into a church."[27]

The bitter clash between these two priests was multiplied many times in Catholic parishes in New York, the city of Brooklyn, and other cities in the Northeast and Midwest. Even a pastor as masterful as Monsignor Kearney was not so smooth that he could allay Russo's suspicion that at bottom, he was biased against the new immigrants. In many places, Italians wanted their own churches; Irish American pastors often objected on grounds that creating special ethnic parishes would prevent immigrants from becoming American. After hesitating at first, Archbishop Corrigan made great efforts to establish national parishes such as Our Lady of Loreto for the Italians. Decades later, his successors would struggle with having so many expensive-to-maintain churches close upon each other after their ethnic congregations had moved on. But amid the mass migration of the 1890s, the national parish was an appealing solution to the "Italian problem." And given the sourness between the Irish and Italian congregations, it was just easier to separate them.

But, as we have seen, even after new parishes were created, Irish-Italian tensions in the church continued as more congregations reached a tipping point in which the Italians outnumbered the Irish. The Irish-Italian dispute became particularly explosive when Irish clergymen tried to rein in the Italians' boisterous celebrations of their beloved feasts.

4

"Race War"

Father Thomas F. Lynch looked with suspicion on the Italian priests at Most Precious Blood Church, a house of worship that Bishop Scalabrini established especially for Italians. Located on Baxter Street, it was a short walk from Transfiguration Church. In an 1891 letter to Archbishop Corrigan, Lynch protested that the Italian priests had failed to stop their parishioners' September 20 celebrations of the conquest of Rome from the pope. Scalabrini's priests "never speak in defense of the rights of the Holy Father either in or out of the pulpit," he complained.

While the Italians' September 20 festivities angered the Irish once a year, their frequent and often rowdy celebrations of saints' feast days concerned the Irish American clergy even more. Once again, Father Lynch was on the watch. On a sultry Monday morning in August 1892, he carefully watched another parade, this one progressing noisily up Mott Street past Transfiguration Church. It honored Saint Donatus.[1] Lynch observed that the priest who led the parade was dressed in cassock and surplice. Four altar boys trailed him, and then a loud brass band that cleared the way for a statue of Saint Donatus that four men shouldered. Women and girls followed, raising candles aloft, and then came rows of men from the Saint Donatus society.

To Lynch, the parade meant one thing: The Italian priests had violated the archbishop's order against outdoor processions. He decided to investigate. Lynch headed uptown a few blocks to

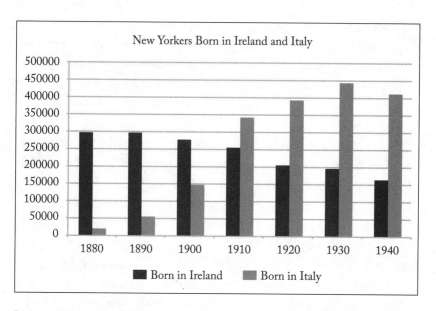

New Yorkers Born in Ireland and Italy

■ Born in Ireland   ■ Born in Italy

Irish and Italian New Yorkers, 1880 to 1940.

Baxter Street just north of Canal to the Church of the Most Precious Blood. When he arrived, Lynch noticed with distaste that the entire church was decorated with bunting and tinsel, and that the statue of Saint Donatus had been placed before the altar. Afterward, he wrote to Corrigan, complaining that the Italian priests "had disobeyed your orders" by holding the Saint Donatus parade, "with all the noise of a brass band and fireworks in the streets."[2]

When it came to Italian feast days, the two very different styles of Catholicism that the Irish and Italians practiced were as destined to clash as a pair of cymbals in a marching band. To Lynch, along with many of the city's Irish American clergy, the Italians' enthused celebrations captured much of what was wrong about their approach to religion. The Irish shunned such loud shows of faith. Having once gone underground to preserve their religion from the British, they expressed a more sedate piety, fed with the staples of attendance at Mass, reception of the sacraments, and obedience to church authority. But for southern Italian immigrants, the feast's outward demonstrations of devotion reflected an inward daily piety built around frequent thoughts about God, Mary, and the saints. Pietro di Donato's brilliant 1939 novel *Christ in Concrete* expresses this well; his bricklayer Geremio engages in a steady internal conversation with God, Mary, and the saints that continues even as he is buried to death in concrete in a macabre construction accident on Good Friday.

The *festa*, with its candles, music, and processions, was a visible sign of this relationship with the supernatural, an expression of thanksgiving and devotion to a patron in return for protection from misfortune. For all the fireworks, the food, decorations, and music, and the fights that sometimes accompanied the feast, it was a serious event. In di Donato's novel, the failure of God to protect Geremio led his son Paul to reject the Catholic faith, echoing the experience of the author, who also lost his bricklayer father to a construction accident in his childhood. There were many nonreligious elements to the feast, from hometown and regional pride to a celebration of being Italian in an American culture that treated the Italians as inferior. But underlying it all was a faith that only God, Mary, and the saints could offer protection from the calamities of life that haunt especially the poor.

But the larger society scorned the Italians' sacred feasts. The newspapers were filled with stories about fireworks injuries and violence that occurred during the Italian feasts. Such stories played to notions that Catholicism was a superstitious religion that made its adherents inferior, an embarrassment to the Irish in their ongoing battle with Protestant detractors. There was also an authority issue for the Irish churchmen, since southern Italian immigrants often detoured around the institutional church when they held their feasts. The journalist Jacob Riis found this out when he went with his friend Theodore Roosevelt, president of the New York City Police Board of Commissioners, to observe Saint Donatus festivities in August 1895 or 1896. A saloonkeeper explained that the saint's statue was stored in the saloon's loft "lest the priest get hold of him." If the saint came under the church's control, he added, the clergy would start charging money. "But the saint belonged to the people, not to the church," Riis wrote. "He was their home patron, and they were not going to give him up. In the saloon they had him safe."[3]

Placed against the more routine struggles that ethnic conflict breeds—the economic and political pecking orders—the struggle over religious practices added a particularly toxic element to the Irish-Italian relationship: a battle over what is sacred. This dispute inflamed feelings on both sides of the Irish-Italian divide as it played out in a variety of neighborhoods in New York, Brooklyn, and other cities. The Italians had only to look to the devotional practices in their homeland, including in Rome, to assure themselves that they were entitled to celebrate feasts in their own way, without interference from Irish priests or the archbishop. The Irish had only to look at the sneering reaction of the rest of American society to tell themselves that they were right to curtail the Italian street celebrations.[4]

The anger seemed to worsen as more parishes developed Italian majorities. Since the religious feasts were so closely tied to the Italians' pride in their village or region, the church officials' rejection of them cut deep. As Italians became a numerical majority in more and more parishes, they became bolder about asserting their interests. In newspaper parlance at the time, the ensuing clash amounted in some cases to a "race war."

* * *

To Archbishop Corrigan's great embarrassment, Most Precious Blood Church was closed in 1893 after it defaulted on its construction loans. The bungling pastor from Bishop Scalabrini's order, Father Felice Morelli, had overspent in hopes that a grand building would attract more parishioners. He was replaced, but his successor couldn't pay back the large loans. Creditors then initiated foreclosure proceedings. While there was a logical financial explanation for the church's shutdown, it inevitably stirred up Irish-Italian conflict to the point that once again, what would ordinarily be a local matter came to the Vatican's attention. The ensuing controversy

Archbishop Michael A. Corrigan agreed to open
parishes for Italian immigrants. They were among
the ninety-nine parishes he started in seventeen
years. Photogravure from *Memorial of the Most
Reverend Michael Augustine Corrigan, D.D., Third
Archbishop of New York* (New York: Cathedral
Library Association, 1902).

ended up destroying the once-friendly relationship between Archbishop Corrigan and Bishop Scalabrini.

Father Lynch had continued to keep watch on the activity of the
Italian priests from Most Precious Blood and wrote to Corrigan
early in 1894 to inform him that they had mounted a campaign
aimed at pressuring the archbishop to reopen the church. Under
the priests' guidance, eleven thousand Italians signed a petition to
the papal nuncio to the United States, Archbishop Francesco Sa-
tolli. This was, after all, the Italians' own house of worship, a lovely

sanctuary that was sacred to them and a source of ethnic pride and identity. Feelings were inflamed. Lynch warned Corrigan that the priests were telling the Italian immigrants that without their own church, they "will be the slaves of the Irish as they have been before the church in Baxter Street existed, and that they will always be slaves."

The Italian Franciscans at St. Anthony of Padua Church came to the rescue and bought Most Precious Blood Church from the main creditor for $76,000. But it was another indignity for Scalabrini, since a rival religious order was needed to clean up the mess his own had created. Meanwhile, the church's closing angered influential Italian priests, who saw it as further evidence of Irish insensitivity. They sent angry letters to church authorities in Italy.[5]

The usually diplomatic Bishop Scalabrini dictated an angry letter to Corrigan that compared the archbishop to such villains as British co-

Bishop Giovanni Battista Scalabrini of Piacenza
pressed the Vatican and American bishops to do more
for Italian immigrants. Photo by F. Gregori, circa
1888. Courtesy of the Center for Migration Studies.

lonial merchants—a certain way to insult an Irishman—and, on top of that, Pontius Pilate and Herod. "I am forced to write you this time with the deepest sorrow," he began. "I would never have believed it, although from the beginning a Prelate had warned me not to trust the New York Curia, because sooner or later it would have betrayed me."

Corrigan wrote back, telling Scalabrini that when the papal nuncio in America received a petition that eleven thousand Italians endorsed, he told the organizers he would help if each person who signed it donated one dollar to help pay the debts of the church they wanted to save. No money was donated. "Having failed in America, the liars now run to Italy," Corrigan wrote, adding, "I have done more for the Italians than any other people and they thank me this way."[6]

Their seven-year exchange of letters stopped abruptly. Three years would pass before they resumed contact.

* * *

The Irish-Italian tensions first seen in lower Manhattan churches became common elsewhere in the city as Italian communities grew in once-Irish neighborhoods. That was so in 1890s Harlem, which was predominantly Irish and German. (It would not develop a significant black population until early in the twentieth century; a small Puerto Rican enclave started in the 1920s).[7] In 1892 the newspapers declared there was a "race war" between Irish and Italian parishioners at Our Lady of Mount Carmel Church on 115th Street in East Harlem. Throughout the 1890s and in later years as well, this term would often be applied to Irish-Italian battles, whether in the church, on the streets, in the workplace, or in politics. The term "ethnic" was not yet in wide use; "race" could have a different connotation, reflecting beliefs that inherent biological traits determined the suitability of different nationalities for American life. At other times, it would simply apply to residents of a particular region or nation, or their descendants.

"English-speaking and Italian elements are at war in the Catholic Church of Our Lady of Mount Carmel," the *World* reported, noting that the Irish pastor, Father Michael Carmody, had been forced out "on account of the hostility of the Italians." When the Italians gathered to celebrate their victory, a priest loyal to Carmody showed up, only to be punched out by the Italians' leader, a saloon owner and politico named Antonio Petrucci. One account related that the priest, Father John Banks, had asked Petrucci why he hadn't been to church.

The dispute traced to the Italians' annual feast of Our Lady of Mount Carmel, which Petrucci ran. The newspapers said the pastor was angry with the Italians for not giving the church enough money from the feast. While the Irish parishioners supported Carmody, the Italians seethed. They became even more angry over his decision to fire five Italian nuns from the parish school because they didn't learn English. Carmody had locked the sisters out of their convent after sending them on a vacation. Upon their return, he dispatched them to Archbishop Corrigan, who also was outraged—at Carmody. "I am shocked at the barbarous treatment of the sisters," the archbishop wrote to Carmody, ordering him to reinstate them. Carmody was later sent to lead a church in London.[8]

Despite the Irish-Italian tensions that had boiled over in the parish under Carmody's leadership, Italians from throughout the city flocked to the East Harlem church as it gained a reputation for answered prayers. Thousands attended Our Lady of Mount Carmel's annual feast on July 16. That led an Italian priest at the parish, Father Scipione Tofini, to come up with a bold plan to ask Pope Leo to coronate the statue of Our Lady of Mount Carmel, a rare papal honor that granted a bejeweled crown for only the most renowned figures of the Blessed Mother.

Surprisingly, the sixty-seven-year-old priest succeeded. Leo went out of his way to honor the East Harlem Madonna by waiving a requirement that statues receiving this papal designation have a long tradition. In doing so, the pope celebrated a style of piety that

Irish American clergymen had discouraged. Suspicious of American ways, the pope was not as concerned as the Irish American churchmen were about how Protestant America would view the southern Italians' traditions. His decree permitting the statue to be coronated was read to a cheering throng when the Madonna's feast was celebrated on July 16, 1903. Pope Leo died four days later.

One interesting turn in the decree was that it requested Archbishop John Farley to coronate the statue. Farley, a native of Newtown-Hamilton in County Armagh, was orphaned at age seven and had later been brought by an uncle to New York to study for the priesthood. He was elevated to archbishop in 1902 after Corrigan's death. While Corrigan had forbidden processions in the streets, his Irish-born successor would preside over one, on orders from an Italian pope. On Sunday, July 10, 1904, Farley led some fifty thousand people from Our Lady of Mount Carmel Church on 115th Street to Thomas Jefferson Park on 112th Street near the East River. A temporary shrine was set up to coronate the statue.

Two crowns—one for Mary, and a small one for the child Jesus—were encrusted with jewels, including an emerald from the pope. Although the day was a triumph for New York's fast-growing Italian community, some of the remarks from Irish American clergy were not exactly the compliments one would expect. Delivering the sermon at an 11:00 a.m. Mass that preceded the procession, the Jesuit provincial, the Reverend Thomas J. Campbell, praised the Italians as a people destined to have a huge influence in the United States. But, looking over his shoulder at Protestant efforts to convert them, he warned, "Remove the influence of the Catholic Church from this people, and I can tell you you have in them a menace to the country."

Having been singled out for a rare papal honor and crowned by the archbishop of New York, the beloved statue of Our Lady of Mount Carmel would reside for nearly two decades in the basement of the East Harlem church. On June 23, 1923, an Italian pastor moved it upstairs.[9]

* * *

By the first decade of the twentieth century, the solution to the "Italian problem" in the American Catholic Church was in sight. There would be Italian national parishes, but not Italian bishops. The Italians could have their feasts. The church would help Italian immigrants arriving at the port, warding off Protestant competitors. But despite these official solutions, the "Italian problem" would simmer for decades more, and the Irish-Italian battle in the church would intensify before it gradually faded. Conflicts similar to those in Transfiguration, Old St. Patrick's, Our Lady of Mount Carmel, and St. Anthony of Padua churches would play out elsewhere in Manhattan, the Bronx, Brooklyn, and many cities across the country, including Chicago, Boston, and Baltimore.

Irish American clergy continued to view Italian priests as second-rate, and the Italians responded with anger. The Reverend John T. McNicholas, a thirty-year-old Irish-born Dominican priest who built the Holy Name Society into a national Catholic fraternal organization and later became archbishop of Cincinnati, sparked one such fracas with his 1908 article urging that American priests and sisters—who were mostly Irish American—rather than Italians, should work with the Italian immigrants. Many of the Italian priests related poorly to their own people, he asserted. "Between a northern Italian and the Neapolitan or Sicilian there exists hardly any bond of sympathy. On the contrary, they often bear each other a racial hatred stronger than that which separates the Irish and the English," he wrote. McNicholas, who lived at St. Vincent Ferrer Church on the Upper East Side, added injury to insult: "And the pronounced tendency of many to work for pecuniary interests has given the entire class of priests the reputation of being lacking in zeal."

McNicholas also called for the American women's religious orders to send sisters to Italy to study. He saw the sisters' parish schools as the quickest way to Americanize the Italians, but lamented that few Italians attended them. One reason, he indicated, was that the American sisters and parents looked down on the Italian children. "In many places parents object to having their children attend school together with poorly-clad, unclean, Italian children," he wrote, suggesting that the sisters would understand the problem better if they knew more about poverty in southern Italy. He added that Italian students could study in separate classrooms "until such a time as no objection could be made to having them mingle with our own children."[10]

The Reverend Aurelio Palmieri, a prominent Augustinian priest born in Savona, a northern Italian seaport between Genoa and Nice, more than answered the stream of criticism directed against Italian emigrants and priests. Palmieri, a world-class expert on the Russian Orthodox Church, took time out from writing fifteen books and hundreds of scholarly articles to publish six articles on the Italians in America. He reached for a rhetorical weapon that opponents of the Irish have often wielded: criticism of drinking. Given the high rate of alcoholism among the Irish, he charged, their priests needed to focus on the "moral rehabilitation" of their own people rather than on the Italians. Moreover, Palmieri accused the Irish, in their opposition to Italian feasts, of being Puritan-like reformers who worried too much about what Protestants thought of Catholic customs. In his view, the Irish were rushing to Americanize the Italians, at a peril to the Italians' souls. "To claim that a foreigner who lands in America can in the blink of an eye deny the memory, traits, accents, the teachings of that mother whose name he bears carved in his heart, in his features, in his lips, in his character, in his feelings, is an absurdity," he wrote.

He complained that the Irish named cathedrals after the great Irish saints, such as Patrick and Malachy, but prevented the Italians from honoring their saints. Processions, he wrote, are a necessary extension of Italian piety. "A Sicilian cannot understand his Catholic faith without a lively veneration of Santa Lucia, Santa Rosalia and Santa Agata," he wrote, noting that for the Irish, Saint Patrick personified "a sublime epic" of holiness and miracles. The

Italians, he said, were not interested in him but felt drawn to their own national saints.

Palmieri especially scorned the article written by McNicholas. He declared that the plan McNicholas pushed to use American priests and sisters in place of Italians to work among the immigrants was rooted in a psychology of "pure Celtic blood." He called the *American Ecclesiastical Review*, which published McNicholas's article, "the major organ of the Hibernian-American clergy." "Hatred blinds," he wrote,

> and when the hatred against our immigrants expresses itself in the kind of paradoxes that Mac Nicholas [*sic*] prepares in his tirade against the Italian clergy, there is no wonder that our emigrants turn their backs on a church that reserves insults and contempt for them, segregates their children from the Catholic children of other races, and sprays bitter slander in their face.[11]

In one way or another, these bad feelings lingered in the church for several decades. "The Italians are not a sensitive people like our own," the Reverend Bernard Reilly, pastor of Nativity Church on the Lower East Side, wrote to Cardinal John Farley in 1917. "When they are told that they are about the worst Catholics that ever came to this country they don't resent it or decry it." He added that he was popular with the Italians in his parish.

The ethnic transition in churches such as Most Holy Rosary in East Harlem displeased longtime parishioners like Ida V. Collins, who was unhappy to see an Italian pastor appointed in 1925. She wrote to the cardinal of how dispiriting it was "when you think of our beautiful church turned over to them and we turned out of the House of God."[12] For this parishioner and many others, religion folded together with ethnic identity like hands clasped in prayer. To change the ethnic makeup of a parish or to appoint a pastor from another tribe seemed almost to change the religion itself. And yet, despite all the Irish-Italian turmoil within the church in the late nineteenth and early twentieth centuries, we can glimpse the seeds for better relations already sprouting.

That is so even for Father Thomas F. Lynch, who had such a difficult time understanding the Italian immigrants' religiosity when their great migration began in the 1880s. When historians remember him, it is for his prickly relationship with the Italians in his Five Points parish. Not recalled, however, is a shining moment when he risked his life to bring the last rites to Italian immigrants trapped in the debris of an underground construction accident on October 24, 1903.

Lynch was pastor of St. Elizabeth's Church at Broadway and 187th Street at the time. Workers building the subway 110 feet below the surface had set off explosions to blast through solid rock. After the blasts, the workers waited ten minutes for the dust to clear. Then a crew of twenty-one Italians and their Irish foreman went into the tunnel with an assistant electrician to rig lights. There was a rumbling sound, and some workers ran. Then ton upon ton of rock crashed down, crushing many of the workers.

Father Lynch witnessed the desperate rescue effort when he arrived at the scene deep beneath 195th Street, where workers had been tunneling southward through Washington Heights. The priest made his way down a steep, rocky hill and ventured inside the tunnel, where he encountered a grisly scene. One groaning Italian worker, his leg pinned beneath a ten-ton boulder, waved his arms limply. Since moving the rock would have killed the man, doctors amputated his leg to free him. (He later died.) Other trapped men were given up for lost and administered shots of morphine to ease their pain. Water from an underground stream poured into the tunnel, creating mud holes. Rescuers tried to set off small explosions to destroy some of the boulders in their path.

Lynch remained in this wreckage forty feet belowground for some five hours, chanting a litany and ministering the last rites to every worker he could reach despite fears that the tunnel would collapse further. "The survivors and those who had taken part in the work of rescue were still talking yesterday afternoon of the heroism of Father Thomas F. Lynch of St. Elizabeth's Roman Catholic Church," the *Sun* reported. The *Herald* offered other details: "For five hours he remained on the spot, his clothes grimy and his white hair wet and muddy, until the rescuers said the last man in the shift had been accounted for and he could be of no further service."

The danger Lynch faced is seen in an exchange between police and the ten-year-old son of the foreman Timothy J. Sullivan, who died in the collapse. Young Samuel begged the police to let him stay in the tunnel. "There's still danger here," the officers kept telling him.[13]

As Father Lynch worked his way through the mud and debris, workers frantically removing rocks with shovel, pick, and bare hands, he saw two Italian laborers, still alive, wedged between piles of rock on a ledge ten feet overhead. The crushed corpse of another worker was heaped over them. One of the trapped Italians, unable to speak, signaled weakly to the priest. The priest asked whether anyone could translate for him. A young man who feared his brother was buried in the collapse came forward. "I can speak a little English, Padre," he said.

"Then come with me and see what the poor fellow would say," Lynch said.

Firemen urged the two men not to go any nearer to the rock because it was wedged insecurely. But Lynch pressed forward and administered the last rites to the dying sandhog in a low voice. Then, having climbed atop what remained of a crushed cart used to haul away rocks, he reached out to the man and held an ivory crucifix to his lips.

It is hard to believe that this was the same priest who had once tried to stop Italians from celebrating their religious feasts and who claimed that they were not humiliated to attend services in the basement. The news reports capture a sense of duty in Father Lynch and suggest to us that perhaps he developed a greater appreciation over time for the Italian peasants and their religiosity. He lived on to become the oldest active priest in the Archdiocese of New York, serving his last twenty years as chaplain at a home for wayward girls in Peekskill. He died on December 28, 1936, at the age of eighty-nine.

By that time, the worst of the Irish-Italian bitterness in New York's Catholic Church had subsided. The language barrier that Lynch once faced had diminished, and, as he and Monsignor Kearney had hoped, there were many Italian Americans who had attended Catholic schools where mostly Irish American sisters instructed them. Italians had their own churches and were free to celebrate their beloved feasts. At the same time, they were becoming more accustomed to Irish ways. Some of the old tensions remained, however. In 1936, for example, Italians at St. Patrick's Old Cathedral were still pushing to finally have an Italian pastor, which they won with the appointment of the Reverend Ercole J. Rossi.

Clashes over what is sacred—over such intimate matters as how to honor the Virgin and the saints, or how to relate to religious authority—can create a particularly noxious resentment. But the church was hardly the only scene for Irish-Italian disputes. In other arenas—especially the workplace—the rivalry between the two ethnic groups was so intense that it often carried the potential to burst into open combat.

PART II

Turf Wars

Rivals in the Workplace

5

"Can't They Be Separated?"

On the warm Monday morning of August 20, 1888, a crowd gathered in the Westminster Hotel at Sixteenth Street and Irving Place in Manhattan to wait in anticipation for the Irish American labor leader Terence V. Powderly to testify in a congressional probe of what the *New York Times* headlined "The Immigration Invasion." The hearings, called to probe violations of the contract-labor law, had begun the previous month at the Westminster, a six-story edifice with canvas awnings shading each window and carriages parked outside.

Powderly arrived late, after the first witness was called, and quietly took a seat. Dressed in a worn gray suit, he was a short man with an outsized, bushy, graying mustache that masked his mouth, a prominent, dimpled chin, blue-gray eyes, and gold-rimmed glasses. Powderly led the Knights of Labor, but by 1888, the American Federation of Labor was on its way to displacing his organization as the leading union. Its leader, Samuel Gompers, was in the audience as well.

On the witness stand, Powderly identified himself as the grand master workman of the Knights of Labor since 1879, and a machinist by trade.

"What sort of men are admitted?" asked the committee chairman, Representative Melbourne Ford, an energetic, ambitious, thirty-nine-year-old first-term Democrat from the busy manufacturing city of Grand Rapids, Michigan.

"We admit all men who work at manual labor," except those who make or sell "drink," said Powderly, a teetotaler. "We exclude all bankers and also professional politicians and loafers."

And what did he mean by "professional politicians"?

"A man is a politician if he seeks all the money he can get out of it," Powderly responded.

As Powderly established his credentials as a wit, one congressman on the panel shifted uncomfortably in his seat and winced in pain as he moved his "rheumatic" legs, a newspaper would report the next day. That was General Francis Barretto Spinola, a New Yorker who was the first Italian American elected to Congress. Spinola still suffered leg pains from being shot in the heel while he led a charge against a Confederate position in northern Virginia during the Civil War, in which he served as a brigadier general. As for Powderly's remark about "professional politicians," Spinola was as partisan a Tammany Hall Democrat as could be, a wily political brawler with a reputation as a born politician.

Congressman Ford, at the time a promising political star, led Powderly with friendly questions. The labor leader recalled the upstanding Irish, Welsh, and English immigrants he knew in his youth and contrasted them with the immoral, unfit newcomers he saw in the present day. His father had come from Ireland with a shilling in his pocket and settled in Carbondale in the Pennsylvania coal country.[1]

Powderly cherished his family's Irish origins. In his autobiography, he wrote that his father migrated to America in 1827 after serving a three-week sentence in the Trim jail in County Meath for the crimes of shooting a rabbit on a lord's estate and being an Irishman who owned a gun. Powderly was active in the Irish land reform movement and served as treasurer of the Clan na Gael, a secret Irish American society dedicated to overthrowing British rule of Ireland. He was involved enough in the Irish cause that a former British spy who infiltrated Clan na Gael once claimed in a book that he heard the union leader advocate burning down English cities in retaliation for offenses against the Irish. "I am in

favor of the torch for their cities and the knife for their tyrants,"
Henri Le Caron quoted Powderly as saying during a heated Clan
na Gael meeting in Chicago. Powderly, alerted to the book by the
Irish nationalist Michael Davitt—whom he had made an honorary
member of the Knights of Labor—denied the account and threatened to sue for libel if the book, published in London, were printed
in America. He maintained that he was at the meeting but did not
speak.[2]

Powderly noted in his autobiography that as a young man, he
bought a Remington rifle and bayonet to go to war in the Irish
cause. But when a friend who was a native of England died, he sold
the rifle and bayonet to raise money for the man's wife and children. Powderly quipped that if his rifle didn't help to free Ireland,
at least it helped to bury an Englishman.[3]

The union leader told the committee that the Irish and other
northern European immigrants from earlier in the nineteenth century differed from the newcomers. They came to stay, became U.S.
citizens, and owned their own homes instead of renting, he testified. Now, he complained, more than half of the coal miners were
foreigners. The new immigrants were "too low" to make good citizens. "They retain their own manners and customs until they die,
or may go back to their own lands."

He accused the immigrant workers of having loose morals, asserting that it was common for eight to ten workers to live in a
house with one woman who took care of *all* their needs. "Not the
wife or mistress either, but she served all purposes," Powderly testified. "I don't know what you would call it; you know what I mean."

Congressman Ford pressed for the racy details. "A wife in common for the whole crowd?" he asked.

"Yes, sir," Powderly replied.

At that point, the country's first Italian American congressman,
Frank Spinola, spoke up. The unstated implication behind Powderly's tale of immorality was that the people involved were Italian.
As the *Times* had noted, the investigation "seems to be more interested in Italian immigration than in that of any other nationality,"

even though the committee had insisted that no nationality was being targeted.

Spinola was not known for defending Italian immigrants. The blue-eyed, white-bearded congressman was half-Irish, and moved easily through the Irish-dominated world of Tammany Hall politics. His paternal grandparents were Genoese; his father, John Spinola, a farmer and oysterman on Long Island's North Shore, had migrated from the Portuguese island of Madeira. His mother, Eliza Phelan, was descended from Irish immigrants and said to be the daughter of a captain who fought under George Washington in the American Revolution. When it came to being one of the boys, Powderly had nothing on Frank Spinola, a former Brooklyn fireman who loved staging big parties at his country mansion in Setauket, Long Island, going to the Saratoga horse races, watching illegal prizefights, and especially playing draw poker, at which, according to the *Brooklyn Eagle*, he "almost invariably won."[4]

Spinola decided to call Powderly on the card he had played with his story about the woman with multiple husbands. "Where did that state of facts exist?" he asked.

"I saw them in the city of Cleveland. This lady told me this two years ago," Powderly answered.

Spinola: "The woman herself told you that?"

If it seemed ridiculous that an immigrant woman in the Victorian era would tell an American stranger she was having sexual relations with eight men, Powderly's unflinching response gave no indication of it: "Yes, sir."

Finally, Spinola worked his way to the question it seemed he really wanted to ask from the outset: What was the woman's nationality? "There are a good many Polanders who become good citizens," Powderly responded.

Congressman Ford, who was leading the committee with the goal of clamping down on immigrant labor, stepped in to rescue Powderly from Spinola's questions and then upped the ante by getting him to claim that the immoral living conditions he allegedly witnessed in Cleveland could be found among immigrants in "a great many places."

"State whether they know what a home is as an American workman understands it," Ford told him.

"They have no conception of home as an American workman understands it," Powderly declared. He told the committee that the immigrant laborers he had seen would never make decent citizens. They had to be identified by numbers clipped to their pants because "it is impossible for an English person to speak to the men to be able to pronounce their name."

Powderly agreed with Ford that immigrants must be able to speak English—"nearly all our Germans do," he added. But Spinola was playing on his home field; the hearing was not just in his district, but in the hotel where he resided. So he stepped in once more even though it wasn't yet his turn to ask questions. "I thought your declaration was rather a broad one," he told the labor leader.

Powderly wavered. "I don't mean that, but I would have our American consuls abroad examine into the character of those who come over," he said, adding that he believed that immigrants must learn English to become citizens.

When Spinola's turn to ask questions arrived, he pressed Powderly further for his views on Italian immigrants. The witness responded that Italians "were not the right class to become citizens."

Spinola: "Leaving that question entirely out, are they an industrious class of people, as far as your observation has gone?"

"They work as a horse does; they are industrious in the same sense that a horse is—because he is driven to it," Powderly replied, before returning to talking of Hungarians.

"I am speaking of the Italians," Spinola reminded him, trying to make the point that if the Italians came to America voluntarily and not under labor contracts that chained them to low wages, they should be accepted.

Although Powderly already had argued that Italians would make poor citizens, he accepted Spinola's point. "If he knows how to come we have no objection," he said, adding that in a union, it

Terence V. Powderly, center, with leaders of the Knights of
Labor. His predecessor, Uriah Stephens, is at the top, center, and
P. J. McGuire is to Stephens's left. Lithograph by Kurz and
Allison, circa 1886. Library of Congress.

didn't matter where a worker came from, "whether from Ireland or
Scotland."

"We don't want it to appear in this investigation as if we were
aiming our arrows at any nationality," Spinola concluded.

Frank Spinola did not ordinarily demonstrate pride in his Italian roots. For the most part, the constituents in his long political
career were Irish or German. He was born in Stony Brook, New
York, in 1821 and came to Brooklyn at the age of sixteen to appren-

tice as a jeweler. His road to political popularity started when he led a Brooklyn firehouse; he was elected an alderman at the age of twenty-two. He remained proud of his years in Engine 4, wearing his shirt collars high in the style of firemen and thus popularizing a look called the Spinola collar. Spinola moved up to the State Assembly and then the Senate. Although he had steadfastly opposed the abolitionist movement, he threw himself into wholehearted support for the Union effort in the Civil War.

Spinola recruited a brigade that he led as brigadier general. While his military leadership skills were suspect, he fought with valor as the Union army followed General Robert E. Lee into northern Virginia from Gettysburg in 1863. He was shot twice while leading a successful charge at Wapping Heights. The following year, however, he was tried in a well-publicized court-martial on charges stemming from a riot in King's County's East New York section in which his recruits rebelled at his failure to pay them a promised bounty. He was accused of recruiting men while they were

Francis B. Spinola was the first Italian American elected to Congress. His constituents were mostly Irish. Library of Congress.

intoxicated. Ultimately, the charges were dropped and he was discharged honorably in 1865. After the war, he moved to New York, then a separate city from Brooklyn, and quickly moved up the ranks of Tammany Hall, becoming leader of the Sixteenth District, the "Gas House District," later known as Gramercy Park.

"To think of Tammany Hall without Gen. Francis B. Spinola is pretty much like thinking of Gen. Spinola without his great shirt collar," the *New York Times* commented.[5] From boss Richard Croker, a native of Clonakilty, County Cork, to the rivals vying for his own leadership post, Spinola dealt day in and day out with Irish politicos. When he presided over meetings of Tammany's Sixteenth District Association, he used Irish songs to build his foot soldiers' enthusiasm. In October 1886, Tammany gave Spinola the nod to run for Congress after Abram Hewitt left his "Gas House District" seat to run for mayor as a Democrat. (Hewitt won but was driven from office when the Irish turned against him in the 1888 election for refusing to observe the Saint Patrick's Day Parade or fly the Irish flag over City Hall on March 17. Hewitt would not attend ethnic parades or fly any other nation's flag, an essentially anti-immigrant stance that cost him the mayoralty.)

Spinola's rough-and-tumble years as a state legislator and controversial Albany lobbyist led to scathing criticism for his congressional candidacy. "If ever Spinola was on the right side of anything it was because somebody made it worth his while to be," the *Tribune* declared. But the "Wonderful Shirt Collar," as the paper dubbed Spinola, won election to Congress by a margin of 469 votes.

In Congress, Spinola was known for supporting Civil War veterans. His signature issue was the quest for federal funding to build a monument in Brooklyn's Fort Greene section to the Revolutionary War soldiers who died in British prison ships in the East River. Memorializing victims of the British was a cause that Irish Americans appreciated; Spinola pushed it constantly.[6]

There was no such political upside to his defense of Italian immigrants. His success was founded on alliances with Irish politicians. The Italians, who were crowding into the Lower East Side, had not yet found their way in great numbers to his Tenth Congressional District, which roughly spanned Fourteenth to Forty-Second Streets, between Seventh Avenue and the East River. While no one would call Spinola a statesman, he did stand up for the Italians and other immigrants.

He took his stand when Congressman Ford's committee released a scathing report that urged new restrictions on immigration. Echoing Terence V. Powderly's testimony, it assailed the immigrants being imported into Pennsylvania's coal regions by way of New York:

> They are of a very lower order of intelligence. They do not come here with the intention of becoming citizens. . . . They live in miserable sheds like beasts; the food they eat is so meager, scant, unwholesome, and revolting, that it would nauseate and disgust an American workman, and he would find it difficult to sustain life upon it. Their habits are vicious, their customs are disgusting, and the effect of their presence here upon our social conditions is to be deplored. They have not the influences, as we understand them, of a home; they do not know what the word means; and, in the opinion of the committee, no amount of effort would improve their morals or "Americanize" this class of immigrants.[7]

The report prompted angry remarks in the Italian Parliament; one member said there was widespread dislike for Italians because of biased coverage in New York newspapers.[8] As he released the report, Ford proposed an immigration law that would charge newcomers a five-dollar tax; limit the number of passengers per ship; and exclude those who did not intend to be U.S. citizens. Spinola dissented, agreeing only to accept a one-dollar tax on immigrants to pay for government costs.

Ford's bill didn't pass. But, as the *Times* editorialized, the congressional investigation "is pretty sure to mark the starting point of a new policy on the subject of alien additions to our population."[9] Both houses of Congress set up permanent committees to investigate immigration. Finding ways to restrict the flow of the poor from southern Italy would be a primary concern for decades to come, leading to a 1924 law designed to curtail immigration from southern, central, and eastern Europe.

*   *   *

Irish animosity to Italian workers stemmed from an economic rivalry that the city's business establishment exploited. As early as 1855, 86 percent of the city's laborers and 74 percent of the domestic workers were Irish-born. So were more than half of the masons, bricklayers, and plasterers. The immense number of Irish newcomers overwhelmed other groups, such as African Americans, much as the mass of low-wage workers from southern Italy would start to elbow out the working-class Irish in the 1880s. Irish workers quickly saw the advantage of unions and viewed African Americans, and then the Italians, as strikebreakers.[10] In 1874, with Italian immigrants arriving in a trickle, the *Times* editorialized with approval that their presence was helping employers to reduce wages. Unlike the Irish, the article noted, the Italians "have nothing to do with trades-unions," working without complaint for a company that brokered the trip from Italy for a percentage of wages and sold them their food, "as the Italians have their own tastes in the culinary direction." The newspaper suggested that employers hire Italians freely since they were accustomed to low wages.

"The Irish malcontents among the laborers can do little injury to the Italians, and the authorities will protect employers in their rights," the *Times* said. The managers of the New-York Italian Labor Company, which brokered the Italians' employment, responded with a letter to the editor that thanked the paper for its observations. It boasted that the Italians labored at 20 percent below the usual wage.[11]

Obviously, this played poorly with the Irish, who had turned to unions to break out of poverty. The boycott and other traditions of Irish resistance to the British helped to shape Irish Americans like Powderly as labor leaders.[12] When New York's first Labor Day parade was held on September 5, 1882, it was clear that the Irish played an outsized role in the union movement. Cigar makers, typographers, printers, bricklayers, masons, shoemakers: ten thousand people marched eight abreast beneath the hot sun to the music of twenty bands, carrying flags and placards to Union Square. The sidewalks were thronged with onlookers, some of whom joined the parade. Flag-draped wagons rolled along with the marchers, many of whom smoked cigars. The union leaders present had such names as McCabe, Davitt, Curran, Ryan, Hickey, Cunningham, Burke, Fitzgerald, and Coughlin. Terence V. Powderly was there. So was Peter J. McGuire, who had come up with the idea for the parade.

The march was a show of force after a labor defeat in a nearly eight-week freight-handlers' strike in the waterfront rail yards that summer.[13] Peter J. McGuire, or P.J., born to Irish immigrants on the Lower East Side of Manhattan in 1852 and a founder of the United Brotherhood of Carpenters and Joiners, later told a congressional committee that Italian workers shipped into Castle Garden, the immigration entry point before Ellis Island opened, had played a key role in breaking the strike. "They brought over hordes of Italians—Calabrians from the mountains of Calabria—in the holds of vessels and transported them from Castle Garden across to the railroad docks in Jersey City and along our piers here, and put them to work," he testified in New York on August 29, 1883. "Those men, Italians and others, slept in the holds of the vessels and were fed there, and were not allowed any liberty at all; they were in fact prisoners."[14]

The 1880s were a time of economic expansion. With railroads spreading across the West and the robber barons making big money on Wall Street, Manhattan's business districts filled with top-hatted men of means. By 1890, Joseph Pulitzer erected a 309-foot tower, the world's tallest building, on Park Row for his *New York World*.[15]

There was progress in the job market for both Irish and Italian immigrants. "The Italian scavenger of our time is fast graduating into exclusive control of the corner fruit-stands, while his black-eyed boy monopolizes the boot-blacking industry in which a few years ago he was an intruder," the journalist Jacob Riis wrote in 1890. "The Irish hod-carrier in the second generation has become a bricklayer, if not the Alderman in his ward."[16] But although Irish success was visible, it is important to note that for decades, there were large concentrations of the Irish in menial jobs. The New York Irish had once driven blacks out of jobs as laborers and craftsmen, creating tensions that exploded in the draft riots during the Civil War. In 1883, three-quarters of the construction laborers in the New York area were Irish. Ten years later, three-quarters were Italian.[17] With such a rapid ethnic transformation of the workforce, it's not surprising that Irish workers were bitter toward Italians willing to do their work for less pay.

Of course, the Italians were not the only immigrants arriving in big numbers. There was a wave of immigration from throughout southern and eastern Europe, especially Jews from Russia. But the Jewish migration was very different from the Italians'. As a result of discrimination dating to medieval times and, more recently, due to the laws of tsarist Russia, Jews were not ordinarily farm laborers. Nor did they live in rural areas. For the most part, Jewish newcomers lived in cities and towns, and were tailors, shoemakers, peddlers, garment makers. But both the Italians and the Irish came mostly from impoverished rural areas and sought out the urban equivalent of farm labor: heavy lifting on the docks, unskilled construction work, and excavation. The Irish had achieved civic power by the 1880s, but many of the men still worked as laborers.[18] As a result, Irish-Italian "race riots," as they were called, became common in the 1890s, especially when financial turmoil in 1893 heightened competition for jobs.

On April 18, 1892, Irish and Italian longshoremen went at it on the docks at the foot of Joralemon Street in Brooklyn, a spot that looked out on the new Statue of Liberty in the harbor, after an Irishman knocked the pipe from an Italian's mouth. The Italians ducked stones and cart rungs as they ran away from seventy-five to a hundred Irishmen. They returned to hurl coal and cinders at the Irish, who heaved bricks in return.

Violence also plagued work on the Brooklyn rail system that would provide a name for the pride of Brooklyn, the Brooklyn (trolley) "Dodgers." Before the streetcars could be dodged, the rails had to be laid—if only the separate Irish and Italian work crews could refrain from fighting.

On September 24, 1893, a "race war" broke out on Flushing Avenue when an Irish foreman ordered his men to redo a section of rail the Italians had completed, according to the *Eagle*. "After several men had been knocked down the Irishmen were reinforced by some of their compatriots in police uniform and the fight was stopped by the arrest of twenty Italians." The paper needled, "the Italians will be arraigned before an Irish police justice and will receive punishment befitting their crimes."

The underlying problem behind such fights, the newspaper said, was that the time had passed when "the heavy work of this country was done by men of Irish birth." If so, Irish workers had not gotten the notice. The same day the *Eagle* recalled the bygone days of Irish labor, Irish and Italian crews installing track at Hudson Avenue and Nassau Street in Brooklyn fought it out near the Brooklyn Navy Yard. Tensions had been smoldering for days. They flared when the brawny Irish foreman, John Cusick, told the Italians that a curved rail they were about to spike was not straight and needed to be taken up. The Italians' foreman, Joseph Sugaretto of 64 Smith Street, told his men to disregard the order, and the two bosses started swearing at each other. Some news accounts said Sugaretto punched Cusick, touching off the fracas. Others said that as they prepared to fight, the Italians rushed Cusick, and the Irish retaliated, with both sides using their picks, crowbars, and shovels as weapons. Some of the Italians went up to a nearby tenement roof, dislodged bricks from the chimney and threw them at Irishmen, felling them. Irish onlookers joined the battle, and the twenty-five Italians fled down Nassau Street with about a hundred people in pursuit, raining stones upon them. Police finally intervened and, according to the *Times*, "without waiting to learn anything about the merits of the case . . . attacked the gang of Italians with their clubs." Twenty Italians were led away to the stationhouse, trailed by the Irish.[19]

Afterward, the recording secretary of an Italian American Democratic club wrote to the *Eagle* suggesting that honoring the Italian independence day would help solve the problem. The forty-year-old Italian-born clerk Gerard Antonini urged that

> the Italian tricolor . . . be permitted next year to float alongside the American flag on the Brooklyn and New York city halls on the 20th of September as the Irish flag is always raised very prominently on St. Patrick's day. Let us indulge the hope, as well, that these conflicts between Irish and Italian laborers will cease and that the day is not far distant when they shall shake hands over the bloody chasm . . . and fraternize as they should.[20]

Despite Antonini's hopes, fights between Irish and Italian laborers became so common that the *Eagle* ran an editorial headlined "Can't They Be Separated?" The paper urged contractors to "keep their gangs of workmen distinct—the Irish in one street and the Italians in another."[21]

But Irish-Italian resentment continued. One example is a battle fought on a Manhattan construction job at 412–414 West Thirty-Seventh Street, a few doors down from a police station, on July 13, 1896. The Italians had complained bitterly that the Irish foreman, James Foley, gave the Irish light duty. That seemed especially so when it came time to mix mortar. The job required two workers—one who sweated it out stirring lime and sand, the other who stood by with a hose, keeping the mix moist. After their lunch break, Foley told an Italian worker, identified in news accounts (which almost always spelled Italian names wrong) as Sandel Sandow, to mix the mortar while an Irishman, Patrick Smith of 334 West 49th

Street, would handle the hose. The two workers began to argue, and Sandow splashed the lime around with his hoe.

"Be careful, you dago," Smith said, and hosed down Sandow's shoes. In a flash, the two men started pummeling each other, and the rest of the thirty workers joined in while local residents piled out of the tenements and cheered. Bricks, ready at hand, were hurled back and forth, breaking ten windows on the street. It took police, billy clubs drawn, a half hour of effort to break up the fight and arrest six men, including the two men who started it. Smith was bruised from being thrown headfirst into a cellar. "Irish Fight Italians," one headline put it.[22]

Such battles between Italian and Irish laborers helped create poisonous resentments that leached into other areas of the Irish-Italian relationship: in the church, in politics, in police-community relations. Yet it began to become clear that both sides needed each other, if only for economic reasons. The Italians needed to become part of the labor movement to break out of the exploitation they suffered. And by the early 1900s some Irish labor leaders realized that they needed to bring workers from the new wave of immigration into their fold, if only so they wouldn't break strikes.[23] But the battles were far from over.

* * *

Appointed in 1898 as the nation's immigration commissioner, Terence V. Powderly continued to fight the importation of low-wage workers from Italy. It was a losing battle. The padrones, labor brokers operating in lower Manhattan, brought in hordes of men willing to work for extremely little pay. The Italian laborers were dispatched far and wide, only to be exploited. "The padrone is king of the Italian quarter," the writer E. Lyell Earle reported the following year. "He regulates everything for his countrymen, and relieves them of much care and more money. He writes their letters, changes their coin, secures them work, and receives a fat commission on everything bought and sold in his little kingdom."[24]

Testifying before the U.S. Industrial Commission in Washington in 1899, Powderly bemoaned that it was now possible to walk through the small Pennsylvania mining towns where he had grown up and hear the "American language" spoken only rarely. He recalled an Irishman who came to America unable to read and write, but whose children were in high positions. "I would not want to be accused of harboring race prejudice or bigotry," he said. "We could not get a better race than came from the British Isles and Germany." He drew a contrast with the "less desirable" southern Italians.

Powderly told the panel that he wanted to crack down on illegal Italian immigration by closing the Italian Bureau of Emigration inside the Barge Office, where immigrants were processed in lower Manhattan while Ellis Island was being completed. The Italian government had staffed the agency in 1894 as part of an effort with U.S. officials to break the padrone system. The idea was for the Italian government inspectors to reach the immigrants as soon as they arrived—even before they went through U.S. immigration clearance—so that they wouldn't have to rely on the padrone. Italian officials believed that the program had helped many of their countrymen, even if it had not broken the power of the padrone.

But Powderly charged in this public hearing that the Italian bureau had advised Italian emigrants on how to evade American immigration laws aimed at preventing convicts, paupers, and the diseased or disabled from entering the country. Furthermore, he asserted, he had received information that the Italian agency was secretly allied with the padrones. He identified his source for this claim as the colorful Italian adventurer and soldier of fortune Celso Caesar Moreno, best known for having briefly held the post of prime minister of Hawaii. Powderly did not disclose, however, that Moreno was convicted in Washington in 1895 of criminally libeling the Italian ambassador to the United States with these same accusations. Moreno had a history of trying to spread false charges against the Italian ambassador, Baron Fava. He was "a familiar figure in nearly every newspaper office on 'the Row,'" the *Times* reported, referring to Park Row, the street along City Hall Park where most of the city's major dailies were located.

When word of Powderly's testimony reached Rome, Italian officials angrily complained to U.S. Ambassador William F. Draper. He thought the Italians were right, calling Powderly's testimony "absolutely without foundation." But Powderly's boss, Treasury Secretary Lyman J. Gage, backed him up and let him close the immigration office, further enraging the Italian officials.[25]

* * *

By 1900, it was obvious that Italians had taken many jobs the Irish once held, and their immigration was about to intensify. Within a decade, the number of Italians residing in the five boroughs would more than double, to 340,765. Many Italians returned to Italy (unlike the Jews, who showed little desire to return to the land of the tsars). But many more arrived, especially when ads were posted in Italy for jobs.[26] A new wave was expected when it was announced that a $35 million contract had been issued to build a tunnel for New York's new subway. "Every Italian who can beg, borrow, or steal his passage money is getting ready to come to New York to dig his share of the tunnel and get part of that $35,000,000," said Edward F. McSweeney, Irish American director of the federal immigration office in New York, adding that the steamship companies had created a gold-rush atmosphere in Italian cities—akin to the Klondike—by posting notices about the contract.[27] This prospect so alarmed the French-born socialite Assemblyman Maurice Minton of Manhattan's Upper West Side that he submitted a resolution two days later to the legislature calling for Italian laborers to be barred from working on the subway tunnels. Italians, the resolution stated, were taking jobs "to the detriment of our Irish-American and German-American citizens."[28]

Father Michael J. Henry, director of the Mission of Our Lady of the Rosary near the Battery at the southern tip of Manhattan, began to advise the Irish not to migrate. Since 1883, the mission had helped thousands of the Irish arriving at nearby Castle Garden to find work in New York, providing a temporary home for those who did not have a friend or relative to meet when they debarked. In October 1900, Henry, a stocky man with a fading hairline and round, rimless glasses, penned a letter to Bishop John J. Clancy in Sligo, Ireland, warning that unskilled young men who came to America "have to enter into competition with their pick-axe and shovel with other nationalities—Italians, Poles, etc. to eke out a bare existence. The Italians are more economic, can live on poor fare and consequently can afford to work for less wages than the ordinary Irishman."[29]

A real estate businessman interviewed by the *Brooklyn Eagle* in 1900 observed much the same. "The day of the Irish hod carrier has long been past," he said, referring to the laborers who lugged supplies to bricklayers. "But it is the Italian now that does the work. Then came the Italian carpenter and finally the mason and the bricklayer." The businessman complained that many Italians were taking jobs that had belonged to American citizens. There seemed little way to resist. "The Italians . . . are the public works laborers of the time," the *Eagle* noted in another 1900 article. "They work diligently with the pick and shovel and the Irish bosses make them perform prodigious tasks."[30]

As New Yorkers waited giddily for their magnificent new underground rapid transit system to be built, the general contractor John B. McDonald hired thousands of Italians to dig the tunnels and haul the rock. McDonald, born in 1844 in Fermoy in County Cork, had come to America when he was three years old. His father, Bartholomew McDonald, at first a laborer, established himself as a local contractor and moved up in politics to serve on the Board of Aldermen. After working for a time with his father, John McDonald set off on his own, taking a job as timekeeper in construction of the city's water system, earning forty-five dollars a month. He never forgot how to keep track of how much money his workers earned.[31] After becoming a foreman, McDonald started his own company and did progressively bigger jobs, including a famed railroad tunnel beneath Baltimore. Among his jobs was the

Jerome Park Reservoir in the Bronx, close to where he had grown up. He hired 1,800 Italians, and paid them $1.25 a day.

McDonald was adept at squelching the Italians' walkouts. When a strike broke out in May 1899, the foreman James O'Leary came over to the office and told McDonald how angry the Irish workers on his crew were at the Italians for striking. "I came here to say, Mister McDonald, that the one hundred Irish under me begs your leave to tackle these damned dagos and clean them out," he said in a thick brogue. McDonald thanked O'Leary for his loyalty, then told him not to worry: the police were coming. With 150 officers on hand, work resumed and most of the Italians returned the next day.[32]

As expected, McDonald hired mainly Italians for the unskilled laborers' jobs on the subway. The stated pay was $1.50 for a ten-hour day, although workers said they often received $1.25 a day. Irish-Italian tensions were part of the daily routine. In 1901 a *Times* reporter poked fun at a crew of workers he observed: "It was comical to watch the other day an Irishman who had been placed at work with five Italians in a narrow trench." Listening to the five as they "chattered in their own language incessantly" led the red-haired Irishman to work with "a ferocious look on his face." Finally, he grew so impatient that he rushed from the trench, cursing and gesturing as he told the Irish foreman that he wouldn't work with the "guineas" anymore. The Irishman was transferred.[33]

On another occasion, police had to call out reserves to quell a riot that broke out after more than a hundred Italians excavating a tunnel near Sixty-Fifth Street and Broadway refused to work. Some of the Italians knocked the project supervisor, Frank Bradley, to the ground when he ordered them to work. Irish laborers rushed to Bradley's aid, and police had to intervene.[34]

There was a mythology at the time that Italians were happy to take jobs at lower pay and longer hours than the Irish would accept. In fact, Italian workers smoldered over laboring longer and cheaper—and usually for Irish bosses. They would strike spontaneously, with great rage, but lacked an organization to follow through.[35]

Tito Pacelli, an immigrant from Campania, led
Italian laborers in a strike for better pay and shorter
hours, stopping subway construction in 1903.
Courtesy of Sherry Pacelli Haddox.

The Italian subway workers needed a union savvy enough to
stand up to McDonald. Tito Pacelli, a handsome twenty-eight-
year-old southern Italian immigrant with deep, hooded brown
eyes, a stylish handlebar mustache, and dark hair swept neatly back
from his forehead, emerged to start one with help from the American Federation of Labor. The newly formed Rockmen's and Excavators' Union was part of the AFL's New York umbrella group, the
Central Federated Union.

The Italian workers struck on May Day, 1903. Pacelli had won
the Italians' support by staging an elaborate parade to launch the
strike. Some twenty thousand marchers took part in a march that

started at 10:30 a.m. at the union's office in East Harlem's Little Italy, 305 East 113th Street. Flags fluttered from all the tenements as crowds turned out to watch as some twenty marching bands passed. The marchers were almost all Italian immigrants, with the exception of about a hundred blacks who were members of the union. About eight thousand of the marchers had come down from the Bronx by train; according to Pacelli, the Bronx workers were paid less than those laboring in Manhattan. All carried small American flags.

While the *Times* derided the strike as an excuse for a day off, Pacelli and his members had begun their drive with an impressive show of force. Still, it was unclear how much support the Italian laborers would receive from the mostly Irish trades locals in the Central Federated Union. The trade workers, locked out when the strike started, were eager to get back to work. They were not pleased to strike for Italians, given their reputation for being scabs.

McDonald quickly informed the Central Federated Union that the strike violated the union's two-year contract with him. Pacelli's problem was that the Rockmen's and Excavators' Union formed only after the subway workers' contracts were negotiated with McDonald, which had left the Italian laborers with the rock-bottom wages the contractor decreed. All the other unions had agreed to a contract.

McDonald also launched a public relations offensive in the newspapers, which admired him for spearheading the long-anticipated subway construction. His personal story was appealing: He had overcome a poor, Irish immigrant background to become one of the nation's leading builders. As the *Times* would later write, "The poor Irish lad, with little scientific culture, but taught in the school of experience, achieved where others had deliberated, hesitated, and failed to attempt."

McDonald was close to Tammany Hall—Richard Croker, a fellow Corkman, was the Democratic boss from 1886 to 1902—and the contractor took advantage of that to secure police help against the strikers. McDonald was a longtime Tammany Hall member,

as his father was, and held a seat on Tammany's finance committee. He admitted donating $2,500 a year—worth about $60,000 today—to Tammany, but was suspected of shelling out twenty times
that amount.[36]

With his Irish-immigrant connections to politicians and police,
his reputation for making wondrous public-works plans a reality,
and his rags-to-riches personal story, John B. McDonald towered
over Tito Pacelli in a battle of this sort. He had another card to
play as well. A prominent Italian who served as a hiring agent—a
padrone—for the subway job was working to undermine the strike.
James E. March, formerly Antonio Maggio, had started out in
Tammany Hall but switched to the Republican Party when the
Irish bosses refused to let Italians hold office. He became the local
Republican leader on the Lower East Side and was appointed port
warden by Governor Theodore Roosevelt, godfather to one of his
children. March had arrived in New York in 1872 at the age of
twelve from Albano de Lucania in the Potenza province of southern Italy and would become a millionaire by serving as labor contractor for the Erie Railroad.[37]

Delegates to the Central Federated Union debated the Italians'
strike angrily. "These men are not American citizens; everyone
knows that," a delegate named Staunton from the Electrical Workers' Union declared. "Some of them are the very scum of the earth.
This talk about wanting to live up to American standards is all rot.
Most of them want to make as much money as they can here and
then hurry back to Italy."

Samuel C. Donnelly, former president of the Typographi-
cal Union and a member of the Board of Education, disagreed.
"Some of our ancestors started here with a pick and a shovel, and
it comes with bad grace from us to look down on people who start
where our ancestors did," he argued. Staunton looked disgusted
and someone muttered loudly about the "dagoes." An Italian newspaper, L'Araldo Italiano, condemned the anti-Italian remarks. "Racial prejudices are always sad," the paper said, "and especially do
not belong in American institutions. But they are absolutely in-

John B. McDonald, an immigrant from County
Cork, contended with a 1903 strike by Italian
laborers when he built New York's first subway.
Bain News Service, George Bantham Bain
Collection, Library of Congress.

excusable and out of place in an association such as the Central
Federated Union."[38]

At first, the central union at least tried to give the appearance
that it supported the strike. But soon the president, James J. Hol-
land, announced there was nothing more he could do. It was a
difficult position for Pacelli, an immigrant from San Salvatore
Telesino, a village located in the Benevento province of Campania,
northeast of Naples.

Il Progresso Italiano, although anti-union, carried a lengthy,
front-page article that praised Pacelli as a "young man of courage
and faith" who had "rare insight, the virtue of speaking prudently,

and the ability to look beneath the surface," qualities "essential for men in battle." The newspaper also hailed "the energy and nobility" of the strikers. Pacelli noted in the interview that he had previously organized masons, whose strike, he added, had led to a daily wage increase from two dollars to four for eight hours of work. He said all the other workers on the subway job—carpenters, masons, bricklayers—worked an eight-hour day rather than the ten hours his men labored. "The contractors hope that the Italians will soon get tired of staying together—waiting for the hour of betrayal," he contended. "But this time they are very very wrong." Pacelli could see the forces arrayed against him. McDonald had tried "to incite the newspapers against us," he charged. "They are trying to raise American public opinion against the Italians. The usual story."[39]

On Sunday, May 10, 1903, McDonald issued an ultimatum for the Italian strikers to return to work by Wednesday or lose their jobs. The Central Federated Union told Pacelli it was over—the strike no longer had its support. But the Italian workers rejected McDonald's demand. Undercut by the other unions, Pacelli tried to persuade his members to settle the dispute. But the sandhogs shouted him down, especially adamant that they get relief from the ten-hour day. When some workers accused him of conspiring with management, Pacelli offered to resign. The majority wanted him to stay, but there were fears for his safety. As the Italians' anger grew, the *Times* reported that every police officer in the city had been put on emergency duty and that Italian-born detectives were used to infiltrate Pacelli's union meetings.

One unnamed officer in East Harlem told the *Post*, "We are sore on the Italians up here and have a grudge to settle with them some time," stemming from an attack on police several years earlier in a saloon on 112th Street between First and Second Avenues. Meanwhile, some of the Italians began returning to work, firing up the strikers' anger even further.

The tensions led to Irish-Italian conflicts, since the police and construction foremen were usually Irish. Twenty Italian workers were arrested at a subway shaft at 185th Street for threatening a foreman, Patrick Meehan. Eleven more Italians were arraigned for trouble at 145th Street and Broadway. Cursing from their windows, Italian women threw stones at Irish laborers working near Spring Street. Four Italian women, two of them with knives, were arrested at Broadway and Sixty-Eighth Street for throwing stones on non-union rockmen, knocking one of them down. The papers reported on a May 22 riot that broke out on Second Avenue north of Houston Street when a mob made up of striking Italian laborers and not a few women attacked Irish American electricians who were employed, not on the subway, but on constructing an unrelated trolley line. A police officer, Thomas F. Lang, was beaten in the melee but managed to pull out his revolver and jam it into the mouth of the gang's leader, Palermo Rosso of 135 Elizabeth Street. Lang threatened to blow off Rosso's head if there were any further resistance. The *Times* cheered police for cracking down on the strikers, saying that officers should know "that the free use of their night sticks . . . will be approved." Meanwhile, James E. March, the Republican leader and padrone, announced that he had succeeded in persuading many of the Italians to return to work, breaking the strike.[40]

Through the five-week strike, Tito Pacelli was able to wring twenty-five cents a day from John B. McDonald for the workers. McDonald became a hero for completing the city's first subway line, and three weeks ahead of schedule. On the day the subway opened, October 27, 1904, three photos and a sketch of a homburg-wearing, mustached McDonald, "The Man Who Dug the Tunnel," were spread across a page of the *World*. In an article he wrote, McDonald vaguely acknowledged "those in whose hands the construction and equipment rested."[41]

* * *

The rapid re-peopling of New York with great numbers of immigrants from southern Italy and eastern Europe was bound to change the ethnic makeup of the city's workforce and cause intense competition for jobs, especially after the economy faltered in 1893. The rivalry was especially powerful between the working-class

Irish and the Italians. Both came from generations of landless farm laborers, a background that suited them to compete for the most arduous physical labor—dangerous work that built a great metropolis, highlighted by such monumental achievements as the water supply system, the Brooklyn Bridge, and the subway.

It's true that to some extent, the Irish laborers moved up to more skilled work as the Italians took on the menial jobs. As Jacob Riis noticed, the Irish had started out as hod carriers, delivering materials to bricklayers and masons, and then became the bricklayers as Italians assumed the backbreaking supply task. It all seems rather nice, since we know that soon enough, Italians became the skilled bricklayers and masons. But the many newspaper reports about continual fighting between Italian and Irish workers show us that such transitions were actually very rocky, especially when jobs dried up in times of economic stress. The workplace rivalry between the working-class Irish and southern Italian immigrants in the late nineteenth century was nasty and intense, and it further divided peoples whose language and customs differed. The sort of bitterness that officials such as Terence V. Powderly showed to immigrant workers would continue to play out in the American story, even to this day. So too would the eagerness of business leaders to take advantage of immigrant workers who were willing to work longer hours for less pay.

Despite the intensity of their feelings about Italian immigrant workers, Irish American union officials came to realize that they needed to organize them. A change can even be detected in Powderly, who spoke so dismissively of Italian immigrant laborers while leading the Knights of Labor in the 1880s and who, as immigration commissioner, took steps to account more strictly for immigrants' national origin, literacy, and ability to speak English.[42] Powderly traveled to Italy, visiting small villages where he stayed in farmhouses. "I do confess that when I went to Europe the first time I was more or less tarred with an anti-immigration stick," he wrote, explaining that he resolved to set aside his preconceived notions. He added, "I learned to know these people by breaking bread with them in their homelands." He decided that "we have not done our duty by ourselves or by our country, in not getting close enough to our immigrants to hear their heartbeats. If we thought they were wrong we could not set them right by remaining aloof from them."[43]

Meanwhile, the more radical voices in the labor movement sensed that the influx of immigrants had presented an opportunity that the mainstream union leaders were slow to grasp. Inspired by socialist ideas, they aimed to organize the new generation of immigrants who were reshaping the nation's workforce. The Italian workers, so often frustrated by both the labor unions and management, were a promising place to start.

6

"The Other Half of Me!"

Elizabeth Gurley Flynn learned young not to hate the Italians. Born in 1890 in Concord, New Hampshire, she moved to the South Bronx with her family at the age of ten. Her mother, Annie Gurley, had grown up speaking Gaelic in Loughrea, County Galway. When an Irish friend sniffed about "garlic-eating Italians," she responded that her grandmother had pulled up garlic from her garden in Ireland and eaten it raw like radishes. When Elizabeth was a little older, she saw neighborhood kids throw stones at "dago" Italian laborers when they passed through selling coal. Her mother would not tolerate this.

Flynn took pride in growing up in a family that rebelled against convention. She'd been brought up on revolution—Irish revolution. "The awareness of being Irish came to us as small children, through plaintive song and heroic story," she wrote in her autobiography. "As children, we drew in a burning hatred of British rule with our mother's milk." She wrote with pride that her forefathers in Mayo had been active in every generation's revolt against the British, with all four of her great-grandfathers involved in the 1798 uprising. One great-grandfather, Paddy Flynn, was known as "Paddy the Rebel," foreshadowing her own nickname, "Rebel Girl."

Her Papa, Thomas Flynn, had started out as a laborer in a Maine rock quarry. He became a civil engineer, but the family lived on the edge of poverty while he pursued socialist causes. The Flynns rented a chilly, rundown, cold-water flat at 511 East 134th

Street in the Bronx with a view of the Harlem River and the New York skyline.[1]

A week after she turned sixteen, Elizabeth and her father were arrested in August 1906 for "speaking without a permit" in a rally at Broadway and Thirty-Eighth Street. Elizabeth, wearing a broad-brimmed Panama straw hat with her long black hair in a single braid down her back, had attracted such a large crowd with her dramatic speaking style that traffic was blocked. Magistrate Walsh released her the next day at Jefferson Market Court in Greenwich Village with a warning to return to her studies. The *Times* editorialized that "the ferocious Socialist haranguer, to wit, Miss Flynn, who will graduate at school in two years, and whose shoe tops at present show below her skirt, tells us all what to think." But the more populist *World* admired her pluck—and her good looks, running large photos of her twice in the same week. "Miss Flynn is a remarkably pretty young girl, with a fresh complexion and big gray eyes," the paper observed.[2] The next month, Theodore Dreiser wrote about "An East Side Joan of Arc" who was a high school sophomore. "The girl is a typical Irish beauty, with the blue eyes, filmy black hair and delicate pink complexion of the race from which she is sprung," he wrote, adding, "Mentally, she is one of the most remarkable girls that the city has ever seen."[3]

The determined Irish American beauty soon made it her business to organize masses of Italian immigrant men—a fertile but unfamiliar field for a young socialist whose Bronx neighborhood was almost entirely Irish and German. James Connolly, destined to become a revered Irish patriot who helped lead the 1916 Easter Rising, a revolt against British rule in Ireland, was her bridge to the Italians.

Connolly moved to New York in 1903 and hurled himself into organizing workers in the name of socialism. Meeting Connolly at a socialist rally at Washington Park in Newark was unforgettable, Flynn recalled. Connolly, born in 1868, grew up in Edinburgh, the son of Irish emigrants. With his wife and three children, he moved to Dublin and merged his twin passions for socialism and Irish nationalism as a writer, speaker, and organizer. Flynn described him as a plain, dark-eyed man with a high forehead and big black mustache, and wrote that he rarely smiled.

They met again in 1907 at an Italian socialist meeting in Newark. It was held on a Sunday morning, as Flynn noted, because the anticlerical Italians were willing to skip church but not their Sunday afternoon spaghetti-and-wine ritual. Flynn spoke her piece and, during an intermission, asked Connolly who would speak in Italian. Connolly's response was to wait and see. To Flynn's surprise, Connolly spoke in good Italian, delighting the audience. He had learned the language to further his organizing. Flynn enjoyed the morning, noting later that the Italians had served cake and coffee, while most socialist gatherings she attended offered no more than water.[4]

* * *

Elizabeth Gurley Flynn met the love of her life in the tumult of a famed textile workers' strike in Lawrence, Massachusetts, in 1912. "His name was Carlo Tresca," she wrote. "I met him on May Day, 1912, on the street in Lawrence, a very dramatic event for me then and one destined to have far-reaching consequences in my life."[5]

Tresca, a handsome, slender, six-foot-tall dynamo of a man with pale blue eyes and brown hair, was the editor of the Italian-language anarchist newspaper *L'Avvenire*, or *Tomorrow*. Born in 1879 in Sulmona in the mountainous Abruzzo region ninety miles east of Rome, he grew up privileged in a prominent family but fled to America in 1904 to avoid a one-year jail term for criminal libel. Both he and Flynn were married to others when they met, but they fell in love in the emotional crucible of what became known as the Bread and Roses Strike, one of the most famous strikes in American history.[6]

Flynn went to Lawrence with the International Workers of the World leader Bill Haywood to fire up the mill workers after the union's two chief organizers on the scene, both of them Italian Americans, were arrested. With the American Federation of Labor slow to organize immigrants, the IWW had stepped in with its more radical, socialist message. Many of the striking workers were Italian, while some of those who opposed the walkout were devout Irish or French Canadian Catholics who objected to the IWW's socialism.

Tresca arrived by train on May 1 to stir up the Italian workers and to be where the action was. Tresca, aged thirty-three, had established himself as an agitator of the first order. Flynn, twenty-one years old, quickly came to admire his dramatic oratory, his fearlessness in the midst of the strike disorder, and his savvy strategizing.

Tresca jotted dreamy, poetic notes in books he gave her. In an inscription dated November 17, 1912, "For fellow worker E. G. Flynn," he wrote,

> Yes, death is a Triumph at any time
> To him who gives his life for Love,
> Brotherhood, Justice, Equality, for
> Human progress[7]

Tresca gave Flynn a novel by Gabriele D'Annunzio, Italy's leading literary personality at the time. *The Maidens of the Rocks* was a curious choice, since D'Annunzio, who would become an ardent Fascist, hardly mirrored Tresca's or Flynn's politics. But the author had other qualities that must have appealed to Tresca. They hailed from the same region of Italy, and D'Annunzio was well known for his scandalous love affairs.[8] He wrote in a passionate, sensual style that Tresca admired. A note Tresca penned to Flynn on November 24, shortly before returning temporarily to his wife, would have fit seamlessly into the novel. "You go into a garden of beautiful and fragrant flowers; your heart swells with joy and your mind is elevated and forgets all the miseries of life," he wrote. "Enter into the garden of my heart, Elisabetta."[9]

Flynn, who wrote poetry, gave Tresca a pocket-sized edition of Elizabeth Barrett Browning's *Sonnets from the Portuguese*, underlining passages that must have captured the whirl of her own emotions: She "*was caught* up into love and taught the whole of life in a new rhythm."

It was a heady time for both, with swirling emotions and high hopes for socialism, given that the Socialist Party candidate Eugene Debs had attracted more than nine hundred thousand votes— about 6 percent—for president in 1912, a race Woodrow Wilson won. The Lawrence strike succeeded in winning significant wage increases for the mill workers and set off a new era of immigrant strikes, continuing with the Silk Strike the following year in Paterson, New Jersey.[10]

American society was in a progressive period, but this openness to new ways went only so far. For all their power in labor unions and big-city politics, the Irish still faced bitter anti-Catholic fervor. Italians, like other immigrants from southern and eastern Europe, were viewed as inferior, un-American, and even dangerous. From radicals like Tresca and Flynn, the answer to the divisions in American society was not in moderate progressive reform but in unification under the banner of class. But as their love story shows, cultural differences based on ethnicity were not so easy to overcome.

The rhythm of their relationship picked up in January 1913 when Tresca left his wife, Helga, and their daughter, Beatrice, at home in New Kensington, Pennsylvania, to organize a hotel workers' strike with Flynn and the IWW in New York. Flynn was separated from Jack Jones, a Minnesota miner she had married at seventeen; she had a young son, Fred, from that marriage. Leaving such concerns behind, she had the flattering experience at age twenty-two of being described as leader of a strike that played out on the front pages of the city's newspapers. "Miss Flynn the Real Power behind the Men," the *Times* headlined one story.[11] Owners of midtown Manhattan's poshest hotels and restaurants pushed City Hall to let police use their clubs on the strikers, and hired their own enforcers. Proprietors such as Jack Dunston, who owned the all-night Jack's Restaurant at Sixth Avenue and Forty-Third Street, looked to hire scabs. Dunston said he had replaced ten striking Italian cooks with "ten Irishmen and Americans, who were not afraid of a fight."

Passions peaked on the night of January 24, 1913. Flynn had brought the workers to "a high state of excitement" with her oratory, one news account reported, and Tresca "did not allay the excitement" when he spoke. During these speeches at Bryant Hall on Sixth Avenue between Forty-First and Forty-Second Streets, a rumor circulated through the crowd that several undercover detectives had infiltrated the meeting and then left. Striking waiters rushed into the street looking for the detectives, then wound up fighting with uniformed police officers posted outside. Tresca ran out to call the workers back to the hall, but the cops didn't understand what he said and tried to arrest him as a ringleader. Then Flynn dashed out into the street to rescue Tresca and disperse the strikers; she was clubbed on the wrist and arm.[12]

In the meantime, a police detective knocked to the ground in the melee grabbed for Tresca, who already had lost his suit jacket. Detective David Kuhne latched onto Tresca's vest, which split. Out tumbled Tresca's treasured copy of Elizabeth Barrett Browning's *Sonnets from the Portuguese*, and it went with Tresca into police custody and from there to the front page of one of the city's less reputable dailies.

"Love and Sonnets in a Strike Riot," declared the *New York American*, a Hearst newspaper. A splashy front-page collage featured a large photo of a pensive, wide-eyed, fresh-faced Flynn with arms folded and head tilted beside a smaller picture of Tresca, left hand in his pocket, with rimless glasses, mustache, goatee, and just the hint of a smile that seemed to suggest he was enjoying himself just fine and didn't mind all that much if the reader was in on his secret. The rip in Tresca's vest had "disclosed a romance that had developed unnoticed in the strife of trade union agitation," the newspaper said, reporting that the book contained the note, "I love you, Carlo. Elizabeth. Dec. 11, 1912," and that "the more fervid passages" were underlined. A passage the newspaper said bore "a particularly heavy mark" sounds like a response to the verse Tresca had written to Flynn about entering a flower garden. It is the last line of a sonnet called "Beloved, thou hast brought me many flowers," concluding, "And tell thy soul, their roots are left in mine."

The newspaper added that when police asked Tresca whether he knew Flynn, he responded, "Yes, and she is a lovely, good girl." A reporter found Flynn at court that night, waiting for Tresca to appear before the magistrate, and asked about the sonnets.

"Mr. Tresca," she said, flushing deeply, "often visits the home of my mother. He is a dear friend of my family. We all love him very much."

"Are you engaged?"

"Oh, no," she said, somewhat confused. "You see, we can't be. I'm married. My husband and I have separated, but we have not been divorced."[13]

In a sense, Flynn had told the truth—Tresca was a frequent and popular guest at her family's Bronx home. He was a charmer: warm, mischievous, and funny. The Flynns loved his cooking—a foretaste of a time when homemade Italian food would win over many an Irish family. When the Flynns celebrated holidays, Carlo contributed his "famous spaghetti," a "marvelous antipasto," and a gallon jug of wine to go with Mama Annie's turkey and pumpkin pie.[14]

Carlo Tresca moved in with the Flynns in March 1913.[15] He sued for divorce from his wife, Helga, a shapely, grey-eyed, blonde, thirty-one-year-old northern Italian who had edited his papers while he was in prison. Helga had worked closely enough with Carlo that she'd shared criminal libel charges with him. An Italian priest in Pennsylvania filed the charges against them for publishing what he said was a doctored picture of him with his female housekeeper in his arms. (Carlo Tresca pleaded guilty, and Helga was acquitted.) Tresca sought custody of their daughter, Beatrice. Helga, who had moved to New York City with her eight-year-old child, responded in court papers in 1914 that Tresca and Elizabeth Gurley Flynn were living as husband and wife in Flynn's family home in the Bronx and that with such ideas of morality, Tresca was not fit to raise their daughter.[16]

Elizabeth Gurley Flynn, center, with fellow IWW leaders of the Paterson Silk
Strike of 1913. Carlo Tresca is to her left. The others, from left to right, are Pat
Quinlan, Adolph Lessig, and Bill Haywood. Walter P. Reuther Library, Archives of
Labor and Urban Affairs, Wayne State University.

Tresca did not look back. Through Flynn, he found a place
among New York's radical elite, getting to know such famous activists as Emma Goldman, Upton Sinclair, Lincoln Steffens, John
Reed, and Norman Thomas. Flynn introduced Tresca to Patrick
Ford, editor of the *Irish World* and a venerated figure among New
York's Irish nationalists. In doing this, Flynn fulfilled the Irish
gatekeeper role of introducing an Italian newcomer to more influential echelons of society.[17]

Theirs was an Irish-Italian love story, embroidered into the tur-
bulence of the times: Bread and Roses, the Paterson silk workers'
strike of 1913, the Bolshevik Revolution and the Great War, the
Palmer raids, the Sacco-Vanzetti case. The prejudices that so often
divided Irish and Italian workers seemed not to apply to them.[18]
Starting in 1917, Flynn and Tresca took time out from their radical
pursuit—a whirl of protests, speeches, arrests, publications, rallies,
meetings, and celebrated causes—to vacation together each sum-

mer in a beach bungalow on Staten Island's South Beach, with a view of Coney Island across the harbor.

Flynn's friendship with James Connolly, by then a martyr who had been killed for helping lead the 1916 Easter Rising, brought a string of prominent Irish nationalists to their door. This thrilled the Irishman living next door. He got to meet Connolly's daughter, Nora, and the Irish patriot and labor leader James Larkin, who stole into town disguised as a sailor. Flynn enjoyed Larkin's company, and delighted in telling the story of a speech he gave at Sing Sing prison in the presence of many Irish American guards to celebrate Saint Patrick's Day. Larkin had declared that when Saint Patrick drove the snakes from Ireland, they went to America to become politicians, cops, and prison guards. So ended that celebration.[19]

More often, Tresca's Italian friends came by, and Flynn relished sharing spaghetti and wine with them under the trees. "I began to put on weight at that time," she wrote in her autobiography. "Italian food was my nemesis."[20]

Despite such domestic scenes, there were crucial differences between Flynn and Tresca—political, cultural, and personal. "My life with Carlo was tempestuous, undoubtedly because we were both strong personalities with separate and often divided interests," Flynn wrote.[21] She was a socialist who believed in a strongly organized labor movement. She opposed using violence. Tresca, on the other hand, was friends with many Italian anarchists—and open to using violence as a tool, at least in principle.

Beyond her uneasiness with the anarchist philosophy, Flynn also was very uncomfortable in the social world of the Italian anarchists she met through Tresca. To her, they were "a strange yet simple and earnest people who could be both exasperating and amusing." Tresca, always the life of the party, felt at home among these men; he was never comfortable speaking English. As his friend Max Eastman would later write in the *New Yorker*, Tresca didn't so much speak English with an Italian accent as Italian with English words. Flynn never came to terms with Tresca's broken English; she seemed to take it personally. "He wrote and spoke only in Italian and made little or no effort to learn English or to participate in American affairs," she wrote in her autobiography.

It also bothered her that, in her observation, the Italian radical movement was almost entirely male; the women stayed home and cooked. She noted with distaste that often they didn't eat with the men. Flynn may have been unusual in her sense of liberation, but she reflected an Irish tradition of strong, dominant women. In Flynn's telling, Tresca's anarchist friends, for all their opposition to society's norms, still had the traditional Italian view of a woman's place: at home with the family. Flynn had a keen eye for women's rights, having left her first husband because he wanted her to give up her organizing and stay home. She wanted women to work, and once called stay-at-home motherhood a form of prostitution.[22]

Some of the Italian anarchists' wives were strong Catholics, and she complained that they looked on her way of life with disapproval. Tresca's Italian friends advised her to be more traditional, staying at home to keep house. She responded, "He had a good Italian wife who cooked spaghetti and was a model housekeeper. Why didn't he stay with her?" But as Nunzio Pernicone wrote in his biography of Tresca, Flynn's "offended sensibilities" did not prevent her from enjoying the sumptuous meals the Italian women served when she visited their homes. Nor did Flynn "get off her fat behind" to help, as Beatrice Tresca told Pernicone. Still, she added, Flynn and Tresca "resolved their differences in bed."[23]

Flynn may well have failed to credit the role of Italian women in the anarchist movement. The historian Jennifer Guglielmo has documented how Italian immigrant women formed radical women's groups at the time in some of the same cities where Flynn was organizing. She found that some of the same women who served meals to Flynn and Tresca were active in these groups.[24]

The ultimate division between Flynn and Tresca was not political or cultural, but personal. The problem was that while Tresca saw himself as a one-woman man, the woman in his life kept changing. He discussed this freely with Max Eastman, who rendered Tresca's accent in the *New Yorker*: "I no like married life. I like one woman, an' then time pass an' I like another. I make many good frien'ship with women because I always say ver' frank: Don't trus' me. My character ver' emotional." Eastman, who interviewed Tresca at length, wrote that Flynn was "Tresca's great romance."[25]

The relationship fell apart in 1925, even as Flynn worked to reduce a prison sentence of a year and a day that a federal judge had imposed on Tresca for publishing an advertisement for birth control. With Flynn's prodding, Congressman Fiorello La Guardia persuaded President Calvin Coolidge to reduce the sentence to three months. The case, La Guardia noted, had been initiated on the complaint of the Italian ambassador, no doubt in retaliation for Tresca's vigorous campaign against Benito Mussolini's Fascist government. In the process, La Guardia sensed that Flynn was heartbroken. "Elizabeth, why don't you stop mixing up with all these Italian anarchists and go back into the American labor movement where you belong?" he told her.[26]

Flynn carried the crushing knowledge that Tresca had had an affair with her sister Bina, a pretty actress who was eight years younger than she. Elizabeth was a towering figure for Bina as she grew up; at the age of twelve, Bina made the *New York Times* by reading a "Socialist poem" at a Union Square rally that protested Elizabeth's arrest. Bina found her own stage through the Celtic Players, who performed Yeats and other Irish playwrights at the Provincetown Playhouse in Greenwich Village. After her brief marriage to James Martin failed in 1922, she returned to the Flynn family home in the Bronx at the age of twenty-four. She fell for Carlo, the handsome older man who had been a fixture at her famous sister's side since she was thirteen years old. Tresca had a passionate, secret affair with Bina even as he lived in the Flynns' apartment with Elizabeth. As a result, Bina became pregnant and delivered her son Peter on January 6, 1923. The boy carried the last name of Bina's estranged husband, Martin.[27]

It's not clear when Elizabeth learned the truth of the matter. She wrote in her autobiography that around the time she was working to reduce Tresca's federal prison sentence, a man came to her with a cache of revealing love letters Tresca had written to his wife. It's possible that this referred to Bina, who was still legally married to James Martin. As Flynn wrote, the letters were "of such a nature that I had no choice."[28]

Peter Martin, the child from that affair and founder of the famed City Lights Bookstore in San Francisco, would later tell the author Dorothy Gallagher, "It separated the sisters for quite a while. They were all respectable people and cultural norms were stricter then. The Irish could be politically left and culturally old fashioned. I think Carlo was more culturally radical."[29]

Emotionally devastated by the end of her Irish-Italian love affair with Carlo Tresca, Elizabeth Gurley Flynn moved to a basement apartment in Greenwich Village and continued her struggle for workers' rights. Fourteen years later, she wrote a poem recalling her summers at South Beach and the loneliness she felt after leaving Tresca. Crossing out Carlo's name, she wrote,

> you who still live and move are dead to me
> Dead in my heart, dead in my faith as well.
>
> I do not miss the kisses or the tears.
> Only the faith that died so slow & hard.[30]

Flynn wrote in a poem of disciplining herself so that she would not continue to be attracted to him:

> Days—months—have passed without a thought
> So well I steeled and disciplined my heart,
> That when I saw you, you were not yourself to me,
> Only a weary shadow of the man I knew[31]

Tresca was fatally shot at 9:45 p.m. on January 11, 1943, as he left the office of his newspaper, *Il Martello*, at 96 Fifth Avenue. "Since for decades he had the equal faculty of making friends and enemies in all strata of society, possible suspects were legion," one investigator noted.[32] The murder was never solved; some writers have seen the cause as Tresca's agitation against onetime Mussolini supporters in wartime New York.

Flynn remembered the last time she'd seen Tresca, a few days before, smiling in the doorway as he waved good-bye. In a poem, she recounted how, after learning of the shooting, she went to stand on the pavement that had been washed in his blood. Despite the "barren desert years" since their romance and Tresca's "decadent decline," the bond between the Italian immigrant and the Irishman's daughter was renewed:

> How strange it seems that you are dead—
> Who were so long the other half of me!—
> How long it was that you were dead
> to me.
> Now that you're dead—you are alive again.[33]

Even for people as open-minded and unconventional as Elizabeth Gurley Flynn and Carlo Tresca, it was difficult to overcome the Irish-Italian cultural boundaries of their era. They seemed to succeed for a while on a personal level. Professionally, they were a dynamic organizing team, with Flynn a formidable media presence and Tresca adept at rousing enthusiasm among immigrant workers. Flynn, Tresca, and other IWW activists nudged the more cautious American Federation of Labor to do more to organize immigrants.

But ethnic conflicts would continue to cause turmoil within the labor movement. It was no easy task to unite workers in New York, even those with similar jobs, skills, and economic interests, when they were divided into competing ethnic tribes. Such divisions would long continue in New York's workplaces. And as we will see, in one field in particular—law enforcement—the lack of diversity in the workforce proved to be a danger to the public safety.

7

Black Hand

On the first Sunday of June in 1896, the twenty-six-year-old attorney Francis L. Corrao buried himself in a lengthy *Brooklyn Eagle* exclusive that claimed to document how the Mafia had taken hold in Brooklyn, then the nation's fourth-largest city. Corrao, said to have stowed away on a boat from his native Sicily at the age of eleven so that he could be with his emigrant father in Brooklyn, had a professional interest in the article because he represented three men accused in a slaying it detailed. But his interest became personal when he came upon a section headlined, "Why Italians Are Useless in Police Work." His younger brother, Charles, was one of the three Italian officers in a City of Brooklyn police force of more than 1,700 cops.[1]

The article portrayed Italians as a menace to society and lamented that even the law-abiding among them would not testify against the "brigands." This was typical for news coverage of the Italians. What really bothered Corrao, an up-and-coming political leader in Brooklyn's expanding Italian community, was a quote from an unnamed police captain who scoffed when a reporter suggested that he was fortunate to have an Italian officer in his precinct to investigate crimes among Italians. The captain's rant:

"Rats!" he exclaimed, with expressive vigor. "Give me an Irishman or an American to work up such a case, but none of your dagoes. They are all tarred with the same stick. They are afraid to say their

souls are their own. They are in dread of the vengeance of the Mafia. I asked my man for some information on this case and he said:
'Captain I dare not act as an informer. They may be would not all
attack me because of my uniform, but some member of my family
would suffer, you may depend on that. To tell you the truth, captain,
I don't want to get into trouble with these people. I'd be a marked
man if I was to act as a spy among them.'"

"I told the fellow," proceeded the captain, "that if he felt that way
about police duty he'd better give up his shield and leave the business.
He didn't take the hint. I have him yet and he's good enough in ordinary
duty, but when dagoes are concerned he isn't in it—not even a little bit.
I let my Irish detective work up these Italian cases and he is not a bit
afraid of the stilettos or pistols."

Like other minority groups that followed them, the Italians had
a tense relationship with the Irish-dominated New York police
force. In many ways, this relationship foreshadowed the troubles
between the city's minority black and Latino communities and the
police in modern times. Italians accused police of not doing enough
to protect them, or of running roughshod over them. Police viewed
the Italians as dangerous, emotional, and unwilling to cooperate
with investigations. Italians saw the police as dismissive and not
really interested in solving crimes in which they were the victims.
And, much as in modern times, the minority cops found themselves caught in the middle of the struggle. Complicating matters
was the widespread graft in the Police Department during this
era, which served to heighten the old guard's distrust of outsiders. At the same time, the Police Department desperately needed
to diversify its ranks if it was going to do its job. The city's law
enforcement community was hard-pressed to keep up with the
immense influx of immigrants coming to New York, especially the
packed Lower East Side. Italian police officers were vitally needed,
as were Italians in other roles in the legal system, but they had
to battle to show they were worthy to serve side by side in this
workplace with officers, lawyers, and judges who were largely of

Irish or German origin. Public safety hinged on the outcome of this struggle in police stationhouses, district attorneys' offices, and magistrates' courts.

Donegal-born William McAdoo, police commissioner from 1904 to 1906 and, preceding that, president-general of the American Irish Historical Society, wrote with some authority on the Irishness of the New York Police Department. It had been "largely officered by Irishmen, and Irish traditions and feelings have been incorporated into the very organization," he declared. Not all officers were of Irish ancestry, he acknowledged; many were German and a few Italian. But much as Ireland's Norman invaders had become "more Irish than the Irish" in medieval times, so had New York police from other nationalities. "And so the Irish spirit permeates all ranks of the police," he wrote, adding, "it is the finest sort of material out of which to make a policeman."

McAdoo saw much good in the department's Celtic tradition, which recalls the adage that on Saint Patrick's Day, everyone is Irish. He wrote,

> President Roosevelt has said that if he wanted a really hard piece of dangerous and fighting work done he would call upon the Irishmen on the force. Besides courage of a high order and the soldierly instinct, the Irish policeman by birth or descent is also kindly, humane, patriotic, cheerful, and witty, and inured to hardship, and has a certain racial alertness and adaptability to circumstances which well fits him for this calling. He fits into a military or quasi-military service as if born to it. The individual prominence of a policeman also attracts the Celt, and at the same time he can understand and sympathize with the class or clan feeling of the organization.

McAdoo also saw Irish influence behind the police officers' tradition of refusing to inform on one another, even in the face of blatant corruption. "The hatred of the informer is ground into the very bones of the Irish race in all parts of the world," he wrote. "An Irish mother would far rather see her son dead than hear that he had gone on the witness-stand to be an informer in a political trial in Ireland."[2]

The Irish ability to circle the wagons against troublesome outsiders, so pronounced in Archbishop Hughes's New York Catholic Church, also applied to the Police Department. Until the fledgling Italian lawmen proved themselves brave and trustworthy enough to be insiders, they were going to be treated as outsiders.

Corrao, who became an assistant district attorney, and his brother Charles were on the front line of this battle for respect. And the young attorney was not one to back down from a fight. The day after the captain's comment ran in the *Eagle*, he wrote a scathing letter to the editor. "A police captain capable of uttering such false and outrageous language is not fit to be such and is a disgrace to the police department," he declared, complaining that the captain "puts the badge of cowardice and incompetence upon every Italian police officer and citizen and gratuitously casts a slur upon the Italian race."[3]

The striving young Frank Corrao already had clashed with the Irish many a time as he tried to establish his career as a lawyer and politician; he was ready for more. Born August 13, 1869, in Palermo, he was a five-foot, six-inch man with large brown eyes, wavy dark hair receding at the brow, and a small mouth. His father, Luigi, was said to have been one of Garibaldi's "Thousand," the band of heroes that defeated the Kingdom of the Two Sicilies in 1860. He migrated to the United States in 1879. The stowaway Francis followed his father in 1881, much as a wave of children from Central America would do in the twenty-first century. He attended public schools and Brooklyn's St. Francis College. Even before completing college, he formed the Francis L. Corrao Association, a charity to improve life for Brooklyn's Italians and, as it happened, to launch himself into politics. A friendly Latin professor from St. Francis College, Segundo Marchisio, had helped him start it. The association's opening ball was quite elegant, with a grand march of dozens of couples, thirty dance numbers, and a roster of lawyers and professors on the committee. A front-page notice in the *Brooklyn Eagle* called Corrao a "bright young Italian resident of this city," and said the event had "proved successful beyond the most confident anticipations of the members of the association." The following year's ball featured a march of a hundred couples led by Corrao and a "Miss M. Collins," evidently an Irish American belle with whom he danced into the early hours of the morning.[4]

Corrao won attention when, as a clerk in a law firm, he jumped into the middle of a potentially deadly fray that had broken out in an office in the Arbuckle Building on Fulton Street near Brooklyn's City Hall. A barber named John Paresi, who had sued his wife for separation, was confronted by his enraged brother-in-law, Louis Borgio. Both men were armed, but couldn't reach their weapons as they grappled. Corrao managed to break Paresi's grip on Borgio's throat, then pulled Borgio into a hallway, where other men grabbed him and hustled him downstairs to the street. "Clerk Corrao is short in stature, but sturdy and possessed of great strength," the *Eagle* exclaimed.[5]

Corrao was admitted to the bar in 1892 at the age of twenty-three, described in news accounts as Brooklyn's first Italian lawyer and also as the Italian community's Democratic leader. The *Eagle* took note: "He has plenty of grit."[6]

But it was a trying time to be a Sicilian working in the legal system. Horror and resentment over the slaying of New Orleans's Irish American police chief, David Hennessy, allegedly by Italian gangsters, on October 15, 1890, colored views of Italians throughout the decade and beyond. Hennessy's death provided a narrative for the entire nation of a brave Irishman martyred for trying to rein in Italian gangs. It was a shocking crime not only because Hennessy was a police chief but also, as the *Times* put it, because "this is the first instance on record where an American has been the victim" in an Italian vendetta.[7] To that point, the growing extortion rackets in Italian communities and the bombings, assaults, and slayings that went with them had victimized Italians only. Then came the thunderclap of the mortally wounded police chief's words to Detective Thomas O'Connor: "The dagos shot me." When a jury acquitted the defendants charged with the chief's murder in 1891, New Orleans citizens took the law into their own hands by lynching eleven Italian suspects.

While worried Italians gathered at banks on Mulberry Street and in the offices of Italian newspapers to hear the bad news and share their outrage, many others approved. "If the verdict had been acquiesced in by the people of New-Orleans, their acquiescence would have shown that there was not power and virtue in the community," the *Times* editorialized. Reaction across the country was similar. Theodore Roosevelt told his sister in a letter that some "dago diplomats" he met while dining out were upset over the lynching. "Personally I think it rather a good thing, and told them so," he wrote.[8]

The lynching in New Orleans was not a matter of Irish versus Italian, since the city's WASP gentry took part as well. But the police department there, as in New York, was an Irish bailiwick, and the intense emotions and national publicity surrounding the vengeance reaped for the Irish American police chief's death served to highlight the divide between Irish cops and Italian communities.[9] The lynching posed an enormous challenge to Italian immigrants in New York, where the newspapers insisted that the Mafia and its Neapolitan version, the Camorra, were taking hold and that Italians allowed this state of affairs by refusing to help police.

Francis Corrao responded by joining in a public protest held at the Brooklyn Atheneum on Atlantic Avenue on the raw, rainy Sunday afternoon following the New Orleans lynching. "We are a hardworking people," he declared, starting the day's last speech by identifying himself as Sicilian. "Jealousy against our growing influence in these United States has prompted our enemies to seize every opportunity to do us harm." The issue was not the Mafia, he said, but the unlawful act of vengeance against men found innocent by a jury.[10]

But for most people, the issue *was* the Mafia, and both Francis Corrao and his brother Charles would have much more to say about that.

*   *   *

Captain Alexander S. Williams took the measure of young Giuseppe Petrosino and liked what he saw. "Clubber" Williams was one of the best-known police officers of his day, and the Italian immigrant he had noticed working the garbage scows on the Hudson River would one day become perhaps the most famous cop in the fabled history of the NYPD. But at the time, Petrosino was a lowly laborer, moving garbage from carts to barges. He caught Williams's eye, and the short, stubby Petrosino began to tell the towering cop what he had gleaned about crime in the city's Italian community.

Williams, promoted in 1887 to inspector in charge of policing the East Side from the Battery up to 110th Street, summed up his view of law enforcement with this quote: "There's more law in the end of a policeman's nightstick than in a decision of the Supreme Court." He had established himself on his first beat by picking a fight with the two toughest local men and throwing both through a window. As a captain, he famously demonstrated his reputation to reporters by hanging his watch and chain on a lamppost at 35th Street and Third Avenue in the tough Gas House District, walking around the block and returning to find the valuables still there—a scene adapted in the Martin Scorsese movie *Gangs of New York*.[11]

With Williams's backing, Petrosino became a police officer on October 19, 1883, at the age of twenty-three.[12] There was no more than a handful of Italians on the force at a time when immigrants from Italy were rapidly filling up the Five Points, especially the crowded crook in Mulberry Street known as the Mulberry Bend.

Petrosino had come of age on that turf. And while one day he would be famous for battling with Italian criminals—beating them up, as needed—it seems he learned his fisticuffs through street fights with the Irish. His youthful brushes with the Irish were not something he talked about while on the police force, but they surfaced in a lengthy newspaper profile written about him several years after his death, based on his private diaries:

At that time the Irish far outnumbered the Italians in this section of the city, and many bitter battles were fought between the sons of the rival aliens. "Joe" bore his part in these conflicts, and from the first demonstrated that his fists were all the weapons he needed in fighting his way through public school. . . . In those days the rivalry between the Irish and Italian children was so keen and the former so far outnumbered the latter that the Italian children never dared to leave the school for home except in groups. The boy Petrosino convoying a flock of little ones of his own nationality was prophetic of the future, for his manhood was devoted to shielding honest compatriots from the ever-increasing demands and depredations of the Camorra and the Mafia.[13]

By the time Petrosino joined the police force, the growth of the impoverished Italian population was beginning to alarm many New Yorkers, especially the working-class Irish who were losing out to newcomers willing to do the dirtiest work cheaper and to pay more for housing. The backlash from Irish street gangs and their allies in the Police Department was so fierce that, according to some prominent Italians, many immigrants returned to Italy.

James E. March, the twenty-four-year-old Italian-born politician and padrone, complained about this situation in an interview with the *Sun* in 1884. Sitting in a Mulberry Street saloon, March told a reporter that some two hundred Italians on that block alone had returned to Italy. A big reason, he maintained, was that the Italians felt they had no way to protect themselves against politically connected Irish gangs that the police tolerated. "Just come through here tonight, or any night," he said. "Last night I saw one hit on the neck with a cobblestone when he was hurrying along the street about his business. He was knocked down by the unprovoked attack, and a gang of roughs shouted in derision." Another was "shamefully pounded" in the saloon when he came in for a pint of beer. March (who, coincidentally, would later be Petrosino's landlord) explained,

The Italians are cowed down by the roughs who are about here, mostly Irish. The Irish hate them because of the competition for the rougher kinds of work. The Italians do not defend themselves because when they do they are the ones arrested. They cannot explain their grievances in the Italian language to an Irish policeman. At the courts they are fined, while the bullies, even if arrested, are bailed out or go clear altogether by political influence.

In the same article, the reporter interviewed Augustus Sbarbaro, one of New York's few Italian-born officers. Sbarbaro, then thirty-six, had served on the police force since 1873 and had been promoted to roundsman, a notch above patrolman. Described in the *Times* as "an exceptionally intelligent Italian," he won attention in 1880 for tracking down Pietro Balbo, a handsome twenty-three-year-old fugitive Italian laborer on the Brooklyn Bridge construction, to arrest him in Wheeling, West Virginia, on a charge of murdering his wife. (Balbo was convicted and executed.) The reporter prodded Sbarbaro on whether an Italian's "personal characteristics" were cause for a chilly reception in New York. "Doesn't he use the stiletto?" the reporter asked.

Sbarbaro rejected that. "If you were to count up the number of cutting affrays in this city in a year you would find that, in proportion to the number of Italians here, they do far less cutting than others, while the provocations to defend themselves with violence are without number," he replied. "When an Italian does anything it is printed in big type." For good measure, he added, "That is not all. No Italian woman is ever arrested for drunkenness, and there is not one of them on the street—not one."[14]

Police hassled immigrant pushcart vendors to the point that one testy magistrate, Edward Hogan, warned in 1903 that it could lead to violence. "Serious trouble will come from the present way of dealing with these people," he declared, adding that they "carry long fruit knives, and I would not be at all surprised if some day, when the police make one of their unnecessarily rough descents on these pushcart men, the peddlers used the knives." A son of Irish immigrants, the sixty-four-year-old Hogan had been an influential politico in the neighborhood near the Battery at Manhattan's southern tip. In his last years, he had taken to assailing graft in the Police Department and, according to testimony before the Lexow Committee corruption probe in 1895, shakedowns of Italian pushcart vendors were part of the systemic corruption in the Police Department.[15]

Frank Moss, a corruption-fighting prosecutor who followed Theodore Roosevelt as president of the Police Board of Commissioners in 1897, had a similar take on how police treated the Italians. "They have been padroned by their own scoundrelly leaders, they have been fleeced and tyrannized by their American (or Irish) landlords and 'bosses,' and they have been treated with unfeeling harshness, and at times with terrific brutality, by policemen," he wrote. "Their experiences with representative Americans have driven them even closer together."[16]

Petrosino, though destined to become one of the NYPD's greatest heroes, started out as an outsider. He was "disliked by the Irish contingency" in the Police Department, the journalist A. R. Parkhurst wrote in his 1914 series based on Petrosino's diaries. His series of articles in the *New York Herald* and the *Washington Post*, "Perils of Petrosino," added that as a result, Petrosino advanced slowly; it took ten years for him to be promoted from patrolman to roundsman. In the meantime, the young officer developed a reputation for capably performing routine police tasks.

Relations between the growing Italian community and the Irish-dominated NYPD became angry during these years, turning police-community relations into another explosive source of tensions between the two ethnic groups. One case in which an Italian saloon owner shot a well-liked Irish American patrolman, Patrick O'Keefe, nearly boiled over into a New Orleans-style lynching in 1899. O'Keefe, who was twenty-five years old and a three-year police veteran, had gone home to his family's apartment in a brownstone row house at 417 East 119th Street in East Harlem for a meal break. He was the primary support for his widowed, Irish-born mother, Ellen, two younger brothers, and a sister. His mother, who had emigrated from Ireland in 1871, told him she was worried that a younger brother, eighteen-year-old Richard, was shooting pool at a notorious saloon owned by an Italian, Michael Farrelli. When O'Keefe went back to work, he checked the saloon. He didn't find his brother, but noted that the Sunday law on liquor sales was being violated. When he went to write up the violation for an offense often ignored, the enraged Farrelli opened fire on him, according to the police account. O'Keefe's wound was nearly mortal, but he lingered as doctors at Harlem Hospital delicately removed two bullets from his head. Police quickly hunted down Farrelli, a heavyset, unstable man who had recently been served a dispossess notice for failing to pay the rent on his saloon at 2348 Second Avenue near 120th Street.

Outside, a crowd that swelled into the thousands called out for Farrelli to be lynched. The mob tried to break through the police line to seize him. O'Keefe, a member of the Knights of Columbus, a Catholic fraternal organization, was a popular figure in the neighborhood. When he had been transferred to another precinct, a petition was circulated to bring him back.

Police dutifully protected their prisoner, but the acrimony was unmistakable. The *Times* account of the shooting concluded,

> Several outrages by Italians have occurred within a short time in that part of the city, and the feeling of the citizens is bitter. The police say that some day, if the Italians do not curb their powers for evil, there will be a large-sized lynching bee in Harlem, and the affairs that claimed Italian victims in the South will be tame in comparison.[17]

O'Keefe survived, but was blinded. Farrelli insisted someone else shot O'Keefe, but at his trial, O'Keefe was able to identify the defendant by voice; the saloonkeeper was convicted and sentenced to ten years in Sing Sing for assault. After several years in prison, he was judged insane and sent to an asylum.

* * *

Joseph Petrosino stepped into New York's inflamed police-minority relations with coolness and tact. A focused, careful man of few words, he spoke through the results he achieved. He began to get attention when he was promoted to detective in 1895 in the midst of what was then called the biggest shake-up in the history of the Detective Bureau. This promotion followed on the state's Lexow Committee investigation into widespread graft in the Police Department. Theodore Roosevelt, then head of the Police Board, secured the resignations of several corrupt police bosses, including "Clubber" Williams, and added many recruits to the police force in an effort to clean up the systemic payoffs the Lexow Committee's hearings had disclosed.

Promoted by Roosevelt, Petrosino was in a delicate position as he began work in the Detective Bureau. He responded by saying little and letting his record speak for him. The following year, Petrosino was promoted to detective sergeant, having made ninety-eight arrests, captured two accused murderers, and recovered $2,500 in stolen property in his first year as a detective.[18]

The lore that would propel Petrosino to fame was built on a foundation of spectacular achievements. In one case, he freed an Italian immigrant who was within a week of being executed for murder in Sing Sing by getting the true culprit to confess. Twenty-five-year-old Angelo Carbone's eight-hour trial on charges that he stabbed Natale Brogno to death near Leonard and Centre Streets on September 12, 1897, within two hundred feet of the Tombs jail in the Five Points section, ended with his conviction on December 15, 1897. No one had actually seen Carbone stab Brogno, but the victim did wind up mortally wounded after the two men fought. Police officers who arrived quickly at the scene saw Carbone standing over the fallen Brogno, who gasped, "Yes" when asked minutes before his death whether Carbone had stabbed him.

Carbone's twelve-year-old nephew Joseph Carbone saw everything, and testified that he had spotted another man, Alexander Ciaramello, Angelo Carbone's cousin, run up and stab Brogno during the fight, then run away. He said he had tried to tell Patrolman Patrick Brady the truth of what had happened. "I didn't believe the boy's statement," Brady, a five-year veteran of the police force, testified.[19] Neither did the jurors, all of whom declared under oath before the trial that they would not be biased against Italian witnesses.

Before sentencing Carbone to death, Galway-born State Supreme Court Justice Frederick Smyth (his father was the high sheriff of County Galway) stated that he wanted his sentence to send a message to Italians that their mayhem with knives would be punished severely. "Your Honor," Angelo Carbone replied, "why should I, who am an innocent man, be put to death to deter others from committing crime?"

With Carbone on death row at Sing Sing, Petrosino got a tip that a watchman who witnessed the fight saw someone run from the scene. He decided to trace Ciaramello, traveling to Jersey City, Philadelphia, Millerton, Delaware, Montreal, and Nova Scotia. After losing the trail, he returned to New York. Then he noticed a cousin of Ciaramello on Elizabeth Street in lower Manhattan's Little Italy. He trailed the man up to the Bronx, watched his house in the early hours of the morning, then followed him downtown the next day. The cousin bought a train ticket for Baltimore, and Petrosino, after informing police headquarters, did the same. Donning fake whiskers as a disguise, he followed the man to the house where Ciaramello was hiding. He knocked on the door, claiming to be a health inspector. Gaining entry, he grabbed Ciaramello by the back of the neck and took him to the nearest police station. The graying fifty-one-year-old confessed on the way there, handing over the murder weapon, a black-handled, six-inch knife. He had stabbed Brogno to seek revenge after finding the victim making love with his wife. Petrosino wired the news straight to the chief of detectives.

Ciaramello was later sentenced to life in prison; Carbone was freed after four months on death row. He returned to his mother's apartment at 166 1/2 Baxter Street, but the pressure of awaiting the electric chair had taken its toll. Doctors believed him to be insane.[20]

One of Petrosino's biggest cases involved the celebrated "Barrel Murder." On April 14, 1903, an Irishwoman named Frances Connors had left home at 5:30 a.m. to fetch rolls from the bakery when she noticed a barrel near the New York Mallet and Handle Works factory at the corner of Avenue D and East 11th Street on the Lower East Side. In the drizzly gray dawn, the coat draped over the barrel caught her eye; she thought it might be turned into scrub rags. "Just as I lifted it up I saw the human head sticking up," she told the *World* later that day. "Beside it was a man's foot. Well, I certainly did scream." A man's body was doubled up inside the barrel, his feet—he wore black leather shoes and galoshes—and head poking above the barrel. The corpse was warm.

The victim appeared to be a man about forty years old—Italian or Greek, most likely. He wore a black overcoat, brown tweed jacket and vest, black and white striped pants, and a tie with green and black checks. He carried a brass crucifix in his vest pocket. There were eighteen stab wounds in his neck alone.[21] The sensational slaying became an instant murder mystery in the pages of the city's newspapers. Petrosino was in the middle of the probe from the start, after a police official called out the refrain, "Send for the dago!" He worked directly with some of the stars of New York law enforcement—Irish Americans nearly all.

Petrosino was teamed with Detective Arthur A. Carey, who would later command the police Homicide Bureau for eighteen years, and Detective James McCafferty, who would become inspector in charge of the Detective Bureau five years later. McCafferty, who lived with his wife and three children at 103 East 75th Street off Park Avenue, came up fast but hard. His Irish-born father died when he was twelve; he became a machinist at age sixteen. As a young patrolman, he caught the eye of the famed Chief Inspector Thomas Byrnes by solving a murder. His methods tended to be severe: subjecting suspects to the third degree, and dragging them to the scene of the crime and then to view the body of the victim.[22]

Carey epitomized the New York Irish cop. As he wrote in his memoir, he knew from early childhood that he wanted to be a cop, as his Irish-born father was. To Carey, there was something about being Irish that made a young man yearn to join the force. Perhaps, he speculated, it was because in the old country, the Irish were deprived of the chance to govern. Or, he thought, maybe the Celtic temperament made the Irish good cops, officers whose smile could take the stress out of a tight situation. For whatever reason, the police he knew as a boy all had names like O'Brien, Sullivan, Byrnes, O'Reilly, Murphy, or McDermott. "Gaelic influence ran strong in police affairs," he wrote in his memoir, adding, "So I say that deep down my father's desire to make me a policeman was ruled by the Irish blood in his veins, even when I lay in my cradle."[23]

It was a different story for Petrosino. While the young Arthur Carey was underfoot inside his father's police station on Chambers Street, Giuseppe shined shoes outside police headquarters. He learned about the police from the outside, looking in. But no less than Carey, he loved being a cop.

As it turned out, another star lawman of Irish ancestry already possessed key pieces of the Barrel Mystery puzzle. William J. Flynn, the thirty-six-year-old, dark-haired, bull-necked chief of the Secret Service in New York, told police that his agents had observed the victim during surveillance of a counterfeiting ring based in a butcher shop at 16 Stanton Street, just east of the Bowery on the Lower East Side, shortly before his gruesome death. The agents were tracking a counterfeiting ring headed by the vicious, Sicilian-born gangster Giuseppe Morello. That provided a suspect, but no one knew who the victim was. Complicating matters, Inspector George McClusky ordered the arrests of Morello, the gangster Tomasso "The Ox" Petto, and ten others before police had gathered enough evidence to hold them. Flynn was furious. And detectives Carey, McCafferty, and Petrosino were left to pick up the pieces.

Petrosino's key contribution was that he picked up word through his sources in Little Italy that a prisoner in Sing Sing might know who the victim was. When Petrosino confronted the convict, he played dumb at first. Then the detective showed him a picture of the eviscerated slay victim and he fainted—it was his wife's brother, Benedetto Madonia. As Flynn later described it with evident pride in a book on the Barrel Murder, "Returning to New York from Sing Sing, Petrosino came directly to me."[24] Such was the influence Petrosino came to hold in Irish-dominated New York law enforcement.

A skillful interrogator, Petrosino then persuaded the victim's wife in Buffalo to acknowledge that her husband was in with a "secret society" and had gone to New York to settle a debt. The man to see, she told Petrosino, was Giuseppe Morello. Petrosino knew the name well, since Morello and his partner-in-crime Ignazio Saietta, better known as "Lupo," had emerged as the leading Italian criminals in New York. The victim of the Barrel Murder was an accomplice in their counterfeiting ring, but wanted out and evidently threatened to go to the police when he had a falling-out with Morello over money.[25]

Morello, who had a deformed, one-fingered right hand and bushy, unkempt mustache, was nicknamed "the Clutch Hand." He had learned the pitfalls of having overly talkative associates in his curious dealings with a group of Irish con men who passed his phony five-dollar notes on the street. This combination of Italian artistry and Irish blarney soon broke down; the Italians' fake bills were a poor imitation and the Irish talked too much. Arrests followed, with convictions for a group of the Irish swindlers and Morello's Italian-born printer. After that, Morello decided to deal only with Italians: no more smooth-talking Irishmen.[26]

When it came to the Barrel Murder, no one talked. Morello had seen to that. The fragile case that Petrosino, Carey, and McCaf-

Detective Sergeant Joseph Petrosino, left, escorts Tomasso Petto, second from left, after his 1903 arrest in the Barrel Murder. Two of the city's top detectives—Arthur A. Carey and James McCafferty—are to Petto's right. New York World-Telegram and Sun Newspaper Photo Collection, Library of Congress.

ferty hurriedly stitched together after Inspector McClusky rushed the arrests tore apart at the seams in full public view at the coroner's inquest.

Petrosino didn't have time for the long-term investigation needed to nab a savvy criminal like Morello. He was kept busy by an alarming number of extortionists who sent out threatening letters imprinted with an ominous black hand. Petrosino told reporters that no Italian who cooperated with police after receiving an extortion threat had ever been harmed. But "the Italians are all in deadly fear," the *Sun* said. Petrosino spent much of his time aiding Italian merchants who received extortion letters decorated with skull, crossbones, daggers, crosses, and a ubiquitous black hand.[27] The Black Hand that this symbol signified was widely believed— erroneously—to be a highly organized secret society. But in reality, the many blackmail plots perpetrated in its name were mostly the work of freelance extortionists. It was not "the Mafia," as supposed at the time. Giuseppe Morello and his gang were the American version of the Mafia, or at least its beginnings.[28]

Though the Black Hand freelancers targeted Italians, they alarmed everyone. Jewish mothers "would rush panic-stricken to the schoolhouses at the cry of the Black Hand to take their children home," as the police commissioner put it.[29] Newspapers and magazines fanned the public's fears, but the Black Hand was not the omnipresent conspiracy of evil it was purported to be. "That there is such a thing as a thoroughly organized, widely separated secret society which directs its operations in all parts of the United States from some great head centre, such as the Mafia or Black Hand is pictured, I have never believed in the light of the facts presented to the police," Police Commissioner William McAdoo wrote.[30]

The frequent bombings and kidnappings perpetrated under the Black Hand brand were quite real, however, and they made life hell for many Italians, especially those who were moving up in business. Frightened leaders of the Italian American merchant community, upset at how ineffective law enforcement had been, gathered at their Chamber of Commerce office at 35 Broadway to urge police to stop the blackmail. The police commissioner, they said, needed to appoint more Italians to the force: There were just 17 out of 8,151 officers. There were two Italian detectives.

On August 21, 1904, the *Tribune* ran a blockbuster, front-page story headlined in capitals, "Italian Crime and Police Incompetence: Detectives of the Force Seem Utterly Unable to Unearth 'Black Hand' Conspirators." It painted a frightening picture of police failure. The alarming story told of constant extortion letters—90 percent of them not known to the public—as well as kidnappings, bombings that destroyed homes and businesses, and the police bungling of the Barrel Murder case. "They say that Giuseppe Petrosini [*sic*] has been for a long time the only Italian detective at headquarters, and that he has shown skill and courage, but has been so overwhelmed with work that his efforts have been seriously impaired," the *Tribune* reported.

The story quoted James E. March's call for more Italians on the police force. But the following week, an ominous *Times* editorial cast blame on the Italian community:

> We have too many bad Italians already, and since the good Italians so generally refuse to give any information to the police which might assist them in their efforts to run down criminals of their race, we may be unable in any protective measures we adopt to distinguish in every case the good Italian immigrant from the bad Italian immigrant. That will make no difference—protect ourselves we must.

The next day, the *Tribune* came to the Italians' defense: "The demand that the Police Department shall employ a sufficient force of detectives who are thoroughly familiar with the Italian language and with the ways and habits and practices of Italian criminals in this city is rapidly gaining in force and volume, and will not be denied."[31]

This editorial was aimed at an Irishman: William McAdoo, the city's police commissioner. A balding man with a distinguished white mustache and probing dark eyes, McAdoo knew what it was to be an immigrant. He had spent his boyhood in Ramelton, a town on County Donegal's inlet-lined north shore, grandson of a patriot who fought for Wolfe Tone, famed leader in the 1798 uprising against British rule. He migrated with his father to Jersey City, learned the law, and became a New Jersey legislator known for fighting political corruption. "Plain Billy" served in Congress before moving to New York.

HIS FIRST BATH.

Police Commissioner William McAdoo, left, and Mayor George B. McClellan are shown in a May 4, 1904, *Puck* cartoon trying to scrub the Tammany Tiger clean. The Tammany boss Charles F. Murphy is in the background, tacking up a notice for the Democratic convention. Udo J. Keppler is the artist. Library of Congress.

To McAdoo, the problem with policing the Italian community wasn't with his cops, but with what he saw as the Italians' refusal to cooperate with police. Petrosino, frustrated with the enormity of his task, pressed him for help. He too believed that Italians had to be persuaded to trust the police—but he also knew how out of touch the Police Department was with his community. Petrosino told McAdoo that New York's Italians simply would not bring their problems to police who didn't understand their language. Wrong, the commissioner responded, telling the detective that police in Sicily got no better cooperation from the public.[32]

Petrosino used his contacts with reporters to make his case through the newspapers. Finally, McAdoo was forced to act. On September 13, 1904, the commissioner announced that he would establish an Italian squad under Petrosino's command. Petrosino told the commissioner privately that five men to be assigned him would not be enough to police a half-million Italians, but McAdoo said that they would have to do.

Given the few detectives assigned to Petrosino—some of whom he was already working with informally—the announcement smacked more of public relations than a new crime-fighting strategy. Like New York City police commissioners ever since, McAdoo was very conscious of what the press wrote about him.[33] On the plus side for Petrosino, McAdoo said he would be happy to have more Italians take the civil service test for patrolman. But for the most part, he blamed Italians rather than the NYPD for the poor policing of their community:

The trouble now is that an Italian criminal at once seeks refuge behind racial and national sympathy, and many of his countrymen, otherwise honest, believe it a sort of patriotic duty to shield him from the officers of the law. The police work with the Italians, even at its best, will not get the results desired, unless it is followed up by a moral movement on the part of the better class of Italians and the Italian newspapers.[34]

Petrosino worked around the clock. His initial staff consisted of Hugh Cassidy (an Italian who hibernized his name from Ugo Cassidi), John Lagomarsini, Peter Dondero, and Maurice Bonoil (whose parents were French and Irish but who learned Sicilian while growing up on the Lower East Side). Petrosino's personal fame continued to grow: the *Times* referred to him as "the greatest Italian detective in the world, who has hanged and put in prison about 100 murderers, and has a medal for bravery."[35]

But behind the façade of his apparent success, Petrosino continued to meet frustration within the Police Department. This wasn't known publicly at the time, but a detailed account was published in the *Washington Post* after his death, based on his diary. "Every hand in the department was turned against him," A. R. Parkhurst Jr. wrote in 1914. "Silently, and with dignity, he withstood the taunts, slurs, and insults that were heaped upon him by those of different nationalities in the uniformed force." His chief obstacles were the old-school inspectors and precinct commanders, according to Parkhurst. The need for an Italian squad underscored their failure to keep order.

Many commanders owed their appointments to Tammany politicians and were expected to go along with the graft common in police work and politics. Petrosino made clear he was aloof from that. "It would surprise the public if it knew the names of some of the men in both parties who have come to me to intercede for some Italian criminals," he once remarked in an interview. As Petrosino knew, powerful members of the Board of Aldermen opposed the creation and later expansion of the Italian squad.[36]

The Italian squad's testy relationship with Irish American police commanders surfaced in a number of ways. The squad did not get a room in police headquarters on Mulberry Street; Petrosino instead arranged for an apartment at 176 Waverly Place in Greenwich Village, operated under the guise of a real estate office. His detectives showed up for work dressed as laborers. Neighbors soon became suspicious and complained to the local patrolman about the rough-looking men with broad-brimmed hats and wicked-looking mustaches. The officer alerted his captain, John J. O'Brien, who organized a nighttime raid in which police destroyed the office, ripping up carpets, clearing out desks, and heaping the contents on the bare floor. When Petrosino returned to find the mess, his landlady urged him to flee. O'Brien, believing he had uncovered a counterfeiting ring, staged another raid, arriving in plainclothes. He didn't recognize Petrosino, who was disguised as a laborer, even though the detective had worked for him a decade earlier. They scuffled, and O'Brien pulled out his gun, pointed it at Petrosino, and asked him whether he would "go to the station without the trouble of sending for a hearse." Finally, Petrosino showed his shield.

O'Brien was transferred to a lesser post in Greenpoint, and Petrosino was promised a new office. He got one five months later, when the Italian squad was installed in the newly opened police headquarters on Centre Street.[37] But the unit was far too small, and Petrosino, who initially portrayed the Black Hand as disorganized crime, began to paint a more harrowing picture in his public statements. "There are thousands of Black Hand robbers and assassins in New York and Brooklyn," he declared, "and they are a rapidly growing menace to public safety."[38]

Petrosino took advantage of the publicity over a bombing at 13 Stanton Street on the Lower East Side that blew up a grocery store owned by two brothers who refused to pay up after a blackmailer demanded a thousand dollars. The powerful explosion blew a passerby named John O'Hara, a local waiter, off his feet and hurled him to the sidewalk, where he lay bleeding with cuts from flying glass.

Petrosino was incensed. The victims of the extortion plot, the Giambalvo brothers, were prospering Sicilians whose family had come to America, one by one, as money was raised to provide passage. After receiving their second extortion letter, they went to Petrosino for help. The detective and his unit guarded the store for five days. But Petrosino, working the next day on four other appointments to meet suspected Black Hand letter writers, notified the commander of the local stationhouse on Eldridge Street,

Captain John J. Murtha, a New York-born son of Irish immigrants, that the store needed guarding.[39]

When he woke up in the morning to learn about the Stanton Street explosion, Petrosino pounded his head with both hands and cursed Murtha. Using his contacts in the press, Petrosino made sure that the influential cop (a future inspector, later convicted of bribery) got his due. Beneath the headline "Police Knew, but Let Black Hand Use Bomb," the *Sun*'s front-page story alluded to "the fact that Detective-Sergt. Petrosino warned Capt. Murtha." The overworked Petrosino told reporters he needed a staff of at least thirty detectives.[40]

After pounding a beat in obscurity for years, "the Dago" had become a superstar in the Irish-dominated NYPD—even if, behind the scenes, he didn't always receive respect. Because of his extraordinary success, the reporters and editors at powerful newspapers loved him. His access to the press gave him power. His bosses, desperately in need of his case-closing skills, did not dare silence him. Whatever he was doing, they only wanted more from him.

But, as the up-and-coming prosecutor Francis L. Corrao was discovering in Brooklyn, it remained difficult for even the most high-achieving members of a minority group to be fully accepted in the insular world of New York law enforcement.

*   *   *

Francis L. Corrao continued to build his political organization, breaking with the Irish-controlled Brooklyn Democratic organization headquartered on downtown Willoughby Street. In 1901 he helped Republican Seth Low win election as New York's mayor, accusing Democrats of allowing the streets in the Italian quarters to be filthy and denying decent schools to the children.[41]

His contentiousness carried over into his private life; the acrid details of his divorce were reported in the *Brooklyn Eagle*. The problem with his wife, Laura, as he saw it, was her parents, the Criscollas—her English-born mother, Sarah, and her Italian stepfather, Lorenzo. Corrao complained that his wife insisted on living

in her parents' house after they married, and wouldn't follow him
when he moved out due to the parents' "interference and abuse."
But it was Laura who sued him for divorce on the ground of cruel
and inhuman treatment. "I would like to know how much longer
I will have to wait for my divorce," she wrote in a note sent to him
on July 28, 1901. The following January, she pressed harder. "Dear
Frank," she wrote. "You are simply making me sick and tired. One
day you say one thing and another day you say something else. . . . I
want to have this divorce case over. I am tired of waiting one month
after another." By then, the couple had a three-and-a-half-year-old
son, Frank. Soon after the divorce, she married an insurance broker
named Thomas J. Green who lived on an elegant street across from
Prospect Park. For his part, Corrao had to issue a public apology to
Laura's lawyer, whom he had falsely accused of trying to sabotage
the marriage.[42]

Despite such setbacks, Corrao's influence grew with the expanding Italian community in Brooklyn. He waged a constant
campaign for his people—and himself—to be accepted in the
mainstream. Sounding like a conservative Irish pastor, he urged
public officials not to take part in Italians' religious processions,
which he denounced as "ridiculous exhibitions of religious devo-
tions" that reflected poorly on Italians. It was "shameful" to spend
thousands of dollars on fireworks, he said, when Italian churches
were in heavy debt. "The American and proper Italian way to show
honor and devotion to their patron saint is by going to church and
not indulging in a vain exhibition of cheap parades, music and fireworks, not unfrequently attended with fatalities," he wrote to the
Brooklyn Eagle on August 15, 1902, after watching Neapolitans celebrate a *festa*.[43]

But, he believed, what really held Italians back was the public's
perception that they were dangerous criminals. The problem, as
he saw it, was that the criminal class found in every nationality
had been permitted to flourish among Italians in New York because of lax law enforcement. He saw that thanks to detectives like
his brother Charles and Joseph Petrosino, police were beginning

to make some strides in targeting "Black Hand" extortionists. But his blood boiled over at what he saw in the courthouse: Prosecutors let Italian criminals get off easily through plea bargains or their incompetence.

Looking to correct that state of affairs, Corrao supported a measure to add an Italian-speaking prosecutor to the Brooklyn district attorney's staff. State Senator Thomas H. Cullen, New York-born son of Irish immigrants (and a future congressman who would break Prohibition by passing a law allowing sale of low-alcohol-content beer), sponsored the bill. It passed, although lacking the provision that the new hire must be Italian. Still, as Corrao pointed out, everyone knew the intent.

On April 2, 1907, Corrao got the job. It was a prestigious post, and it paid well; his salary was $5,000, or more than $115,000 a year in today's money. For Corrao, the appointment came none too soon; he was convinced that many Italian immigrants were leaving Brooklyn because they believed that the authorities could not protect them from crime. For, as he wrote later, "Murder, assault and robbery of Italians is looked upon by the District Attorney's office with the most cynical indifference."[44] Despite his high hopes, Corrao soon found that the low-level tasks assigned to him were better suited to a $1,500-a-year clerk. He was the token minority.

Corrao seethed when he saw other prosecutors bungle cases involving Italians while he was sidelined with minor tasks.[45] Even so, he flourished socially, thanks to the prominence of his new post. Italian organizations held a banquet in his honor in Coney Island.[46] He also mixed with the well-to-do Irish, celebrating Saint Patrick's Day in 1909 with the Celtic Club of Brooklyn at Stauch's, a restaurant and dance hall in Coney Island. Corrao attended with his eighteen-year-old sister, Nellie, and also with his brother, Detective Charles Corrao, and his wife. The enormous hall featured a huge, high-tech harp suspended from the ceiling, blazing with green and gold electric lights. The festivities included Irish songs, Irish vaudeville entertainers, and a gift of potted shamrocks provided to each of the 3,300 attendees, courtesy of the Tammany boss Richard

Croker. The featured speaker, Father William T. McGuirl—born in County Leitrim and raised in Rockaway, Queens—spoke of how the Irish built America, saying that they were able to do so because they were good and honest, and not, as the *Eagle* paraphrased it, "the scum of a race like that which is coming over from another country."[47]

Corrao's boss, District Attorney John F. Clarke, sat in a prominent place as a vice president of the Celtic Club, led by powerful State Senator Patrick McCarren, a Democrat from Brooklyn's Williamsburg section. The fifty-year-old Clarke, also a Democrat from Williamsburg, was at home in Irish circles; he played a leading role in the Brooklyn chapter of the Irish nationalist organization Clan na Gael.[48]

Clarke had not been looking to add an Italian prosecutor to his staff; newspapers had to call for him to appoint one. It may well be he had no idea that the young man he had appointed to the job filled with anger and humiliation as he watched other prosecutors take the cases he longed for. He was fond enough of Corrao to take him along on a three-month journey to Italy in 1908, supposedly to research Italian organized crime.

According to Corrao, one purpose of the trip was to study a plan by the city's new police commissioner, Theodore A. Bingham, to expand the Italian squad Joseph Petrosino headed into a much larger "secret service" that would report directly to the commissioner, rather than through the Detective Bureau. Given the panic in the newspapers over Black Hand crimes, this was one of the city's hottest issues. The Tammany-dominated Board of Aldermen, and especially Manhattan's "Little Tim" Sullivan, were dead-set against this secret service. The opponents raised legitimate civil liberties issues, but there was suspicion that their real motive was to maintain the graft and power they enjoyed through a politically manipulated Detective Bureau.

Like Petrosino, Corrao had decided that the best way to stop crime in New York's Italian community was to prevent Italian criminals from entering the country. The chance to investigate that possibility firsthand brought Corrao a taste of the respect he had been craving, winning him credit in the newspapers.

Prominent Italian merchants contacted District Attorney Clarke, warning that it was dangerous for him to travel to Italy. Italian authorities also thought so, and dispatched soldiers to greet and escort Clarke and Corrao when they landed in Naples. Clarke, a dapper, bearded, blue-eyed man of five feet, eight inches, treated it as a joke and asked Corrao whether they were under arrest. Corrao informed his boss that the escort was a mark of honor; Clarke continued his joking by offering to buy the soldiers a drink, which they refused.

The truth of the matter, though, is that the trip was much more about pleasure than business, at least for Clarke. They met here and there with Italian government and Vatican officials. The two lawmen did visit Naples and Corrao's hometown, Palermo, but spent most of their time abroad taking in the sights of the Amalfi coast, Florence, Venice, Milan, Rome, and the northern Italian lake district.

While Clarke lingered in picturesque Interlaken amid the cool summer splendor of the Alps near the end of their trip, Corrao went ahead to wait for him in Paris. When he met the *Brooklyn Eagle* correspondent Emma Dullet there, Corrao used the occasion to announce his findings. He indicted the Italian justice system, saying it allowed gangsters to get away with murder and then migrate to America. "They talk about the corruption of Tammany Hall, but I tell you that Tammany Hall politicians could go to Italy and learn a trick or two," he said, charging that lax enforcement and rigged juries allowed crimes to be committed in Italy "with impunity."[49]

Two weeks passed before Clarke extracted himself from the pleasures of his European sojourn, reunited in Paris with his assistant, and traveled with him to Cherbourg to board the German liner *Barbarossa* for their return. In the meantime, Italian newspapers in New York assailed Corrao for his scathing comments on Italy's justice system. Reporters who met him and Clarke when the vessel landed in Hoboken on September 2, 1908, told him that some were calling for his resignation.

Clarke sidestepped questions on what he had learned about Italian criminals and laughed off his assistant's predicament. "I see that Mr. Corrao has been interviewed," he told reporters with a laugh, "and there appeared to be a disposition in some quarters to differ with his conclusions about Italian judicial procedure. I have nothing to say at all about it." Clarke's return was noted chiefly for the fact that his beard was shaved off during the three-month voyage, a daring new style. He said he was shorn on Capri after he couldn't resist patronizing a barber named Michelangelo.

Left on his own, Corrao dug in. "I wish to repeat all I said and make it even stronger than I have," he told reporters, calling the Italian justice system "a regular clearinghouse for Italian criminals."[50]

The assistant district attorney had returned from his native land with a menacing story to tell. Just how ominous his journey was would soon become painfully clear when Joseph Petrosino was dispatched on a secret mission to Sicily.

*   *   *

Joseph Petrosino's world changed rapidly after retired Brigadier General Theodore A. Bingham became police commissioner on January 1, 1906. One of Bingham's biggest goals was to cripple the Black Hand, and the Italian squad was a priority for him. "From that day," A. R. Parkhurst Jr. wrote in 1914, "its status changed and the slurs that had been heaped upon it if made at all were made in secret for none at headquarters dared offer affront to Petrosino and the men under him."[51]

Bingham immediately ordered Petrosino to prepare a report on what he needed, an invitation the star detective had longed for.[52] United by their common goal of ending the Black Hand blackmail and bomb plots that afflicted the Italian community, the cop and the commissioner made an unlikely pair. Bingham was a blue-blooded military man of Anglo-Irish descent, the descendant of

Revolutionary War soldiers, an engineer trained at West Point, the son of a Protestant clergyman from Connecticut who was the valedictorian of his Yale class. He was a tall man with sandy gray hair, a handlebar mustache, and a ramrod bearing that persisted even after he was maimed when a seven-hundred-pound derrick fell on him in a construction accident that ended his military career. He declared on his first day in office, "If I stay honest, I'll raise hell." Friends and his many enemies agreed that he did.[53]

Bingham expanded Petrosino's squad and promoted him to lieutenant; Sergeant Antonio Vachris was appointed head of the squad's Brooklyn staff of ten detectives, including Charles Corrao, Francis Corrao's younger brother.[54]

Petrosino celebrated his promotion in a dinner with fellow detectives at Saulino's restaurant at Lafayette and Spring Streets, down the block from his apartment. The owner, Vincent Saulino, had migrated to New York in 1880 from Agnone, a town a hundred miles due east from Rome, known for bells made there for a thousand years. With his French-born wife, Malinea, doing the cooking, he set up a small restaurant. It was a favored spot for Petrosino, no less for the food than for his interest in Saulino's widowed daughter, Adelina. Petrosino's competitive streak entertained the Saulinos; when he lost at cards, he tore them up in frustration. After that, Vincent Saulino offered to do it for him. Petrosino asked for Adelina's hand in marriage the same night he celebrated his promotion. With Monsignor John F. Kearney presiding, they were married at St. Patrick's Old Cathedral on a Monday evening, December 30, 1907; the groom was forty-six years old and the bride, thirty-seven.[55]

The spate of Black Hand bombings continued. Banks at 240 and 246 Elizabeth Street were hit, as was a cheese importer at 244 Elizabeth Street, so close to police headquarters that one headline declared, "Bomb Shakes Up Bingham's Office." Frightened Italian merchants formed an Italian Vigilance Protective Association. Newspapers ratcheted up the pressure on Bingham. "Lives of 10,000 in Peril by Black Hand, Bingham Helpless," the *World* headlined on May 26, 1908. Bingham, under pressure to hire more Italian cops, retorted that it wasn't easily done.[56] With police fumbling in the face of repeated bombings and Petrosino overworked, it was obvious at this point that the lack of diversity on the police force posed a danger to the public.

With his wife pregnant during the summer of 1908, Petrosino slowed down, sick with bronchial pneumonia. Bingham, meanwhile, clashed with the city's aldermen over the funding he wanted for his secret service. "Little Tim" Sullivan, a onetime bootblack on Broome Street and saloonkeeper whose older cousin "Big Tim" Sullivan was the Democratic boss of the Bowery, stood in the general's path as majority leader of the Board of Aldermen. Bingham was just the kind of blue-blood the Sullivans delighted in taunting. The editorial writers at the *Times*, meanwhile, hinted darkly that Little Tim opposed the commissioner's Italian squad because of shadowy connections between Tammany and up-and-coming Italian criminals. "The Little Feller" spent the last two years of his life defying Bingham before dying of kidney disease at the age of forty.[57]

Finally, though, Bingham came up with fifty thousand dollars in private funding—quite possibly from desperate Italian American merchants—to launch a secret plan aimed at stopping the Black Hand hysteria. Jeremiah W. Jenks, a Cornell University professor who served on a congressional commission that was taking a hard look at immigration, forwarded the plan to Bingham. It had been developed by an Italian expert who evidently was afraid to have his name attached to it. The proposal was based, quite accurately, on the idea that the great majority of Italian immigrants were not criminals and did not turn to crime once they settled in America. Nearly all criminals in the New York Italian community had also been criminals in Italy, and fled to escape punishment.

The report pointed to one particular gang boss from the Lower East Side: Paul Kelly, who as we saw earlier had changed his name from Paolo Antonio Vaccarelli. This was a clear shot at the Sullivans, whose alliance with Paul Kelly's gang was well known. The solution, according to this plan, was to take better advantage of a law Congress passed in 1907 that allowed three years to deport criminals who had entered the country illegally. To do that, New York police needed the "penal certificates" Italian courts issued to those convicted of felonies and birth records to identify these suspects beyond doubt. This was too difficult to do by mail, the report found, urging instead that police "send to Italy a trusted person, acquainted with local conditions of criminality," to gather the records. Once police had those documents, according to the report, a small squad of detectives could begin rounding up criminals and returning them to Italy.[58]

The report did not mention Petrosino, but in effect had his name written all over it. The proposal became Bingham's pet project, and he insisted that Petrosino carry it out. The detective, who had become a father at the age of forty-nine when his daughter, Adelina, was born on November 30, 1908, was reluctant to leave his family but dutiful. As close friends said later, he knew it was a very dangerous mission. Three days before his departure, he spoke about it with Monsignor John F. Kearney, his pastor at St. Patrick's Old Cathedral. The priest, who knew the workings of the Police Department well, urged Petrosino not to go, warning that he might not return alive. Petrosino smiled and said, "Probably not."[59]

Petrosino shipped out for Genoa on February 9, 1909, in a foul mood, headed into even fouler weather that sickened everyone on board except for him. He assumed an identity as a Jewish businessman, but the time had passed when the famous detective could travel unrecognized.

As Petrosino went on to Rome, the secrecy of his trip was unraveling in, of all places, police headquarters. Bingham, after sparring with a committee of hostile aldermen in a public hearing, couldn't restrain himself from telling reporters with great glee that he had come up with funding to launch his secret service. The matter had surfaced when reporters asked where Petrosino had disappeared to. The cover story had been that the detective was on vacation, but now it was indicated that Petrosino had gone on a

Lieutenant Joseph Petrosino in undated photo.
George Grantham Bain Collection, Library of
Congress.

secret mission to Italy to clear the way for Italian criminals in New
York to be deported there. Compromising the operation's security,
major papers carried this story on February 20, 1909, courtesy of
the police commissioner.

In a letter from Rome on February 23, Petrosino regaled his wife
with the wonders he had seen in St. Peter's Basilica and the Sistine
Chapel, but noted, "In spite of everything I am sad, and I must say
that, when it comes to comfort, I prefer my dear New York, which I
hope to see very soon." Petrosino said he hoped that a partner promised to him would arrive, "because I feel already annoyance at being
all alone." The veteran detective knew he shouldn't have been sent on
this mission alone. Furthermore, as a cop from a peasant background,
he was poorly equipped for what was essentially a diplomatic mission.

Pressing on, he went to Palermo, Sicily. There, in the Piazza Marina, Lieutenant Joseph Petrosino was fatally shot on the evening of March 12, 1909.

The sad truth of the matter was that the Police Department had sent Petrosino out alone and unprepared and then compromised his security by telling the press about the mission so that the commissioner could win some short-term edge in his public relations spat with the Tammany-backed aldermen. Everyone knew that Petrosino was in danger. "Petrosino Killed at Last," the *New York Evening Post* headlined, adding, "It had been rumored that Petrosino's mission to Italy was not a voluntary one, that he went against his will."[60]

Petrosino's Italian friends and relatives believed it was wrong for him to have died in this way, and the newspapers gingerly reported their reaction. "He was so well known to the evil Italians that he was a marked man," the former city coroner Antonio Zucca told the *Times*. Frank Frugone, publisher of the Italian-language New York paper *Bolletino della Sera*, blamed the publicity for his friend's death. "He had no chance," Frugone told the *World*. "He should have gone away secretly. It should never have been published that he was going to Italy." And Adelina Petrosino's brother, John Saulino, told the *Sun*, "We knew the danger under which Joe was working. Joe understood it himself."

Gino C. Speranza, a pioneer Italian journalist in the city's English-language press, was more pointed. Petrosino was "ill-advised" to fight single-handed a battle that required patient planning between two nations, he wrote. "We must not send or allow brave officers to go to their death in inspiring but impractical skirmishes," he wrote. "For Petrosino to sail on an Italian boat from New York where every dock laborer knew of his going was absurdly to undervalue the watchfulness of the enemy."[61]

But these notes were faint in the symphony of public reaction that followed, thoughts shared among close friends of Petrosino such as Dr. Raffaele Asselta and the relatives gathered around the stricken widow and crying three-month-old daughter.[62]

The score was set from the first telegram to Bingham from the American consul in Palermo that confirmed Petrosino's death: "Dies a martyr."[63] That said it all, for Petrosino immediately became a secular saint in whose procession both the Italians and the Irish could walk. In the aftermath of the hero's sacrifice, the public took notice of the quiet dignity of the impoverished Italian immigrants who flocked by the thousands to pay their respects to Petrosino. Crowds formed spontaneously when a hearse carried the coffin containing his corpse from the dock to the building where he lived and would be waked in a political hall downstairs. The *Sun* reported,

> From the office buildings men with dark skins came running out on the sidewalk, there to stand hatless, even to cross themselves, as the procession moved by at a measured pace. Pushcart men . . . stood behind their carts and stands with bowed heads. The fire escapes that fret the faces of the tenements were heavy with silent, reverent spectators.[64]

Thousands of people, mostly Italians, but a cross-section of the city as well, filed past the coffin—closed because of a poor embalming of the corpse in Italy—in the hall of James E. March's Republican club, located downstairs from the Petrosinos' third-floor apartment at 233 Lafayette Street. Meanwhile, the Irish American leaders of church and state did all in their power to honor Petrosino and his legacy. State Senator "Big Tim" Sullivan, whose cousin "Little Tim" had done his best as an alderman to deprive Petrosino of the resources he needed, proposed legislation to grant a special pension to Petrosino's widow—the honest detective having died, unlike some other celebrated detectives of the day, with little money in the bank. Said Sullivan, "It is no more than this woman deserves."

Monsignor Kearney planned a grand funeral Mass at St. Patrick's Old Cathedral for Petrosino, who was described in news accounts as his close friend. Three days before Petrosino set out for

Italy, Kearney had warned that if he took the mission, the next time he would see the lieutenant would be at his funeral. "I want you to refuse to go," he said. Kearney would be the main celebrant of the Mass but could not preach about his friend Petrosino because "I would break down."

Kearney got a taste of what Petrosino had been up against when he received a Black Hand letter threatening an attack on his church. It was not to be taken lightly. He forwarded the letter to Bingham, who promptly denied to reporters that such a threat had been received. Kearney went along with this at the time, but years later was said to have remarked, "If the church goes—I go with it."[65]

The funeral procession arrived at the old cathedral on Mott Street behind the Police Band playing Verdi's Requiem March, with six lieutenants, bearing names such as Cooney, Delaney, Judge, and Riley, serving as honorary pallbearers. Inside the church, hundreds of police officers and public officials sat to the left, with Mayor George McClellan Jr. in the tenth row. Italians filled the right side of the church; Kearney made sure they got tickets. A hundred children from the parish school sang in the choir.

Monsignor Michael J. Lavelle, a son of Irish immigrants and renowned rector of St. Patrick's Cathedral on Fifth Avenue, preached the homily. Responding to the undercurrent of anger in the Italian community, Lavelle defended the Police Department. "Many people, I fear, have the wrong idea of the police force," he said. "It is criticized on every side, and, in a sense, that is right, but if we stop to realize what the police force means, we immediately see that much said against it is unjust. It is the most important and efficient institution in our system of democratic government."

That Lavelle felt a need to defend this Irish Catholic bastion at such a sensitive moment—when everyone knew that high-level bungling may have helped the murderer of the greatest hero in the history of the NYPD—is not a surprise, given the priest's deep involvement in Irish American causes. In later years, Lavelle would become the first clergyman to serve as grand marshal of the Saint Patrick's Day Parade. He was well known for his interest in Irish history; the American Irish Historical Society would honor him with the gift of a Celtic gospel manuscript more than a thousand years old. But Lavelle, an Italian-speaking churchman who had come of age on Broome Street just as the first Italians moved in, also would be named in 1913 to head a council that raised money for the care of Italian immigrants, and to found Catholic Charities for the poor. For his aid to New York's Italians, King Victor Emmanuel would recognize Lavelle in 1929 with the Knighthood of the Crown of Italy.[66]

Lavelle was too sophisticated a churchman to end his sermon on such a defensive note, nor would his affection for the Italian community allow him to do so. He had started out his sermon by speaking briefly in Italian. In an emotional conclusion, he called for unity through the blood of the martyred detective:

> May God grant that the sacrifice will be productive of the greatest good, as the blood of the martyrs became the seed of the Christian Church. I hope and pray that the death of this faithful, true, large-hearted, devoted, and beloved man may be the means of inspiring self-respect among his countrymen, so that no mere small handful of criminals shall longer degrade their race. May it teach to the rest of the people the debt and the love that we owe to these strangers on our shores, so that we may not wrongly discriminate. Let us make every one as welcome in our hearts as they are under our flag.

Some two hundred thousand people lined nearly five miles of streets to witness an enormous procession. The hearse, drawn by six black horses, carried the dark oak, silver-handled coffin from St. Patrick's Old Cathedral. It traveled up Fifth Avenue, and then across the Queensboro Bridge to Calvary Cemetery in Queens. The Finest and the Bravest—the cream of Irish Catholic New York—marshaled their might in Giuseppe Petrosino's memory. More than three thousand police officers took part by marching in the procession or guarding the route. Fire Chief Edward F. Croker, nephew of former Tammany Hall boss Richard Croker and son of an Irish immigrant, led a contingent of more than three hundred firemen. The Fighting 69th Regiment's marching band took part.

So, too, did some sixty Italian societies. Colorfully dressed veterans of the Risorgimento led their way, in red Garibaldi shirts, of course, and blue zouave pants tucked into flaring spats. There were organizations named for saints—Donato, Rocco, Faustino—and groups representing occupations, such as the United Boot-Black Protective League and a society of barbers. They proudly marched past the lowered flags of the St. Regis hotel and the Waldorf-Astoria on Fifth Avenue. "The Italian marching clubs who had paraded their tinsel sashes and kaleidoscopic uniforms to the appreciative eyes of Mulberry street found no embarrassment on the avenue," the *Sun* reported. "The whole city was kin while the body of a plain lieutenant of detectives who had died on duty was passing."[67]

* * *

Commissioner Bingham sent an Italian-Irish detective team back to Italy to complete Petrosino's work, dispatching Lieutenant Anthony Vachris, head of the Italian squad in Brooklyn, and forty-year-old Detective John R. Crowley, whose parents were Irish and who spoke Italian fluently.[68] Vachris grew a black beard to disguise himself in the role of Jewish businessman John Simon.

The two detectives had succeeded in getting certificates identifying four hundred Italian criminals who could be sought for deportation when word came from police headquarters that they were to cut short their mission and return home. Commissioner Bingham had been deposed—not for mishandling Petrosino's mission to Italy but, as he would later say, for not bending to Democratic bosses who had been accustomed to controlling police personnel moves.

Without Bingham as a protector, the world of the Italian squad turned upside down. The proud detectives, so recently the toast of the city, were dispersed. Vachris and Crowley were ordered to speak with no one about their courageous trip. Crowley, who lived in Brooklyn, was sent to patrol the Bronx. Vachris, a resident of

Bay Ridge in southern Brooklyn, was transferred to far-off City
Island in the Bronx.[69]

A few dozen low-level criminals were rounded up and deported, thanks to the certificates Vachris and Crowley had located. But the bulk of the 742 certificates (including 300 the
Italian authorities sent after the two detectives hurried back to
New York) were never used, even though Vachris had translated
and indexed them with photographs before his transfer to the
Bronx. Police headquarters "lost" the records—the documents
Petrosino had died for. They were located in 1913 after an investigative commission asked twice for them. By then, it was too late
to use them, since the three-year statute of limitations that existed
at the time for deporting criminal immigrants had passed. As the
Times reported, "many prominent Italian citizens would like to
know why these certificates were allowed to drop out of sight for
so long a time."[70]

*   *   *

Joseph Petrosino's martyrdom did not resolve the problems Italians
faced in gaining acceptance in New York law enforcement. His quiet
struggle for respect was obscured amid the outpouring of acclaim
for him. Later generations of minority police officers—especially
African Americans and Latinos assigned disproportionately to dangerous undercover narcotics work—would also have grievances.[71]
When a disguised Petrosino saw a police superior turn a gun on
him as a suspect, his experience anticipated contemporary incidents
in which police mistook black undercover officers for criminals
and shot them. But despite that, Petrosino's success in life and his
acclaim in death had established that minority police officers could
be worthy of holding a place with the Irish in the NYPD.

Francis L. Corrao's younger brother Charles, who was close to
Petrosino, survived the breakup of the Italian squad and was on
hand when it was formed again several years later. Charles, who
had a round, clean-shaven face, "perhaps comes nearer to holding the position formerly occupied by Lieutenant Petrosino than

any other member of the Detective Bureau," one of the era's most prominent crime reporters wrote. Lieutenant Charles Corrao enjoyed an illustrious career, most notably catching a Black Hand extortionist a moment before he could ignite a bomb.[72]

For Francis, the older brother and the pioneer, the road was rockier. Reporters sought out the assistant district attorney after Petrosino was killed to ask about his travel to Italy six months earlier, giving him the attention and respect he craved. "It seems from experiences I had in Italy last summer that the officials look on the Italian-American citizen when over there more as a curiosity, especially when he is studying the question of Italian criminality," Corrao said, adding that he knew Petrosino well and that the detective had deserved better from the Italian authorities.[73]

But Corrao remained on the margins of the district attorney's office. He resigned in anger on April 26, 1910. In a long, typewritten letter, he assailed District Attorney John F. Clarke, saying that their visit to Italy in the summer of 1908 had been more to study art than crime. "I soon found out that I was not appointed to prosecute Italian criminals, but simply to be an ornament in the office," he wrote. Clarke appeared astonished, responding, "I am at a loss to explain his action."[74]

The following year, Corrao published a short book attacking Clarke. Under Clarke, he wrote, prosecutors acted "on the supposition that the Italians of Brooklyn have no right to the law's protection or that they are not worth the time and attention of the District Attorney's office." As evidence, he cited the 1911 case against James Quinn, "a Tammany Hall contractor-politician" who had fatally shot Luigi Maraia, the seventeen-year-old son of Giuseppe Maraia of 508 President Street, Brooklyn, in a dispute over pay on a paving job. The prosecutor accepted Quinn's disputed claim of self-defense and agreed to dismiss the case without submitting it to a grand jury.

Corrao gained some measure of satisfaction. Clarke, at that point the longest-serving Brooklyn district attorney with twelve years in office (and another thirteen as an assistant district attorney), was voted out of office, losing to a Republican who had Corrao's support.[75] Corrao's influence was growing with the size of Brooklyn's Italian community.

*   *   *

The criminal justice system was the setting for an especially corrosive battle between the Irish and Italians, given the power of law enforcement over everyday lives and the dangers inherent in police work. It was essential to public safety that the mostly Irish commanders of the Police Department attract more Italian officers to the force to put an end to the terrifying spate of Black Hand bombings that afflicted the city in the early 1900s. Despite that, progress was slow in bridging the divide between the NYPD and the growing Italian community.

Like later minority groups in New York, Italian immigrants believed that police, judges, and juries were biased against them. They assumed that the system was based on favoritism, especially toward the Irish, rather than on justice. And they were led to believe that the police were indifferent to the crimes that victimized Italians. To the largely Irish police force, the Italians were dangerous and mysterious, an impenetrable mass of foreigners who were more interested in protecting each other from the police than in securing their own safety.

And yet, as in other arenas, we can see that Italians' frequent involvement with the Irish planted seeds for better relations in the future. Police commanders came to realize they needed more Italian officers, much as pastors like Monsignor John F. Kearney learned after a time that they needed to work cooperatively with Italian priests, and much as Irish American labor leaders gradually understood a need for Italian organizers such as Tito Pacelli.

In the realm of law enforcement, Lieutenant Joseph Petrosino became a martyr whom both the Irish and Italians could venerate. His ultimate sacrifice ended the notion that an Italian could not live up to the heroism attributed to cops of Celtic origin. Francis L. Corrao contributed in a different way, publicly addressing the ethnic strains that Petrosino tactfully kept to himself. Until his death in 1927 at the age of fifty-eight, he never stopped trying to build the political power needed to gain more influence for his people in the justice system.

The two men exemplify the dilemma that ethnic and racial outsiders so often face as they seek acceptance from the larger society: whether to work inside or outside the system. The overachiever Petrosino worked with quiet determination inside the Irish-run Police Department to win acceptance. Corrao became fed up and quit his post as a prosecutor to inveigh against the district attorney, then proceeded to organize Italians politically to force the changes he sought in the criminal justice system from the outside. Each found his own way of dealing with Irish American gatekeepers to their workplace. But for one of the best examples of an Italian American who learned to work the system by forming alliances with Irish gatekeepers, we cross over to the other side of the law and to the world of New York's Irish-controlled waterfront.

8

On the Waterfront

Thomas V. O'Connor, the forty-nine-year-old Toronto-born son of Irish immigrants who led the International Long-shoremen's Association, was beside himself on the morning of October 21, 1919. His men, some seventy thousand of them, had severely embarrassed him by walking off the job—over his staunch objection—two weeks earlier in what became the largest water-front strike in American history. The workers derided him: before the day ended, he would barely escape a mob calling for him to be lynched.

T. V. O'Connor, as he was usually known, was a proud man who had worked his way out of poverty by running a two-cent ferry service on the Buffalo River. Having grown up in Buffalo, he organized dockworkers on the Great Lakes. Conservative and business-friendly, he was savvy enough to later become a confidant of Republican presidents, serving as chairman of the U.S. Shipping Board. With his round glasses and slicked-down dark hair, he would look very much a part of the Hoover and Coolidge administrations in which he served. But on that morning in 1919, circumstances swamped him. He pleaded with the representatives of fifty-three locals at union headquarters in Manhattan to honor their contract, which called for them to accept a paltry arbitration award of five cents more an hour, and ten cents for overtime—the five-and-ten "Woolworth" deal, as the workers dubbed it. For all of this indignity, O'Connor blamed primarily one man: Paul A.

Vaccarelli, an Italian American labor leader who had been maneuvering to depose him as president of the ILA.[1]

Years of bitterness between Irish and Italian workers on the
New York waterfront were the subtext for O'Connor's struggle with
Vaccarelli, the onetime gangster who reinvented himself as a union
leader. O'Connor spat out Vaccarelli's name time and again as he
spent three hours urging the union reps gathered at 164 Eleventh
Avenue to vote an end to the illegal walkout. These men were supposedly his people, the Irish American longshoremen who lived in
Chelsea and other West Side neighborhoods, the kind of workers
who had dominated waterfront work in New York since the 1850s.
He warned them away from Vaccarelli, who he claimed had been
profiteering from their walkout by secretly supplying Italian strikebreakers. Vaccarelli's men—the Italians—would get their jobs, he
warned, and then Vaccarelli would "whip you back to work." That
is, those who still had jobs.

O'Connor was throwing red meat to his men, for his warning
harked back to earlier confrontations with Italian strikebreakers.
The Knights of Labor strike of 1887 crumbled when shippers hired
immigrant Italian scab workers. And when a port-wide strike in
1907 ended, riotous violence broke out on the West Side between
Irish longshoremen and fleeing Italian strikebreakers.[2]

The Irish took over the waterfront in the mid-nineteenth century. Up to around 1880, some 95 percent of the longshoremen
in the New York port were Irish. After the 1887 strike, shipping
companies began to hire more Italians to make it difficult for the
Irish to strike. By 1912, more than a third of the longshoremen were
Italian, and the Italians were beginning to dominate in Brooklyn.
But the Chelsea Piers on the West Side between Seventeenth and
Twenty-Third Streets, completed in 1910, gave the Irish a powerful
bailiwick that they fought to retain.[3]

O'Connor tried to attack Vaccarelli and the walkout by steaming up the simmering Irish resentment against the Italians. For in
this job action, something remarkable had occurred. Italian longshoremen in Brooklyn were the first to disregard their contract and

walk off the job to protest the five-and-ten raise. They marched to Chelsea, set up picket lines there, and called for their fellow workers—mostly Irish—to join them. The "Woolworth" raise, coming after the weak contracts granted during the war years, was enough to make the longshoremen throw aside years of tribal conflict and join forces, at least for the moment.[4]

O'Connor's accusation against Vaccarelli also echoed other suspicions about him and about Italians in general. Waterfront racketeers had long profited from providing strikebreakers (or assaulting them, depending on the pay). Everyone knew that Vaccarelli had led one of the city's most powerful gangs only a few years earlier. Anyone who read the newspapers would have known about the exploits of Paul Kelly, which was the name Vaccarelli had gone by in the years when he headed the Five Pointers gang and the Paul A. Kelly Association, the notorious club devoted to mayhem of all sorts and to fixing elections for Tammany Hall through intimidation, beatings, and voter fraud on a mass scale.

O'Connor told the union delegates that he had hired an investigator at sixty dollars a week "to get me the dope" on Vaccarelli. "I know everything that is going," he boasted. One item of interest to him was that "the Italians gave him a dinner on Saturday night in the Italian Gardens in Broome Street in honor of his appointment."

Angering O'Connor and surprising many others, U.S. Secretary of Labor William B. Wilson had appointed Vaccarelli—the former gangster—to a three-person federal conciliation board tasked with ending the walkout. Mayor William Hylan, also on the board, had recommended him; the appointment seemed to give Vaccarelli the upper hand in his bid to push O'Connor out of the ILA leadership. O'Connor, along with his aide John F. Riley, was left to complain that Vaccarelli had "deceived" the mayor. The appointment was a milestone in Vaccarelli's effort to go legit and was seen among Italians as an honor for the entire community. Hence the dinner on Broome Street.

Beyond that, there was a practical logic to the government's move. Since Vaccarelli had encouraged the walkout, he was the union official best positioned to end it. "The appointment of Paul Vaccarelli, very opportune and very wise, is certainly a hammer blow to the head for O'Connor and John F. Riley, and we understand that they are full of indignation," the newspaper *Bollettino della Sera* said.

And that was the case. "Gompers wanted Vaccarelli and myself to be friends," O'Connor told the longshoremen in his headquarters, referring to the respected president of the American Federation of Labor. "I said, 'Sam, not on your life.'"[5]

* * *

Few people were more adept than Paul Vaccarelli at walking the divide between New York's Irish and Italians. He made a career of knowing just when to jump over that wall, and when to take cover behind it.

His parents, Michael and Angela, migrated to New York from Potenza in the southern Italian region of Basilicata in 1875, then in their early thirties. Their son was born in 1877, and he grew up poor on the Irish-dominated Bowery. Michael worked as a laborer for less than a dollar a day. Young Franco Paolo Antonio Vaccarelli studied at the Crosby Street school for Italians; the soup was free. He stayed in school until he was fourteen, then took a job delivering stoves. At eighteen, he found work on Pier 29 on the West Side hauling heavy sacks from the ships, and was promoted to be a checker, inspecting barrels and bags of cargo. That would have been a prized job for many a son of Italian immigrants at the time, but he wanted more. Much more.

Since the Irish lads outnumbered him when he was a kid, he learned to fight. The short, wiry, dark-haired Vaccarelli thus pursued an avenue of advancement that often draws poor young men from minority backgrounds: sports. He became a prizefighter in the late 1890s, adopting the name Paul Kelly. He hung out in Bowery dives called Billy the Dude's, the Dirty Rag, and Suicide Hall. Practical lessons in fighting were easy to come by.[6]

Big Tim Sullivan, shown in an undated photo, allied with the
gangster Paul Kelly. George Grantham Bain Collection, Library
of Congress.

Since the Irish were the class of the field, many an Italian or
Jewish pugilist took a Celtic name. That tactic persisted; Frank
Sinatra's father would call himself Marty O'Brien. The bantamweight Paul Kelly beat a few tough Irishmen at their own game
and lost some bouts, too. After playing it for what it was worth, he
found a more lucrative way to capitalize on his talent for beating
people up: he became a gangster. He used his earnings to set up a
so-called athletic club, and while there was the occasional social
outing, the real sports engaged in were assault, intimidation, robbery, and election fixing. Kelly and his Five Pointers picked up the
mantle of some of the legendary gangs of New York such as the
Whyos and Dead Rabbits.[7] Their turf was bound by Broadway on
the west, Bowery to the east, Fourteenth Street to the north and
City Hall Park to the south. Most of the members were Italian;
many took Irish names, styling themselves after the swaggering
Irish hoodlums of yore in the Five Points.

The Tammany boss Big Tim Sullivan, who had a keen eye for
talent, put Paul Kelly to work for him. That became the young
man's ticket. With Sullivan's protection, Paul Kelly and his troops

could pull off their crimes with little fear of the police. In return, they provided an in-kind campaign contribution to Sullivan: they rigged the vote. The preferred method was to provide a throng of "repeaters," men who would vote in one polling place after another, throughout the day. Kelly could line up more than a thousand repeaters for an election on the Lower East Side.

Forward-thinking politician that he was, Sullivan made it a point to get along with the Italians in his district, as long as they didn't challenge him for power. He had much in common with them. An imposing, broad-shouldered, blue-eyed man who stood six feet one and weighed 220 pounds, Sullivan was born into an impoverished Irish immigrant family in a flat on Leonard Street in lower Manhattan in 1862 or 1863. His father, Daniel Sullivan, died when Tim was five. His brother died when he was seven, at which point he began selling newspapers in City Hall Park after school. When he was eleven years old, his teacher Miss Murphy told him to stay after class. He thought he was in trouble, but Miss Murphy put her hand on his shoulder and told him she just wanted to spare him the embarrassment he'd suffer when other students saw that his tattered shoes had such deep cracks that the snow soaked in. Miss Murphy sent him down to the local ward boss for a pair of shoes and, as Sullivan would later say in a speech that drew tears from his supporters, he had found his destiny. As a politician, Sullivan became famous for handing out shoes in the wintertime—more than five thousand pairs of shoes and warm socks in a day—to anyone who asked. He provided bountiful Christmas dinners, too, and warm clothing. How he afforded such generosity isn't clear, but he had an ample income from the saloons and theaters he owned, not to mention the stream of payoffs he was suspected of receiving for assuring police protection of gambling dens.

Having come up the hard way, Sullivan knew how to win over the poor of whatever nationality. The son of impoverished Irish immigrants could speak a bit of Italian and sponsored a resolution to make Columbus Day a state holiday, delighting his Italian

Thousands of people received free shoes at Big Tim Sullivan's
headquarters at 207 Bowery. These men were beneficiaries in
1910. George Grantham Bain Collection, Library of
Congress.

constituents. He put a slew of Italians into jobs in the city street-
cleaning department.[8] As one writer commented,

> Italians, Greeks, Russians and Polish Jews, he took them as fast as
> they came, flung them into his melting-pot. They went in Silvestros
> and Gordzinskis and they came out Sullivans. He naturalized them,
> registered them, and voted them for Tammany Hall. They won-
> dered and adored him. He was not unfair to them; they got their
> mess of pottage with the rest.[9]

One of the stops on Sullivan's ride to power was an election
on September 17, 1901, for Democratic district leader in the Five
Points area. Sullivan, a state senator, backed his good friend Tom
Foley, a saloonkeeper, against the Tammany boss Richard Croker's
man, former Police Justice Patrick Divver. With the help of Paul
Kelly's repeaters and strong-arm men, Foley won by a three-to-one
margin. "I was beaten by crooks and repeaters and the police," a
dejected Divver lamented. "It's the worst thing that has happened to
Tammany in the history of the organization. We were blocked out."

With Sullivan's protection, it seemed that Paul Kelly could get away with anything; he was a turn-of-the-century Mr. Untouchable. "Who is behind Paul Kelly?" the *World* demanded. "What hold has the dapper little Italian thug and jailbird with an Irish name on the powers higher up in his party?"[10]

The answer was simply that Kelly had made himself useful. Only once did he and his protector slip up. Right after Tom Foley's victory in 1901, the cocky Kelly committed the assault that would allow the *World* to later label him a jailbird. Kelly and two companions had beaten a Brooklyn resident named Robert K. Bruce, looking to rob his watch and chain. Bruce identified Kelly, but couldn't identify his accomplice. Somehow, police arrested the accomplice and released Kelly, supposedly for lack of evidence. But when Kelly was caught for another assault, he was brought to justice.

He came up against the wrong judge, John W. Goff, a fifty-three-year-old native of Ireland who had both a great appreciation for his heritage and keen outrage over the corruption some of his fellow Irish Americans engaged in through Tammany Hall and the Police Department. The corruption-fighting Reverend Charles Parkhurst, a Protestant and Republican, had called Goff, an Irish Catholic Democrat, "the noble Irishman."

Goff took the occasion not only to impose a nine-month sentence on Kelly, "one of young 'Tim' Sullivan's friends," as the *Times* put it, but also to lecture the police. "I think action of the police in this case was most shameful," he told Kelly. "It is evidence that they tried in every way in their power to shield you." The *Tribune* needled Sullivan: "'Young Tim' will lose his political prestige among the thieves and thugs if he does not protect them better." But the case didn't slow down the rise of Kelly's career in crime, nor did it derail Sullivan, who was elected to Congress the following year, even though the *Times* opined that he "is simply not fit to be at large in a civilized community."[11]

In 1903 Kelly's gang went to war with another band of election-fixing thugs, twenty-nine-year-old Monk Eastman's gang. Eastman, whose origins are unclear but who possibly was Jewish, also used an Irish alias on occasion. Whenever police arrested him, he gave his name as William Delaney. Cops continued to go by that, so that when he was taken into custody, he would reply, "Well, if my name is William Delaney, put it down William Delaney."[12] After some wild shootouts, Eastman left the scene when Goff sentenced him to ten years at Sing Sing. He was caught trying to rob a tipsy young man of means who was under the watchful eye of two Pinkerton detectives his family had secretly dispatched for his safety.

With Big Tim Sullivan's protection assured and his rival out of the way, Paul Kelly opened a notorious bar at 57 Great Jones Street, first called Brighton Hall and later, Little Naples Café. Acting Police Inspector William G. Hogan, a son of Irish immigrants, had Kelly arrested in a Saturday night raid on the bar. But when Kelly appeared in court, a local precinct commander showed up to vouch for him and the character of his bar. "I have been in there myself, and I can say that I never saw anything out of the way going on there," said Acting Captain Edward J. Bourke, a British-born son of Irish parents. After the charges were dismissed, some five hundred Kelly supporters who crowded outside the Jefferson Market Court in Greenwich Village gave the judge three cheers.[13]

Newspapermen wanted to know more about this man; they inquired about him and his name. "He wears clothes which the Bowery accepts as the pink of fashion and gentility, pointed patent leather shoes of the type still stylish in that region, some flashy jewelry, and a watch which by right of possession, at least, is his own," the *Sun* noted, adding, "There isn't anything in Kelly's face to indicate the nationality which that honorable name implies."[14]

Kelly made his Irish moniker official on March 27, 1905, when he obtained a court order to change his name from Vaccarelli. A politically connected Irish American judge did the honors: Justice Francis B. Delehanty, an Albany lawyer whose father was born in Birr, County Offaly (then King's County), and who rose to the bench through the grace of his brother-in-law Edward Murphy, an influential former state senator from Troy, New York.[15]

Kelly got his comeuppance not from police but from rival gang-sters. Jack Sirocco, a onetime lieutenant in the Five Points Gang, went to war with the Kellys. Sirocco, a twenty-three-year-old who wore plaid caps low over the eyes, was, like Kelly, a politically connected gangster with home base in a saloon and restaurant he owned. He had advanced his career by leaving Kelly to take over one of three gangs to emerge from the remains of Monk Eastman's mob, and thus posed an obvious challenge to Kelly. Sirocco was also in the ballot-rigging business, and was sore that one of Kelly's men, Bill Harrington, had spread word of Sirocco's misdeeds. On November 17, 1905, Sirocco dared to show his face at a Kelly func-tion. In the scrap that followed, Sirocco was shot in the arm. That set the stage for Sirocco's retaliatory raid on Kelly's Little Naples hangout on Great Jones Street near the Bowery.

James "Biff" Ellison, a big, dark-haired, dark-eyed, stylishly dressed man with a deep cleft in his chin, led the way. With him were "Razor" Riley and two other Bowery bruisers. Ellison found Kelly at the bar with Harrington, beneath a portrait of Big Tim Sullivan. The accounts vary at that point. From what Kelly would later tell the district attorney's office, Ellison and his men invited Kelly and Harrington for a drink, then set out their complaint: that Kelly was responsible for the Sirocco shooting days earlier. Kelly claimed innocence, and offered to prove it. But Ellison had a job to do. He pulled out his blue-barreled revolver and held it to the nattily dressed Kelly's white waistcoat.

Kelly, the five-foot, five-inch former bantamweight, shifted aside nimbly. As a witness later testified, "Paul made a quick jump and there was three shots and Bill Harrington fell down with a bullet he stopped." Harrington was shot dead, a bullet piercing the left side of his chest. Kelly was wounded in the side; his white waistcoat was stained with gunpowder residue.[16]

It is intriguing to unravel the ethnic complications in this scene. Harrington, who was backing up Kelly, was an Italian, as were Kelly and most members of his association. Ellison, forty-four years old, grew up in Maryland and apparently was of Irish ancestry—at least, judging by a story the newspaperman Alfred Henry Lewis told about him. He recalled that Ellison once tried a sort of Saint Patrick's Day defense in court after he and Pat "Razor" Riley were arrested for tearing up an Italian merchant's pet store on the saint's feast day. They had smashed the canaries, moved the monkeys, and torn the tails from macaws. The defense lawyer explained it to the judge as "over-celebrating" Saint Patrick's Day, indicating that the men were too drunk to know what they were doing. But the Italian merchant noted that Ellison and Riley were sober enough to avoid a bear he kept on a chain in the center of the room. The defendants were found guilty.[17]

By the time police arrived at Little Naples, everyone had fled. Holes in the ceiling and walls revealed that dozens of shots had been fired. Windows were broken; furniture was overturned and destroyed. Kelly, at least by his own account, told the bartender to call an ambulance for Harrington before leaving the premises.

Kelly lay low for a few days, then had his brother Joseph Vaccarelli tell authorities that he was staying in his cousin's place in East Harlem. When a detective named McGee arrived to arrest him on December 1, 1905, Kelly, smoking a long cigar with his wife at his side, told him with a smile, "I was just starting downtown to give myself up."

Surprisingly, Kelly talked—the first indication of his new direction. Looking thin and weak, he arrived at the district attorney's office bearing Exhibit A, his white waistcoat marked with gunpowder residue. He identified "Biff" as the man who shot Harrington. According to news accounts, he told Assistant District Attorney Michael H. Cardozo Jr. who the four gunmen were. When the coroner's inquiry was held afterward, his testimony was taken in secret, most likely to disguise that he continued to talk. As he exited the hearing, he told reporters he hadn't said anything.

It took nearly six years for authorities to find and prosecute "Biff" Ellison. The prosecutor expected Kelly to testify, but the star witness disappeared during the trial. One of his confederates, John "Rough House" Hogan, played that role—clearly with Kelly's approval. "Kelly is missing, and apparently has no interest in this prosecution," the assistant district attorney told the jury. "But this little wiry man who was one of his followers, seemingly not afraid of God, man nor the devil, made up his mind that he would tell the story of that gang fight, and he has done so." Ellison, by then fifty years old, was sentenced in 1911 to eight to twenty years in Sing Sing for manslaughter.[18]

In the meantime, Paul Kelly began to reinvent himself after the 1905 shooting. He had little choice. Police Commissioner William McAdoo shut down his tattered Little Naples dive. Further, Kelly had become an embarrassment to Tammany Hall and looked like a weakling in the gang world. There was no way he could continue with the overt violence that had carried him up the ladder in the 1890s, even with Sullivan's help. Newsmen had discovered him, with one magazine calling the Kellys the city's most active gang.

"The honored leader of the Kellys, who recently disappeared after the Harrington murder, is an Italian born with the musical name of Paolo Vaccarelli," it was reported. "The change to Kelly was made partly because it sounded tougher and partly because 'Kelly was Vaccarelli for short,' as one gangster put it. The Irish name has meant a good deal in his political and social preferment among his fellows."[19]

Kelly was beaten, but he was not without resources. He opened a new bar in Times Square, a sign that he continued to have political juice. He went into the real estate business in East Harlem and, showing his shrewdness, opened an auto repair garage at 236 West Forty-First Street. And he made his first forays into union leadership.

Italian workers sought him out with complaints that a padrone who hired them to work on garbage scows was paying them just seventy-five cents to a dollar a day, well below the promised wage. With the backing of Big Tim Sullivan, Kelly "explained the situation" to a local Democratic district leader who backed the padrone. Within days, the padrone was willing to pay a wage higher than the one originally agreed upon, $1.25 for a ten-hour day.[20]

In 1906 Kelly gained admission for the scow workers in the American Federation of Labor, which accepted him as leader of the local. Kelly picked a good time to reinvent himself as a waterfront labor leader, since Italian workers were rapidly replacing Irishmen on the docks. "In its swiftness, this substitution of the Italian longshoremen for others is one of the most striking examples of racial displacement in American industry," the Harvard professor Robert F. Foerster would write in 1919.[21]

As Paul Kelly continued to organize Italian workers, his Irish name became a liability. With his eponymous "political" association falling apart, he no longer needed to brand himself as Paul Kelly. On September 14, 1910, Judge Edward B. La Fetra granted him a court order changing his name once again. Paul A. Vaccarelli said he asked for his old name back because his parents had continually admonished him for changing it.[22]

Vaccarelli, who supposedly had gone straight, complained that police harassed him by raiding what he said was his respectable social club at 588 Seventh Avenue, just above Forty-First Street in Times Square. He told a reporter from the *Times* that he was going to lodge a complaint with the mayor, William J. Gaynor. "Kelly is a mild-mannered, soft-spoken little man who is diplomatic in conversation and only reproachful of his enemies—the police," the newspaper reported.

Police saw it differently, and in 1912 arrested Vaccarelli five times for running a gambling house and once for running a disorderly house, or bordello. "Kelly has long been a figure in police annals," the *Tribune* reported, noting a case in which William McAdoo, now the city's chief magistrate, had issued a warrant to search the club. The cases went nowhere; the club was back in business within a half hour of the raids.[23]

* * *

In 1913 Vaccarelli had the sad task of attending the funeral of Big Tim Sullivan at St. Patrick's Old Cathedral, with Monsignor John F. Kearney presiding. Sullivan had slipped visibly in his last days,

Irish and Italian mourners stood shoulder-to-shoulder at Big Tim Sullivan's
funeral at St. Patrick's Old Cathedral on September 15, 1913. Flickr Commons Project and George Grantham Bain Collection, Library of Congress.

suffering from dementia due to syphilis. He was confined to a
farmhouse on rural Eastchester Road in the Bronx, but appeared
to have wandered away. Strangely, the famous politician had gone
missing for thirteen days before his crushed and broken body was
found in the Fordham Morgue in the Bronx. He'd been run over
by a train near Pelham Bay Parkway on the Harlem Division of the
New York, New Haven, and Hartford Railroad. It was never clear
whether Sullivan was a suicide or the victim of some plot stemming
from his underworld connections.[24]

Fifty to seventy-five thousand people packed the streets between the start of the funeral procession at 207 Bowery, Sullivan's
clubhouse, and the church. There were twenty carriages just to
carry flowers, and a hundred more for the official party of mourners. Tarnished as Sullivan's reputation was, the day was an occasion
for remembering his achievements, which were considerable. He
had authored New York's gun control statute, the Sullivan Law,
and supported women's suffrage. For his Italian constituents, he

introduced the legislation that made Columbus Day a New York State holiday. There would not be another new government holiday to honor an individual until Martin Luther King Jr. Day was created—in 1985, for New York City municipal workers. In 1912 Sullivan pushed through a bill that set fifty-four hours as the maximum work week for women in New York State, an early wage-and-hours reform. Frances Perkins, who became U.S. secretary of labor under Franklin D. Roosevelt, later recalled Sullivan's explanation for why he pushed hard to make sure the bill passed: "I'm a poor man meself . . . I seen me sister go out to work when she was only fourteen and I know we ought to help these gals by giving 'em a law which will prevent 'em from being broken down while they're still young."[25]

As the funeral procession threaded through narrow Spring Street on the way to the old cathedral on Mott Street, it marked the ethnic change that Sullivan had weathered so well. According to one writer,

> They passed shops and saloons that were draped in mourning; tenement houses whose windows framed hundreds; Italian wineshops and cafes where business was suspended because the Italians had enlisted under Big Tim when the Irish faded from the East Side and many, many Italians had given up their name to take the name of Sullivan.[26]

Italian immigrants filled the eighty windows and fire escapes of the six-story tenement overlooking the Mott Street entrance to the church. Down on the street, Michael Ryan, who had known Big Tim for forty-five years, held the reins of the hearse. "Ryan was one of many elderly Irishmen and Irish women that had some part in the funeral, Irish people of a past day, of a type that is rapidly disappearing in this city," the *Sun* noted.

Sullivan's mourners ranged from panhandlers to philanthropists. "Judges and lawmakers touched elbows with gunmen and gang leaders and pickpockets," according to the *Sun*. An up-and-

coming Assembly leader named Alfred E. Smith was there, as was
the Republican leader James E. March. So too were "the gang leaders" Paul Kelly and Jimmy Kelly, the latter a former boxer who had
changed his name from John DeSalvio.[27] Hundreds of people wept.

Fifty altar boys dressed in white surplices met the casket, which
was covered with three thousand roses and two thousand white
chrysanthemums. Monsignor Kearney, described as a lifelong
friend of Sullivan, waited behind them with two of his priests, the
Reverend Severino Faccacia and the Reverend Gaetano Arcese. A
choir of thirty boys, nearly all of them Italians, sang "O, Grave,
Where Is Thy Victory?" Thousands of people were packed into the
church, where Kearney led the service.

There was no eulogy for Big Tim.[28]

*   *   *

Paul Vaccarelli managed to thrive even without Big Tim's protection. He wound up buying the Bronx farmhouse from which
Sullivan had disappeared, picking it up at auction, and moved his
family there from East Harlem. Following the death of his first
wife, Irish-born Minnie Cordner, Vaccarelli married Anna Teresa
Maloney, a native New Yorker whose parents were Irish. Her
brother, Thomas Maloney, lived with them and managed Vaccarelli's auto business. Vaccarelli's sister-in-law, Mary Weir, whose
ancestry was Irish, also lived in the spacious farmhouse at 2549
Eastchester Road in the Williamsbridge section. So too did his
parents, Michael and Angela, and a niece and nephew.

Meanwhile, Vaccarelli's ability to make deals with powerful
Irish Americans continued to propel him on his journey from street
thug to respected labor leader. He became influential enough to
try to oust T. V. O'Connor as head of the International Longshoremen's Association. To do that, he allied with Dick Butler,
a colorful dock walloper who was born in London in 1875 of parents who hailed from County Tipperary. Butler's father, Tom, had
worked the docks on the Thames and then in New York, where
he drowned at age fifty because of an accident on the job. Dick

Butler grew up hard; in his autobiography, he recounted bashing a foreman savagely with a metal bar because he was turned down for work, and then beating the charge in court.

Vaccarelli and Butler made an unlikely pair. Butler was a husky six-foot-tall, two hundred-pounder, brash and loud. Through his Tammany connections, he served a couple of years as a state assemblyman; he later boasted that since the legislators all voted as party leaders ordered, all he had to do in Albany was drink. He moved up from the legislature to owning a saloon at Twenty-Eighth Street and Tenth Avenue, the first of several. For him, running a nightspot went fist-in-glove with being a politician and labor leader. The flamboyant Butler played a supporting role in a celebrated murder case by hustling the playboy Harry Thaw out of an asylum for the criminally insane in 1913. Thaw was held there after being found innocent by reason of temporary insanity of murdering the architect Stanford White in 1906 out of jealousy for his affair with his wife, the sexy, red-haired artists' model Evelyn Nesbit. During a trial in March 1915, it emerged that Butler took $6,000—worth close to $130,000 today—in return for springing Thaw from the asylum in Fishkill, New York, and smuggling him out of state, allowing him to escape to Canada. The jury bought Butler's dubious defense that he didn't think he was doing anything illegal, since as far as he knew, Thaw was by then sane and didn't need to be institutionalized any longer.

Vaccarelli was as short, quiet, and restrained as Butler was big and loud, coming across more as a banker or clergyman than a saloonkeeper. He had been brash in his years as a boxer and gangster, but was more discreet in his new life. He spoke French, Spanish, and Italian, and, as Herbert Asbury wrote in his 1928 book *Gangs of New York*, seemed to have the breeding to move well in higher social circles.

Butler had formed the Longshoremen's Union Protective Association, which he merged with O'Connor's ILA in 1912. He moved his union office upstairs from his second saloon, Dick Butler's, at 711 Seventh Avenue in Times Square, and prospered. Customers

The longshoremen's union leader T. V. O'Connor
opposed a waterfront strike that Italian American
dock workers launched in 1919. George Grantham
Bain Collection, Library of Congress.

included Sam Gompers, head of the AFL, and the lawman William J. Flynn, who dropped in to tell him to be careful. Charley
Stoneham, owner of the New York Giants, came by too. The Giants manager John McGraw was a customer.

Straitlaced T. V. O'Connor didn't appeal to Butler. As he
wrote in his autobiography, both he and Vaccarelli looked down
on O'Connor as a minor-leaguer from the sticks, Buffalo. They
worked the great Port of New York; O'Connor had come up working on Great Lakes tugboats. Butler was West Side Irish, but he'd
enjoyed slumming on the Lower East Side at Vaccarelli's Little
Naples. A character himself, he had an appreciation for the toughs
who'd hung out in Vaccarelli's joint, men like Big Jack Sirocco,
Eat-'em-up Jack McManus, and Bill Harrington. And he admired

the Paul Kelly Association's ability to fix an election, even though he thought he was better at it. Vaccarelli was a guy he could work with. When Butler formed what he called the Kenmare Detective Agency—a unit of armed men to counter the detective agencies the shipping companies hired as muscle during strikes—he headquartered it in Vaccarelli's office, which was in the New York Times Building in Times Square. Al Marinelli, Tammany Hall's chief Italian contact, was his partner in the agency.[29]

Dick Butler, "the dock walloper," in a 1915 photo. Butler teamed with Paul Vaccarelli to challenge leadership of the longshoremen's union. Flickr Commons Project and George Grantham Bain Collection, Library of Congress.

The Irish-Italian alliance between Vaccarelli and Butler was put to the test in 1915. A prominent Irish American businessman from Boston offered the union a million dollars for a strike on East Coast ports. T. V. O'Connor disclosed that he received the offer from the Boston contractor and politician Matthew Cummings, a former national chairman of the Ancient Order of Hibernians, who was born in Bandon, County Cork, and migrated to the United States at the age of fourteen. As Butler later wrote, the goal was to cut off the flow of munitions to Great Britain by tying up the ports, thus aiding Germany in the First World War and, indirectly, the Irish cause against British repression. The United States was officially neutral at the time.

Butler said he received a similar offer from someone other than Cummings. The suspicion was that the Irish were intermediaries for a German agent who wanted to induce a strike by funding a full month of strike pay for the longshoremen. Butler, forewarned by his lawman friend William J. Flynn, smelled a rat. He met with O'Connor and Vaccarelli and, in his telling, the three agreed to let the subject drop.

To Butler's consternation, Vaccarelli and O'Connor brought the story straight to the *New York World*. As it worked out, all three labor leaders were treated like heroes in the press for foiling the plot. Vaccarelli in particular was credited with clearing the piers of agitators. "Only prompt action prevented the success of the plot," the *Times* reported.

The caper went a long way toward changing Vaccarelli's reputation; President Woodrow Wilson cabled during the war to thank him for warding off labor trouble on the docks. Vaccarelli built on this goodwill by publishing a patriotic labor newspaper, *Uncle Sam*, during the war. He topped its platform with a call for "Unwavering loyalty to the Government and institutions of the United States of America." Vaccarelli also served as chairman of a government committee responsible for finding workers to service navy transport ships.[30]

At the same time, Vaccarelli warned publicly that it was becoming difficult to maintain labor peace at a time when German
agents were striving to stir up strikes among longshoremen angered
by their low wages. In 1916 he frightened officials of the Morgan
Line to the point that they told reporters that Vaccarelli was trying
to coerce their workers into a strike. The *Times* reported that men
who had worked twenty years on the docks "quit their posts almost
in tears, declared that Kelly had threatened them with beating and
even more serious harm if they did not accept his leadership." The
paper added,

> It was less than six years ago that the former gang leader and widely
> feared bad man entered City Court Justice La Fetra's court and
> asked permission to change his name back to its original form—
> Antonio Vaccarelli. Under it Kelly had been a peaceful citizen;
> under it he desired again to live at peace with the police, he said,
> and the Justice granted him the boon he asked. Then Kelly, who
> was once the proprietor of New York's toughest saloon and dance
> hall, who gloried in the reputation of "the hardest bad man" in New
> York, apparently reformed. But of late he has taken an active part in
> the affairs of the longshoremen, and his appearance has always been
> followed by trouble.

T. V. O'Connor hastened to the scene with assurances that
Vaccarelli, by then a vice president of the ILA, was not in charge.[31]
Following the armistice, Vaccarelli knew that his workers would
demand raises deferred during the war. Having navigated the rocky
Irish-Italian relationship since his boyhood on the Bowery, Vaccarelli was able to unify the workers in a single, massive strike in
1919. It was no easy feat, given the ethnic bitterness between the
two factions. Each side thought that men on the other failed to
pull their weight. The Irish longshoremen considered the Italians
too small to lift 220-pound sacks of potatoes or 280-pound sacks of
sugar. If so, that posed serious safety concerns in a dangerous job.

The clubbiness that ethnicity encouraged helped men doing dangerous work to feel safer. The Italians, for their part, thought Irish foremen gave the Irish light duty whenever possible. The researcher Charles B. Barnes encountered their hatred for each other when he spent a year on the docks:

> It was difficult to make the Irish work harmoniously with the Italians. At first it was impossible. Then Italians were put on in separate gangs or to handle coal; but care had to be exercised. If a gang of "Ginnies," or "Dagoes," as they were called, was put in the hold with the Irish, the latter would quit. Accordingly, sharp foremen played one race against the other.[32]

Vaccarelli's alliance with Dick Butler helped bridge that divide. But although Butler was a candidate to lead the ILA, this was not a case in which the Irishman played foreman to the Italian, a sign of an evolving Irish-Italian relationship. In this case, Vaccarelli pulled the strings. Because the 1919 strike originated with Italian workers, it was necessary for the federal government to appoint him, and not Butler, to the arbitration board. One Italian newspaper referred to Butler as "his lieutenant."[33] Sixty thousand or more longshoremen struck—Italian, Irish, black, Scandinavian—as well as thousands more from various trades active in the harbor, idling 650 ships. The strike ended with an agreement for further arbitration that ultimately raised the workers' wages. Vaccarelli ordered his men back to work on November 5, 1919, and, in a statesmanlike note, told them to return "not in a surly or vindictive spirit," but to give employers full value for their pay.[34]

Paul Vaccarelli and Dick Butler did not succeed in replacing T. V. O'Connor as head of the ILA; he went to his federal post in 1921. That honor eventually went to Joseph P. Ryan, a son of immigrants from County Tipperary. Ryan, whose power base was among his fellow Irish in Chelsea on Manhattan's West Side, stood by O'Connor during the 1919 strike but also was close to Butler, who called him "somewhat of an improvement" over O'Connor. Joe

Ryan replaced Vaccarelli as a vice president of the ILA, then moved up to president in 1927.[35]

Vaccarelli continued to lead the scow workers' union but, cut out of the ILA's top level, began to take leadership positions elsewhere in the labor movement even as he pursued his real estate and insurance interests. Dubbed the "lightning change artist" of organized labor, he switched in 1923 to serving as business agent for the Musical Mutual Protective Association. To get into the musicians' union, Vaccarelli had to prove he could play an instrument. He auditioned successfully on the drums, which he learned to play in the days when the Paul Kelly Association's fife-and-drum corps paraded on the Lower East Side for Big Tim Sullivan.

Five years later, Herbert Asbury contended in *Gangs of New York* that Paul Kelly was a reformed man. F. Paul A. Vaccarelli died of pneumonia on April 3, 1936, following his final journey from the Bronx mansion where Big Tim Sullivan spent his last days to Misericordia Hospital. His four-hundred-word obituary in the *New York Times* mentioned his friendship with Sullivan and highlighted his role as the "Dockside Strike Conciliator." The *Times* made not a mention of his criminal past.[36]

In the end, the Irish-Italian battle over the waterfront labor unions and the jobs that came with them was resolved by the separation of the combatants. The Italians were admitted to the union, but there were separate Italian locals and Irish locals. Brooklyn went to the Italians; the Irish controlled the Manhattan docks as well as the overall union leadership.

Still, Paul Vaccarelli had demonstrated that it was possible, at least temporarily, to get Irish and Italian dock workers to set aside their differences to go on strike together over shared economic grievances. His ability to insert himself into the leadership of the longshoremen's union went only so far, however, and ever adaptable, he took his considerable talents elsewhere. He left behind a very uneasy peace on the waterfront. Jobs were at stake, after all, and the shape-up system for hiring made the waterfront an especially competitive workplace.

The docks were also a profitable workplace for racketeers, given the massive tons of cargo changing hands, the restive workers, and the volatile labor situation. And so Irish and Italian men in another highly competitive line of work that Vaccarelli knew well—crime—waged a bullet-riddled battle of their own to control the underworld spoils of the Brooklyn waterfront.

9

White Hand

Anna Lonergan knew plenty well what she was supposed to say to reporters or cops—and, more importantly, what not to say. She was the newspapers' "Queen of the Mob," after all, having briefly been married to the leader of Brooklyn's Irish "White Hand" gang before his untimely death. She was also the sister of his successor, whose own premature death had drawn her and a newspaper reporter to the family's apartment in a brick walk-up at 738 Myrtle Avenue in Brooklyn on the night of December 26, 1925. It was bitterly cold when Richy Lonergan's corpse was brought home from the city morgue at about 6:00 p.m., a bullet wound over one eye. Wind howled at up to forty miles an hour, and the temperature was plunging toward eleven degrees after a relatively warm Christmas Day.

Anna, a twenty-nine-year-old former Broadway show girl with blonde hair and big blue eyes, had wept earlier that day when she and her mother, Mary, identified Richy's corpse at the Kings County Morgue. Like Anna, Mary Lonergan was not unfamiliar with the sight of blood. She had fatally shot her six-foot, two-inch, red-haired, Irish immigrant husband, John—a onetime bare-knuckle boxer who had sparred with John L. Sullivan—in what a jury accepted to be an act of self-defense. For Anna, this blustery day after Christmas marked the third time she had identified a shooting victim in the morgue; her father and first husband had preceded her brother.

Now, Anna was just angry—"berling mad," as she would have put it—so much so that she came to the dangerous brink of violating the underworld code she knew so well by nearly identifying the culprits who had killed her brother. They were "foreign gangsters," she declared, boldly vowing to use the ample proceeds from Richard Lonergan's life insurance to trace and identify them.[1]

"I think they were foreigners," she told a *Brooklyn Eagle* reporter. "No, I don't know who, but you can bet it was no Irish-American like ourselves that would stage a mean murder like this on Christmas Day."[2]

Anna, who grew up wanting to be a nun and went to church daily when she was a child, meant that the godless Italians were responsible.[3] She offered no names, but in that time and place, the term "foreign gangsters" could only have meant Frankie Yale's gang, the Italians engaged in a long war with the Irish for control of lucrative rackets on the Brooklyn waterfront. And indeed, within days, a gang of Frankie Yale's hoodlums that included a young thug named Al Capone would be rounded up and charged in the murders of Richard Lonergan and two of his gunmen. For just as the Irish and the Italians of New York had competed for legitimate jobs as bootblacks, construction workers, or longshoremen, so too did professional criminals of both ethnicities battle each other and Jewish gangsters, too, in their shady workplaces. But while construction workers threw insults, punches, or bricks, gangsters used guns, the tool of their trade.

However violent the shift from Irish to Italian longshoremen was, the ethnic succession for waterfront criminals and for organized crime in general was much more so. Such hardened criminals were not typical of the immigrant peoples they sprang from and preyed upon, but they were glamorized in the popular culture of the Prohibition years and thus loomed large in the public imagination. As in more legitimate lines of work in New York, the Irish arrived before the Italians in this one, too, and so served as role models for the Italians to some extent. Irish gangsters created a style that young Italian hoodlums like Paul Kelly had adopted in the 1890s, and then motion picture depictions of Irish mobsters further embellished their swaggering image for later generations. Al D'Arco, who in 1991 became the highest-ranking mafioso to turn federal informant, recalled sitting through many showings of James Cagney gangster movies as a boy and entertaining his Brooklyn family with imitations of the actor.[4]

But there was nothing funny about the bloody mob war that Irish and Italian criminals fought on the Brooklyn waterfront, with the medical examiner recording seventy-eight unsolved murders over a ten-year period beginning in 1922 in the borough's Irishtown section amid the cobblestoned streets near the Brooklyn and Manhattan Bridges and the Navy Yard.[5] It's not clear how many of these slayings resulted from Irish-Italian clashes; gangsters from both ethnicities needed little provocation to kill one of their own. Anna Lonergan would recall that her late husband, Bill Lovett, had killed a fellow Irish American for pulling a cat's tail, for example. But the death of Richard "Peg Leg" Lonergan—so called (although not to his face) for the wooden leg he acquired after the Smith Street trolley ran over him when he was eight years old—was different, the end result of a pitched battle. The bad blood between Irish and Italian gangsters working the Brooklyn waterfront had been established long before Richy Lonergan left home on Christmas night of 1925, going out, according to his mother, to buy lights for the Christmas tree.

Everyone knew that Lonergan's occupation as leader of the White Hand was hazardous duty. The gang dated to around 1910, its name an obvious shot at the Italians and their Black Hand, not to mention their skin tone. Irish laborers had built the Brooklyn waterfront; the unions were Irish, and so were some owners of the shipping companies and piers. So Dennis "Dinny" Meehan took it as his right to run the rackets. It was not a subtle trade; the main task was to collect tribute from men who worked hard for a living on the waterfront and to beat them, kill them, or destroy their property if they didn't pay. Meehan succeeded to the point that Captain John Coughlin, the head of the Brooklyn Detective Bureau, labeled him "unquestionably the worst criminal in Brooklyn"—a mean feat in a county of two million. Police couldn't nail him; he beat the charges in a robbery and then in the slaying of a rival Irish gangster.[6] But gradually, as one waterfront neighborhood after another turned from Irish to Italian, a gang of Italians began taking over the protection rackets from Meehan.[7]

That put Meehan on a collision course with Frank Ioele, the gang boss who sometimes called himself Frank Uale and was nicknamed Frankie Yale. The Calabrian-born Ioele, a short, stocky man with a dimpled chin, emigrated to New York in 1905 at the age of twelve and built an empire of businesses that included a funeral parlor and the Yale Cigar Manufacturing Company at 6309 New Utrecht Avenue in southwest Brooklyn's Bensonhurst section. (A picture of the owner, along with his Frankie Yale nickname, was on the cigar cartons.) Ioele had been a gunman for the gang leader Johnny Torrio, using the cigar company as a front for his illegal liquor operation. He was deep into waterfront shakedowns.[8] He lived in a growing Italian-Jewish section of southwest Brooklyn, far from the turmoil of the docks he aimed to rule. Residing with his parents and wife in a big house at 6605 Fourteenth Avenue, Ioele flaunted his wealth by decking himself in diamonds—his belt buckle alone was said to have seventy-five of them—and by making lavish donations to St. Rosalia Catholic Church and school, located at Fourteenth Avenue and Sixty-Third Street in southwest Brooklyn.[9]

Meehan died in his bed on March 31, 1920, sleeping peacefully while awaiting trial on three indictments. Gunmen entered his apartment at 452 Warren Street as Meehan, his wife, Sadie, and his mother-in-law dozed. Only four-year-old Dennis Jr. was awake, and one of the intruders patted him on the head to keep him quiet. Five shots were fired, one of which went through Meehan's head and then struck his wife in the shoulder. Four days later, "one of the largest funeral processions ever seen in Brooklyn" accompanied Dinny Meehan's coffin to Holy Cross Cemetery in Flatbush. It was widely believed that Bill Lovett was the gunman who had dispatched Meehan, although more recently the authors William Balsamo and John Balsamo have written that the Ioele gang was responsible, killing him in retaliation for murdering one of its strong-arm men. Two years later, the resilient Lovett managed to survive after he was shot six times.[10]

Anna Lonergan had known Bill Lovett since they were children growing up on the Lower East Side. He was a homely man, five feet, seven inches tall with black hair, a broad, flat nose, and a funereal pallor. He was also the hero of a World War I machine gun battalion, receiving the Distinguished Service Cross for rescuing two buddies by crossing no-man's-land during a harrowing night attack in the Argonne. And he was a fearless killer who succeeded Dinny Meehan as head of the White Hand gang.[11] After being bailed out on a gun possession charge, he married his sweetheart Anna, sister of his buddy Richy Lonergan. "'Wild Bill' Lovett, Brooklyn character, who in fourteen arrests has spent but seven months in jail, is under a life sentence today," the Telegram reported. "He's married."

Lovett promised to go straight and work in the insurance business. He quipped to a reporter, "If there's any murders going on in the next couple of weeks you'll know Bill Lovett and his wife were out to Long Beach and had nothing to do with them." His remark wasn't an exaggeration, since Lovett had been arrested seven times in homicide cases after his military service ended, although there was never enough evidence for him to be tried.[12]

The newlyweds moved to Ridgefield Park, New Jersey, with Anna's mother. Lovett promised his new wife that he'd stop drinking. But three months after the wedding, Lovett left home, telling his wife he was going to work, then returned to the old neighborhood and went on a binge. After he passed out in a bar, word spread that Wild Bill was there for the taking. Ioele ordered the hit; his enforcers shot Lovett multiple times and crushed his skull with a meat cleaver. His body was found on November 1, 1923, in the back of the Dockloaders Club at 25 Bridge Street in Brooklyn's Vinegar Hill section, three blocks east of the Manhattan Bridge.[13]

In the meantime, Anna had gotten wind that her husband had gone on a bender with his old pals. She went to Brooklyn's Bath Beach, where Lovett's mother lived, and got his brother to help her search for him. Informed that her husband had been slain, she collapsed.

Anna's gray-eyed, red-haired brother Richard, who listed his job as bicycle repairman in his father's shop at 259 Bridge Street but was actually part of Lovett's gang, tried to reassemble the pieces. And so on that Christmas night of 1925, the twenty-five-year-old hoodlum decided to take the fight to the enemy's den, an Ioele-friendly waterfront speakeasy at 152–154 Twentieth Street, Brooklyn. That bravado wasn't unusual for Richy Lonergan, who, according to the *Brooklyn Eagle*, "believed he had a charmed life and carried on his operations with unusual recklessness even for a gangster."[14]

In the early hours of December 26, Lonergan and a troop of White Handers walked through the black double doors of the Adonis Club. It was Jack Stickem's Place, as regulars called it, using the nickname of the main proprietor, thirty-six-year-old Jack Stabile. The bar in the front piped up beer from barrels in the basement. But the action was in the second room, where the singer Helen Logan was performing in a cabaret as the piano played ragtime and jazz favorites for couples dancing in a crowded fifteen-foot square in the center of the room.

The arrival of Lonergan and his four gunmen created a stir, one woman who was there later recalled. "They were welcome. Don't ever let anybody tell you differently," Rose Adoleas, a flapper who lived near Manhattan's Chinatown, told an interviewer the following year, adding that, by the way, she was not a gun moll. "Welcome" might not be the right word, however. "Expected" is more to the point, since Ioele's gang was getting inside information from an Irish turncoat and knew that the White Handers would be showing up in force.

However delighted the crowd at the Adonis was to see him, Lonergan lacked Christmas spirit. He heckled Irish women who were with Italian men, passing cracks about "ginzos" and "dagos" and telling them to "come back with white men." This was an out-right insult to Italian-born Jack Stabile, since a pretty, fair-haired woman was clinging to him that night. Mae Wilson, who lived three blocks down Third Avenue, had taken up with the flashy-dressing Stabile because she was lonely while her husband did time in state prison. Wilson, as one observer later reported, was "strik-ingly rouged and dressed."

As Lonergan handed over his coat (but not his gun) to petite Alva Callahan, who cleared a handsome forty dollars a week as a coat checker, she noticed something odd about him. "You seem so jumpy," she told the gangster. And so the party continued.[15]

* * *

Meanwhile, Mae Capone was worried. She and her husband, Alfonse, had returned to Brooklyn from their home near Chicago during the Christmas holiday so that their seven-year-old son, Sonny, could undergo surgery. Their only child was sickly. Now he needed mastoid surgery to drain an infection in the left inner ear. Worried that the operation would leave their boy deaf, the Capones came to New York to find the best doctors money could buy.

And Al Capone had plenty of money. Taking Mae and Sonny with him, he had departed Brooklyn in 1920 at the age of twenty-one to work for his mentor, Johnny Torrio, in the Chicago rackets. Before Torrio went west, his clubhouse had been on Fourth Avenue in Brooklyn, around the corner from the Garfield Place row house where Al grew up with his father, Gabriele, a barber from the town of Angri at the foot of Mount Vesuvius, and his mother, Teresa. Al Capone was a fledgling gangster then, one step removed from the youthful street fights he had with the Irish when growing up on Navy Street along the waterfront. Torrio had been a gangster since around the time Capone was born, fighting for Paul Kelly in his war with Monk Eastman back in 1903. After Kelly withdrew from the day-to-day business of running a gang, Torrio headed to Brooklyn and allied with Frankie Yale. In Chicago, the savvy Torrio fought his way up the food chain, growing rich through bootlegging after Prohibition started in 1919. But the Irish gangs were larger, more deeply entrenched, and powerful; he called on Capone to join him.

Capone not only went to work for Torrio, but succeeded him in 1925; the boss was nearly slain in a shooting and bowed out for the time being. And so as Capone went back to Brooklyn that Christmas of 1925, he was a success as a criminal but not yet a celebrity for it. He was able to offer a hundred thousand dollars to the doctor who treated Sonny. The surgeon turned it down in favor of the usual thousand-dollar fee.[16]

Mae and Al Capone were an odd match. She was Irish American. He was Italian American. She was tall, slim, pretty, quiet, and blonde. He was stout and ill-tempered and had thinning, dark hair and an ominous four-inch scar on his cheek. Mary Josephine Coughlin—everyone called her Mae—was born in 1897 to Mike Coughlin, a clerk on the Erie Railroad, and Bridget Gorman. Both of her parents had migrated separately from Ireland earlier in the 1890s and lived in lower Manhattan close to the growing Italian community. They married on January 28, 1894, at St. Anthony of Padua Church, the Italian parish supported largely by Irish members' donations. The 1900 census lists them as living across the East River in Brooklyn at 6 Manhasset Place, a street later removed when the Brooklyn-Queens Expressway was built at the point where it sweeps past the Brooklyn and Manhattan Bridges. In the 1910 census, they were recorded as living at 553 Clinton Street, walking distance to the Red Hook docks, where Mike Coughlin worked as a laborer. The Coughlins had six children, plus two nieces and a nephew living with them. Mae, then thirteen, had a sixteen-year-old sister, Anna, and a seventeen-year-old cousin, Josephine Dilworth, who both worked as salespersons in a department store. Mae, a high school graduate, later did the same. By the time Mae Coughlin met Al Capone, the upwardly mobile Coughlins lived in a three-story brick home at 117 Third Place in the neighborhood now called Carroll Gardens, between Court and Smith Streets. It was a lovely block on which the brick homes were graced by gardens in oversized front yards. The Capones lived at 38 Garfield Place in a lower-rent waterfront neighborhood on the other side of the Gowanus Canal, just off busy Fourth Avenue.[17]

Capone's biographers have ascertained that the two met at a party on Carroll Street. She was twenty-one; he was nineteen.[18] It is hard to imagine what attracted Mae Coughlin, a churchgoing Catholic with a high school diploma and an upright family, to a roughneck who was two years younger and had a big scar on his face. Irish-Italian unions were unusual at the time, but not unheard of. An Irish woman could be a status symbol for an Italian man. At the time, the fair Irish lassie was beginning to be seen in popular culture as the picture of beauty; the song "Pretty Kitty Kelly"—"there's not a colleen sweeter"—would be released in 1920.

In any event, the couple wed at St. Mary Star of the Sea Church on Court Street on December 18, 1918. The Reverend James J. Delaney, thirty-five-year-old son of Irish immigrants, presided. By that time, Sonny, or Albert Francis Capone, was two weeks old.[19]

The idea that a virtuous woman from a religious, middle-class Irish American family waited until after the birth of a child to wed, and then married in the local Catholic parish where all the neighbors knew her, is also difficult to comprehend. One possible explanation comes from a grandniece of Al Capone, Deirdre Marie Capone. In her 2012 book *Uncle Al Capone*, she writes that Sonny was born of another local woman Capone had gotten pregnant and who died in childbirth. Capone's mother took the child in, but then looked to arrange a marriage for her son so that the child would have a mother. She found Mae Coughlin, a devout young woman at her church. According to Deirdre Marie Capone, Mae Coughlin, who was sterile due to a birth defect, agreed. Mae's mother, Bridget Coughlin, had died several years earlier, in 1915.[20]

Whatever the case, Mae was a devoted wife and parent. She kept a low profile, except for one time in 1927 when she complained to a reporter that her son came home in tears every day because other kids taunted that his father was a killer: Al Capone's son was bullied at school. She surfaced only occasionally with her husband at the track or theater, protected by bodyguards. When visiting her husband at Alcatraz prison in later years or accompanying him to court, she covered her face partially to avoid photographers. She dressed conservatively in clothes that were expensive but not flashy; her jewelry consisted of her wedding ring and a diamond ring worn with it. One newspaper feature claimed that she wouldn't let her husband in the door if he came home too late at night and that, while she had a maid, she was willing to do the dishes herself.

Her decency is seen in one incident involving a house the Capones had rented in Florida. The landlord was petrified to find out who the new tenants were, and she expected the worst. The Capones, it turned out, gave back the house in excellent shape and even left behind valuable china and silver. Though a four-hundred-dollar phone bill was unpaid, the woman was not about to complain about it to Al Capone's wife. But one day a slender, well-dressed lady arrived at the door and announced that she, Mrs. Capone, had come to pay the phone bill. She presented a five-hundred-dollar bill and declined the change.[21]

In short, Mae Capone was not one of the gun moll types with whom her husband was familiar. And so while he went out to the Adonis Social Club that Christmas night of 1925, she stayed home. It was a business trip. When Capone arrived at the Adonis around 2:00 a.m., the festivities were in full swing. Lonergan had ordered up a weepy, sentimental song even though Jack Stabile said he wanted to ditch the teary stuff. Then the piano player pulled out the music for one of the memorable hits of 1925, "Yes Sir! That's My Baby."

The accounts vary on what happened next. According to Rose Adoleas, "Needles" Ferry was the first to recognize Capone and the trio of Frankie Yale's gunmen who walked in with him. A stunning fusillade filled the tiny room; women screamed and dove to the floor; chairs were hurled and broken in the mayhem that followed. Witnesses claimed that the lights were shut off, but police wouldn't believe that. Rose Adoleas ran out, leaving a gold cigarette case engraved with her name. Alva Callahan, the coat checker, left her own coat behind in her rush to get to the door. Mae Wilson, seated at a table on the edge of the room, would tell police that she turned her face to the wall, covered her ears with her hands and screamed. And Alfonse Morelli, his wife, and two children, who lived in the upstairs apartment, slept through it all. At least, that is what they told detectives. For police, it was always that way in gangland hits: no one saw or heard anything.

When it was over, Lonergan and his buddy Aaron Harms lay dead on the dance floor. "Needles" Ferry ended up outside in the gutter. James Hart, a twenty-four-year-old White Hander, was shot in the right side and found crawling in the street at Flushing and Throop Avenues, about five miles from the Adonis. And two others from Lonergan's gang, Patrick "Happy" Maloney and Joe Howard, escaped unharmed.

Before long, word of the shooting reached Anna Lonergan and her mother. Early that morning, Mary Lonergan called police to report that she heard her son had been wounded. No, she was informed. He was dead. Mary Lonergan fainted.[22]

Mae Capone lost her husband, but only for the remainder of the Christmas holiday. Al Capone and Stabile were among the nine men arrested and held in the Raymond Street jail. Capone's friends showed up loaded with cash to pay a high bail, but Magistrate Francis A. McCloskey refused to release him. Capone was still little known enough for some news accounts to describe him as a bouncer or doorman at the Adonis Club, but the *Brooklyn Standard Union* reported that police said he had "made a large fortune in bootlegging" in Chicago. But the charges were dismissed for lack of evidence. Capone was released on New Year's Day, and celebrated the holiday at a party on Fourth Avenue at which he, Torrio, and Frank Ioele all gave speeches.[23]

Capone was free to continue his war with the fearsome Irish gangs in Chicago for control of illegal traffic in liquor. Capone scoffed at them and at Chicago police detectives as well, calling them "another bunch of Irish bastards with guns."[24] The battle reached a shocking low point when his gunmen, disguised as police officers, lined up seven men connected to George "Bugs" Moran's gang in a garage and gunned them down in cold blood on February 14, 1929—the Saint Valentine's Day Massacre.

Anna Lonergan was right, as it turned out. Italian gangsters were the culprits (although Capone was American-born, not a "foreigner"), and they had lured her reckless brother into a trap.

Anna's second husband, Matty Martin, gathered up the remnants of the White Hand gang, though the Irish-Italian war for control of the waterfront rackets in Brooklyn was largely over after the Adonis shootout. Martin also met an untimely end when he was gunned down in Tanner's speakeasy at 62 DeKalb Avenue in downtown Brooklyn on December 14, 1931.

Even though police theorized that Martin was shot by fellow gangsters in a squabble over a woman, Anna Lonergan Lovett Martin stood by him as he lay on his deathbed in Cumberland Hospital. She pleaded with her husband to say who shot him. "If I knew I wouldn't tell you," he replied. Martin played the tough guy when detectives pressed him. "Who shot me? Al Capone's brother-in-law," he said—Capone was by then a celebrity. A discouraged Anna Lonergan sounded ready to give up. "I'd like to know one thing," she told a reporter. "Just when am I going to get a break? I've had nothing but bad breaks since I was born."[25]

Five months later, she walked into a police station with a deep slash on her right arm and told the desk sergeant that she received it when fending off a man who jumped her as she walked along waterfront Main Street in Brooklyn, between the Brooklyn and Manhattan Bridges. She claimed that the assailant had tried to slash her face with a knife. Police theorized that she'd been collecting hush money for not revealing who had slain her husband, and that the killers had tired of paying her off.[26]

That same year, Anna revealed that she was ready to marry again—this time to an Italian. As the *Eagle* reported on November 26, 1932,

Anna Lonergan Lovett Martin, widow of two gangsters and sister of a third, will wed again soon, taking as her third husband Nicholas Perrillo, an auto dealer, whose record is said to be spotless.

The wedding will take place about Dec. 15, Mrs. Martin said today, but she declined to reveal where.

"We do not want to be bothered," she said. "We want to live quietly and happily and you can't do that when too many people are interested in your affairs.

"I've known some sad days and some unhappy ones and I hope at last to find peace."[27]

But this was one Irish-Italian union not meant to be. Perhaps the auto dealer with the spotless police record reconsidered after reading the newspaper article. There was no marriage. Anna Lonergan wound up living alone in a neat one-family house in Brooklyn's Bushwick, far from the docks.[28]

Anna Lonergan had not started out as a fan of Italian men. Her only arrest was for assaulting an Italian shopkeeper who made eyes at her when she was fourteen and out with some older girlfriends from Irishtown, the crowded neighborhood beneath the Brooklyn Bridge. She had grabbed a piece of liver from a butcher across the street and smacked the man across the face with it, leaving him red with bovine blood. She spent a night in jail.[29]

But Anna Lonergan Lovett Martin did have Italian friends. She befriended the gangster Leonard Scarnici and visited him in Sing Sing until he went to the electric chair in 1935 for slaying a detective during a bank holdup. Irish or Italian, that was the kind of man Anna Lonergan was fated to love.

The story of the Irish-Italian transition in organized crime goes well beyond these events involving Anna Lonergan and the debased men who circumscribed her world. It involved alliances as well as warfare, and Jewish gangsters, among others, played a major role. The actions of a relatively small number of ruthless gunmen took on a greater significance at the time than they would otherwise deserve because of the way gangsters were celebrated in the movies and the newspapers. For Italians, this bolstered an injurious stereotyping that posed an obstacle to their advancement in American society.

*   *   *

We've seen that Irish-Italian conflict played out in many a workplace, whether that was a construction site, a wharf, a speakeasy, a police station, or a government or union office. In most cases, the Irish appear to have been the haves, and the Italians the have-nots. It is easy to forget that despite Irish success in New York, many of the Irish remained impoverished. Furthermore, the Famine experience cast a long shadow, honing fears of economic uncertainty. A have versus have-not lens is not wide enough to capture the whole story; the misery the Irish suffered was so deep that it was bound to create a sense of economic insecurity and a defensiveness that would persist even in better times in America.

Consider the story of one Irish immigrant, Maggie Gallagher. Life was desperate in the windswept, impoverished parish in County Donegal on the west coast of Ireland where she grew up. It was a place where, the New Yorker Asenath Nicholson wrote in 1850, "the wildest scenery stretches along the bold coast; and where it would seem that man, unless driven from the society of his fellow-being, would never think of making his abode."[30] The people of Gweedore had always been poor, but their plight grew more severe starting about six years before Maggie was born in November 1860. The landlord, Lord George Hill, took control of some five hundred acres of land where tenant farmers in Gweedore had long been permitted to graze their sheep and gather turf for the fireplaces in their chilly stone huts. Then he doubled the rent for the narrow strips of land from which they wrestled a living. This was one small step in a centuries-long process of confiscating the lands from which Irish peasants drew a livelihood, although Lord Hill insisted he was making improvements that would help lift his tenants out of their poverty.

Whatever his intent, the result was devastating. Maggie's parents, Manus Gallagher and the former Mary McFadden, lived in a hamlet in which fifty of the seventy families resorted to eating seaweed to maintain a diet of two scant meals a day. Without enough grazing land, the farmers had to give up their cattle. James McGinley went from fourteen cows to four in three years. Patrick McFadden went from six cows to none. Only fourteen of seventy families had beds. Edward McGarvey not only lacked a bed, but also had no blanket. About half the families had no shirts. The widow Margaret Mc-Bride sold her gown to pay the higher rent. Many of the women would not leave their huts because their torn clothing exposed them to shame. Testifying in 1858 before a House of Commons inquiry, the local priest, Father John Doherty, said he excused many families from attending Sunday Mass because, despite their deep devotion, "they had not sufficient clothing to come out."[31]

Maggie Gallagher migrated to Brooklyn at the age of twenty in 1880. On February 27, 1884, she wed Henry Collins, an Irish immigrant, at St. Patrick's Church at Kent and Willoughby Avenues in Brooklyn. The Reverend Thomas Taafe, a celebrated local priest from County Longford in Ireland's Midlands area, presided.[32]

Within five years, Maggie had birthed four sons. Henry Collins worked variously as a mason and bricklayer, according to the Brooklyn city directory. It is not known whether Maggie and Henry Collins feared the influx of Italian construction workers who were willing to work for low pay. But, given the poverty Maggie had known, they presumably were quite vigilant about protecting their income.

Henry Collins, who came to the United States in 1866 at the age of seventeen, died of pneumonia on May 5, 1891, in a first-floor apartment at 30 Floyd Street, Brooklyn.[33] He was forty-two. The youngest of his four sons, also named Henry, was less than two years old. He was to become the grandfather of my wife, Maureen.

Maggie married a second time eight months later, this time to another Irish immigrant, Owen Boyle. Family lore has it that they had been in love back in Gweedore, where Boyle is a very common name. (Passport records show that Owen Boyle grew up nearby.) On their wedding certificate, her surname was initially given as Gallagher, then crossed out to list it as Collins, her married name. She signed the document with her maiden name.

Owen Boyle had two sons. Maggie gave birth to two more children, a daughter, Mary, in October 1893 and a son, James, in December 1894. The 1900 census records them as living in an apartment at 525 Smith Street, Brooklyn. Owen Boyle listed his occupation as liquor dealer. He is evidently the same forty-two-year-old Owen Boyle who owned a saloon one block away, near a railroad depot at Smith and Ninth Streets.[34]

The year 1900 turned out to be a tough one for Owen Boyle. On the evening of December 5, he became embroiled in an angry argument with a policeman named Nils Jepson, a forty-year-old Swede and former seaman. Jepson wanted to enforce an after-hours law. Boyle said that the cop was harassing him. In the scuffle that followed, it was charged, Boyle grabbed Jepson's nightstick and hit him with it in the back of his head. "Officer Jepson May Die as Result of Assault," the *Eagle* headlined the story the next day. Boyle was held on $2,500 bail (equivalent to about $65,000 now) on a felony assault charge. As it turned out, the officer recovered and testified against him. But Boyle, who argued that he acted in self-defense, was freed after a jury acquitted him on April 18, 1901.[35]

After the trial, Owen Boyle brought his liquor business down to 85 Hudson Avenue next to the Brooklyn Navy Yard. The family settled in the slums of Vinegar Hill, moving to a nearby tenement at 132 Bridge Street. And that is where Maggie Gallagher Collins Boyle died, of cardiac stress, on May 3, 1904. She was forty-three years old.

These Irish immigrants in my wife's family had achieved some measure of middle-class status, at least temporarily, before the Italian peasants in my family had even arrived in the United States. But as Maggie Gallagher's story shows, it was a struggle—a struggle that data from the period multiply many times over. While the Irish had huge success in the civic arena, the church, and many other walks of life, the rates of poverty, disease, and imprisonment remained disproportionately high in the Irish population. For example, the Irish-born male residents of New York State had twice the death rate of the Italians in 1910.[36] To the arriving Italians, the Irish were authority figures who served as their teachers, priests, foremen, police officers, judges, and elected officials. But in fact the New York Irish continued to struggle well into the twentieth century, coloring working-class attitudes to competitors in the job market.

My Calabrian-born grandfather, Christopher Moscato, struggled as well to feed and care for his six children, especially after his wife died shortly after giving birth to their last child, my mother. He too had his brushes with law enforcement. After running a fruit stand for a number of years, he got work managing a pool hall on Mott Street. His daughter Marie Bradley recalled a visit there as a girl of eight or nine:

> We always had to bring his hot food to him. When I got to the poolroom and opened up the door, all the men had their backs to me. All their hands were up. So I ran outside the building and said "Ma, they're holding up Papa."

For a time, Christopher Moscato took to crime to make a living. He and another man were arrested on February 22, 1928, in upstate New York at an isolated farmhouse hiding a still that was capable of turning out more than three hundred gallons of alcohol a day. My grandfather, forty-six years old at the time, tried to escape by leaping from a second-floor window. He was caught.[37]

Court records show the charges against my grandfather were dismissed on January 30, 1929, while his codefendant, a Long Islander named John Cazzaro, paid a hundred-dollar fine. His daughter Marie explained it this way:

He had to appear in court. So what happens is he goes; all the kids go with him. The lawyer is making this impassioned plea to the judge: "This man has five children. Who's going to support their kids while he's away?" He got off. That's my father. This is the kind of jobs he had. It was hard for immigrants when they first came.[38]

The matter became more complicated when a corpse was discovered in the farmhouse, which was owned by the local gangster Albert Perry, in October 1929. The victim, never identified, was described as a well-dressed thirty-five-year-old man of Italian descent. He was believed to have been fatally shot on September 4, 1929. When other leads failed to pan out, the local sheriff decided a year later that it would be a good idea to question those two Italian men who were arrested a year and a half earlier. It's not clear how hard the sheriff's officers tried, but they never did find them, according to a local newspaper that was still recounting the unsolved case on its fortieth anniversary in 1969.[39]

Following the birth of another daughter in 1928 (my mother) and his wife Rachela's death in 1929, Christopher Moscato resisted suggestions that he break up the family and moved with his six children to the Bay Ridge section of southern Brooklyn, near Fort Hamilton. He had learned about this growing neighborhood along the Narrows from a relative who was working on construction of a new subway line there.

Leaving behind his bootlegging and pool-hall days on Mott Street, he dreamed of having a unionized job, but that was not to be. He paid the rent by working as a building superintendent. Borrowing a friend's plumbing license, he installed steam heat, first in the building where he lived to earn the rent, and later in the Bush Terminal waterfront industrial complex. The 1930 census lists him as a plumber employed in a box factory.

My mother, Anne Moses, recalled that when she was a girl, he was very courteous to a neighborhood man who had influence on the docks. But when the man left his presence, he sternly ordered my mother not to enter the man's house or play with his daughter.

He never did get a job on the docks. Nor did he manage to become a union member. He took a second job as a night watchman, and used the income to send my mother to ballet classes in Manhattan.

* * *

As we've seen in examining various workplaces, there were alliances between the Irish and the Italians as well as battles: Paul Vaccarelli and Big Tim Sullivan, Carlo Tresca and Elizabeth Gurley Flynn. Yes, the American Federation of Labor was often harsh toward immigrants, leaving a void that the radical Wobblies of the IWW tried to fill. But the AFL also provided a place where the new wave of immigrants from southern and eastern Europe could mingle with more-established, savvy Irish labor leaders.[40] And over time, attitudes began to change. As the historian James R. Barrett writes, such Irish-run institutions as the Knights of Columbus, Clan na Gael, and the Ancient Order of Hibernians were fighting in the 1920s against immigration restrictions aimed primarily at southern Italians and Jews from eastern Europe. Irish American politicians and the Catholic Church tried, unsuccessfully, to stop the 1924 legislation that cut off the flow of Italian immigrants.[41] These collaborations offer a glimpse of the shared Irish-Italian political interests that were to come.

PART III

Sharing the Stage

Politics and Entertainment

10

The Pols

Thirty-two-year-old Fiorello H. La Guardia had high hopes as he started his new job as a deputy New York state attorney general in January 1915. He jumped at the opportunity to prosecute the first criminal charges under the state's new weights and measures law, a bill the Housewives' League had campaigned for because consumers were so often shorted. To La Guardia, proving the offense seemed a simple matter of arithmetic: the state accused meatpacking houses of overstating the weight on packs of bacon by several ounces.

But the opposing lawyer, State Senator James J. Walker of Greenwich Village, had several advantages. One was his friendship with the judge, who, like Walker, was an affable Tammany stalwart. The other was that Walker had written the weights and measures law, which allowed him to do a steady business as a lawyer for meatpacking firms. And so, rather than contest the facts, Walker simply instructed the judge that the law did not apply to meat sold in wrappers but only to products in solid containers. The case was quickly dismissed.

Afterward, Walker invited the fuming La Guardia out for a drink with him and the judge. La Guardia continued to argue his case, and pointed out to Walker that he had just defeated his own law. Walker suavely stilled this breach of etiquette with a bit of friendly advice. "Fiorello, when are you going to get wise?" he responded. Then he explained the facts of life: if he made connections now while serving in the attorney general's office, he would later make plenty of money as a defense lawyer.

The judge agreed with this conventional wisdom, but the upstart La Guardia couldn't stomach it, pointing out that plenty of local shopkeepers had been fined for selling short-weighted bacon or ham in wrappers while the meatpacking companies got off scot-free. Walker, the voice of experience, told the young man to stop worrying about such matters. "What are you in politics for, for love?"[1]

This story, which La Guardia recounted in his autobiography, tells much about the two men who fought it out in New York's 1929 mayoral election and about the larger roles of the Irish and the Italians in New York politics and government. In his memoir, La Guardia cast Walker with the would-be gatekeepers, as indeed the politically savvy Irish were. And the gatekeeper had assured La Guardia that Irish-dominated Tammany Hall would treat him and his kind just fine if they went along with the system. That had been Tammany's message to Italian immigrants for decades. La Guardia would have none of it; Tammany's cynicism and dishonesty drove him to become a Republican, a party in which his populist, left-wing ideals scarcely fit.

La Guardia was yearning to crash the gate, and he turned out to be the leader the Italians needed to open the doors of City Hall beyond the measured gap Tammany had allowed. In La Guardia's account of the weights-and-measures case, Walker had posed as the sophisticate while casting him as the rube. But by the time he set this story down, La Guardia could tell it with the knowledge that many considered him to have been New York City's greatest mayor, while Jimmy Walker had been an embarrassing although colorful flop in the same role.

In many ways, the two mayors who led New York City for all but a few months from 1926 to the end of the Second World War personified the public images of their tribes. The anti-immigrant, anti-Catholic polemicists of the nineteenth century had characterized the Irish as brawling brutes from the bog who were fit only for backbreaking work as hod carriers (if they could stay sober long enough). By the 1920s, Irish Catholics were still battling nativist smears, this time fighting a resurgence of the Ku Klux Klan and anti-Catholic opposition to Al Smith's 1928 presidential campaign. But now the Irish were the toast of pop culture. When the theaters moved uptown to Broadway with the coming of the subway in 1904, it was an Irish American, George M. Cohan, who greeted the new locale and fondly remembered the old: "Give my regards to Broadway, remember me to Herald Square." Walker, who idolized Cohan, captured the new image of the Irish American as an urban sophisticate with street smarts. He was "the mayor of Broadway."

As the author Peter Quinn wrote in his searching essay "Looking for Jimmy," two Jimmies—Walker and Cagney—defined the urban Irish style. With their quick and ironic wit, their strutting lingo, and their smooth, loose-jointed dancing around the line that divides legal from illegal, the two Jimmies captured the transformation of the Irish and their image.[2] Of course, in Cagney's case, it was an act. Walker took his real-life act to the political stage, where for a long run he was a hit. Walker was not as menacing as Cagney's gangster characters, but his comment to La Guardia after defeating him in the courtroom reflected the same philosophy of life that Cagney would espouse in his role as the gangster Rocky Sullivan in the 1938 film *Angels with Dirty Faces*: Don't be a sucker.[3] The Irish may have arrived in New York as rural bumpkins, but that didn't last long.

Much as Walker was the edgy emblem of son-of-immigrants success, La Guardia represented a people who still had to prove themselves in America. While Walker was genially upbeat, La Guardia brimmed with righteous anger. He boiled in fury at how the system treated Italian immigrants and the poor in general. As a young man, he found work on Ellis Island as a translator, and brought Italian-speaking immigrants who wanted to marry to City Hall. He was outraged when he saw that the drunken aldermen who presided would insert lewd language into the ceremony so that they could amuse their friends at the expense of the unknowing Italian peasants.[4]

A stout five feet, two inches tall with an operatic style and a vowel-filled name, La Guardia was often cast as the city's Italian-in-chief, much as Walker had led the Celtic chorus. Although he was an Episcopalian with a Jewish mother, critics used negative stereotypes of Italian immigrants against him, implying that he was uncouth. Born on the Lower East Side, reared on military bases in Arizona, and acclaimed for his service as a major in aerial combat in World War I, he was sometimes portrayed as less than American. The *New Yorker* writer Henry F. Pringle wrote during the 1929 election campaign that many Republican officials viewed La Guardia as "a menace to Americanism, common, vulgar and undisciplined." Pringle's own view wasn't too far off. He referred to "La Guardia's complete lack of suavity, his all-too-evident crudities," adding that his frequent use of the word "lousy" made "the Best People cringe." Assailing what it said was a groundless charge La Guardia made against his main opponent in the 1933 election, the *New York Times* editorialized that La Guardia needed to control his "Latin temperament."[5]

There were no doubt Irish Americans with a temper problem and nattily dressed Italian Americans who were cool and casually corrupt. But at a time when even respected experts believed that "race" really defined the personal characteristics and abilities of entire peoples, La Guardia's clash with Jimmy Walker and Irish-dominated Tammany Hall reflected a broader ethnic struggle that played out in many northern and midwestern cities where the Irish dominated local politics. As they prepared to do battle in the 1929 mayoral election, it could be said that Fiorello H. La Guardia and James J. Walker mixed like olive oil and soda water.

*   *   *

Irish Americans were so dominant in the politics of New York and other big cities that it seemed only natural to them to be in charge, even after later immigrants from eastern and southern Europe began to cram into the tenements where they once lived.[6] George Washington Plunkitt, a Tammany state legislator who did business from a bootblack stand in the Manhattan courthouse instead of an office, held forth on this observation in a book published in 1905:

> The Irish was born to rule, and they're the honestest people in the world. Show me the Irishman who would steal a roof off of an almshouse! He don't exist. Of course, if an Irishman had the political pull and the roof was much worn, he might get the city authorities to put on a new one and get the contract for it himself, and buy the old roof at a bargain—but that's honest graft. It's goin' about the thing like a gentleman. . . .
>
> Yes, the Irishman is grateful. His one thought is to serve the city which gave him a home. He has this thought even before he lands in New York, for his friends here often have a good place in one of the city departments picked out for him while he is still in the old country. Is it any wonder that he has a tender spot in his heart for old New York when he is on its salary list the mornin' after he lands?[7]

For a while, it looked as if Plunkitt was right: Irish Americans continued to hold political power well after massive numbers of Jews and Italians arrived on the Lower East Side. Considering the number of newcomers, that was extraordinary. From 1881 to 1911, about one and a half million Jews arrived in New York, primarily from eastern Europe, and about 70 percent of them stayed in the city. Fleeing from violence and arriving with their families, few of them returned to the old country. Unlike both the Irish and Italian immigrants, many were skilled workers who came from cities and towns.[8] Their votes were soon to alter the course of New York politics.

That became clear in 1913, when the Republican-Fusion candidate John Purroy Mitchel thrashed Tammany Hall to win election as a reform mayor at the age of thirty-four, putting together a coalition that relied heavily on Jewish votes. (Mitchel, a Democrat of mainly Irish ancestry, pledged a nonpartisan administration.)

Premature obituaries were posted for Tammany power. Writing in 1914, the muckraking journalist Burton J. Hendrick observed that voters' shift away from Tammany had begun about a decade earlier, when the linchpin to Tammany success—the saloon—began to fade as a local political headquarters. The newcomers gravitated to the synagogue, not the saloon, he explained. "Skillful as he is, the Irish leader found himself at sea in attempting to organize this new element," he wrote, telling the story of a Tammany leader who, acting as if he was going to church, made the mistake of removing his hat in the synagogue as a sign of respect. "He didn't understand the Jews; they didn't understand him."[9]

When Big Tim Sullivan died in 1913, he was viewed as a throwback to an earlier era when the Irish were able to maintain control by providing goodies to the newer immigrants. "No one will ever do it again," one writer declared. "Sullivan succeeded because he was early in the field and had his confederacy well under way before the oncoming hordes."[10] Still, Irish dominance of city politics remained strong enough that in 1927, the Tammany boss George Washington Olvany spoke of it with pride. "The Irish are natural leaders. The 'strain of Limerick' keeps them at the top," he said. "They have the ability to handle men. Even the Jewish districts have Irish leaders. The Jews want to be ruled by them."[11]

Facing that attitude, many Italians joined the Republican Party. For example, by 1930, there were nearly as many Brooklyn Italians registered in the GOP as in the Democratic Party. Even Francis L. Corrao, who first organized Brooklyn's Italians for the Democrats, had endorsed some Republicans when he was blocked in his efforts to secure patronage appointments for himself and others.[12]

Still, adept Irish American politicians like Big Tim Sullivan knew how to hold on to Italian votes. But as ever more Italian immigrants arrived in Manhattan, that began to change after Sullivan died in 1913. We see that especially in a Lower East Side district where one of his closest allies, Big Tom Foley, was the local Tammany boss. Foley, a husky six-footer, was the son of Irish immigrants who settled in Williamsburg. Foley established himself by starting a series of saloons in lower Manhattan. The first was several blocks from his apartment, at Oliver and Water Streets.

The Democratic politico Tom Foley, right, with the Tammany boss Charles F. Murphy as pallbearers for the funeral of Big Tim Sullivan. Flickr Commons Project and New York Times, September 16, 1913. George Grantham Bain Collection, Library of Congress.

He eventually moved to a bigger and more popular joint at Centre and Franklin Streets, strategically located across from the Manhattan Criminal Court, and near what is now Foley Square, the civic center that would be named for him in 1926. Noted for its circular bar and strict men-only policy, the saloon became one of the city's major political gathering spots. In 1901 Foley pushed his way into becoming Democratic leader of the Second Assembly District on the Lower East Side, defeating the longtime incumbent, the saloonkeeper Paddy Divver.

Both Irishmen went all out for Italian votes in that campaign, racing each other to bring the first present to newlyweds and attending christenings and funerals. In one case, Foley paid a newly widowed Italian woman a month's rent and provided a half ton of coal and a barrel of flour. Foley also posted a man at the City Hall marriage bureau to call him when weddings were held. Then, he'd hurry over with a ring or piece of silver. Divver was always too late until he figured out Foley's method and installed a spy of his own. Then the two had to race to City Hall when the tips came in that Italians from the district had married.[13]

Big Tim Sullivan, who led the adjacent district, backed Foley in a campaign one observer called "famous as one of the most savage political fights in the barbaric political history of the Democratic Party of New York." Sullivan sent in the gangster Paul Kelly to provide muscle and repeat voters. Using similar tactics, Foley was elected sheriff in 1907.[14]

Tammany Hall has been compared to a feudal hierarchy, with the party boss as king. Each ward had a leader, a powerful vassal who, like his counterparts in days of yore, could sometimes be a challenge for the king. The leader's castle was usually his local saloon, where he ruled over subleaders and the captains of election precincts, who were considered successful to the extent they produced votes for Tammany. It was a system that put Tammany Hall into the midst of neighborhood life and the problems of everyday people, yet with centralized authority, reminiscent of the Catholic Church's structure of parishes within dioceses. Everyone—especially political appointees and the elected officials indebted to this system—was bound by a code of loyalty. Daniel Patrick Moynihan has likened the Tammany machine's structure to the oligarchy of a rural Irish village, in which each person had an assigned role.[15]

A sign of the system's effectiveness was that Tammany's Irish stalwarts continued to hold power long after the mathematics of immigration indicated that Jews and Italians should have taken over. One journalist predicted in 1900 that Italians would become involved in politics, adding that "more than one Murphy or Donnelly is really a Morfeo or Donati, who for the sake of greater authority and power has translated his name into good Celtic."[16]

Nowhere was the change in population more complete than on the Lower East Side. As the *New York Sun* reported in 1916,

The Second district stretches east and south of Chatham Square. It takes in a territory that for years has been in a state of racial transition. Originally it was an Irish stronghold, but an Italian invasion that started about five years ago has blotted out its first identity. Practically all that remains of the Celtic flavor is Tom Foley, the Tammany power, who is leader in the district.[17]

Faced with that trend, Foley promoted Michael Angelo Rofrano through the ranks of his Downtown Tammany Club; he couldn't retain power without Italian support. Rofrano, five feet, six and a half inches tall, stocky, with a handsome round face, dark hair, and a quick, upright gait, was born in Potenza in the Basilicata region of southern Italy in 1873. He migrated with his parents to New York, becoming an American citizen at the age of fourteen. A personable young man, he prospered as a plumbing contractor and grew popular through his involvement in various Italian organizations. On January 26, 1902, he married twenty-year-old Mary A. Corrigan at St. James Catholic Church. His wife was the daughter of two Irish immigrants.[18]

The upwardly mobile Rofranos lived at 11 Oliver Street in a four-story home built with cream-colored brick in the upper stories and brownstone on the first floor and steps. It was close to Chatham Square in what would later be considered Chinatown. By 1910, the couple had four daughters: Lillian, age six, four-year-old Grace, and two-year-old twins Mary and Eloira. In 1911 they would add a fifth daughter, Louise. Michael Rofrano became a lawyer that same year after studying at New York Law School. Eugene Driscoll, a contractor whose parents were Irish-born, lived next door with his wife; they had seven of their nine children by then. His politically connected brother, First Deputy Police Commissioner Clement Driscoll, also lived with the family. Tom Foley kept an address at 9 Oliver Street, although he had moved uptown to 122 East Thirty-Fourth Street. The Mulligans—John, a bricklayer, and his wife, Mary, both had Irish parents—lived next to the Rofranos on the other side, with five children aged seven and under. Dr. Joseph S. J. Manning, son of Irish parents, his wife, Margaret, and their five children lived at 19 Oliver Street. And Assemblyman

Alfred E. Smith resided in a three-story brick building at 25 Oliver Street, renting from St. James Parish, where Smith had been an altar boy. The pastor and other priests were all of Irish ancestry, as might be expected for a parish where the Ancient Order of Hibernians had founded its first U.S. chapter.

Smith and his wife, Katherine, had five children. Katherine's Irish-born mother, Emily J. Dunn, lived with them, as did Katherine's brother Lawrence. Throughout his storied political career, Al Smith would portray himself as Irish American, and his mother was indeed descended from immigrants from County Westmeath. But his father, Alfred E. Smith Sr., was the son of a Genoese immigrant named Emanuel and a German-born mother. Smith used his middle initial but even close associates—the campaign manager during his 1928 presidential bid, or Jimmy Walker—didn't know that it stood for Emanuel, the name of his Italian grandfather. Smith may not have realized his Italian roots, but his father was known to defend Italians when neighbors complained that they were ruining the neighborhood.

Smith's daughter Emily recalled Oliver Street fondly in her 1956 memoir about her famous father. Just five families living on one side of the street—the Rofranos, Driscolls, Mulligans, Mannings, and Smiths—had twenty-nine children among them. The Rofrano children's ages were close to those of the Smith family's, and so there were plenty of friends. Emily Smith Warner wrote that her closest friends included Marion Riordan, daughter of Congressman Daniel J. Riordan, an Irish American real estate man and Manhattan College graduate who lived at 29 Oliver Street with his wife, Edith.[19]

Emily Smith Warner's description of Oliver Street in those days practically resounds with strains of "The Sidewalks of New York," the theme song for her father's 1928 presidential campaign. The kids played in the streets and ran home for dinner. They went swimming in Far Rockaway in the summer, and took walks across the Brooklyn Bridge on Sundays after church. The songwriting state legislator Jimmy Walker stopped by the house to play the piano while his wife, a former showgirl, sang; young Emily was thrilled.

But beneath this nostalgic veneer, a deadly political feud was building on Oliver Street, one of the most bitter battles in New York's political history. The fight began in 1912, when Michael Rofrano, having served as Tom Foley's faithful lieutenant, decided it was his turn. He had organized Italian voters behind Foley, but even so, the Tammany leader continued to run only Irish Americans for office. Rofrano told Tom Foley that he wanted to run for Congress. Foley laughed at him—he was not about to pull his support from Congressman Riordan, who was a boyhood pal and next-door neighbor of the most talented politician in Foley's stable, Al Smith. The previous district leader, Paddy Divver, had made a fateful decision in 1900 not to renominate Riordan for Congress. Riordan, who had been president of Divver's political club, then joined forces with Tom Foley and Al Smith to oust Divver as district leader. Foley was not about to forget how he became a Tammany district leader.

A few days after their confrontation in 1912, Foley and Rofrano fought with their fists in front of Foley's political club on Madison Street on the Lower East Side, north of the Brooklyn Bridge. It is not known whether the older, bigger Irishman or the shorter, younger Italian got the better of that battle. Rofrano quickly set up the rival Home Rule Democratic Club at 48 Madison Street, around the corner from his home and a block away and on the opposite side of the street from Foley's Downtown Tammany Club. Rofrano supported the reformer John Purroy Mitchel in his winning mayoral campaign in 1913, and was rewarded with a job as deputy street-cleaning commissioner. In the meantime, his rivalry with Foley intensified.

Many Italians in the neighborhood supported Rofrano politically, as did his neighbor Eugene Driscoll and his brother, Clement, a police official. But Foley was able to hold the loyalty of quite a few Italians, thanks to the efforts of one of his chief political aides, Michael Giamari. Soon enough, the tensions between Rofrano and Giamari burst into violence.

A bloody battle began on December 17, 1913. Giamari was stabbed in the back, but survived. The same night, a Rofrano supporter named Vincenzo Cardella was fatally shot. There were other stabbings in 1914. Then, on New Year's Day in 1915, Rofrano's cousin James Minott, a thirty-four-year-old New York-born hotel waiter whose parents were Italian, was shot on Rofrano's corner, Madison and Oliver Streets. He died four days later, suffering from fifteen bullet wounds. Two of Giamari's brothers, Albert and John, were arrested but later acquitted in the slaying. The violence continued on March 8, 1915, when Michael Giamari was shot four times and killed.[20] Police caught the alleged triggerman, the Sicilian immigrant Gaetano Montimagno. The district attorney quickly put him on trial in May.

The city's most prominent Italian American lawyer, Caesar Barra, represented Montimagno. He declared that Rofrano was "the real defendant" in the case and charged that the prosecutor wanted to convict his client so that he would testify—falsely—that Rofrano had ordered the hit. "Michael Rofrano has been a thorn in the sides of the politicians of the Second Assembly District," he told a Manhattan jury.

> They want him out of the way and the only way they can get rid of Michael Rofrano is to send him to his death by having twelve men say that he is guilty of having counseled, planned, decreed the death of Michael Giamari. . . . Have you ever heard in the history of civilization, such a murderous, diabolical scheme and plan and conspiracy, to send a man to his death, as that as has been concocted by the politicians in this case?

A string of convicted criminals testified that Rofrano hired Montimagno to assassinate his political rival. Montimagno was found guilty and sentenced to die at Sing Sing the week of July 19,

1915. As his lawyer had predicted, he quickly turned state's evidence and implicated Rofrano to avoid being executed.[21]

Rofrano disappeared on September 14, 1915, the day he was indicted on charges of ordering the death of Michael Giamari. He was last seen in the ornate Municipal Building near the Brooklyn Bridge in lower Manhattan. Detectives entered Rofrano's home at 11 Oliver Street through the skylight; he was gone. Police circulated wanted posters for him. "Looks like an Italian" was part of the description given out. "The indictment of Rofrano is the political sensation of years," the *World* exclaimed, adding that the district attorney had found evidence that there was also a plot to murder Tom Foley and Congressman Riordan.

For eight months, police did not find him. Then Rofrano turned himself in at the southwest corner of Washington Square on May 15, 1916. He was taken to the Tombs Prison, where he recognized sections he had helped to build twenty years earlier.[22]

During the trial that followed in October, Montimagno testified that Rofrano, frustrated that the plot to slay his rival was delayed, met him personally. He said Rofrano poured out a glass of wine and told him, "Do this thing and all will go well. Do you know who I am in New York? They all have to do as I say. I shall make a slave of Tom Foley when you get rid of this man. I will see you have a good job and associate with good people. I will look out for you."

During the trial, Rofrano's Irish American wife, Mary, sat in the back of the courtroom with Rofrano's mother. A reporter noticed her as "an attractive woman with blue eyes and dark hair," adding that she "is apparently convinced that her husband had no connection with the plot to slay" Giamari. When the prosecutor questioned her husband about relations with other women, she showed no reaction. She testified the next day, supporting her husband's alibi. Shortly after that, the prosecution case started to unravel when one of the key conspirators, the thirty-nine-year-old saloonkeeper "Rox" Cornell, testified that Rofrano was not involved in Giamari's slaying, which he said resulted from a gambling feud.[23]

On November 12, 1916, Rofrano was acquitted. "Italian Colony Pleased," the *Times* headlined its story. About a thousand supporters gathered outside the courthouse on a Sunday afternoon burst into cheers, and tried to tag along as police hustled Rofrano away in a limousine as quickly as possible to avoid any attempts on his life. His wife, who had not been permitted to be in the courtroom for the verdict, had to travel in a second car. The best Mary Rofrano could do was to shout to her husband, "Oh, God is good, Mike!" As Rofrano was whisked through the streets of lower Manhattan, men and women waved from the windows. By the time police brought Rofrano the few blocks to his home, Oliver Street was packed with people. Across the street from Rofrano's residence, they filled the steps of the Mariners Temple, a Protestant church with big brown classical columns. American flags unfurled from the windows of Oliver Street as Rofrano entered his home to see his five daughters for the first time in months. Then a procession of well-wishers began, with box after box of flowers to follow. "Why, they tried to make it appear that I was mad to get public office," said Rofrano, a red rose in his buttonhole.[24]

*   *   *

At the same time Michael Rofrano feuded with Tom Foley, Fiorello H. La Guardia was finding his own political footing in this hazardous political world. As much as he despised Tammany, La Guardia also detested the local Republican leader, Italian-born James E. March, the padrone who became a political power broker. Even March and other Republican leaders curried favor with Tammany's corrupt Democrats, La Guardia believed. Told by fellow Republicans that he had no chance of winning, La Guardia ran for Congress in 1914 from a district that included the heavily Irish Chelsea section of Manhattan. He lost to Tammany's Michael Farley, president of the National Association of Liquor Dealers and the wealthy owner of a popular saloon at Twenty-Second Street and Eleventh Avenue. But, lifted by Italian votes, La Guardia had done better than expected, with 34 percent of the tally to Farley's 47 percent in a five-man race.²⁵ That led to his patronage appointment as a deputy state attorney general and set the stage for him to run against Farley two years later.

This time, he sought to out-Irish Congressman Farley, a native of Birr, County Offaly, who migrated to Brooklyn in 1881 at the age of eighteen. He noticed that Farley's ego had ballooned after a term in Congress to the point that he no longer bothered to show up in his saloon and buy a round. Tammany men usually didn't make mistakes like that; Farley had lost touch with his own tribe. La Guardia exploited that error. Campaigning months after James Connolly and other Irish patriots were executed for their roles in the 1916 Easter Rising, La Guardia gained Irish supporters by charging that Farley was not sufficiently anti-British.

During his years in public office, La Guardia displayed a respect for the Irish fight against British oppression that went beyond political expedience. He made speeches for the Irish cause, attended rallies, and sponsored a resolution in Congress protesting the imprisonment of Eamon de Valera, a leader of the Easter Rising whom the British did not execute because he was American-born.

The politically shrewd La Guardia also saw from the start of his career that it didn't hurt to have at least some of the Irish on his side. He described one particularly outspoken volunteer in the 1916 campaign as an Irish Joan of Arc, acknowledging that the activist was not really supporting him but opposing Farley. During that campaign, the congressman called La Guardia a wop and a dago— and La Guardia won by 357 votes.²⁶

Thus began a formidable political career. While still in Congress, La Guardia served with distinction in the U.S. Air Service on the Austrian-Italian front in World War I, promoted to major. In 1919 he was elected president of the city's Board of Aldermen, filling a prestigious citywide job Al Smith left to win the governor's seat a year earlier. La Guardia, adept at ethnic politics, appealed again to Irish voters, this time by joining them in their opposition to President Woodrow Wilson's peace treaty. But when La Guardia wanted to run for mayor in 1921, Republican leaders put the brakes on him. The party boss Sam Koenig told him that "the town isn't ready for an Italian mayor." He ran in the primary, losing badly to Manhattan Borough President Henry Curran, who lost the general election.

That same year, La Guardia, who had married in 1919, was devastated by the loss of his budding family. His infant daughter, Fioretta Thea, died in May of tuberculosis. Then his wife, the former Thea Almerigotti, succumbed to the same disease on November 29, 1921.

La Guardia was elected to Congress in 1922, and he went on to achieve national recognition as the most progressive member of the House of Representatives. Battling the conservative ethos of the prosperous 1920s, he championed a progressive agenda that anticipated the New Deal and fought the anti-immigration tide. By the time he ran for mayor against Walker in 1929, he had a national reputation.[27]

* * *

Jimmy Walker was at the peak of his game in 1929, riding on the instinctive charm he had shown ever since his first appearance on the political stage at the age of seventeen. Back then, he had stood in at a campaign appearance for his father, who was running for alderman. Billy Walker, a carpenter who emigrated from Castlecomer, a coal-mining town in County Kilkenny, was ill that day. Jimmy had always been much more interested in baseball and Tin Pan Alley than in politics, but he had learned enough to win over his audience by sweetly evoking Ireland. His father was elected, and later held posts in the State Assembly and as a city buildings commissioner.

Jimmy Walker grew up in Greenwich Village in the days when it was an Irish Catholic enclave. He was born on June 19, 1881, in a flat at 110 Leroy Street, between Hudson and Greenwich Streets, and christened at St. Joseph's Church, where the pastor would dub him "Jimmy Talker." Walker played football and baseball for Xavier Prep and a season of semipro baseball in Hoboken.

Resplendent in a double-breasted suit, Mayor Jimmy Walker stands with Major General Umberto Nobile, noted Italian explorer, in a 1926 City Hall ceremony. New York World-Telegram and Sun Newspaper Photograph Collection, Library of Congress.

He yearned to make it as a songwriter; his song "Will You Love Me in December as You Do in May?" was a hit in 1908. His greatest art form, though, was the political quip. His quick and quintessentially Irish wit worked well for him as he followed his father into politics and began serving in the state legislature, eventually rising to the powerful post of Democratic majority leader in the Senate. As a beginner, he often found himself following keynote speakers to the podium at political dinners. He made light of his low billing, saying, "We cannot always be first. For after all, even the immortal George Washington, who was first in war, first in peace and first in the hearts of his countrymen"—pause—"married a widow." He particularly liked to poke fun at reformers, the political enemy. "A reformer is a guy who rides through a sewer in a glass-bottomed boat," he once said. When he was mayor, a speaker from the Citizens Union, a good-government group, confronted him at a public hearing. When Walker referred to the group as "Citizen Union," the speaker corrected him, saying it was plural, Citizens Union. "Then there are two of you," Walker shot back.[28]

Walker's wit served him well in the state legislature's frat-house politics. He employed it in a 1923 debate to defeat the Clean Book Bill, which aimed to criminalize publication of supposedly salacious novels written by D. H. Lawrence and others. The bill had already passed the Republican-controlled Assembly by the time Walker rose to speak against it in the State Senate on May 2, 1923. Two weeks earlier, the *Times* had warned that the Senate Democrats were ready to push the bill to passage. It was a reasonable assumption; New York's Archbishop Patrick Hayes supported the measure and it had bipartisan backing, including a Tammany sponsor in Senator Salvatore Cotillo of East Harlem.

Publishers warned that the bill's restrictions were so severe that they wouldn't be able to distribute the Bible if the measure became law. Gertrude Atherton, president of the Authors League and a novelist who wrote dozens of books, argued at a hearing that young women could not be corrupted by reading literature too sophisticated for them to understand; she cited her own experience reading Boccaccio's *Decameron* at sixteen. "A sixteen-year-old girl has to be sophisticated before she can understand sex matter if it is written in a literary style," she said. John Sumner, secretary for the Society for the Suppression of Vice, later responded that he was "surprised to hear Mrs. Atherton say that no bad book could do any harm to a girl of sixteen."

Walker played on this theme when he addressed his fellow senators. Everyone, he said, had a "dear mother" who "grew into a life of saintliness and went down to her last resting place just as clean and pure in mind and heart as the day she was born"— despite the temptations posed by "many salacious books." It was a rhapsody straight out of his friend Ernest Ball's 1910 song "Mother Machree," an homage to Irish mothers. (Ball also wrote the music for Walker's one hit song and, in 1912, the enduring "When Irish Eyes Are Smiling.") "That is all there is to this talk about books of the kind against which this bill is directed ruining our young girls," Walker declared. "They haven't got time to read them and they won't read them if proper influences dominate their homes. *No woman was ever ruined by a book.*"

Walker continued, "It is one of these strong men who are worrying about salacious books in the hands of little girls who are ruining them." That remark brought the house down with laughter, for every man in the legislature knew what Walker was talking about: Morals had a way of loosening in the boys-away-from-home, men's club atmosphere in statehouse political circles. (And the showgirl-chasing Walker was no angel.) "This debate makes me think of the Volstead Act and in connection with this of how many vote one way and drink another," Walker continued, referring to the law that created Prohibition. By this point, Walker had managed to accuse his colleagues of hypocrisy while simultaneously making them laugh to the point of tears. "Some of the best tellers of shabby stories in this Senate have been worrying their hearts out during the debate today about somebody reading something which may not have been good for him or her."

Salvatore Cotillo, the bill's sponsor, was heckled when he rose to speak. Cotillo was not a man to be taken lightly. He had studied at Manhattan College and Fordham University before becoming a lawyer in 1912 and a State Assembly member the following year. He moved on to the State Senate in 1917, served as an emissary to Italy for President Woodrow Wilson during World War I, and in 1924 would become a justice on the New York State Supreme Court—a startling rise for a kid from Naples.

But Walker had clearly made sport of the senator from East Harlem. The bill was defeated easily, thirty-one to fifteen, in a vote that blurred party lines. When Cotillo moved to reconsider, he was laughed off. The scene is reminiscent of the Irish-Italian narrative in some movies of the period: the slick, urbane Irish American contrasted with an immigrant rube from Italy. For example, the hapless Italian storekeeper in the 1938 film *Angels with Dirty Faces* is the kind of "sucker" Jimmy Cagney's Rocky Sullivan treats as a joke, or, in the 1915 silent film *The Italian*, the bootblack "Beppo" Donnetti is thwarted by the ward boss Bill Corrigan.[29]

Jimmy Walker knew how to make people laugh at an opponent, and nothing is more devastating to a politician than to be laughed at. His combination of political and verbal agility was as Irish as Mother Machree. He brought that skill with him to the 1929 campaign against Congressman Fiorello H. La Guardia.

* * *

La Guardia had first met Jimmy Walker in his days as a prosecutor; he was ready to return to that role in the 1929 mayoral campaign, casting Walker as defendant. Walker, elected to his first term as mayor in 1925, had delighted the public but built a record that infuriated reformers. Delivering as many as fifteen speeches a day from mid-September through Election Day on November 5, La Guardia set out a case charging that Walker was lazy, pampered, corrupt, gang-connected—and that his wardrobe was in bad taste. He held Walker responsible for the graft he charged proliferated in many city agencies. La Guardia was especially passionate about linking Walker to corrupt Democratic politicians. He tried to turn the unsolved murder of the notorious gangster Arnold Rothstein into a major campaign issue, claiming that police and even Walker knew who shot the gambler in Manhattan on November 4, 1928, but were afraid of the scandal that would follow an arrest. (When Tammany-backed District Attorney Joab Banton said it was no more than the slaying "of a gambler who cheated," La Guardia said that was the point: "Whom did Rothstein cheat?")[30]

Since La Guardia's attacks were short on details, Walker sidestepped them easily. But on September 27, 1929, La Guardia landed a powerful blow with evidence linking an influential Italian American supporter of Walker, Magistrate Albert H. Vitale, to Rothstein. Vitale, a forty-two-year-old son of Italian immigrants, was a vice-chairman of Walker's campaign in the Bronx and a key figure in rounding up Italian support for the mayor's reelection. He had proven his mettle to the Walker campaign by making a fool of La Guardia when the upstart Republican spoke before eight hundred people at the Italian-American Plasterers' Social Club on a Saturday night in mid-September at the Winter Garden, a theater at Tremont and Washington Avenues in the Bronx. When La Guardia rose to speak at 11:30 p.m. to what he could reasonably have expected to be a friendly audience, he was booed and hissed. Cheers went up for Walker. La Guardia pressed on, devoting his speech to his charge that Walker ridiculed knowledgeable, respected citizens who testified before him at city budget hearings. But he was the butt of the joke that evening. It wasn't clear just how La Guardia had fallen into this trap, but Vitale was on hand as the evening's toastmaster and refused to introduce La Guardia when he arrived to speak. He said La Guardia was not invited, while La Guardia insisted he was.

Two weeks later, La Guardia announced that a secret document showed that Rothstein had loaned Vitale $19,940 (worth more than a quarter-million dollars today). Furthermore, he charged, the Manhattan district attorney had this document even though he had claimed publicly there was no evidence in Rothstein's records that compromised local public officials. He called on Walker to either "repudiate or support Judge Vitale."

Walker was left to equivocate. When reporters reached him at the Ritz-Carlton Hotel, he offered them a preachy lesson in the law, saying he had no power to remove Vitale from the bench. Vitale threatened to sue La Guardia for libel, but acknowledged getting the loan through a friend he said was dead. Nor would he name the "friend." Recalling how he had snubbed La Guardia at the campaign event, Vitale added, "Small as he is, I should hate to think that Mr. La Guardia is small enough to have tried to get back at me in resentment for that."

And small as he was, in terms of political clout, La Guardia had managed to make Tammany worry. Still, Tammany operatives thought that the charge could be turned against La Guardia, at least among Italian voters who might be offended at the attack on Vitale. The magistrate crowed over an editorial in a Bronx news-paper that called on La Guardia to supply proof that Vitale had committed a corrupt act.[31]

Walker, who tap-danced around the Vitale charge with less than his usual grace, wanted to make sure everyone knew that he wasn't breaking a sweat, even as he denounced "demagogues" and "slanderers." Smiling, he said that people should not take political campaigns too seriously. "I don't let them excite me," he told re-porters. "Please don't let this one get you excited or make you run a high temperature." When La Guardia assailed him for raising the mayor's salary to forty thousand dollars a year, Walker just quipped, "That's cheap! Think what it would cost if I worked full time." Walker also made sport of La Guardia by asking in his speeches, in a serious tone, why he'd been someplace—say, Providence, Rhode Island—on a certain date. He had no evidence La Guardia had been out of town; it was just a tactic to rile his opponent.

And La Guardia was indeed heating up. He charged Walker with "tax racketeering"—seventy-five million dollars in giveaways to powerful businessmen. Walker stayed cool, confident enough to declare publicly, "I am the candidate of Tammany Hall and if elected I will be a Tammany Hall mayor." He pledged to seek ad-vice from the Tammany boss John F. Curry, "one of the finest men I have ever known." His opponent, he said, was "groveling in the mud." Speaking to thousands of Democratic district captains in Tammany Hall, he added, "You are now the cultured and dignified people of this city. We would never stoop or degrade ourselves to the level of this slanderous type of Republican campaign."[32]

As Walker told it in a code his listeners would understand, the world had turned upside down: Tammany men had become the city's new patricians; the Republicans had thrown in their lot with a vulgar Italian.

The elegance of Walker's campaign was reflected in its use of a new medium, the talking picture. Thousands of people turned out to see *Building with Walker*, in which the debonair mayor hailed his own achievements from a set created at Broadway and Forty-Seventh Street in Times Square. Made with the help of Fox Studios, the movie featured one of the era's leading dance bands, the Paul Whiteman Orchestra, and the actor Eddie Cantor.

While La Guardia worked overtime to fire up indignation over Tammany-sponsored graft and favoritism, Walker tried to be boring. It was a difficult task for him, but he managed to cite statistics in a way that normally eluded him. He ridiculed La Guardia's charges of graft by saying that he had passed up the obvious "jackpot" when he opposed private companies' requests for a utility rate increase and a hike in the five-cent transit fare. "If we were interested in graft, I am satisfied that you would give us credit enough for having intelligence enough to go after graft that is worthwhile," he quipped.[33]

Teflon would not be invented for another nine years, but Walker seemed coated in it. La Guardia's charges just would not stick to the gloss of the mayor's Irish American charm. With his slick black hair and blue eyes, his trimly athletic five-foot-nine-inch frame, his spats, walking stick, double-breasted suits, silk handkerchiefs, silk top hats for evening wear, and panama hats for parades, he projected an image that many Jazz Age New Yorkers reveled in. In the midst of a busy social schedule, he could change into more outfits in a day than La Guardia—in his wrinkled size-42 stout suits, his gut sagging beneath baggy pants with a 27 ¾-inch inseam—wore in a week.[34]

Walker made light of La Guardia's charges that he was "Jimmy the Jester," "the Night Club Mayor," and the "Tango Mayor." Speaking to the Women's Democratic Club at the Commodore Hotel next to Grand Central Station, he jested, "I tried the tango once several years ago and sprained my ankle." And "Their complaint against the present mayor is that he wears clothes. I must admit that." In a more stinging speech to 2,500 people that night at Brooklyn's Prospect Hall, he complained,

> Can anyone expect me to keep my good-nature in this campaign ever again, to recognize a man even by proxy who apparently has not enough dignity, enough decency and enough self-respect to tell but one one-thousandth of the truth? I have run against many kinds of men, but this is the first time that I have ever had an opponent among my fellow-men who resorted to slander, vilification and vulgarity that are not fit to enter any decent home that I have ever been in.

Electing La Guardia would lead to "hoodlumism," he charged.

Privately, Walker respected La Guardia's political talent, especially his ability to employ German, Yiddish, Italian, and two kinds of English—the king's and New York's—depending on what the situation called for. "This Little Flower is no shrinking violent," he told the newspaperman Gene Fowler.

Each man accused the opponent of making blatant ethnic appeals to his own tribe. La Guardia did indeed insist that Italians should vote for him. Walker attacked him for this ethnic pitch by saying that as mayor, he never preferred any group and sought votes based on his accomplishments, not "racial sympathy." In a speech to Irish activists at Bryant Hall on Sixth Avenue, La Guardia denied seeking Italian votes based on a "racial appeal."

"If a large number of citizens of Italian ancestry or extraction are supporting me, it is not on racial grounds, but it is because their men have been working down in the ground on subway contracts and they have been robbed every week of part of the prevailing rate of wages to which they are entitled," he declared, a charge that echoed the earlier battle between Italian excavators and the Tammany-connected builder John B. McDonald. "It is because of the greed of Tammany and their connection with subway contractors, which has not been denied, that they are able to take every hour from the pay of the skilled and unskilled workers part of the pay which the city pays to these contractors to pay to the workers." In a cunning line of attack, La Guardia essentially told his audience of Irish nationalists that Walker and Tammany had lost touch with authentic Irish virtues. Walker, he asserted, looked down on working people and boasted about his wardrobe. "He is a loudly dressed man, displaying all the bad taste and vanity of the political parvenu who got rich quick," he remarked. "He is not a well-dressed man according to the standards of this country, but he is the loudly dressed man according to the styles of the English fop or the Paris gigolo. Why, Tammany Hall was created as a racial group, but they are ashamed of it now. I am proud of the race I come from." It was one way to seek Irish votes: to charge that Walker, the supposed emblem of Irish American success, was the antithesis to the disciplined Irish republicans: a frivolous English dandy. And in his "gigolo" charge, La Guardia seemed to suggest a betrayal of Irish Catholic morality in Walker's dalliance with the English-born actress Betty Compton, a relationship that scandalized Walker's good friend Al Smith.[35]

But it was Walker's election to lose. As Al Smith's failed 1928 campaign for president showed, Democrats had built a coalition that united an earlier generation of immigrants, the Irish, with new immigrant groups such as the Jews and Italians. It wasn't enough for Smith to overcome the anti-Catholic, anti-immigrant attitudes rampant in 1920s America, but it was quite successful in big cities. And this coalition remained a powerful force in New York.

Even the Italians did not vote for Fiorello H. La Guardia in 1929, as it turned out. The gloom quickly settled over La Guardia's campaign headquarters at the Hotel Cadillac at Forty-Third Street and Broadway when early returns showed that Walker had trounced him in a heavily Italian district that ran along Fourth

Avenue on the Brooklyn waterfront. La Guardia mustered just
26 percent of the citywide vote—ahead of the Socialist candidate
Norman Thomas, but far behind Walker. Tammany operatives
acknowledged to reporters privately that they thought anti-Italian
prejudice also played a role in La Guardia's poor showing, much as
anti-Catholic bias had hurt Al Smith's 1928 presidential campaign.
On election night, the electric lights of Broadway flashed out a
message most agreed with: "Vote for Walker, a real New Yorker."

Walker, who took every Assembly district and won a plurality
of nearly a half-million votes, received 62 percent of the tally. He
issued a statement saying that the public had rejected the "slanderous" charges made in the race, and joked privately with his police
commissioner that the vote vindicated a man's right to wear the
clothes he wanted.[36]

*　　*　　*

As decisive as Walker's victory was, he did not leave the 1929 campaign unscathed by La Guardia's attacks. Richard F. Warner, a
New York Evening Post political reporter, noticed that even before
the campaign ended, La Guardia's constant pounding against corruption had punctured the myth surrounding the genial Walker,
leading Warner to observe, "One doubts if Mayor Walker will ever
again be quite so popular."[37]

La Guardia was quickly vindicated in his charge against Vitale when a curious incident occurred at a banquet to honor the
magistrate early on December 8, 1929, at the Roman Gardens
restaurant at 187th Street and Southern Boulevard in the Bronx.
The Tepecano Democratic Club was feting Vitale, its "honorary
chairman for life." As he spoke to some fifty guests seated around
a horseshoe-shaped table, seven gunmen burst in and robbed the
assemblage of thousands of dollars in cash and jewelry. A detective at the dinner surrendered his gun, while other guests tried to
hide rings and wads of cash. Initial reports described the guests as
businessmen, but as the story unraveled, it turned out that Vitale's
admirers that night included many lawyers and bail bondsmen who

relied on his decisions as magistrate—rulings he sometimes rendered right from his political clubhouse rather than the courthouse. Some of the "businessmen" were also criminals. Most notable was the presence of Ciro Terranova, a gangster dubbed the "artichoke king" for his influence in the produce trade. After the robbery, Vitale returned to his clubhouse and, with a few phone calls, was able to arrange the return of the stolen goods, including Detective Arthur Johnson's gun.[38]

This suspicious train of events triggered an investigation by the state court system, which had power to dismiss city magistrates. Vitale was removed from the bench on March 14, 1930, for his no-collateral loan from Arnold Rothstein. From there, the scandal snowballed. As the Great Depression descended on New York and the nation, the spectacle of having so many politicians living high on graft appalled the public. At the request of Governor Franklin D. Roosevelt, the court launched a broader investigation of corruption in the New York City courts in August, appointing a Tammany foe, the former judge Samuel Seabury, to lead the probe. Seabury's investigation showed that magistrates were in cahoots with vice cops, who raked in payoffs by threatening prostitutes with jail. Among the disclosures was a plot to arrest dozens of innocent women on prostitution charges to keep up arrest numbers; a female magistrate doctored court records to cover up her own role.[39] Then Seabury became counsel to a state legislative committee that conducted an even broader investigation.

One of the highlights in an ongoing tale of plunder came on October 6, 1931, when the Tammany district leader and sheriff Tom Farley explained how he had been able to amass $360,660 in less than seven years when his salary averaged $8,500 a year. Farley famously said that the money came from a "wonderful" tin box he kept in his safe at home. Roosevelt later removed Farley from office.

By the spring of 1932, Seabury implicated Walker personally, producing testimony from a businessman who said he gave the mayor $26,535 in bonds out of admiration for his charm (rather than to secure regulatory protections for taxi fleet owners). Then there was $10,000 from a businessman seeking a bus franchise without owning a bus—another "gift" from a friend. And Walker reaped $246,692 in profit over two years from a brokerage account he had not invested in—a "beneficence" from a friendly newspaper publisher.[40]

As the charges mounted, Walker impressed his buddies in the City Hall press corps with his cool confidence. Though under immense pressure from Seabury, the mayor still led a massive "beer parade" down Fifth Avenue on May 14, 1932. The stated reason was to boost his plan for the Depression-deprived federal government to raise revenue by taxing beer. But for most, it was simply a full-throated cheer for beer from Prohibition-parched New York.

After Walker arrived at his parade "only 15 minutes late," as the *Brooklyn Eagle* said, he stepped off to start the extravaganza. There were forty "We Want Beer" floats. Some sixty bands played drinking songs such as "How Dry I Am," plus the mayor's own early hit song and the Tammany fight song, over and over. The carmaker Walter Chrysler, the stockbroker E. F. Hutton, the fighter Gene Tunney, the waterfront labor leader Joseph P. Ryan, the Italian newspaper publisher Generoso Pope, and casts of Broadway shows all marched. Six hundred organizations took part in a parade that ran all day and into the night.

At one point, an aged Italian man worked his way through the police line to shake hands with Walker. "Where can I get a beer, Mr. Mayor?" he asked.

"Just go two blocks west and, when you find it, I'll be there with you," Walker responded, shaking the man's hand vigorously.

"Three cheers for the mayor," the man shouted.

It was that kind of day for Walker. "The hero of the day, of course, was Mayor Walker," the *Times* said. "It was both his idea and his march."[41]

The beer parade was also his last hurrah. Eleven days later, Walker arrived at the Manhattan courthouse in a double-breasted blue suit to do battle from the witness stand with Samuel Seabury and the legislative committee investigating him. A youthful-

looking fifty-one, he claimed to take it all in stride, for, as he liked
to tell reporters whenever he was subpoenaed, there are three things
in life one must do alone: "Be born, testify and die."[42] Thousands
of Walker's supporters thronged outside the courthouse. Inside, the
atmosphere was more prizefight than legislative hearing. Hundreds
of people filled the courtroom as Walker made a star's entrance,
thirteen minutes late.

However nimble Walker was in his battle of wits with the sober-
minded, silver-haired Seabury, it was the day his political music
died. He offered a fog of witticisms and indignation, but no real
explanation for the wealth that flowed to his pockets. Governor
Roosevelt, eager to separate himself from Tammany as he raced toward the White House, was poised to use his power to remove the
mayor from office. The party was over. James J. Walker resigned as
mayor of New York on September 1, 1932.

* * *

Joseph V. McKee, a Bronx Democrat (and thus not from
Manhattan-based Tammany), served until the end of 1932 as acting
mayor after automatically moving up from his post as president of
the Board of Aldermen. Meanwhile, an election was held to fill
the remaining year of Walker's term. Tammany ignored the com-
petent McKee and picked John P. O'Brien, judge in charge of the
patronage-rich probate court, to run for the seat. O'Brien, a Massachusetts native fond of saying that his father was from County
Tipperary and his mother from Limerick, was described in news
accounts as having a "'fighting Irish' temperament" that made him
one of Tammany Hall's staunchest supporters. A father of five,
he was known as a prominent Catholic layman deeply involved
in church and Irish activities. He was president of the Guild of
Catholic Lawyers, on the executive committee of the Holy Name
Society, president of the Friendly Sons of St. Patrick, and a member of the American Irish Historical Society.

O'Brien made a point of campaigning in the Italian community
and tried to show the parallels between the Irish and Italian im-

migrant experiences. In both cases, he declared, Democrats had welcomed newcomers. "I never saw the time when the Republican Party ever opened its doors or had a welcome on the mat for people from Ireland or people of the Italian race," he told Brooklyn's Italian-American Tammany Club. "It has been the strength of Tammany that it has welcomed persons of every race and if you have merit you are sure to advance."[43]

O'Brien beat his Republican opponent, the businessman Lewis H. Pounds, by more than six hundred thousand votes. But nearly a quarter-million voters wrote in the name of Acting Mayor Joseph V. McKee, who was not on the ballot. O'Brien, facing the Depression, was unable to accomplish much in the one year remaining in Walker's term. He did hold Tammany's loyalty, since party bosses directed him. He is best remembered for what he said when asked who his police commissioner would be: "I have had no word on that yet."[44] With Tammany running O'Brien again in 1933 for a full four-year term, newly elected President Roosevelt pulled strings to get McKee to run on a separate line, the Recovery Party.

La Guardia secured the Republican and Fusion Party lines, and an interesting three-way race developed. O'Brien was a dull campaigner who struggled awkwardly with Tammany's heavy baggage, but McKee, loyal to the Bronx Democratic machine led by the wealthy lawyer Edward J. Flynn, was an attractive candidate. The *Times* praised his character and competence, a view widely held.[45]

A handsome forty-three-year-old attorney, McKee had served as a classical languages instructor at Fordham University en route to master's and law degrees, and as a newspaper reporter, judge, assemblyman, and president of the city's aldermen. Along the way, he authored a history textbook used in the city's schools. In City Hall, he challenged the collusive dealings that surrounded him. As acting mayor, he cut his salary from the forty thousand dollars a year Walker took to twenty-five thousand dollars. One Sunday-supplement story described him as a mix of Calvin Coolidge—for his thrift, especially—and Jimmy Walker, for his winning smile and athletic gait. (McKee golfed in the 70s.) His interest in good government and careful budgeting, and perhaps his close ties to the Catholic Church, led Tammany operatives to call him "Holy Joe" behind his back.

News accounts said his ancestry was Scottish—they praised him for Scottish thrift—but there was some confusion over whether McKee was Irish or Scottish. McKee's parents, Catholics born in Scotland, migrated from Glasgow in 1887; McKee's father worked as an engraver. Records from the 1910 census show, however, that three of McKee's four grandparents were born in Ireland; one, his paternal grandfather, was listed as Scottish.[46]

In any case, McKee maintained close political ties with the Irish, partly through his connections to the Archdiocese of New York. Since Walker was so often away on vacation, he had frequently served as acting mayor during Walker's administration, at one point, for eighty-eight days in a row. Trying to please Irish groups, he sought to pass legislation banning films with negative ethnic stereotypes. He wanted to censor the 1927 silent movie *The Callahans and the Murphys*, about two feuding tenement housewives who drank bottle after bottle of beer and poured some of it down each other's blouses, while saying things like, "This stuff makes me see double and feel single!"[47] McKee was also grand marshal of the Saint Patrick's Day Parade in 1928. In the same year, the king of Italy decorated him for his interest in helping Italian immigrants.

From the outset of the 1933 campaign, it was clear that the "three I's" of New York's tribal politics—Ireland, Italy, and Israel—would be key to determining the winner, given the size of the Irish, Italian, and Jewish votes. McKee fought it out with O'Brien for the Irish vote. His supporters argued to Irish voters that Tammany Hall had shortchanged them. Flynn, the Bronx Democratic boss, told an Irish organization at the Hotel Commodore near Grand Central Station on October 6 that McKee would bring the Irish "an equal place in the sun and an equal opportunity for the advantages which other races in this city enjoy."[48]

This time, La Guardia had the Italian vote locked in from the start, aided in part by the activism of a young, American-born generation. Young men signed up for ballot security—that is, to butt heads with Tammany toughs—and local clubs sprang up for La Guardia in the city's Italian neighborhoods. If the Italian boxer Primo Carnera could knock out Jack Sharkey to become heavyweight champion, as he had in June in Madison Square Garden, so too could the Little Flower defeat the Irish.

According to the 1930 census, 440,250 Italians lived in the city. That was more than twice the number of Irish-born New Yorkers, but the Irish remained a potent force with the inclusion of the American-born of Irish descent. Jews outnumbered the Italians, and were more likely to vote. From the turn of the century, Tammany had shown a knack for winning over Jewish voters, in part because its candidates, such as Governor Al Smith, supported social reform legislation. La Guardia, whose mother was Jewish, had to woo this vote away from the Democrats. For starters, each ticket ran a Jewish candidate in the number two spot for president of the Board of Aldermen.[49]

The 1933 election was held at a sensitive time for New York's Jewish community; the Nazis had come to power in Germany. Jews were a political power in the city, having been able to organize politically in ways that a history of discrimination had prevented in Europe. In that sense, they were like the Irish, who had aroused Anglo-Saxon fear because of their voting power. Southern Italian immigrants, forced to leave their homeland in part because their own government's tax policies had deepened their poverty, were much slower to do the same.[50]

With jobs scarce during the Depression, economic rivalry stoked ethnic resentments. This was especially so for the Irish and the Jews, who competed for middle-class jobs as teachers, health care workers, and government employees and in the lower rungs of finance. It was less so for the Italians, who were slower to enter these fields. In the 1930s the Italians and Jews did not compete for jobs to the degree the Irish and Jews did. The Irish-Jewish economic rivalry spilled into religion, especially through the radio preacher Father Charles Coughlin's anti-Semitism. Later in the 1930s, this attitude found expression in a largely Irish movement, the Christian Front, with its "Buy Christian" campaign for boycotting Jewish merchants. The group was especially strong in Brooklyn's Flatbush section, encouraged by the *Tablet*, the newspaper of the Catholic Diocese of Brooklyn.[51]

La Guardia, expert at the politics of ethnicity, found a way to exploit the Irish-Jewish divide. He picked up on an article McKee had written as a young man, eighteen years earlier, in the journal *Catholic World*. It contended with alarm that most students in public high schools were Jewish, adding, "and it is a rare thing even to hear an Irish Catholic name!" The article portrayed the Jewish high school students as morally adrift and without religion. "In overwhelming numbers these students are Socialists, or Socialists in the making, whose gospel is contained in *The New York Call*," the Socialist newspaper, "and whose ambition is the furtherance of Socialist doctrine," McKee wrote in 1915, when he was a history teacher at DeWitt Clinton High School in Manhattan.

La Guardia waited for the right moment to spring his charge that the article was anti-Semitic. It came when McKee sent him a telegram urging that he disavow his political sponsor, Judge Seabury, for criticism he had leveled against Governor Herbert Lehman, a revered figure in the Jewish community. La Guardia retorted that McKee was trying to draw attention away from "the cowardly, contemptible and unjust attack" he'd made in the *Catholic World* article against the Jews, a people "so gloriously represented by our Governor."

McKee assailed La Guardia for trying to "inject racial bigotry" into the campaign. He insisted that his article did not disparage Judaism, but in fact praised it. And that was true; McKee wrote that the Socialist Jews had lost their moral compass by abandoning Judaism, and also complimented the Jewish students on their industriousness. But the article's inference was obvious: that godless Jews were going to take over society unless Catholics sent their sons to high school in greater numbers. McKee's article had tapped directly into the Irish-Jewish economic rivalry: "It must follow that in the years to come our handicapped boys will be forced to give way in competition for better positions and higher advancement in law, medicine, education and business." He concluded the article darkly: "The presence alone of Catholic boys would be a deterrent to many dangerous forces now at work."

La Guardia's charge was boosted the next day when the attorney Samuel Untermeyer, an important figure in the Jewish community, denounced McKee as a bigot and raised the specter of "Hitlerism." McKee supporters pointed out that he had aided Jewish charities. Governor Lehman's brother Irving, a judge, publicly defended McKee. And Jewish men who had studied under McKee in high school praised him. None of that helped.[52]

Although he spoke Yiddish and was the son of a Jewish mother, La Guardia, an Episcopalian, did not emphasize his Jewish side. It was not a secret, as Al Smith's partial Italian ancestry was. But it was not well known, either. As the historian Arthur Mann has written, it was difficult enough for La Guardia to be Italian American without adding a second minority identity. He was taunted in the 1930s as "the half-Jewish wop."[53] Multiple ethnic identity did not yet offer the political advantage seen in later decades.

But La Guardia moved much more easily in Jewish circles than did his Irish American opponents. In his work as a labor lawyer and an interpreter on Ellis Island, he came to know eastern European Jewish immigrants well. Speaking to an audience of five hundred Orthodox Jewish leaders, he poked fun at politicians who went around announcing what great friends they were of other ethnic groups. "Everybody is friendly to everybody—in October," he said. "But when a person tells me he has friends among the Italians, he shows me that he considers himself superior."[54]

Such remarks show how the politically astute La Guardia built a base not just among Italians, but among all the groups making up the "new" wave of immigrants from eastern and southern Europe— those who followed the Irish.

Election Day was brutal as toughs loyal to the various factions battled it out in many polling places, leading to eighty-five arrests.

With a crowd of reporters and his wife watching, La Guardia faced off against "Harlem hoodlums" in one polling place, shouting, "I know you. You're thugs. You get out of here and keep moving."

La Guardia had carefully organized his supporters to take on ballot-fixing chicanery that was a throwback to the days when Big Tim Sullivan won elections with help from the gangster Paul Kelly. Albert Marinelli, the first Italian American among Tammany's thirty-five district leaders, had organized his strong-arm men to the point that they all wore gray fedoras to identify each other. Marinelli was the political heir to Big Tim, having come up through his organization and then defeated the remnants of the Sullivan clan to take over Tammany leadership on the Lower East Side. The gangster Lucky Luciano was said to have induced Harry Perry, who married into the Sullivan family, to relinquish the seat to Marinelli in 1932. Fifty years old, Marinelli was one of ten children of an Italian-born father. A muscular man who boxed as a hobby, he was running for Manhattan county clerk in 1933. Prosecutor Thomas E. Dewey would later charge that a federal probe found that Marinelli had managed to steal thousands of votes from other slates in the 1933 campaign. It was, the Associated Press reported, "the most violent election period in a generation." But even so, it noted, "liberal use of blackjacks, brass knuckles, lead pipe, bricks, knives and hob-nailed boots" failed to intimidate voters from turning out.

With the new "Who's Afraid of the Big Bad Wolf?" as his campaign's theme song, La Guardia seemed to have little trouble with the Tammany tiger. Mayor O'Brien was a clumsy public speaker, and the poised McKee was on the defensive. But La Guardia was still vulnerable to anti-Italian prejudice, as Paul Blanshard wrote in the *Nation*. On the last day of the campaign, O'Brien played on that weakness by trying to link La Guardia to the anarchist Carlo Tresca, charging that an Italian newspaper connected to Tresca was supporting La Guardia for mayor.[55]

That might have played well in the Irish-dominated neighborhoods on Manhattan's West Side waterfront, where O'Brien and

Tammany Hall triumphed. But this time Italians, who normally voted for Tammany Hall, closed ranks behind La Guardia. The Little Flower inspired a strong turnout among Italians and wound up with close to nine out of every ten Italian votes, a margin similar to what the city's first African American mayor, David Dinkins, would achieve in the city's black community fifty-six years later. With a boost from Jewish voters and a strong showing in Brooklyn, La Guardia beat McKee by nearly 260,000 votes, with O'Brien trailing in third place. It was a historic defeat that broke the fabled power of Tammany Hall, which lost all major races and failed to carry any borough, even Manhattan, for O'Brien.[56]

Italians across the city—and even around the world—erupted in joyous celebration. There were torchlight parades, bonfires, and dances in the streets, much as occurred when Primo Carnera had beaten Jack Sharkey for the heavyweight championship earlier in the year. (The Italian boxer wrote to La Guardia to congratulate him.) In Brooklyn's Brownsville section, some three thousand Italians marched with a hearse and a coffin, carrying the sign, "Here lies Tammany—The Big Stiff." At the same moment, political obituaries were written for the home base of Irish political power in America's largest city. "The Tammany dynasty in New York city has fallen," the AP declared. The force of Tammany was such that the story played on front pages across the country.

Pundits of all sorts piled on. "Tammanee! Tammanee!" Will Rogers wrote in a song he sent to the *Times*. "Big chief got to get out of his tepee to make room for the Italian LaGuardee." Salvatore A. Cotillo, the East Harlem politician and judge, remained loyal to Tammany by voting for O'Brien. But, he wrote to La Guardia, "none of the fifty-seven varieties of slang for 'Italian' could influence the voters against you." Generoso Pope, supporter of Fascists in Italy and of Tammany in New York, headlined his front-page article in *Il Progresso*, "Italian Victory." But the *Gaelic American* newspaper bemoaned the victory of an Italian American in "this most Irish of cities."[57]

Even before he formally took office on the first day of 1934, La Guardia began referring publicly to "we Irish, Italians and Jews."

Declaring that many city residents live in dangerous "firetraps," Mayor Fiorello H. La Guardia urges Congress to act on a housing bill in 1937. Harris and Ewing Collection, Library of Congress.

But the election had bared an Irish-Italian fissure in the city's politics. On Mayor O'Brien's last day in office, some fifty friends of Assistant District Attorney Robert V. Santangelo showed up at City Hall expecting, as a Tammany-connected alderman had told them, that O'Brien would name him a magistrate. The morning papers had said so, too, but someone else got the judgeship. Santangelo, who lived at 66 Oliver Street and was active in the Downtown Tammany Club, may simply have been the victim of maneuvering among Tammany insiders. But his humiliation was quickly viewed as a slight against Italians in general because of their support for La Guardia.[58]

La Guardia, expert at understanding and exploiting the city's ethnic tensions, was aware that Irish voters would resent it if livelihoods were lost with Tammany's fading patronage. The Depression made city jobs all the more valuable. But fear of offending

the Irish didn't stop La Guardia from reforming the civil service
so that many more city employees advanced through competitive
exams instead of political appointments. As a result, the historian
Thomas Kessner wrote, "the civil service lost its brogue." There
was a sharp drop in the number of Irish Americans heading city
departments. It may be an exaggeration to say that La Guardia
destroyed the Irish patronage system, but he dealt it a heavy blow.
As the plum ten-year mayoral appointment of city magistrate went
increasingly to Italians, the number of judges with Irish ancestry
plummeted.[59]

During his years in office, La Guardia close to doubled the representation of both Jewish and Italian New Yorkers in high-level
city patronage jobs.[60] That meant there were fewer of the Irish in
a position to dispense lower-level jobs. The City Hall press corps
captured Irish frustration with La Guardia in the Inner Circle
show, an annual roast of the mayor in which the reporters' humor
can sometimes reveal more about city politics than their news coverage does. Since one of La Guardia's pet causes at the time was
to find a city anthem, the political writers happily suggested one
to the tune of "The Harp That Once through Tara's Halls." Much
of the audience—Al Smith and Jimmy Walker, among others—
would have recognized that as a song based on a poem about the
traditional seat of the ancient high king of Celtic Ireland:

> The harps that once in City Hall
> Sat in the Mayor's chair,
> You never see them round at all
> Nor find them anywhere.
> But some day we'll come back once more
> Or know the reason why;
> But now the sign upon the door—
> No Irish Need Apply.[61]

La Guardia also threw himself into battling systemic corruption in the Police Department, which meant trying to disentangle

the largely Irish American force from Italian and Jewish gangsters, some of whom were becoming increasingly influential in Irish-run Tammany Hall. Addressing two hundred grim-faced police officials at police headquarters, he launched this effort on his first day in office, declaring that protection of gangsters had to end. Cops must either drive racketeers from the city or leave their jobs, the mayor declared, telling his mostly Irish American audience that New York's police should be the equal of Britain's Scotland Yard. He quickly appointed Michael Fiaschetti, who had followed in Lieutenant Joseph Petrosino's footsteps on the police Italian squad, to help break up corruption in city markets.

La Guardia named the incorruptible Lewis J. Valentine, son of an Irish immigrant mother and a father of German ancestry, as police commissioner.[62] Valentine's detectives helped the special prosecutor Thomas E. Dewey convict Charlie Lucania, or Lucky Luciano, in 1936 of running a prostitution racket.

As the city's first Italian American mayor, La Guardia quickly created public bocce courts. More controversially, he banned organ grinders, long the degrading emblem of Italian immigration. He offered the weak justification that he did so because they interfered with traffic. More to the point, he remembered his humiliation at being taunted as a dago at the age of ten when an organ grinder and his monkey arrived in the Arizona town where he grew up. Even worse, as La Guardia wrote in his autobiography: his father had invited the man to dinner.

Elevating personal preference to policy, La Guardia refused to grant permits to organ grinders after December 31, 1935, saying he didn't want the city to license begging. Organ grinders were still numerous enough before then for the *Times* writer Meyer Berger to note that until they were banned, they were an "integral part" of Saint Patrick's Day festivities. They played "Wearin' o' the Green" throughout the year, but especially wherever people gathered on March 17, much to their profit. Some five thousand people signed a petition urging that the organ grinders be licensed again, but La Guardia, who had a tyrannical streak, refused.[63]

La Guardia could afford to anger people occasionally because of the results he produced. His combination of honesty, competence, and progressivism led the Roosevelt administration to send an outsized portion of New Deal dollars for low-cost housing, parks, and jobs to New York. The unfashionable crusade for the oppressed he had pursued in Congress in the 1920s was now what the public wanted, and La Guardia provided that, with moxie. During his first term, the Triborough Bridge was completed, subways were extended, 235 playgrounds were built, corrupt city employees were arrested, and the city budget steadied despite the Depression.[64]

In 1937 Democrats united against La Guardia, who had beaten a divided field four years earlier. Democrats backed another Irish American from Tammany, the former judge Jeremiah T. Mahoney. No reform mayor of New York had ever been reelected, and Tammany was determined for that pattern to continue. Democrats had taken back control of the Board of Aldermen in 1935; the Fusion Party that helped elect La Guardia withered, and the Republicans, as always, thought he was too far to the left.

Jerry Mahoney, an athletic, six-foot-three-inch lawyer whose father was a Famine Irish immigrant, had gained attention as head of the Amateur Athletic Union by opposing U.S. participation in the 1936 Olympics in Berlin to protest against Nazism. He didn't get his way, but was able to use that stance to seek Jewish votes. He accused La Guardia of being soft on the Nazis, but that was far from true; La Guardia was one of the most outspoken officials in America against Hitler. The State Department formally apologized to Germany in 1937 for La Guardia's comment that the New York World's Fair should have a "chamber of horrors" exhibit for "that brown-shirted fanatic."

Mahoney also charged that La Guardia was "coddling" communists, essentially a message to Irish Catholic voters that it was their religious duty to defeat him. He brought this point home by arguing that La Guardia had "handcuffed" the police force to prevent it from cracking down on labor unrest. The Communist Party had indeed endorsed La Guardia; he didn't outright reject

the endorsement but was cool to it. But Mahoney's charges veered
into red-baiting. He accused La Guardia of using the public school
system to spread communist ideas and described the home relief
bureaucracy as a "minor Moscow." And he vaguely charged that La
Guardia was trying to rule through an "unholy alliance between
minority groups." Mahoney created a booklet, "Municipal Menace Number One," that accused La Guardia of being "a lawless,
promise-breaking, rabble-rousing Mayor."

When the opportunity arose, Mahoney spoke nostalgically of
Ireland: his "angel mother" and her roots in Donegal, "where they
eat potatoes skin and all," and the poverty of his youth. "But who-
ever saw a rich Irishman anyhow?" he said to an Irish group.[65]

The Democrats also accused La Guardia of anti-Catholic and
anti-Irish bigotry, pointing to his decision to name Dr. Charles
Fama as medical examiner for the city employees' pension system.
Fama, who replaced Jimmy Walker's brother William, had long
assailed the Catholic Church in his role as head of an association of
Italian Protestant ministers. He also attacked the Irish.

Fama, who was born in Mistretta, Sicily, in 1889 and migrated
at the age of ten, became Exhibit A for those who charged that La
Guardia was biased against the Irish. The controversy traced back
to an article Fama wrote in 1925 that summarized his anti-Catholic,
anti-Irish views. In particular, he focused on the Catholic view that
the Italian government had "robbed" the pope of papal lands in the
nineteenth century. This view, Fama noted, appeared in a book
the hierarchy sanctioned that told Catholic Sunday school teachers
how to explain questions and answers in the *Baltimore Catechism*.
He wrote,

> Now, is it to be wondered at, that the young people who are being
> taught in this way look upon their young Italian fellows in utter
> contempt and as an inferior race of Catholics. It has often been
> observed that the Irish Catholics show a special hatred toward their
> Italian fellow-citizens of the same faith, though Italy and Ireland
> know so little of each other. This is doubtless the explanation and it

also reveals why so many Italians join our Protestant churches, since all their beloved patriots who made Italy one and free,—Garibaldi, Mazzini, Cavour, Victor Immanuel,—are called "robbers and thieves in the night."

Fama gloated over the growth of Protestant churches with Italian immigrant congregations and poked at "Catholic Ireland" and Spain for not supporting the Allies in World War I. He scorned the "Irish Catholic rabble" who rioted outside the tony Union Club on Fifth Avenue on Thanksgiving Day in 1920 over the presence of a British flag. The rioters had just left a service at St. Patrick's Cathedral in honor of the late mayor of Cork, Terence MacSwiney, who had died a month earlier following a hunger strike that became an internationally celebrated protest against British authorities. Fama assailed Cardinal Patrick Hayes for his response, which included chiding a group of Catholics who called on him to denounce the riot.

Fama's fusillade harked back to the anti-Catholic, anti-Irish rhetoric Archbishop John Hughes had faced in the 1850s, not forgotten in Irish Catholic New York. La Guardia's support for Fama was a potent issue for firing up Irish voters. "It is very evident that our Mayor has little regard for the opinions of people of Irish blood," the *Gaelic American* editorialized. Interestingly, the Democrats had the criticism of Fama's appointment as anti-Catholic come from a prominent Jewish supporter of the ticket, the attorney Samuel Untermeyer, who four years earlier had denounced McKee's article as anti-Semitic.[66]

Whatever the Democrats tried, it didn't work. La Guardia won the head-to-head election with 60 percent of the vote. Jewish votes were decisive: it is estimated that he won 68 percent of the Jewish votes and—down from 1933—62 percent of the Italian vote. Mahoney won the Irish vote by roughly the same margin La Guardia won among the Italians.[67]

La Guardia broke Tammany power by showing it was possible to be both a man of the people and honest. For decades, corrupt

Democratic bosses had beaten back high-minded reformers because the advocates of good government seemed aloof from the voters' everyday miseries while Tammany was ready with a free pair of shoes or a picnic in the park. In his first term, La Guardia demonstrated that a mayor could be a ferocious advocate of working people and at the same time a reformer.

And so it was that La Guardia was pictured in the papers, leaning back in the chair at his desk in City Hall, puffing restfully on a pipe, with a tiger skin, symbol of the slain Tammany, spread on the floor before him. The photo symbolized that La Guardia had put an end to Irish control of New York City politics.[68]

* * *

Despite La Guardia's victories, Irish Americans continued to lead the Democratic organizations in each of the city's five boroughs. Chastened, the Democratic leaders realized that they needed to do more to court Italian voters. Bit by bit, more Italian Americans were named to the state and federal judiciary and other appointments. But there was still a resistance to letting the Italians wield real political power, as up-and-coming Democrat Carmine De Sapio found.

His upstart club gradually took over at the grassroots, winning victories in primaries for Democratic committeeman posts. The committeemen then choose a district leader. Sheriff Daniel E. Finn Jr. held that post for the First Assembly District, which included Greenwich Village and the Battery. Finn's father, Magistrate Daniel E. Finn, once ruled the same district. The senior Finn had emigrated from Limerick in about 1850 at the age of three, then followed a path toward respectability as fighter, saloonkeeper, Tammany district leader, and city magistrate. He was a colorful cuss who delighted in angering the police by showing mercy to the people they arrested. One time, he dismissed a case against two men who fought over a woman with the advice, "Don't try to compel a girl to love you if she prefers someone else. Get another to take her place."[69]

De Sapio, whose father was an Italian immigrant, came up
through the political ranks of Finn's organization, and learned his
lessons well. In the fall of 1939 he made his move. Outbreaks of
violence during the primary election required that balloting for
district leader be done under heavy police guard. De Sapio won
handily, but the Tammany leader Christie Sullivan, the last Tammany power from Big Tim Sullivan's clan, refused to seat him. De
Sapio had to go to court to take his rightful place as district leader,
but was refused a seat on Tammany's executive committee, which
handled jobs, the political lifeblood. His election as district leader
in 1943 went more smoothly, and in 1949 he became leader of Tammany Hall, ending Irish control that dated to 1872. For a time, he
was a kingmaker in New York State politics and influential nationally. Although hampered by allegations of connections to the mob
and other corrupt activities, he became extraordinarily powerful—
perhaps more so than any of his Tammany Hall predecessors.[70]

*   *   *

On election night in 1941, the Tammany Hall leader Christopher J.
Sullivan sat in his office with a puzzled expression on his face as he
thumbed through early returns in the mayoral race. They showed
that Irish-born Brooklyn District Attorney William O'Dwyer
was doing well in Italian districts, beating La Guardia. And, he
noticed, La Guardia was doing better than expected in Irish districts at that point.[71]

The 1941 campaign featured the same ethnic stress points as the
two previous races, with La Guardia once again winning the lion's
share of the Jewish vote and losing the Irish vote. The surprise, as
it turned out, was that he lost the Italian vote, receiving just 46 percent of it.[72] It wasn't enough of a setback to drag him to defeat—he
won the race with 53 percent of the vote, a margin of fewer than six
percentage points. It was by far the closest of La Guardia's three
victories in four mayoral races against Irish American opponents.
Jewish votes saved the day for him.

The reason for La Guardia's poor showing among Italian Americans is difficult to pinpoint. One clue comes from the historian Ronald H. Bayor, who found that the level of Italian dissatisfaction with La Guardia crossed all income levels, but was strongest in neighborhoods that had fallen economically. It reminds one of the discussion concerning the black vote during the 2012 election campaign—whether President Barack Obama would suffer at the polls because he'd failed to fulfill the dreams his supporters had for the nation's first black president. (Black voters continued to support him in 2012.) Italian voters, still suffering from the depressed economy, had not seen the improvement in their lot that they had hoped for from La Guardia. Compared to 1937, La Guardia took a particularly hard hit in Brooklyn, where much of the Italian population lived.

It must be remembered that La Guardia had lost the Italian vote to Jimmy Walker in 1929. Walker had succeeded in making him look faintly ridiculous as he deflected the challenger's never-ending barrage of unproven political charges. That changed in 1933; the fact that some of La Guardia's charges were proven had earned him respect. La Guardia became a countryman Italian voters could be proud of, and they embraced him in 1933. By 1941, La Guardia's excesses—his mean-spirited, undignified attacks on people who dared to disagree with him—may have worn on Italian Americans as much as they did on many other voters. He was losing their respect.

But the Italian voters' rejection of La Guardia in 1941 is only half of the equation. They also had to choose O'Dwyer, an immigrant from Bohola, County Mayo. And Bill-O was an attractive candidate in those days before the controversies that later beset him, such as his 1951 testimony before the U.S. Senate concerning his ties to Frank Costello, the powerful Calabria-born gangster who, much like Paul Kelly, took an Irish name. No one foresaw that in 1950, O'Dwyer would resign as mayor under hazy circumstances.

Perhaps O'Dwyer's anticommunist message resonated with Italian American voters, who were generally more conservative than

La Guardia. The tacit support La Guardia's opponent received from the Catholic Church may also have been a factor: Italians (at least some of them) were gradually adapting to the Irish American culture of the U.S. Catholic Church. In Brooklyn, for example, the diocesan newspaper the *Tablet* had long been hostile to La Guardia. And perhaps some Italian American voters saw their own aspirations encapsulated in Bill O'Dwyer's immigrant saga. He had emigrated in 1910 and found work as a hod carrier, the type of backaching construction labor left by then mainly to Italians. He moved on to plasterer's apprentice and bartender in Fifth Avenue hotels. Then he became a police officer, studied law at night, and earned a law degree at Fordham University. After that, he was appointed a magistrate, and then was elected Brooklyn district attorney. He was acclaimed across the nation for prosecuting Murder, Inc. gangsters; only years later would questions be raised about whether he protected the gang's notorious leaders.

By 1941, something had changed between the Irish and the Italians of New York to make it possible for a majority of Italian voters to want to put their city's future in the hands of a cop from County Mayo. New York politics was an arena that at times divided the Italians and Irish, but, as decades passed, increasingly drew them together. The 1941 election was one step along that path.

After all, it had even become possible by then for La Guardia and Jimmy Walker to become friends. In 1939 Walker introduced La Guardia to an audience at a Carnegie Hall concert of Tin Pan Alley nostalgia as "the greatest mayor New York ever had," according to newspaper reports. The *New Yorker* magazine opined that too much was made of this remark, adding the qualification that Walker had called La Guardia "the greatest *little* mayor."[73]

Be that as it may, La Guardia appointed Walker a year later to a twenty-thousand-dollar-a-year job as labor arbitrator for the women's garment industry. Samuel Seabury denounced the appointment as a political deal arranged at the behest of President Roosevelt and the Bronx Democratic boss Ed Flynn. La Guardia brushed the criticism aside. It was time to let old battles fade away.

*   *   *

Measured by voting tallies and the demographic of officeholders and campaign tickets, politics offers one of the best ways to quantify the changing relationship between New York's Irish and Italians. What we find is that politics traces out a story of how the Italians slowly found the footing to compete with the savvy Irish as equals. As noted earlier, in the 1880s, the Irish Italian congressman Frank Spinola had an Italian name and some concern for Italian immigrants, but acted essentially as an Irish American politician in the Tammany Hall mode. In the 1890s Paul Vaccarelli changed his name to Kelly and found his niche by serving the needs of the Irish American boss Big Tim Sullivan, rigging election results. Bosses like Sullivan won Italians' loyalty by offering low-level city jobs, pairs of shoes and other such aid, or a picnic in the park. But Irish politicos were very stingy about allowing the Italians any actual power. In the early 1900s Francis L. Corrao organized Brooklyn's Italians politically, but was continually frustrated in his dealings with established Irish American politicians. Other Italians in Brooklyn evidently were as well, since many joined the Republican Party instead of the Irish-dominated Democrats. In the 1910s Michael Rofrano thought the time for Italian political power had come, but was blocked by Tom Foley. Not until La Guardia's campaigns in the 1920s and 1930s did an Italian American compete as an equal with Irish-run Tammany Hall. A new generation of young Americans with Italian ancestry wanted something more than the services and low-level jobs that Tammany had doled out to their parents and grandparents, and voted for La Guardia, first for Congress and then for mayor.

Italians, less likely than Jewish immigrants to vote, played the underling role for decades before claiming their place as leading figures on New York's political stage. And then, strangely enough, the election results in the city's 1940s mayoral campaigns hinted that the Irish-Italian rivalry was beginning to fade.

By then, the Irish-Italian relationship was in transition. We will see further signs of change on yet another highly visible stage.

Cool

Like Fiorello La Guardia and Tito Pacelli, like Francis L.
Corrao and Joseph Petrosino, and like Paul Vaccarelli, Frank
Sinatra had to learn to work with and compete against the Irish to
achieve success. That was the pattern in the Irish-Italian relationship, and it was so in the world of entertainment, as in many other
arenas. Sinatra's lesson began when he was a kid growing up in
Hoboken, New Jersey, and continued right through to his contest
to unseat a great icon of Irish America, Bing Crosby, as the king of
male vocalists.

As in many other lines of work, the Irish had arrived first as
popular entertainers and were in place to act as the Italian aspirants'
mentors and tormentors. Irish tenors such as John McCormack of
Athlone, County Westmeath, were renowned. McCormack, who
studied opera in Italy, brought immense popularity to such songs
as "My Wild Irish Rose" and "When Irish Eyes Are Smiling."
Tin Pan Alley, on Twenty-Eighth Street near Broadway, was well
stocked with Irish American songwriters. The blossoming of Irish
talent in New York was one reason for a bumper crop of mass-
market songs that celebrated the attractions of Irish women, such
as the Brooklyn-born vaudeville singer Maude Nugent's 1896 tune
"Sweet Rosie O'Grady." Such beloved songs, filled with nostalgia
for Ireland, helped to further acceptance of the Catholic Irish in
Protestant America.[1] There were Italian superstars, too, such as the
Neapolitan operatic tenor Enrico Caruso. But in general, Italian

entertainers were newcomers in America compared to the well-established Irish.

Italians were soon to make their mark in the music world, with a flowering of popular Italian American singers in the 1950s following on Sinatra's stardom. The same transition was occurring in baseball. From the late nineteenth century, players of Irish and German ancestry had reigned on the diamond. There was a scattering of Italian players after the turn of the century, and then a pair of Italian American kids from the San Francisco Bay Area achieved fame as the double-play combo on the powerhouse New York Yankees: Tony Lazzeri at second base, starting in 1926, and Frank Crosetti at shortstop, in 1932. Then another Bay Area boy, Joe DiMaggio, arrived in centerfield in 1936. As was often the case for up-and-coming Italian Americans, they worked for an Irish American boss, the great Yankees manager Joe McCarthy, a strict but gentlemanly taskmaster. Following on DiMaggio's stardom, Italian American players enjoyed a heyday in the 1940s and 1950s, with African American athletes, Latinos, and Asians following them over the succeeding decades.[2] As was the case for players from other racial and ethnic groups that succeeded them, Italian American athletes had to overcome negative stereotypes. "He never reeks of garlic," a 1939 *Life* profile of DiMaggio advised.[3]

Entertainment and sports have long offered channels for minority groups to advance with their heroes and win acceptance in American society. But for those who lead the way—Jackie Robinson, most prominently—the pressure can be enormous as the news media and fans conduct a sort of hazing process.

* * *

Sinatra's parents both migrated from Italy as children. His father, Marty, was a ruddy, blue-eyed Sicilian who arrived at Ellis Island at age nine. His mother, Dolly Garaventa, emigrated from Genoa with her parents as an infant. The two families differed significantly: the Sinatras were grape growers who came from the rural poverty of Catania, while Dolly's well-educated father was a lithographer in Genoa. Since her northern Italian family looked down on her Sicilian boyfriend, strong-willed Dolly eloped with him. They married at City Hall in Jersey City in 1913.

Anthony Martin Sinatra was an aspiring prizefighter who boxed under the name Marty O'Brien. This wasn't unusual; Italian and Jewish fighters often took Irish names since the Irish so dominated the ring. Jim Flynn, a Hoboken native who preceded Marty in the ring and was the only fighter to knock out Jack Dempsey, was born Andrea Chiariglione. But there was more to the name than that. As Frank's daughter Nancy wrote, it helped to have an Irish name in a town that Irish politicians ran.[4]

Ambitious Dolly latched on to her husband's ring name when she opened a saloon at Fourth and Jefferson Streets in Hoboken, calling it Marty O'Brien's. It was during Prohibition, and Marty pitched in by helping bootleggers truck in whiskey from Canada.[5]

Dolly was the mover and shaker in the Sinatra household. Using her talent for speaking English and various Italian dialects, she quickly established a reputation for helping immigrants deal with the authorities. She also worked as a midwife. Politicos from Hoboken's Irish-controlled Democratic machine took note of her influence, and she soon became a committeewoman known for reliably delivering Italian votes. A fixture at wakes and weddings, an expert at finding a lawyer or a bail bondsman, Dolly was a broker between the Irish and the Italians in Hoboken, a gritty waterfront town across the Hudson River from lower Manhattan. Under five feet tall and full of life, she was known for singing "When Irish Eyes Are Smiling" again and again during a night out on the town. Dolly was influential enough to secure a job for Marty in the Irish-run Hoboken Fire Department after he lost employment as a boilermaker because he'd broken his wrists while boxing. With Dolly on his side, Marty rose to the rank of captain.[6]

When Frank was born in 1915, Marty picked an Irish American friend, Frank Garrick, to be his godfather. The Sinatras knew the value of having an influential godfather; Dolly would come to have eighty-seven godchildren as she grew powerful in Hoboken.

Garrick, the nephew of a Hoboken fire captain, was circulation manager of the *Jersey Observer* newspaper.

As their fortunes improved, the Sinatras moved from an impoverished Italian section with ramshackle wooden tenements to an apartment in an Irish-German neighborhood. Frank found himself in the minority, encountering boys who were better-dressed and supposedly well mannered—but who were a lot tougher. Trying to fit in, he became a sporty dresser who owned so many pairs of pants he was nicknamed "Slacksey O'Brien." Later the family moved to a tall, narrow, three-story, four-bedroom home at 841 Garden Street, with a living room and dining room.

Failing to complete high school, Sinatra took a series of menial jobs. In one case, his Irish godfather got him work as a newspaper bundler at the *Jersey Observer*, but then had to fire him when Sinatra walked into the newsroom and falsely claimed he was hired as a sportswriter. Dolly was enraged with her son, who liked nothing better than to catch the vaudeville acts in Journal Square, the hub of nearby Jersey City. He idolized singers such as Bing Crosby and the Italian crooner Russ Columbo. When Dolly saw a photo of Crosby on her son's bedroom wall, she is said to have thrown a shoe at him and denounced him as a bum. At one point, Marty told him to get out of the house. But Frank, under the spell of Crosby's cool, casual, easygoing style, yearned to be a singer. On one occasion famed to Sinatra biographers, he took his seventeen-year-old girlfriend Nancy Barbato, his future wife, to see Bing Crosby at the Loew's Journal Square theater in Jersey City in the summer of 1935. It is often portrayed as a turning point, for although Sinatra listened to Crosby's records all the time, seeing the crooner perform live inspired him to become a professional singer. He predicted to Nancy that someday, he would be on the stage. He knew he had to be a singer.[7]

Sinatra performed for a group called the Hoboken Four, and thus began the rise of one of the twentieth century's greatest entertainers. He also crossed the river to audition on his own in New York, convinced that if he could make it there, he'd make it anywhere. By 1939, Sinatra was playing with the trumpeter Harry James and his orchestra. That was big time, but for a young man with dreams of being the next Bing Crosby, it wasn't big enough.

Like many another Italian American looking to advance, Frank Sinatra would have to face an Irish American gatekeeper. Tommy Dorsey, a tough, hard-drinking, brawling Irish American trombonist from Pennsylvania coal country, would play a pivotal role in his career. Dorsey, having split off from his older brother Jimmy after a drunken fistfight between them ended their fabled orchestra, captained one of the country's most praised dance bands. Behind a pair of rimless, round glasses, his blue eyes maintained a hawk-like lookout for talent he might swoop in and grab from a rival bandleader. And Frank Sinatra had caught his eye.

At first, Sinatra had failed to impress. Dorsey stopped in while Sinatra was auditioning in a Manhattan studio for another band, led by Bob Chester. When the twenty-three-year-old Sinatra saw Dorsey's face, he was so nervous that he froze, forgetting the lyrics to the song he was singing. Less than a year later, the demanding Dorsey decided to fill a vacancy for a male vocalist by stealing Sinatra from Harry James.

It was a dream come true for Sinatra; Dorsey got him on jukeboxes and radio. But it wasn't easy to work for a man who drilled his orchestra like a boot-camp sergeant. There could be as many as nine shows in a day, followed by an all-night bus ride. Dorsey was quick to discipline slackers, imposing fines on those who missed a deadline or curfew. Still, the ambitious Sinatra saw a certain magic in the disciplined, driven Dorsey, and studied him closely. He saw a man who combined barroom toughness with a wiry, bespectacled, well-dressed panache, a taskmaster who could drive his band members relentlessly and yet hold down the nickname "The Sentimental Gentleman of Swing." He learned to be tough on himself and, like Dorsey, to be a perfectionist. He observed Dorsey's artistry with the trombone close up. Sinatra would later say that while Dorsey didn't make much effort to teach him, noting his breathing techniques as he played the trombone helped him to develop his singing style, a sweet sound soon to be greeted as not only new but, according to millions of fans, even better than Bing Crosby's melodious crooning.[8]

Sinatra started with the Dorsey band in January 1940. By May 1941, *Billboard* magazine had named him Male Vocalist of the Year. He beat out Crosby. And soon enough, Tommy Dorsey was faced with the realization that his audience had come out to hear that cocky, skinny, bowtie-wearing young singer he'd hired. A strange thing happened: the teenaged girls screamed out *Frankie-ee*. Dorsey saw them faint or at least appear to as Sinatra hung on to the microphone and intoned his sad songs.

As quickly as he had come, it was time for Sinatra to move on. As he acknowledged years later, he was vying for Crosby now, but so were singers from other leading orchestras, including another Italian American, Perry Como. He was afraid that the competition would overtake him unless he went forth as a solo singer.[9] But unlike Harry James, Tommy Dorsey refused to let Sinatra out of his contract after he broached the subject in February 1942.

The standoff between two such ambitious, headstrong men would doubtless have occurred no matter what their ethnicities were, but it still represents a classic moment in the Irish-Italian story: the Irish American gatekeeper clashing with the striving, upstart Italian American over the work rules. Sinatra was determined to overcome the foreman; he made his break in September 1942. "I had gone as far with the band as I ever could. So I blew," Sinatra told New York's *PM Daily* in 1943. "There's nothing to detract from me. Thirty-three musicians in the Dorsey band. It was like competing with a three-ring circus. Now I'm up there alone."

Dorsey was furious: a father spurned, to his mind. And indeed, Sinatra would acknowledge years later to the writer Pete Hamill that Dorsey, godfather to his daughter Nancy, was almost a father to him. Embittered, Dorsey told others that Sinatra could never make it without a band. And then he insisted that if Sinatra was going to get out of his contract, he had to accept a deal that would have cost him 43 percent of his future earnings (for a decade, some accounts say, and forever, according to others). The Sinatra biographer James Kaplan writes that after Sinatra's final show with Dorsey, the bandleader drank heavily backstage, which "always put a fine edge on his cold Irish anger." When Sinatra cried on his shoulder, Dorsey told him, "I hope you fall on your ass."[10]

There are various theories as to how Sinatra broke Dorsey's contractual chokehold. The most spectacular notion is fictionalized in Mario Puzo's 1969 novel *The Godfather*. An Italian singer named Johnny Fontane gets out of his contract with the bandleader Les Halley after Don Corleone puts a gun to Halley's head. After that, Johnny Fontane becomes the country's greatest singer and, like Sinatra, makes Hollywood musicals and divorces his hometown sweetheart. Various stories have it that Sinatra received help in his dealings with Tommy Dorsey from Willie Moretti, a North Jersey gangster who'd taken an interest in his career from early on. Others say Frank Costello intervened. Much to Sinatra's distress, these stories were embroidered over the years. Sinatra's version is that he pressured Dorsey legally, with his lawyer playing hardball by threatening to cut off Dorsey's airtime on NBC.[11]

On December 30, 1942, Sinatra opened solo at the Paramount Theater in Times Square. In short order, amid the squeals, sighs, and swoons and the sweet sounds of his bedroom ballads, Frank Sinatra's fans could make the credible claim that he was America's leading male vocalist, meaning: better than Crosby. Using poetic license, Sinatra spun the story of how seeing Crosby inspired him to seek a career as a singer, telling the *New York Evening Post* that back when he was a sportswriter in Jersey City, he saw Crosby sing one Sunday afternoon and decided to quit his job the next day to sing.

A *Downbeat* magazine poll named him the leading male singer, replacing Crosby. Declared *Newsweek*, "He can't read a note but he's dethroning Bing."[12]

With the world at war, a playful, publicist-driven "feud" between America's two leading male singers provided the public, soldiers included, with a respite to the grim news from the South Pacific, North Africa, Italy, and the Russian front. Their supposed rivalry came to a head on February 1, 1944, in Hollywood when the edgy Italian American upstart and the suave Irish American pro faced each other on the same bill. Publicists dubbed it the "battle of the century."

*   *   *

Bing Crosby was born in 1903 in Tacoma, Washington, a dozen years before Sinatra's birth on the other side of the continent. His popular performances of traditional Irish songs and his movie roles as a Catholic priest have contributed to his image as an Irish American *par excellence*, but his ancestry was in fact half-English and half-Irish. The Crosbys traced their arrival in America to 1635, when Simon Crosby, an Anglican, settled in Cambridge, Massachusetts. The Crosbys married into *Mayflower* families and rose to prominence as sea captains and leaders in the American Revolution. Bing's father, Harry, was born of this blue-blooded lineage in 1870. Bing, whose birth name was also Harry, recalled his father as a relaxed, casual man who liked to strum the mandolin and, in general, had a good time—much like the Bing his fans came to know.

Crosby's mother, Catherine Harrigan, brought the Irish blood to the family. Her great-grandfather, Dennis Harrigan, migrated from Schull in County Cork to New Brunswick, Canada, in 1831. Her grandfather, Dennis Jr., the eleventh child of Dennis and Catherine Harrigan, made his way to Stillwater, Minnesota, and established himself as a church architect. The fourth of their seven children, Catherine, was Bing Crosby's mother.

In his autobiography, Crosby wrote that his mother was the level-headed parent and the disciplinarian. She kept track of the family money—Bing was astute about his business dealings when he became wealthy as a performer—and wielded a hairbrush on kids who misbehaved. She was also a devout Catholic; her husband was a Protestant who converted to Catholicism.[13]

Since Crosby was only half-Irish, and three generations removed from the old country, his ethnic ties to Ireland were indistinct, in contrast to Sinatra's son-of-immigrants connection to Italy. Still, those ties were passed along to Crosby through his mother's Irish Catholic ways and, significantly, through the Jesuits who taught him at Gonzaga High School and Gonzaga University in Spokane, Washington. He credited Gonzaga's prefect of discipline, a 280-pound Jesuit and son of Irish parents named Father James A. Kennelly, with keeping him in line. "Big Jim" strapped his errant charges with a ten-foot-long key chain, according to Crosby, but was also a fun sort ready for a game of baseball or football.[14]

The convergence of Catholicism, discipline, and sports, so much a part of Irish American culture, shaped Crosby's youth. He was athletic enough to play a year of semipro baseball in Spokane and was an excellent swimmer. Later in life, he golfed in the low 70s. That athletic talent no doubt contributed to his gracefulness as a performer.[15] And, though he had the image of being casual and even lazy about his work—he loved his time on the golf course and often recorded songs in just a take or two—his sense of discipline is evidenced in the enormous body of work he produced (and perhaps also in the beatings his son Gary wrote of in later years).

Crosby's achievements included the most popular recording, "White Christmas"; more studio recordings than any other singer (over four hundred more than Sinatra); the most number-one hits, at thirty-eight, well ahead of the Beatles' twenty-four; and an Academy Award for his role in *Going My Way*, the highest-grossing movie ever at the time. Crosby was simply a phenomenon, not only as a performer but as a businessman. He used his earnings in show business to invest in recording technology, including the development of tape. In 1937 he created what would become the major celebrity pro-am golf tournament.[16]

His nearly fifty-year career lasted so long that his early brilliance became a distant memory. In the 1920s he mastered that cutting-edge technology called the microphone, turning it into a new kind of musical instrument. No longer would singers have to belt out songs in Al Jolson's rafter-raising style. Instead, Crosby and others such as Rudy Vallee, Kate Smith, and Russ Columbo could "croon" them. To the old guard, it seemed like cheating. The famous Irish tenor John McCormack, whose music ranged from "It's a Long Way to Tipperary" to Verdi's *Rigoletto*, complained that there was no longer demand for operatic singing, which he saw as more artistic.[17]

Beyond the intimacy he established with a well-modulated voice and the microphone, Crosby, a drummer in the bands he played in during high school and college, also had an excellent sense of rhythm. He played with the new beats of jazz in a way that other singers did not. And, most importantly, he struck up a friendship with Louis Armstrong and learned all he could from the jazz genius. Crosby's music served as a bridge between masterful but marginalized African American jazz musicians and the broader public. Baby Boomers would come to know Crosby for his Christmas albums, sentimental Irish songs, corny antics with Bob Hope, and celebrity golf. But with his mellifluous synthesis of jazz and the crooner style, Bing Crosby was the height of cool. His unworried, easygoing manner was a tonic for the Depression era, and his cool, casual persona transferred nicely to the screen just as talking pictures took hold.

On the way to his crown as the undisputed king of male vocalists, Crosby overcame a number of competitors, including Russ Columbo, son of Neapolitans who migrated to southern California. The Crosby-Columbo "Battle of the Baritones" early in the 1930s foreshadowed Crosby's rivalry with Sinatra a decade later. For a while, the two men's careers seemed entwined.

Columbo, like his father, was a professional violinist. He was playing with the popular bandleader Gus Arnheim's orchestra at the Cocoanut Grove in Los Angeles when Arnheim signed on Crosby. On nights when Bing failed to show, Columbo took his place at the microphone.[18] He proved to be more than up to it. So from the dawn of his singing career, Columbo was compared to Crosby.

Both men had built enough of a following to be courted by the radio networks in New York in 1931. As Crosby recounted in a 1933 article he wrote to publicize a new movie, "I was pig-headed in those days. I was in love with fun and didn't want to leave the coast. Their offer was raised, but still I refused. So, they took Russ Columbo along." After Columbo got a contract with NBC, Crosby, who disliked New York, decided he had to act. Crosby attested, "Russ is a grand entertainer and we both used to imitate each other until it was pretty hard to tell which of us was singing—unless you were there in person. When Russ went on the networks, then I got some sense and went East."[19]

Columbo, with his big, dark eyes and slicked-back hair, his dalliance with the actress Carole Lombard, and his slow, lyric "sob ballads," was pitched to the public as a Latinate heartthrob, the new Valentino. "His ability to warble rueful love songs is, of course, the selling point," a *Brooklyn Standard Union* columnist wrote when he opened at the Brooklyn Paramount in 1931. "An ovation somewhat akin to a riot indicates that his voice registers as well in the theater as it does over the air."[20] Referring to "the so-called battle between Crosby and Columbo," the *Brooklyn Eagle* noted, "Who, everybody wanted to know, was the creator of this slow, sotto-voiced type of singing? Was it the 'Romeo of song' (Columbo), or Crosby?"

Columbo's rise ended on September 2, 1934, in Hollywood when he died in an accidental shooting at the age of twenty-six. A celebrity photographer he was friendly with was toying with an antique pistol that he discharged by carelessly dropping a lit match on it. It was such a blow to Columbo's family that his death was kept secret from his mother, Julia, for the ten years she lived afterward. (She received a monthly letter supposedly from Russ, but written by her husband, Nicholas, or a son.)[21]

By the time Sinatra became a contender, Crosby was in a class of his own, regularly turning out number-one hit records—five in 1944—and hosting one of the most popular radio programs, *Kraft Music Hall*. He was beloved for all he did to entertain the troops, and in 1944 won the Academy Award for his portrayal of a priest in *Going My Way*.

That success is what made Sinatra's ascent all the more a story; he was taking on the pop-music monarch. A war-weary public loved the rivalry it created. It seemed that whenever someone praised Sinatra, a dig at Crosby was required, and vice versa. *Billboard* magazine declared in 1943 that Sinatra posed the greatest challenge in years to Crosby's rule as king of male vocalists.[22]

"Clearly Mr. Sinatra is on the way up," the *New York Times* radio editor wrote, adding that "a few prognosticators are even mentioning him in the same breath with Bing Crosby." He suggested that Sinatra wasn't quite there yet. From Ocean Parkway in Gravesend, Brooklyn, fourteen-year-old Marjorie Wohl, a member of the FS-FFSF, Frank Sinatra First Faithful Swooning Fans, responded in a letter to the editor, "A great many Sinatra fans think Bing shouldn't be mentioned in the same breath with Frankie. Also, why may I ask the sarcastic references to 'Mr.' Sinatra. I guess you men are just jealous of him. After all, what's he got that you haven't (except a glorious voice and about 50,000,000 fans?)"[23]

But Crosby had plenty of fans, too. When Sinatra sang before a Brooklyn Dodgers baseball game at Ebbets Field, he drew cheers with "Take Me out to the Ball Game." But when he started in on love songs, the crowd chanted contemptuously, "We want Crosby!"

Billboard, having polled students in four hundred high schools, reported in June 1944 that Crosby was ahead of Sinatra for top male singer by a narrow edge. Songwriters still considered Crosby the singer most likely to make a song successful; Sinatra was viewed as too young, the magazine found. And Crosby was the favorite among soldiers, with more than twice the votes Sinatra received.[24]

However laidback he was, all this competition was not lost on Crosby. The gossip columnist Earl Wilson reported that he wanted to have lunch with Sinatra to give him some advice.[25] There wasn't a lunch, but Crosby offered his counsel by way of a "Dear Frank" letter he published in a fan magazine, *Motion Picture-Hollywood*, in December 1943. Assuming a paternal role, Crosby advised Sinatra to find a good business manager, to never neglect fan mail, to stick with his singing style when show business pros try to change it, to get along with reporters, and not become upset over the occasional bad press.

Crosby wrote that the "silly gossip about you and me hating one another" brought to mind a story he had heard about George M. Cohan and Jimmy Durante. Durante was embarrassed that a movie script called for him to get all the best lines and told Cohan he didn't want to steal the show away from him. But Cohan generously insisted that Durante take every advantage he could.[26]

Crosby chose an interesting way to tell his fans that he was cool with the challenge from Sinatra, picking a story about entertainers of Irish and Italian ancestry who had close to the same age gap as he and Sinatra. By the time Crosby wrote his "letter" to Sinatra, Cohan had risen to mythic status as a patriotic Irish Catholic thanks to James Cagney's Oscar-winning portrayal of him in the 1942 musical *Yankee Doodle Dandy*. In his letter, Crosby was self-deprecating, as he often was, but still cast himself in the Cohan role, as he had the achievements to do. By Crosby's account, Durante, like Sinatra a son of Italian immigrants, showed respect to a man who had preceded him in the limelight.

This tale encapsulates the Irish-Italian story from the Irish perspective: accomplished Irishmen and women helped the children of Italian immigrants up the ladder to success. Crosby even gave Sinatra's ethnicity his seal of approval in his letter. Recalling an occasion when Sinatra punched out someone for making anti-Semitic remarks—Crosby vaguely alluded to Sinatra's defense of "a minority racial group to which, incidentally, you don't belong"—he wrote, "I was proud to be in the same business as an Italian kid who would fight for the under dog in the good old Yankee way."

*   *   *

In New York, there was enormous interest in the Crosby-Sinatra "feud." WINS Radio capitalized on it to draw listeners to a two-hour Sunday afternoon program sponsored by a used-car dealer who called himself the Smiling Irishman, using an Irish motif in his advertising, with plenty of shamrocks in the print ads. The "Battle of the Baritones" program tallied a running poll based on the many sacks of Sinatra-Crosby fan mail that were sent to the station. Defense workers at the Bendix and Sperry plants, employees of National Biscuit Company, soldiers based in Colorado, and hordes of high school students sent in ballots by postcard, letter, or various other methods. Among the items covered with signatures were blouses, a handkerchief (with lipstick imprints), a pink slip, a Crosby-type porkpie hat, an eggplant (said to be a favorite food of Sinatra), baseball bats, and pillowcases. The radio station said it received more than a million votes, with a slight edge for Sinatra. Often there were notes: "Frank can't sing; we want Bing"; "That guy Crosby had his day; give us Frankie we say." So many letters came in that WINS started sending them to the Smiling Irishman's office uncounted.[27]

The "feud" went head-to-head when the two singers performed together in Hollywood with the singer Dinah Shore on *Command Performance*, a radio show for the armed forces, on February 1, 1944. Newspapers dubbed it the "musical battle of the century" but noted that since *Command Performance* was exclusively for the troops, most Americans wouldn't hear a word of it.[28]

The show began with Dinah Shore introducing "Papa Bing," who, after singing a couple of numbers in a very rich, deep voice, asks, "But say, how about this, what's his name, Sinatra? What's he doing here tonight?"

Shore: "Well, Bing, Sinatra's a great singer. A singer like that comes only once in a lifetime."

Crosby: "Yeah, and he has to come in *my* lifetime."

That became Crosby's stock line, a gracious acknowledgment of his competitor. Some gentle jibes followed: how skinny Sinatra was, and, from Shore, how well Sinatra dressed, in his wool tweeds, in comparison to the casually attired Crosby.

And then Sinatra arrived, edgy and hot in comparison to Crosby's smooth and cool. "Hey, what's goin' on here?" he blurted. "Crosby, you givin' me the needle?" They traded zings. When Sinatra asked whether it was possible that Enrico Caruso was able to sing any better than he did, Crosby responded, "Even now, yes." (Caruso died in 1921.)

They followed up with a skit in which Crosby and Sinatra competed with songs for the hand of Dinah Shore. It was set up with boxing-match sound effects. After singing out a string of insults— Sinatra called Crosby "the Sinatra of 1909"—they closed out singing "People Will Say We're in Love." Shore declined to pick either suitor.[29]

The Crosby-Sinatra rivalry was good business for both singers, and similar face-offs followed in other venues. Sinatra was a guest on Crosby's *Kraft Music Hall* show on November 16, 1944. Then they both appeared on a Sinatra broadcast four days later. Fan magazines took their verbal jousting seriously.

The teasing continued in the *Kraft* show, and went to a new, if more subtle, level after Sinatra made an offhand reference to ham and eggs, followed by Crosby's suggestion that they talk about eggs for the next fifteen to twenty minutes. This was no doubt a reference to a 1944 Looney Tunes cartoon in which Porky Pig's egg factory shuts down because a skinny, bowtie-wearing, Sinatra-like rooster had sung sweet love songs to entice the hens away from laying eggs. Porky Pig brings in other singers in an attempt to lure the swooning hens away from the Sinatra knockoff—roosters caricaturing Al Jolson and Jimmy Durante, among others—until a warbling, leisurely dressed Crosby rooster did the job. This was one contest Crosby won.

Since Porky Pig's egg factory was presented as a military contractor—the "Flockheed Eggcraft Factory"—and ships eggs to Britain and Russia, the implication was that Sinatra endangered the war effort. That was a sensitive topic for Sinatra, given that his classification as 4-F for the draft, due to a punctured eardrum, was often met with skepticism and, among servicemen, anger at a man making the girls back home swoon. Crosby, on the other hand, enjoyed sterling patriotic credentials thanks to the great effort he put into raising money for war bonds and entertaining the troops. (He was too old to serve.)

Their joint appearances entertained the troops, who, according to polls, favored Crosby over Sinatra. The singers returned to *Com-*

mand Performance on September 6, 1945, with Judy Garland and Bob Hope. Following a round of insulting banter, a radio skit had Garland invite Crosby and Sinatra to audition to play the leading man in her next film. Garland played a swoon at the sight of Sinatra.

The zings in these shows could be quite sharp, sometimes scripted and sometimes not. Crosby, a master of breezy irony, seemed to hold the upper hand in their banter, but Sinatra shone when it was time to sing. In the end, the two always reconciled with a duet. That was so even in the cartoon, *Swooner Crooner.*

In their wartime appearances, Crosby and Sinatra needled each other over their age, their physique, their singing, and their hair (Crosby wore a toupee). Much of it now seems corny and scripted, but parts were quite personal and at the time, millions of fans took it to heart.

Certain subjects were avoided. They did not venture into politics, although newspapers made note of their differences: Crosby was a staunch Republican; Sinatra, a staunch Democrat. Crosby had joined the Republican presidential candidate Wendell Willkie in an election-eve rally in 1940, broadcast from Broadway's Ritz Theatre. "We've read the script, Mr. Willkie, and we think it's plenty good," he remarked. Over tea, Sinatra and President Franklin D. Roosevelt discussed girls who swooned as the campaign heated up in 1944; Sinatra stumped for FDR as he sought a fourth term. Crosby was a member of the Hollywood for Dewey committee in 1944. In what may come as a surprise to those who know Sinatra's politics from his later friendships with Richard Nixon and Ronald Reagan, he was closely associated with left-wing causes and organizations, speaking up frequently for racial and religious tolerance.[30]

"I've always considered myself of the liberal clan," Sinatra told the left-wing New York daily *PM*, which was reporting on his support for FDR. "I come from a pretty rough neighborhood in Jersey. All kinds of kids we were there, Jews, Italians, Negroes, Irish. We lived and fought together. We learned to like our fellow man." He boasted, "Boy, the fist fights we used to have! Let anybody yell wop or Jew or nigger around us. Well, we taught him not to do it again, you might say. I guess we were the worst punishment an anti-Semite could run into."[31]

Ethnic differences were clearly on Sinatra's mind—he even won a special Oscar in 1945 for his role in a short film, *The House I Live In*, in which he is shown stopping an angry mob of boys from beating up a Jewish kid.

But ethnicity was not deemed a subject fit for the jokes Sinatra and Crosby exchanged on the air. Media coverage certainly identified Sinatra with his Italian American ancestry, and the release of the hugely popular film *Going My Way* in May 1944 created Crosby as the period's quintessential Irish American Catholic.

That film tugged on America's heartstrings with its evocative use of the sentimental song "Toora Loora Looral (That's an Irish Lullaby)." Crosby sings it in his role as Father Chuck O'Malley, a progressive priest sent to help an aging pastor fix a struggling New York parish. Father O'Malley also straightens out a tough Italian kid, Tony Scaponi, using sports to turn him from youth gang leader to choirboy. In that role, Crosby capsulized in an idealized way the influence of the Irish-run church over the Italians.

Crosby had not really emphasized his Irish heritage before this; the movie studios preferred stars with all-American appeal rather than ethnic niche audiences. He hadn't played Irish-named characters before. But following the success of *Going My Way*, being Irish Catholic became a big part of the Crosby persona. In his autobiography, he recalled with humor how a gray-haired Irish immigrant maid had intervened during a party held on a Friday to stop him from taking a hot-dog canapé, saving "Father Crosby" from violating the church's requirement to abstain from meat on Fridays.[32]

Even with such strong ethnic identifications, Crosby and Sinatra steered away from references to their Irish and Italian backgrounds during their joking "feud" in the 1940s. That was to change a decade later. For example, in a 1959 television performance on *The Frank Sinatra Timex Show*, Crosby zinged Sinatra and Dean Martin (whose parents, Gaetano and Angela Crocetti, were immigrants from Abruzzo) over their ethnicity. Singing "Together (Wherever We Go)," a song for the new musical *Gypsy*, Crosby inserts the line, "I'd rather face a dozen battalions, than Italians together." Later, Sinatra pronounces the word "medley" as "meldey," and Crosby tartly comments, "Man how these pizza pushers love to wallow in their chianti," which he mispronounces as chie-ant-ee.[33]

Martin seemed to move more comfortably into ethnic *shtick* than did Sinatra, breaking easily into Italian, his first language. In an appearance on Crosby's television show on October 1, 1958, he urges Crosby to play Italian folk songs. When an enthused Martin responds by calling Crosby "paesan'," Crosby informs him deadpan that he is not Italian. Why is it, Martin replies, that so many Italians sing like him then? It was a compliment from a man who once said he "copied Bing Crosby 100 percent"—an imitation that was the sincerest form of flattery. Many other prominent Italian American singers of the 1950s did the same, as Martin notes.[34] Crosby then suggests that he sing Irish folk songs and that Martin sing Italian ones, which he likens to a pizza topped with a shamrock.

The result was appetizing. Martin, singing in Italian, did passionate versions of "Torna a Surriento" and "Oh Marie," alternating with Crosby's "My Wild Irish Rose" and "Galway Bay." There's a bit of joking worked into the songs: When Crosby intones, "If you ever go across the sea to Ireland" in "Galway Bay," Martin inserts that one must make sure he is Irish. The medley leads up to a playful mix of Crosby's "Toora Loora Looral" and Martin's "O Sole Mio," closing in both musical and ethnic harmony.

The Irish-Italian story had to come a long way before two leading entertainers could tease and joke about their ethnic differences, however gently, before a national audience. It was the case in the late 1950s, but not in the 1940s, when Sinatra and Crosby began to turn their supposed rivalry into entertainment. In any event, wartime was no time to make light of ethnic divides, especially with American forces fighting in Italy in 1943 and 1944.

But if ethnic competition was not overtly a part of the Crosby-Sinatra repartee in their 1940s appearances, it can still be detected in the broader themes of their gamesmanship. Crosby assumed a paternal role, offering advice to Sinatra in much the way Jimmy Walker had tutored the up-and-coming Fiorello La Guardia on the road to success. Both Crosby and Walker were so well established that they could afford to be casual, jaunty, and even apparently helpful to the Italians who were striving to defeat them. This idea that the Irish, wise to the ways of the world, were secure enough to impart sage advice to succeeding immigrant groups traces back to the early days of Italian immigration in New York. Horatio Alger's 1872 novel *Phil, the Fiddler* tells the story of Filippo, an Italian boy who runs away from a padrone who enslaves him as a musician in the Five Points section. He finds refuge with a tough but wise and warmhearted Irish couple who steer him toward a path to success.[35]

Sinatra yearned for what was his. Confident about his skills and abrasive at times, he knew from his experience with Tommy Dorsey that the would-be gatekeepers would not look after his interests. The brash kid from Hoboken versus the paternal and wittily ironic Crosby: it was a contest steeped in the imagery of Italian-Irish conflict.

As an upstart, Sinatra entered his *Command Performance* encounters with a need to prove himself—not only to show that his appeal went beyond teenaged girls, but to demonstrate his patriotism. As an Italian American, he was suspect in ways that Crosby was not. The same was the case for Fiorello La Guardia, despite his wartime service. The Irish had proven their patriotism in previous wars and the popular culture celebrated their achievements in movies and music. Italians had not yet arrived, at least as judged in the popular culture. When Sinatra exited his draft board in December 1943 with a 4-F deferment, news accounts quoted an unnamed draftee shouting, "Hooray for Crosby."[36] All of this background lurked, mostly unstated, behind the seeming frivolity of the Crosby-Sinatra "feud."

Frank Sinatra signs his draft induction papers in Jersey City in 1943.
Many soldiers were angered that the Swooner was found ineligible
to serve. World-Telegram photo by Fred Palumbo, New York
World-Telegram and Sun Newspaper Photograph Collection,
Library of Congress.

After the war, Sinatra's reputation plummeted. That decline
resulted partly from veterans' lingering resentment over his draft
deferment but also from a feud with two Hearst newspaper col-
umnists, Westbrook Pegler and Lee Mortimer, who accused him
of ties to communists and gangsters. Sinatra sought to redeem
himself with a Crosby-like role as a humble Catholic priest in the
sentimental 1948 film *The Miracle of the Bells*. Writing in the *New
York Evening Post*, Earl Wilson assailed newsmen for publishing
invective with the aim of preventing him from getting the role of
priest.[37] In any case, Sinatra flopped in his role as Father Paul, with
reviewers finding him wooden, unconvincing, and atrociously mis-
cast. He was no Father Crosby.

Crosby also imitated Sinatra, playing a Sinatra-like singer who
made the girls swoon in the 1944 film *Here Come the Waves*. He also

recorded an album of songs that Sinatra normally sang. Neither was among Crosby's better works.

Sinatra's career famously bounced back with his Oscar-winning performance as Private Angelo Maggio, a wisecracking Italian American from New York, in the 1953 film *From Here to Eternity.* "Only my friends can call me a little wop!" he says in that role.[38]

The Sinatra-Crosby showmanship reached a peak in the 1956 film *High Society*, in which both men compete for the attention of the socialite Tracy Lord, played by the Irish American actress Grace Kelly. In a story based on the Irish American writer Philip Barry's popular Broadway play *The Philadelphia Story*, Crosby takes the role of WASPy millionaire-playboy songwriter C. K. Dexter-Haven. Sinatra is the interloper peering into the world of the rich, playing the Irish American gossip reporter Mike Connor. The high point is their Cole Porter number "Well, Did You Evah?," when the two suitors playfully poke at each other while drinking champagne in the Crosby character's study. The two men rehearsed the three-minute song for three days, reveling in their ad libs.[39] It was a hit: Crosby would later call it the favorite number in all his many performances.

One senses a real rivalry, not a publicist-created one, in an incident that occurred six years later. Sinatra, still an active Democrat, had struck up a friendship with John F. Kennedy when he was a senator from Massachusetts. Kennedy had stayed overnight at Sinatra's home in Palm Springs, California, during the 1960 presidential campaign. Two years later, with Kennedy planning to visit Palm Springs again, this time as president, Sinatra expanded and redecorated his home in anticipation of another visit. As it turned out, Kennedy stayed nearby with Bing Crosby and called Sinatra from Crosby's home, leaving Sinatra disappointed and angry.[40]

Perhaps Sinatra's hurt traced back to his vulnerable days as a kid from Hoboken seeking the approval of Irish gatekeepers who stood at the portals to his advancement. In that sense, President Kennedy was one more influential Irish American he wanted to impress. This process of seeking Irish approval went back fifty years in Sina-

tra's family, to when his mother impressed Hoboken's Irish politicians and his father moved up in the local fire department. This
progression applied to Frank Sinatra, too, albeit in different and
increasingly competitive ways. It meant being nicknamed "Slacksey
O'Brien" as a boy, battling with Tommy Dorsey as a young upstart,
and maturing as a performer in high-profile competition with the
leading male singer of the era, Bing Crosby.

During the course of the supposed competition between Sinatra
and Crosby, much changed in the Irish-Italian relationship. Italians
were celebrated in sports, as the Irish had been. In New York, Italians shared the political stage with the Irish, and then some: The
three major candidates for mayor in 1950 were all born in Italy. On
the entertainment stage, performers like Crosby and James Cagney
had made it cool to be Irish. With the stardom of Sinatra, Dean
Martin, and a raft of other singers, it became cool to be Italian, too.
By the 1950s, the Irish and Italians appeared as equals on two stages
the public watched most closely: politics and entertainment.

In the context of the story of New York's Irish and Italians, perhaps the most important facet of the Crosby-Sinatra hullabaloo is
that, at least among young people, the dispute was not drawn along
ethnic lines. In his lovely short biography of Sinatra, Pete Hamill,
son of Irish immigrants, recalls as much from his childhood in
Brooklyn. He was too young to take sides, he writes, but the battle
echoed all around him among the older kids. Rather than one more
line of demarcation between the Irish and Italian kids, some of the
Irish were Sinatra fans while some of the Italians were for Crosby.[41]

It was one thing for the Italians to vote for Irish-born Bill
O'Dwyer for mayor over Fiorello La Guardia in 1941, or for Irish
New Yorkers to thrill to Joe DiMaggio's fifty-six-game hitting
streak in that same year. It was quite another for young women to
cross the ethnic borders previous generations had policed to give
their hearts to the crooner of their choice. For out of that mass of
squealing bobby-soxers, with their swoons and their sweet songs of
love, would come the generation that married New York's Irish and
Italian communities to each other.

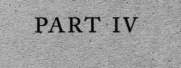

PART IV

At the Altar

Becoming Family

Love Stories

After word arrived that Lieutenant Joseph Petrosino was fatally shot while on an investigative mission in Palermo in 1909, the wails of his infant daughter, Adelina, further darkened the mood in the family's apartment on Lafayette Street in lower Manhattan. Petrosino's widow, also named Adelina, was in a precarious position: she knew that the Police Department had failed to protect her husband's safety. And she had reason to fear that the gangsters her husband had infuriated would come after her and her baby.

So baby Adelina was raised in Brooklyn after her family moved to a two-story, cream-colored brick row house at 623 Fiftieth Street in the section now called Sunset Park. She lived upstairs with her mother, who kept a close watch on her. Downstairs were the Saulinos, her mother's Italian-born brother Louie, his wife, and two sons. There were many Scandinavians on the block, some Germans, an Irish family—and no other Italians.[1]

Adelina's mother spoke to her in Italian; she learned to answer in English. Her childhood was sheltered; she went no further than the corner to attend public school. Summers were spent vacationing with Italian relatives on the Rhode Island shore, and in the neighborhood she played with friends who were German Lutherans. Her mother sent her to church on Sundays, although she didn't go herself. Adelina went to Manual Training High School on Seventh Avenue (later John Jay High School). She took a job as a bookkeeper at the Harper and Brothers publishing company. There, she met the love of her life, Michael Joseph Burke.

Michael Burke's heritage was Irish, and he wore it well. While Adelina was an only child raised by a mother who tended to be controlling, he was the fourth of seven children. As the oldest son, he had all the confidence and charm a worshipful Irish mother could instill. Adelina's upbringing was orderly and quiet; Michael's was chaotic, with his family moving constantly from one apartment to the next in Brooklyn's Bushwick section, and then South Ozone Park, Queens. Where the Petrosinos and Saulinos were prim and proper, the Burkes were ragtag.

Michael was a mischievous kid who usually got away with his indiscretions, but on one occasion he stirred up scandal by marching in the Protestants' Sunday school Anniversary Day Parade to get the ice cream handed out afterward. He would later claim that he was thrown out of Holy Rosary School for that offense (but it was hard to tell whether this was true, given his love for telling tales).

His Irish American parents were born in the United States. Going back, the Burkes' origins trace to County Tipperary, while the family of Michael's mother, Johanna Lynch, was believed to be from Limerick. Michael simply joked about it. "They were a bunch of horse thieves; they had to get out of the country," he would say.

Adelina, who had an easy smile and gentle manner, was eight years older than Michael when she met him in 1940 at the age of thirty-two. Michael, who worked in the production end of the publishing house, was captivated. She hesitated to go out with him, having begun to assume that she wouldn't marry. But he was so much fun. They kept their dates a secret. He took the long subway ride from south Queens to Brooklyn, sometimes falling asleep on the way home and waking up at the end of the line. With his dark brown hair and blue eyes, he was a charmer. Hazel-eyed Adelina, a quarter-inch under five feet tall, was ready to be charmed.

Michael Burke served in the Army Air Corps during World War II, reaching the rank of staff sergeant while assigned to a supply station in Guyana, then a British colony. Meanwhile, Adelina kept her relationship with Michael secret. People in the office would relate news they had received from him, and Adelina pretended that she didn't already know. Every month, Michael would send her roses. He had his sister write out the card, *Te amo, cara mia*. The sister didn't know what it meant.

In August 1945, Michael called to say, "I have a weekend pass. Will you marry me?"

Adelina had two problems. She was able to take care of the first one easily: she needed to get the pastor of St. Agatha's Parish to permit them to wed without meeting the church's requirement that the banns proclaiming an upcoming marriage be posted three weeks in advance. A dispensation was granted. The second was more difficult: Mama Adelina disapproved of the marriage and adamantly refused to go to the wedding.

Mama Adelina was used to being in control, and was not ready to give up her only child to marriage. So Michael and Adelina arranged to be married quietly—and without her—on a Monday afternoon at St. Agatha Church. But when Michael's parents and siblings found out, they insisted he couldn't keep them away; they were Catholics, after all, and it was a Catholic church. Once Mama Adelina found out that all the Burkes would be there, she relented and agreed to attend.

As the family recalls it, the Burkes had no objection to Michael's marriage. But, it is said, one family friend commented that Michael was marrying a "guinea." The Burkes rose up in defense of Adelina's ancestry.

Adelina and Michael Burke wed on August 20, 1945. The reception was held in the Petrosinos' apartment, and Adelina Petrosino sang Italian songs for the occasion. The newlyweds honeymooned for two nights at the posh Hotel Bossert in Brooklyn Heights. Then Michael Burke returned to the military until December.

On October 11, 1946, their daughter Susan was born, the granddaughter of the famous Lieutenant Joseph Petrosino.[2]

*   *   *

From early on in the Italian migration to New York, various observers dared to predict that the day would arrive when the Italians and Irish would fall in love with each other and marry in large numbers. One of Joseph Petrosino's friends thought so. Monsignor John Kearney, pastor of St. Patrick's Old Cathedral on Mott Street, was beginning to notice an increased number of marriages between Italian men and Irish women as early as 1899. These unions were encouraged by the fact that Italian immigrants were mostly men, while Irish immigrants tended to be women. Almost no Italian women married non-Italians at the time in New York.[3]

The scholar Thomas Jesse Jones predicted more. "The Irishman hates the Italian because the latter is willing to work regardless of the workingman's tradition," he wrote in 1904. "When the Italian learns the American point of view these two peoples become friends, and it is likely that the next generation will witness as many intermarriages of Italians and Irish as now take place between the Irish and the German."[4]

Likewise, the writer Laurence Franklin looked past the rivalry over jobs and division in the church to foresee a day when the gap between the Irish and the Italians of New York would close. The Italian children "possess much less feeling of race difference than their parents, and their children in turn will probably be thoroughgoing Americans—or Irishmen; for strangely enough it is the Irish who seem to make the strongest impression on them," Franklin wrote, recounting a conversation he had with a small Neapolitan boy who addressed him in a perfect Irish brogue.[5]

While there would indeed one day be many Irish-Italian marriages, these predictions at the turn of the century were very premature. The New York Irish did show some willingness to marry outsiders, but mostly the Germans or English. They were more likely to marry a German Jew than an Italian.

That nugget is contained in a mass of data gathered by Julius Drachsler, a young assistant professor of sociology at City College who undertook an enormous research project on intermarriage among immigrants, reviewing 101,854 marriage certificates granted in the Bronx and Manhattan between 1908 and 1912. Drachsler, a Czech Jewish immigrant who had come to America at the age of fourteen, was trying to gather actual facts to undermine racist theories that leading academics espoused at the time: the notion that southern and eastern European immigrants were genetically inferior human beings who could not assimilate successfully into American life.

Southern Italians and blacks fared especially badly in the racial and ethnic hierarchy that these social scientists expounded on, with blacks at the bottom of the list and Italians just above. The Irish fared somewhat better in this Anglo-Saxon-oriented rating of the races. Drachsler was still in his twenties when he set out to challenge notions that were advocated by respected scholars such as Edward A. Ross, a president of the American Sociological Society, who wrote, "That the Mediterranean people are morally below the races of northern Europe is as certain as any social fact."[6]

Such academic views helped provide supposed justification for the 1924 federal law that sharply restricted immigration from southern and eastern Europe. In 1927 the anthropologist Margaret Mead came up with an overlooked but obvious answer to the low test scores of Italian children: the results depended heavily on whether English was spoken at home.[7]

The Irish may have had a skeptical view of the Italians, but never so negative as in the perspective of the many Anglo-Saxon scholars who used bogus science to disparage them. The Irish had no Italian-hating version of Thomas Nast, whose cartoons in *Harper's Weekly* depicted the Irish as apes. While eugenicists provided intellectual cover for the crackdown against immigration, the Irish viewed the Italians as members of the same faith, albeit with dismay at their differences.[8]

Drachsler worked against the background of such controversies. Before taking ill in 1922 with a fatal case of tuberculosis, he published two books that painstakingly produced data that social scientists would use for years to come. He tallied that southern Italians intermarried in fewer than 6 marriages in 100, while northern Italians (17 marriages in 100) and the Irish (22 marriages in 100) were much more likely to do so. For southern Italians, the second generation's intermarriage rate was even lower than the first, at 3.5 in 100. This is because the earlier generation of Italians was so heavily male that it accounted for more intermarriages than the second generation experienced. For the Irish, the second-generation intermarriage rate was 36 percent. In general, the earlier immigrant groups such as the Irish and Germans tended to marry each other, and not into the newer groups, such as Italians, Poles, or Greeks.

Counting through the marriages of 6,778 Italian men between 1908 and 1912, Drachsler found that 92 percent were to Italian women. The nearest group from which Italian men found wives was the Germans, at 2 percent, and the Irish, with 1 percent. Irish men married Irish women in 82 percent of the 8,812 marriages counted. Germans were the next most common, at 8 percent. Italians accounted for less than 1 percent; nearly all those weddings involved northern Italians.[9]

This is the period when the phrase "melting pot" first was used, the title of Israel Zangwill's 1908 play about a Russian Jewish immigrant family. Its hero, a Jewish immigrant who marries a Christian, declares, "America is God's Crucible, the great Melting-Pot where all the races of Europe are melting and re-forming!"[10]

But the crucible of intermarriage was set to a low heat, especially for Italians.

*   *   *

Giovanni Giliotti arrived in New York in 1909 at the age of twenty-three on board the French-built, double-funneled, twin-masted ship *Chicago*. He had grown up in Borgotaro, a town in the Emilia-Romagna region of Italy known for its porcino mushrooms. With a love for good food, he initially left home to study cooking in France, then set out for New York from Le Havre. He found work as a hotel chef, traveling the eastern seaboard down to Atlanta to work.

He went back to Italy for a time, married, and returned with his wife, Filomena, in 1922. Their daughter, Mary, was born the following year. They lived in Rosedale in the southeastern corner of Queens, a rural area at the time, raising chickens and growing vegetables in their yard. On May 8, 1930, Filomena died at the age of thirty-four.

John Giliotti traveled to the hotels with his young daughter, but was dissatisfied with the setup. Instead, he left her home with relatives. John was a protective father, all the more so because of the difficult circumstance. One time, he was enraged when a teacher at his daughter's school confided to him that she was a "tomboy." His knowledge of English idioms being a bit weak, he thought the teacher was warning him that his daughter was consorting with boys. He went home and smacked her.

Mary spoke Italian and had some Italian-speaking friends, but she was thoroughly American. She went to Andrew Jackson High School. She dated racecar drivers. And she found work as a secretary at the *New York Journal-American*, a Hearst newspaper. In 1948 she met Gerard Cronin, an advertising salesman at the paper.

He was six feet, four inches tall, a handsome man with black hair and dark eyes. He grew up in an Irish American family on Sterling Place in Brooklyn's Park Slope section—not up the hill near spacious Prospect Park, where the well-off Irish resided, but down the slope closer to the waterfront, where the poor Irish and the Italians lived. It was Gerard's great-grandfather, Lawrence Cronin, who came over from Ireland during the Great Famine and found work in Manhattan as a laborer. His son William, born in 1867, was a teamster. William's son, also William, was born in 1891 and was listed in census and draft records as the supervisor at a telegraph cable company based on Broad Street in Manhattan. His son was Gerard, who would later tell his daughter, Linda Cronin-Gross, that his father was involved in bootlegging. By prior arrangement with police, his father would hide upstate when arrests were planned.[11]

Gerard served in the army in Fiji during World War II. He saw no combat, and came home with a photo of himself in a grass skirt with coconut-shell breasts. He could be hilarious, but was essentially a quiet man. He smoked a lot, but rarely took a drink. Gerard asked Mary—a pretty woman who was five feet, four inches tall and had brown eyes and dark hair that would gray prematurely—on a date. Then he made the long trip out to southeast Queens to pick her up.

John Giliotti greeted him—with a shotgun.

Gerard and Mary's daughter, Linda Cronin-Gross, recalls that her parents had told her the same story of the first date. "My grandfather got his shotgun and ran him off because, you know, he's Irish," she said. "Definitely because he's Irish was part of it."

Gerard Cronin and Mary Giliotti continued to date, but in secret. They wed in 1950 at St. Clare Roman Catholic Church in Rosedale, Queens, and stayed in the neighborhood, close to Mary's father. "My grandfather was never thrilled," recalled Linda, a public relations executive who attended St. Clare's School and then the Mary Louis Academy, a Catholic high school in Queens. "The Irish didn't care very much. The Italian grandfather was never happy with the arrangement."[12]

*   *   *

Given Italians' devotion to family—a steadfastness that traces to centuries of invasion, foreign rule, and exploitive governments—it is no surprise that they resisted marrying outsiders in the New World. A language barrier, low social status, and crushingly low incomes—southern Italian immigrant men earned less than black men did in 1910—were also obstacles to intermarriage.[13]

But with each passing generation, that was to change. The Catholic Church, where the Italians once worshipped in the basement and the Irish in the main sanctuary, became a catalyst for Italian-Irish intermarriage. The federal census official Eliot Lord, who advocated settling southern Italians in the American South, predicted as much in a 1905 book he wrote to reverse prejudice against the newcomers:

The common religion is also a bond of union, and Italians are usually attracted to Irish-American churches and parish schools while
they are too few or too poor to establish churches of their own. The
influences of a Catholic church organization are steadfastly bent
against racial antagonisms, and for the promotion of Christian fel-
lowship of its followers.[14]

Lord's case that the Italians would Americanize, in part because
of a religious connection to the Irish, struck some reviewers at
the time as impossibly sunny. But by the 1940s and 1950s, social
scientists were exploring the idea that America's melting pot was
really a "triple melting pot"—Protestant, Catholic, and Jewish. The
Irish, given their influence in the American Catholic Church, were
bound to be a dominant ingredient in any Catholic melting pot.
They were the brokers between the older migration from northern
and western Europe and the newer arrivals from southern and eastern Europe.[15] Given that role, it was natural that Italians who were
active in the Catholic Church would tend to wed Irish partners
when not marrying one of their own.

By the 1940s, the Italian American population in New York
had changed a great deal from earlier decades. The massive Italian
migration, averaging about two hundred thousand people a year
through the first decade of the twentieth century, had come to a
virtual stop with the Immigration Act of 1924. The new law set
quotas obviously aimed at stopping the influx of Italians and eastern European Jews while at the same time permitting even more
migration from Germany and Great Britain. There were still some
newcomers from southern and central Italy, but as time passed,
there were far fewer first-generation Italian immigrants bringing
the old country to America. (There was a fair amount of post–
World War II Irish migration to neighborhoods such as Woodside
in Queens and Woodlawn in the Bronx.)

Over time, the rigidity of the Irish American Catholic Church
became less of a turnoff for the second- and third-generation

Italian Americans than it was for their parents or grandparents. Two separate large-scale studies conducted in the 1960s by priest-sociologists—one of Irish ancestry, the other Italian-born—demonstrate that by the third generation, Italians had adopted a much more Irish outlook on the church, in part because of the influence of Catholic schools. They'd been "hibernized."

Daniel Patrick Moynihan and Nathan Glazer noted this in their landmark 1963 book *Beyond the Melting Pot*. If Protestantism had once been a symbol of social success for Italians, they wrote, "Today, a more significant symbol of rising social status is marriage with a girl of Irish descent, who has gone to a good Catholic school. . . . The social pages of the *New York Times* often report such marriages."[16]

The Reverend Andrew Greeley, a famously cantankerous third-generation Irishman from Chicago who delighted in using sociological surveys to puncture conventional wisdom, was the first to gather detailed data about the Irish-Italian relationship. He oversaw a study in which more than two thousand white Catholics aged twenty-three to fifty-seven were interviewed in the winter of 1963.

The priest-sociologist—he had not yet become the best-selling author of sexually explicit novels—had a keen sense for Irish-Italian differences. When he grew up on the South Side of Chicago, he wrote, an Italian family was no more welcome than a black one. He found that as of 1963, the Irish were still significantly more successful than the Italians: they had more prestigious jobs, more education, more money. Irish Catholics were more likely to be Democrats, and were more liberal. (He argues that the Irish were generally liberal, except in New York and Boston, where for historical reasons they tended to be suspicious of other groups.) Greeley found that Italians were much more likely than the Irish to live in the same neighborhood as their parents and to see them each week, and they were stricter parents.[17]

Other experts continued to explore the mass of data Greeley gathered. One of them, Harold J. Abramson, delved into intermarriage and found that the Italians still married each other—more than six in ten of their marriages. The Irish were more likely to marry others, but still, more than two in five unions were with other Irish. Keep in mind, though, that those surveyed were born between 1906 and 1940. That means that quite a few of the older Italians were either immigrants or had grown up in heavily Italian neighborhoods, and were therefore unlikely to meet and marry outsiders. When Italians did marry others, they usually wed the Irish or Germans—10 percent of Italian marriages for each group. By the third generation, there was a tendency for Italians to marry the Irish when they married outsiders, and in coeducational colleges, there were often Irish-Italian marriages, he found.[18]

While Greeley's study was national in scope, a priest-sociologist named Nicholas John Russo, who was a professor in the Diocese of Brooklyn's Cathedral College, examined some of the same territory in New York City. After surveying more than a thousand people in twenty-one New York City parishes in 1967, Russo found that when third-generation Italians in New York married someone from another ethnic group, the partner was *almost always* Irish. Just under half of the third-generation Italians surveyed had married an Italian spouse, and about 12 percent had wed Irish partners. Only 3 percent married into any other ethnic group. The rest of those surveyed were unmarried.

The Irish who were surveyed didn't marry Italians at nearly the same rate: just under 5 percent. And they were much more likely than Italians to marry someone who was neither Irish nor Italian (12 percent).

These numbers included people who had not married. Narrowing it down to third-generation Italian American New Yorkers who had married, Russo found that nearly one in five wed Irish partners. Fewer than one in twenty had married spouses from all other ethnic groups combined (other than Italian and Irish).[19]

It is important to keep in mind that Russo surveyed Italians reached through Catholic parishes. Because of their involvement in New York's Irish-influenced Catholic parishes and schools, they were far more likely to meet and marry Irish Americans than were Italians who were indifferent to the church. Italians who went to Catholic high schools were especially likely to marry Irish spouses.[20]

The turning point came in 1946, according to Russo. That was when many Italians began to move out of their ethnic neighborhoods and flock to residential areas of the city or the suburbs. That, Russo writes, is when "the Italians tended to conform to Irish Catholic norms in increasing numbers."[21]

While Russo emphasizes the role of religion in bringing the Irish and Italians together, contemporary scholars of "whiteness" have emphasized the importance of race in analyzing relations among ethnic groups of European ancestry: Italians struggled to be viewed as "white," and thus American. In other words, first the Irish, once pilloried in American society as nearly subhuman, "became white," or acceptable. And then the Italians did. Indeed, a 1923 U.S. Supreme Court ruling specifically stated that Italians were white and thus eligible under federal law to be naturalized citizens, even if they were "dark-eyed, swarthy people." (The ruling found that a "high caste Hindu" from India could not be considered white, although he lay claim to being an Aryan.)[22]

While the Italians' economic advances and acceptance into American society no doubt made them more likely marital partners for the Irish, religion emerged as a key factor in Irish-Italian marriages. Russo determined that third-generation Italians were just about as likely as the Irish to send their children to Catholic schools. The Italians had so internalized the Irish way of being Catholic that they even prayed like the Irish. Their Italian-born grandparents were far more likely to pray to the Blessed Mother and saints than to God. Not so for the later generation, which was just as likely as the Irish to pray first to God rather than a saintly intermediary. The longer the New York Italians were in America, wrote Father Russo, himself an Italian immigrant, the more their religious attitudes tended to be like those of the New York Irish.

Once often a battleground, Catholic parishes were now bringing the Irish and Italians together. The ensuing transition to Irish-

Italian marriage was seamless in some families, but in many it was not. In some cases, families experienced much tension as young couples crossed the social boundaries that had existed for their parents and grandparents—and sometimes, those tensions never really ended. In other families, any awkwardness quickly gave way to good-natured teasing about ethnic differences: a family's shared story.[23]

* * *

Mary Collins met Frank Macchiarola in kindergarten at the red-brick Holy Cross School in Brooklyn's Flatbush section in the fall of 1946. The Brooklyn Dodgers were locked in a pennant race with the St. Louis Cardinals over at Ebbets Field, a mile's walk north on Bedford Avenue. The next year, they were separated: Frank went to Holy Cross's boys' school, where his third-grade teacher would call him "Murphy" because "Macchiarola" was too hard to say.[24] Mary went to the girls' school. It was that way until the eighth grade, when Mary won the general excellence award for girls, and Frank won for the boys. They accepted their awards in Holy Cross Church. "I thought, 'Huh, I have to go down the aisle with this Italian?,'" Mary said years later. It turned out that they walked the aisle separately. But Mary did go down that same aisle with Frank at her side sixteen years later, when they married.

Frank's Italian-born paternal grandparents, Francesco and Maria, ran a grocery store on Dean Street. Their son, Joseph, worked in a shipyard and then became a city sanitation worker. He married Lucy Bernardo, whose father, Patsy, was an immigrant from the Naples area.

Mary's father, Michael Collins, was from Curry in County Sligo. He arrived at Ellis Island in 1921 at the age of seventeen, and was promptly held there, possibly on suspicion of having the name of Michael Collins, the Irish revolutionary leader. At least that is what family lore suggests. He settled in Flatbush, which continued to draw new Irish immigrants. Mary's mother, Rita Egan, migrated in the mid-1920s from Ballaghaderreen, a small cathedral town then in County Mayo and now in Roscommon. She worked in a rectory in Boston, and met her mate in an Irish dance hall in Manhattan.

Religion was important in the Collins household: Sunday Mass, for sure, but also weeknight rosaries said together, and the novena to Saint Theresa of the Little Flower at St. Peter Claver Church in Bedford-Stuyvesant every Monday night. Rita and Michael Collins began this lifelong novena after a friend brought them what was believed to be a relic of the saint to further their prayers as Rita lay in bed from the third month of a pregnancy that led to the birth of her oldest son. Her father had a deep faith, "more a blind faith," as Mary described it. "It wasn't a questioning kind of faith." Frank's family also practiced the Catholic faith, but with far less dutiful devotion at that point. Frank's father was "do as I say, not what I do," according to Mary.

Both Frank and Mary continued their Catholic schooling in high school and college. Both went to work in the city school system. They were assigned to the same district, and went to some of the same meetings. One day, a dinner was to be held to honor their supervisor. Mary, who already held a supervisory position at the age of twenty-seven, was reluctant to go; as a woman, she felt she didn't fit in. But Frank invited her, and she went with him.

Frank, working on his doctorate, already showed the talent that would one day make him one of the leading figures in New York's civic life before his death in 2012: schools chancellor in charge of educating a million children, and then college president, law school dean, and leader in the business community. He was a La Guardia-like figure: round and short, shrewd yet playful, sharp as could be, funny, outspoken. He was at once salt of the earth and entirely brilliant. Frank had stood out all his life: oldest grandson in his family, a seven-year-old who could take the city bus on his own, apple of everyone's eyes.

But he wasn't exactly embraced in the Collins household. That was especially so for Mary's father, Michael. "My father, for all his Catholicism—you brought home your own," Mary said. "My brother Mike married a Murphy and that was all well and good. But I brought home a Macchiarola. Interestingly enough, my father never said a word about it. But it was there, no doubt about it."

Mary decided to raise the subject with her mother. "Frank is a nice guy. I'm going to continue going out with him," she announced before asking what Dad thought of him.

"Don't worry about Dad," her mother replied.

Michael Collins was a parks worker who bartended two nights a week to supplement the family's income. His response to the question on Mary's mind was continued silence on the subject of Frank Macchiarola. "He never said a word. In my mind that was my father's approval," Mary recalled. "I loved my father to death. He was a typical stubborn Irishman."

Mary found that her education—in particular her master's degree—meant a lot to Frank's family, especially his father. His mother was more distant, possibly in part because of her Irish ancestry, she thought. Still, Mary didn't sense hostility. It helped that the families knew each other through neighborhood sports and church activities. "I was reminded often enough by his mother what a prize package I was getting," she recalled.

Frank and Mary Macchiarola married at Holy Cross Church on June 13, 1970.

On their first Thanksgiving together, they hosted their families for dinner. At the table, her father got up and offered a toast to Frank: "I would go a long way to find an Irishman like Frank," he declared. Even more than forty years later, Mary's eyes welled with tears as she recalled that scene. "To me that was a very special moment because it was almost like he was atoning for his sins," she said. "There was silence. It was an incredible moment."[25]

* * *

Although Irish-Italian marriages became common in the postwar years, the Italians and Irish were still much more likely to marry spouses from their own ethnic background. That was especially so for the Italians, as an analysis of the 1980 U.S. census showed.

The odds that an Italian woman would marry an Italian man were nineteen times greater than the chance that a non-Italian woman would wed an Italian man. An Irish woman was four and a half times as likely to marry an Irishman.

The study by the sociologists Stanley Lieberson and Mary C. Waters showed that when Italians did marry outside their ethnicity, they were most likely to marry an Irish partner. Looking at women aged twenty-five to thirty-four—Baby Boomers born between 1946 and 1955—the two sociologists found that more than one in five of spouses with entirely Italian ancestry had married partners who were at least part Irish. (The 1980 census was the first to record ethnic identity, permitting two nationalities to be listed.) This wasn't so for the Irish. Their greatest affinity was not with Italians but with the Germans, whose emigration to the United States roughly tracks their own.[26]

The difficulty with all of these data is that the census does not ask questions about religion. For understanding the Italians, that's not a huge problem, since nine in ten identified as Catholic as of 1980, according to an analysis of the General Social Survey. But just two in five of the Irish did, and one in five of those whose ancestry is German. Nationally, most Irish Americans and German Americans are Protestant.[27]

Still, this study shows how the Italian-Irish marriage trends Fathers Greeley and Russo had detected in earlier decades had continued. The fact that most of the New York–area Irish were Catholic made it even more likely that Italians would marry them.

*   *   *

The one Irish relative I had while growing up was Frank Bradley. He married Marie C. Muscato, my mother's sister. Uncle Frank, an analyst for the city's Budget Bureau, was a charmer with all the wit so often associated with the Irish. He was clearly the only member of the family who would jokingly tell the kids that the "O.F.C." in the brand name of a popular whiskey meant "Officially

for Catholics." The Muscatos—initially Moscato—and the Bradleys lived in very different worlds.

The Bradleys were from Kilbaha, a tiny harbor town in County
Clare near the mouth of the River Shannon. They trace their lineage at least back to John and Johanna Bradley, who married in
1830 and farmed a six-acre leased plot. Their son Thomas, born
in 1841, migrated to the United States at the age of fourteen, following three older brothers and many others from his village to
work in the factories of Newtown, Connecticut. He found a job
in the rubber works and at the age of eighteen married Bridget
Kelley, a button maker from County Clare. They lived in Sandy
Hook, next to Newtown. During the Civil War, Thomas Bradley
served in the Seventeenth Regiment Connecticut Volunteers, an
infantry unit that fought in some of the worst battles as part of
the Army of the Potomac. In later years, he became active in local
Democratic politics, serving as Sandy Hook's postmaster and a
Newtown selectman. "Mr. Bradley's life and success illustrates the
opportunities that a fair field and fair play in America offers to the
European emigrant here," the *Newtown Bee* wrote in his obituary
in 1905.[28]

Thomas and Bridget had nine children. Michael F. Bradley, the
second oldest (and the oldest to survive infancy), was born in 1866.
He sought his fortune in New York City, where he rose through the
ranks to become administrator of the 4,400-bed Manhattan State
Hospital, described as the world's largest insane asylum.[29] It is said
that a local priest's appeal to Cardinal Patrick Hayes helped him to
advance after promotion was denied, as Michael Bradley believed,
out of anti-Catholic bias. Michael Bradley married Isabelle Wilson, a nurse at the hospital. Her family came from Manorhamilton,
County Leitrim.

Frank, born in 1913, came of age on the grounds of the psychi-
atric hospital his father ran on Wards Island in the East River.
His family was well-to-do—"lace curtain," as my Italian relatives
later put it—thanks to his father's successful investments on Wall

Street. One older brother became a psychiatrist, the other an engineer. Frank graduated from Manhattan College in 1935. Then he followed the Bradley path into government, taking a civil service job. (Evidently some Irish Americans were still being hired in the La Guardia administration.) During World War II, he served in North Africa and Italy. After the war, he was elected commander of the Father Stedman Post of the Catholic War Veterans in Brooklyn; the slate of officers was mostly an amalgam of Irish and Italian names.[30] He continued on that career path into the 1970s, becoming budget examiner for the city university system.

For my brothers and me, Frank was the uncle who could get you a summer job in the city parks system. He could teach you to throw a curveball. He mixed the highballs. He had special, smooth-bottomed white sneakers for tennis, dusted with the red clay of the courts. He was unfailingly cheerful. He worked across the street from City Hall, and knew all the players. He was the emcee and toastmaster when a banquet was held to honor Abe Beame as he left the top job at the Budget Bureau to become comptroller, a steppingstone to the mayoralty. He loved that I was friendly in school with the son of Jim Cavanaugh, city budget director and later deputy mayor. When my Italian relatives gathered around a very well-stocked dinner table to tell stories of how poor they were in the Depression—as they always did—Frank would make up his own stories. "We were so poor that I had to have water in my cereal," he would quip. Everyone knew that Frank came from a different social class, and that he was Irish, not Italian.

He and Marie met in 1950 at a Catholic War Veterans dance in the Bay Ridge section of Brooklyn. She was a shapely, fair-skinned, energetic, dark-haired woman of thirty-one, a lively conversationalist, self-educated in the works of the great writers of the day, supporting her family with her job as the paymaster for a company in Brooklyn Heights.

Marie grew up in Little Italy, where her father, Christopher, an immigrant from Cerasi in Calabria, ran a poolroom. Her family lived at various Little Italy addresses, including a small, three-bedroom apartment at 293 Mott Street, near Houston Street. Murals of Mount Vesuvius decorated the hallways. Unlike her older sister Josephine, Marie wasn't sent to school at Old St. Patrick's. Her father decided he'd had enough of the church, and forbade it. But two weeks into her first public-school year, she came home with a cold sore on her lip, which was an answer to her mother's prayers. Rachela, an immigrant from Laurenzana in Basilicata, got her way this time. She insisted that Marie go to Catholic school. She brought her to St. Patrick's Old Cathedral to be baptized at the age of six in October 1925.

After Rachela's death due to edema on April 7, 1929, Christopher took his six children (my mother, Anna—the baby—was eight months old) to live in a five-room cold-water flat on Gatling Place near Fort Hamilton in southern Brooklyn. This time, Marie was registered in the public school. The family name changed from Moscato to Muscato at the will of the clerk who registered her.

Bay Ridge had a substantial Irish population—most of the children were in Catholic schools—as well as many Scandinavians. When she was about twelve years old, Marie recalls, she heard excited whispers in her home. "Sotto voce," she said. "It turns out one of the Italian girls was marrying an Irish boy. It was like they were in mourning. . . . The thing is, they were being married in the Catholic Church. It was the same religion. But the thing is, it wasn't Italian. He was Irish."

But Marie Muscato was destined to fall in with the Irish. Through her job as a clerk in the library, she met the librarian Elaine Lewis, who was five years older than she and highly educated, with a degree from Vassar. She was an expert in folklore, and even had a radio show on WNYC, introducing the music of the legendary black blues musician Leadbelly to a wide audience. Elaine met and married Jim O'Beirne-Ranelagh, who had taken part in the 1916 Easter Rising and became an Irish Republican Army general.[31] After fighting on the losing side in the Irish civil war, he came to New York, where he and Elaine met through their shared interest in Irish music. Both Elaine and Marie soon began attending Irish events with Jim. They were active in the Gaelic Society and Jim ran the Irish Sweepstakes in Brooklyn.

Marie learned about Ireland, and helped Elaine Lewis to learn about the Italians. One day, the folklorist visited Gatling Place in Brooklyn to record Italian songs as sung by one of the women on the block, Lucy Bartolomeo. She played them on her WNYC Radio show, *Folksongs for the Seven Million*. Elaine and Jim O'Beirne-Ranelagh eventually moved to Ireland, where Elaine wrote a book under a pen name that gently poked fun at rural Irish life, telling the story of a New York woman who relocated with her husband to County Wicklow.[32]

So Marie was at home with Irish ways when she met Frank Bradley at a Catholic War Veterans dance in southern Brooklyn's Bay Ridge section in 1950. Still, she was well aware of the Irish-Italian divide. "When I was a girl, we were always fighting with each other, Irish and Italian," she recalled, adding that there were quite a few Irish families on Gatling Place, none of them close friends.

By the time Frank met Marie, both of his parents had died. The only surviving parent was Marie's father, Christopher. He took an immediate liking to his daughter's new beau. "Frank is the only gentleman I ever saw you with," he told her. They wed at St. Patrick's Church in Bay Ridge on August 30, 1952.

Marie quickly became popular with Frank's maiden aunts, in part because of her talent for cooking. She was neither the first nor last Italian American to win favor with the Irish through that skill. Her repertoire went well beyond the Italian favorites she'd grown up with: the aunts especially liked her beef bourguignon. "Wasn't it a lucky day when Frank Bradley married Marie Muscato?" one of the maiden aunts, Catherine Bradley, declared to the other after a hearty meal. "Indeed it was," came the reply.

Marie's ultimate test of Irish acceptance came in 1958, when she and Frank vacationed in Ireland. They visited the family of Frank's late mother, the Wilsons, in County Leitrim. Manorhamilton, a small town about sixteen miles outside Sligo, is set in the midst of enchanting green glens. The main street rises to the ruins of a seventeenth-century castle that overlooks the verdant country-side. The Wilson family home was across the street from the castle; Frank's aunt, his mother's sister, lived there. That night, there was a gathering to greet the Yanks. Relatives and their friends sat in a circle, entertaining each other by taking turns at singing songs.

"So it comes to me," Marie recalled. "They say, 'Give us a song.' I say, 'I can't sing.' They said, 'Oh surely you must know a song.'" So Marie sang "Kevin Barry," one of the great songs of Irish resistance to the English. It tells the story of an eighteen-year-old medical student who was hanged in Dublin's Mountjoy Jail in 1920 following his conviction in the slaying of a British soldier, singing his praises for refusing under torture to turn informer.[33]

"Well!" Marie recalled. "They clapped. This little Italian girl? I sang the whole song. They couldn't get over it! Even Frank didn't know that, you know." But Frank Bradley had not been a member of the Gaelic Society, as she was, and had not learned the song from Elaine and Jim O'Beirne-Ranelagh. "They said, 'Welcome home. How many Italians know "Kevin Barry"?'"

Recalling years later the ethnic taunts she heard from Irish American kids while growing up in Bay Ridge, Marie Bradley would quip, "I got even with the Irish. I married one!"[34]

*   *   *

These stories of Irish-Italian romance and marriage reflect a postwar trend that resulted from various factors. One is simply geographic: the Italians moved out of their crowded ethnic enclaves and mingled with the Irish in residential neighborhoods in the city and suburbs. Construction of the subway accelerated that. For example, it permitted my relatives to move from crowded Mott Street to Bay Ridge in far-off southern Brooklyn, where many of their neighbors were Irish. Construction of new highways had the same effect. (And a plan to build an expressway across lower Manhattan in the 1960s led many Italians to leave their enclave there, although it was ultimately rejected.) Another reason was economic:

Italians were catching up to the Irish, and more likely to be equals in the workplace rather than underlings. We see that in the office romance of Michael and Adelina Burke. When Adelina's father, Joseph Petrosino, was alive, it would have been unusual for an Italian woman to work in the office of a major New York publisher, as Adelina did. And finally, religion was a key factor. Studies show quite clearly that the Italians most likely to marry Irish Catholic spouses in the postwar years were active in the Catholic Church and had attended its schools.

Scholars debate which of these elements—proximity, socioeconomic status, or religion—is most responsible for ethnic intermarriage. The studies by Fathers Russo and Greeley point to religion as a decisive statistical factor in bringing the Catholic Irish and Italians to the altar. That is consistent with the "triple melting pot" theory, in which some sociologists have held that different ethnic groups intermarry based on religion: Protestant, Jewish, Catholic. But scholars who questioned the "triple melting pot" have made good cases for geographic proximity or comparable economic status rather than religion as the real undergirding for ethnic intermarriage. The Catholic Church is certainly very important to the Irish-Italian story in New York, but ultimately it is difficult to disentangle these three dynamics, since all can be present in a single relationship. We see that in the love story of Mary and Frank Macchiarola, who shared the same neighborhood, church, and workplace.

The social boundaries of old are blurred and even erased when people from once antagonistic ethnic backgrounds mingle in these places, especially when they do so as social equals. Arenas that once served as Irish-Italian battlegrounds—neighborhoods, workplaces, and churches—became places where young women and men in postwar New York met and fell in love. In varying degrees, they still had to overcome the legacy of past battles and prejudices that may have divided their parents and grandparents.

We can analyze the data scholars have gathered to understand, at least in broad strokes, why the Irish and Italians in New York married each other in large numbers in the years after World War II. In doing so, we deal with statistical probability, not the mysteries of love and marriage. As I wrote at the outset in discussing the "melting pot" theory, human behavior cannot be contained in formulas in the way chemical reactions are, a crucible in which each element melts precisely as expected. There is more to it than counting the number and percentages of ethnic intermarriages.

So we need to look more closely at what happens when, having melted into one another's arms and mated, spouses from two cultures that differ a great deal go about melding their traditions in a new, dual-ethnicity family.

13

Food and Family

It might be said that the increasing popularity of pizza in New York paralleled the rise of Irish-Italian marriages. Like the Italian immigrants who brought it, pizza was looked upon with some reserve in New York in the early 1900s. "Pie has usually been considered a Yankee dish exclusively, but apparently the Italian has invented a kind of pie," a *New York Tribune* writer commented in 1903, trying to explain "the 'pomidore pizza,' or tomato pie," made from dough rolled out an inch thick with "plenty of red pepper on top." The pizza's perceived spiciness was cause for suspicion; an adjacent article carried the headline "Do Fiery Foods Cause Fiery Natures? Italian Love for Red Peppers May Explain the Combativeness of Spirit of Men of That Nation."[1]

Two years later, Gennaro Lombardi opened a pizzeria on lower Manhattan's Spring Street. Pizza was popular among Italian immigrants, but took a while to catch on elsewhere in the city. As late as 1939, the *Herald Tribune*'s food columnist treated pizza as foreign to most New Yorkers' tastes. "If someone suggests a 'pizza pie' after the theater, don't think it is going to be a wedge of apple," Clementine Paddleford wrote. "It is going to be the surprise of your life."[2] But by the 1950s, pizza had become a Friday night staple in the homes of both Irish and Italian New Yorkers. Brought home somehow still steaming warm in a thin cardboard box, a pizza pie fulfilled the Catholic requirement to abstain from eating meat on Fridays and also tasted good.

Canned spaghetti, fed to American troops during World War II, also became popular—probably more so in Irish homes than with Italians, who often held that product in disdain. In any case, Irish Americans were far ahead of the British in their knowledge of spaghetti: On April Fools' Day in 1957, the BBC pulled off one of the most famous televised hoaxes by running a documentary that purported to show how spaghetti grew on trees. Many viewers in the United Kingdom fell for it.[3]

Italian food—or, more accurately, its Italian American version—entered the American mainstream in the 1950s, mostly by way of New York. When the singer Dean Martin defined love as a vision of the moon as an extra-large pizza pie in the 1953 movie *The Caddy*, everyone wanted to sing along: "That's Amore."[4] Martin's character sang that song surrounded by his loving Italian family. It differs sharply from the way Italians were depicted in pre–World War II Hollywood movies, when they were often sinister characters or untutored bumpkins. The new message was that Italians were accepted, with their food a sign of romantic love and strong family bonds. Italian food had become a sign of *amore* rather than "combativeness." *The Caddy* reinforces that when the Martin character hands out bowls of *pasta e fagioli* to his adoring family as he sings his song of love.

As the Irish and Italians married and created families in the postwar years, the couples had to overcome not only the animosity prevailing in previous generations but also some considerable cultural differences about food, family, and religion. For all the data that have been gathered about the frequency of ethnic intermarriage, there has been relatively little study of how couples from different ethnicities mix their cultural values in family life.

Since intermarriage is considered a sign that the bride and groom have assimilated into American culture, there may be a tendency to assume that their varied ethnic backgrounds matter little. Experts in family therapy tell us otherwise, however. Ethnic groups have different ways of being a family, and however Americanized they may be in the workplace, traditions from the old country can still be passed through the family from one generation to the next. Life's landmarks—births, baptisms, weddings, funerals—or hardships such as divorce have a way of making people focus on ethnicity. Sometimes grandchildren revive the family's ethnic tradition. For Jews, this is reflected in the *baal-teshuvah* movement, in which Jewish Americans, often of the third generation, go from being nonobservant to Orthodox.[5]

The broad outlines of some cultural differences between Irish American and Italian American approaches to family life can be seen in a 1980s survey of 220 mental health professionals. The Italian Americans found nothing more important in life than family, and saw eating as a symbol of the family's closeness. Men were dominant, women were protected, and babies indulged. Self-control was not a high value for the Italians, while it was important for the Irish, who also put a premium on the rules of the church. The Irish Americans who were surveyed looked down on complaining, and prized being strong and psychologically tough.[6] There are clear differences. The ugly history of ethnic and racial stereotyping may be the reason relatively little recent study has been done of ethnic differences. But surveys like this one demonstrate that ethnicity matters, among many other factors, when one is trying to understand a family.

Food has long stood out as the most obvious difference: Italian American family life revolved around it, while it was unimportant in Irish culture. The historian Hasia Diner traced the low Irish priority on food to the Great Famine. The lack of food was so painful and central to the Irish people that a good meal could not be the source of joy, pride, or ethnic identity.[7]

Southern Italians also were deprived of food, but its easier availability in America helped make the meal a center of family life. Germans, Jews, Poles, African Americans, Puerto Ricans, Chinese—food played an important role in the identity of every major ethnic group in New York except for the Irish.

But Irish eyes soon smiled on Italian food. The turn-of-the-century police commissioner William McAdoo remarked on the bunches of kale, spinach, carrots, and cauliflower, and the cheeses and many shapes of macaroni he saw as he went to and from his headquarters. "It is one of the singular sights of Little Italy to see an array of most excellent-looking vegetables generally a week or two earlier than they appear in other parts of the city," he wrote in his 1906 memoir. "I could never ascertain where these vegetables came from, but they looked very inviting."[8]

In a panel discussion with Frank Macchiarola and the former mayor Edward I. Koch, the writer Pete Hamill, son of Catholics from Belfast, recalled how Italian food entered his childhood in the 1940s:

> The most important factor in my childhood might have been when Mr. Caputo came into the hall of my mother's kitchen and taught her how to make the sauce. We didn't want to eat anything else for the rest of our lives. Part of this discussion is how the Italians taught the Irish how to eat. The Irish had the worst food in the history of the world. I didn't realize until I was 17 that roast beef could be pink. They thought you could get trichinosis from hamburgers. Everything was charred and cremated because, who did they learn it from? The British.[9]

It's no wonder that in Hamill's novel *North River*, cooking has a lot to do with the relationship that develops between a tough-minded Sicilian woman named Rose and an Irish American doctor, James Delaney.[10]

Italians' near sanctification of food and mealtime often required some adjustment for the Irish partner, especially around Christmas Eve, Thanksgiving, and Easter. Before she married Frank Macchiarola, Mary Collins wasn't much of a cook. "Tuna fish was about my style," she recalled. She'd been raised on what she calls a "bland" diet. "My father, growing up, if you put anything on his meat and potatoes, that was terrible." But she learned to cook Italian, with help from Frank's mother. It is common in Italian-Irish and other ethnic intermarriages for cooking to be transmitted from mother-in-law to daughter-in-law.[11]

There were certain terrors involved: one time, Mary's mother-in-law brought her long green peppers so hot that they burned her hand, requiring treatment. And then there were the animal innards. Once in a while, Frank would cook, especially if he wanted tripe. "I absolutely despise tripe and he loved tripe," Mary recalled. She learned to make other dishes he favored, such as *pasta e fagioli* and lentils. "I learned to like them too," she said. "I'm Italian by taste. It certainly beats Irish cooking." Still, she added, "it blew my mind" at how much time the Italian relatives spent around the table. "I could not conceive of how Italians used to eat."

Once the Macchiarolas had their own home in Brooklyn's leafy Midwood section, they would invite both sides of the family on Sundays and holidays. "The thing that I learned was that Christmas Eve is very important in the Italian house," Mary said. "It was more important than Christmas." Frank cooked on Christmas Eve: clams, mussels, crabs, fish fillet, lobster sauce, shrimp. Mary always thought it was too much to eat, but, as she put it, "that was always his night." Her father, Michael Collins, learned to like it as well: "Joining the two families was fun because my father became the biggest lover of Italian food."[12]

Drinking is another sign of the cultural differences between the Irish and Italians. It has been said that the Italians, fond of wine, drink while eating but that the Irish, known for their pubs and their Guinness, eat while drinking.[13] Alcohol is, simply put, important to Irish life, an uneasy situation so often explored in the works of Ireland's great writers. Excessive drinking is a great Irish concern, testified to by the fact that so many "took the pledge" not to imbibe. Drunkenness is not so great a problem in Italy and, likewise, Italian Americans are less likely to have a drinking problem than Irish Americans are. In southern Italy, drunks are scorned, an outlook that immigrants brought with them to America. Irish pubs can now be found in Italian cities, and beer has become popular there. But Italian Americans came to enjoy beer much sooner than Italians did, likely because of Irish and German influence in America.[14]

* * *

While food is an important way Italian Americans carry their ethnic culture from one generation to the next, music plays a large role for the Irish. The audience for traditional Irish music may be a small one within the larger entertainment world, even in Ireland, but one can still see American college students jumping up in the pubs to sing by heart the words of rebel songs or to dance a jig. Music has always played an enormous role in Irish culture since it was long a tool to resist British oppression and to express the sorrows and longings of everyday life.

The noted Irish fiddler Tony DeMarco was a convert to this sound. Interviewed by the author in the midst of the annual Feast of San Gennaro on Mulberry Street—where DeMarco has an apartment—the husky musician seemed to be as thoroughly Brooklyn Italian American as anyone could be. Yet he is also an Irish fiddler who cut an album for the Smithsonian Folkways project and who has judged one of the most prestigious Irish music contests, the annual Fiddler of Dooney competition in Sligo.

DeMarco's mother, the former Patricia Dempsey, was the daughter of an Irish-Italian marriage that went awry. Her father, Jimmy Dempsey, was a police officer and the son of Irish immigrants. Her mother was "Minnie" Fenimore, whose parents migrated from Naples. Tony DeMarco's Italian American father—his family came from Abruzzo and Calabria—was a lightweight title boxer in the army who passed up the chance to fight professionally and instead chose a career as a commodities broker.

With three of his grandparents Italian and one Irish, the Irish influence in Tony's childhood was limited. That was all the more so because the Irish grandfather, Jimmy Dempsey, had long since left the family and moved to Europe. DeMarco's grandma Minnie lived with his family and brought him his first guitar when he was nine years old. DeMarco was brought up with the idea that "the Irish side was no good." His Irish grandfather had been troubled ever since he shot a young man as a police officer and, as DeMarco learned, "He never quite got over that."

Still, his family did celebrate Saint Patrick's Day when he was growing up. Meanwhile, DeMarco picked up the violin in high school, then found his way into folk and bluegrass fiddle music and from there, to Irish music. A turning point came one day when he practiced the fiddle in a park near his home in the East Flatbush section of Brooklyn. Paddy Reynolds, an immigrant from County Longford who was one of the top Irish fiddlers in the United States, was out walking his dog. Reynolds helped bring Tony De-Marco into New York's Irish music scene.

Brown-eyed, dark-haired, with a voice full of Brooklyn, De-Marco is aware that he is no one's image of an Irish fiddle player. "My whole persona is not a freckled, red-haired Irish kid," he said. Despite his accomplishments as a fiddler, he added, he faces a degree of discrimination in the cliquish world of traditional Irish music—not so much from the musicians, who are "a little more forgiving," but from promoters. "When they hear [the name] De-Marco, they're not so psyched." DeMarco has organized his own music festival, the New York Tradfest, leading fellow musicians to dub him the "Tradfather."

*   *   *

Food, music, the church, social clubs, and religious or ethnic associations are among the ways that Italians and the Irish have preserved their sense of ethnicity in America. But it is clear that the once-strong ethnic ties that the Irish, Italians, and other European ethnic groups held may well be fading away. Still, there are ways in which ethnicity counts, even in groups as Americanized as the Irish and Italians.[15]

This phenomenon emerges especially in family life. One factor is simply the desire to impart an ethnic identity to children, a hope that is especially strong among Italian Americans. One study conducted in upstate New York's Albany region in the mid-1980s found that two-thirds of Italian parents wanted their children to identify ethnically, while just one-third of Irish parents did.[16]

In his 1967 study, Father Greeley found that Italians living in urban neighborhoods were more than twice as likely as the Irish to live near parents and siblings. They were also much more likely to visit relatives weekly. It is not that Irish Americans are slackers when it comes to maintaining ties with relatives. Rather, they are like most other Americans. Italian Americans exhibited unusually strong family ties.[17]

Both Irish and Italian cultures emphasize the bond of mother and son. For the Irishman, there is the sainted Irish mother exemplified in the song "Mother Machree." The mother holds a place in her son's heart "which no colleen may own." There is also a tradition, dating back to the Great Famine, of marrying later in life or remaining single, or perhaps entering clergy or religious life. For the Italian, there is the stereotype of the prying mother-in-law who can't let go of her married son. This type of relationship was caricatured in the situation comedy *Everybody Loves Raymond*, in which the Queens-born actor Ray Romano plays Ray Barone, a *Newsday* sportswriter who is hemmed between the demands of his meddling Italian mother and his endlessly frustrated wife.[18] Ray's mother, Marie, lives across the street and constantly barges into his life. In two memorable episodes, she brings the entire family to Italy—a trip Ray is very reluctant to make because he considers vacation a time to be *away* from his annoying mother. The ethnicity of Ray's wife, Debra, never becomes a factor in the show. Her maiden name, Whelan, indicates Irish ancestry. But Debra, a former Madison Square Garden executive whose parents are wealthy, cultured suburbanites from Connecticut, is assimilated to the point that her ethnicity doesn't matter. When she winds up in constant competition with her Italian mother-in-law, the show's co-creator, Phil Rosenthal, has said, her greatest liability is that she can't cook.[19] Rosenthal, who grew up in Queens, drew on his own Jewish family to create the characters.[20]

Ray Barone's predicament makes comedy out of one of the tensions that family therapists see in third-generation Italian Americans: those who reject the demands of *la famiglia* may experience
conflict, while those who embrace it may feel left out of America's in-
dividualist, achievement-oriented culture. Either way, they may find
themselves surprised to be using the same stock phrases of parental
advice that they grew up with.[21] For those who marry into other ethnic cultures, such as Irish, there may be some explaining to do.

*　　*　　*

Gatherings of the Burke clan were a bit overwhelming for Susan
Burke, the granddaughter of Lieutenant Joseph Petrosino, when
she was a girl. Her father, Michael Burke, was the oldest boy in an
Irish Catholic family with seven children, and thus "the savior," as
she put it. Her father's was a "crazy Irish family that had keg parties every time you turned around." The Burke family's raucous
gatherings contrasted with the quiet Sunday dinners she was used
to at home. Her Italian-born Grandma Adelina, whose father ran
a small restaurant where she met Petrosino, was an excellent cook.
She made her own pasta on Sundays, or a porridge-like polenta,
and "the greatest tomato salad in the world; I can still close my
eyes," Susan recalls.

Susan was an only child, as was her mother, also named Adelina. Her father's siblings mostly had large families, which made
for loud and lively gatherings. Others may have perceived Susan
Burke's ancestry as Irish, but she felt Italian. Susan noticed the
difference between her Italian American mother, who doted on
her father, and the more dominant women in the Irish family. At
parties, the sisters-in-law looked askance when Adelina got up to
fix a plate of food for her husband. "What, is he crippled?" they
asked. Susan's mother laughed it off; she found great warmth in the
Burke family. And her father adapted with pleasure to the Italian
household he headed, meaning that he was accorded great respect
but that his wife and formidable mother-in-law had a great deal
to say about day-to-day life in the family. Susan said she saw only

one argument between her parents, when her father objected after her mother told her the truth about Santa Claus. "Michael, she's eleven," Adelina Burke retorted.[22]

From the start of their migration, Irish and Italian women in America played different roles. Differing from other immigrant groups, women outnumbered men among Irish immigrants. Many came on their own, without men. They came to work. Among Italians, men far outnumbered women. Following southern Italian traditions, the father was the head of the house, a figure who commanded respect. The mother was the center of the family, controlling the day-to-day life at home. "Life in the South exalts the family," the Harvard professor Robert Foerster wrote in 1919. "Gallant to his wife, the husband has almost complete power over the members of the family; the wife's affection tends to be slavish."[23]

Irish women worked as domestics and then as schoolteachers, nurses, and office workers. Unlike immigrants of many other ethnic groups, Italian women didn't generally work in other people's homes. In traditional southern Italian culture, to do so would risk being seen as disloyal to one's own family. Italian women often did piecework at home, or labored in factories if circumstances required them to work outside the home.

Irish parents were much more likely to see to it that their daughters were schooled, and Irish culture put a great emphasis on the written word. In the nineteenth century, there were more Irish girls than boys in American parochial and public schools, especially in advanced grades.[24] Education was a low priority for southern Italians, particularly for girls. Foerster found that very little money was spent on education in Basilicata, Calabria, and Sicily. "Attendance is slight" in schools, and "buildings are inadequate and unhygienic," he wrote.[25]

The leading clinical textbook on the role of ethnicity in family therapy advises counselors to be aware of such history. Its co-editor, Monica McGoldrick, traced the tradition of strong Irish women to nine hundred years of British oppression that blunted the power of men in Irish society. She notes, too, that Ireland has a tradition of powerful women dating to Celtic times. McGoldrick, who is Irish American, found that this helped make Irish women independent.[26]

Poverty and political oppression shaped southern Italian culture too, but with different results. Family was the refuge against a harsh environment, and everything else, including religion, was secondary. In New York, Irish immigrants shaped powerful institutions that helped to pass on their culture: in the church and its schools, in the police and fire departments, and in ethnic associations such as the Ancient Order of Hibernians and county societies. The bar was a place where alliances and friendships could be made, deals brokered, troubles confided. Italian immigrants had the family. The worlds of work, the church, and the ethnic associations mattered to the extent they contributed to the strength of the family.

Against that historical background, it is not surprising that researchers have found some persisting differences in Italian and Irish approaches to the family. For example, Italians are said to have a somewhat more authoritarian approach to raising children: survey data showed that even more so than the Irish, Italian parents valued that their children obeyed them. Irish parents put a strong value on self-control, and were more open to the children being intellectually curious and self-reliant.[27] If that finding doesn't sound quite right to Irish ears, it may be because working-class Irish American parents have also been found to be strict with their children and insistent on obedience.

Family therapists have also taken note of how cultural differences related to ethnicity affect the Irish-Italian family. The Irish are, in general, much more circumspect about sharing feelings of pain or loss. Italians may tend on the other hand to find comfort in expressing their feelings in a dramatic way. Monica McGoldrick has noted that Irish and Italian couples might deal in very different ways with a problem that can't be solved. The Irish spouse could tend to withdraw in silence, creating a distance from the problem. The Italian spouse might be angered by a silent withdrawal.

This is not to say that only the Irish family has an elephant in the room. McGoldrick has advised therapists working with Italian families to probe carefully because, despite their apparently open debates, secrets may still lurk.[28] One sees that dynamic in the 1977 film *Saturday Night Fever*, which turns the tables on the happy family dinner scene that accompanies Dean Martin's singing of "That's Amore" in *The Caddy*. The John Travolta character, Tony Manero, who works in a Brooklyn hardware store by day and stars on the dance floor at night, feels trapped by his family. He's required to show up at 6:00 p.m. for dinner, knowing that mealtimes inevitably become a battlefield for family tensions. He's encouraged to eat more pork chops, but the conversation gives him little appetite. His father is an unemployed construction worker who boils over when his wife suggests that she find a job, which he takes as an attack on his honor. Tony can't wait to bolt from the table and head for the dance floor. He carries the conflict in his home with him, but keeps it a secret.[29]

Religion has been another area in which ethnic differences can figure in Irish-Italian marriages. Irish Catholic Americans have tended to pass along their ethnic heritage through the Catholic Church. In many cases, the Irish spouse led the Italian to become more of a churchgoer—a development that would have pleased New York's Irish Catholic pastors and bishops of the late nineteenth century.

This was so for Lieutenant Joseph Petrosino's daughter. Susan Burke, who became a teacher and then assistant principal at Bishop Kearney High School in southwest Brooklyn's Bensonhurst section, said the Irish side of her family was very devout while the Italian side was not especially religious. Grandma Adelina Petrosino was not a churchgoer, but had required her daughter, Adelina, to worship on Sundays. "My mother was a Sunday Catholic until she fell in love with my father, and then there was a reason to go to church: to bring him home safely," Susan said. Her father, Michael, attended the 6:30 a.m. Mass daily.

It was also the case even for the late Frank Macchiarola, the former schools chancellor and St. Francis College president who was one of New York's leading Catholic laymen. His wife, Mary Macchiarola, recalls that when they met, Frank wasn't a church-goer. This worried her. She was relieved when Frank called one day and said, "Guess where I am." He had gone to seek the counsel of a priest who was friendly with Mary. A few days before their wedding, Frank went to Mass with Mary, which pleased her greatly. Later, he became very religious, spending a work week once a year in prayer at the Trappist monastery in Spencer, Massachusetts. When he led New York's public school system, he was a daily communicant. "He said he had the lives of a million kids in his hands," Mary recalled. "He couldn't make decisions by himself."

*   *   *

My wife, Maureen, and I met through the church. We were working on a Catholic retreat for college students in Brooklyn when our eyes first met on May 2, 1974. Researching this book has made me realize that I am something of a social science statistic: as a third-generation, churchgoing Italian American from New York who went through twelve years of Catholic schools, I was highly likely to wed an Irish Catholic if I did not marry a woman of Italian ancestry.

There was certainly nothing unusual about an Irish-Italian marriage when I wed Maureen Collins in 1976. The immediate neighborhood where I grew up in the Flatlands of Brooklyn housed mostly a mix of Irish, Italians, and Jews. (I didn't know a Protestant until I was fifteen.) My 1967 diploma from Mary Queen of Heaven School depicts headshots of fifty-six students, twenty-nine with Irish surnames and twenty-three of Italian ancestry (including one awkwardly named Moses). There was a map of Ireland high up on the wall of the school's basement cafeteria, and its many jagged inlets intrigued me. The education was Irish Catholic. Most of the lay teachers had Irish names. Since the Dominican Sisters of Sparkill used religious names in those days, one couldn't be sure in their case. But one anecdote may provide the answer, and also a glimpse at the Irishness of Catholic school education.

As Saint Patrick's Day approached and Irish-Italian rivalry peaked among the students, my eighth-grade class pestered Sister Andrew Marie to reveal whether she was Irish or Italian. Sister Andrew Marie, who was as good-natured as a human being could be when spending the day keeping nearly sixty thirteen- and fourteen-year-olds in line, wisely refused. What was the truth? All we could see of the sister was her round face, since she and all the other sisters still wore a religious habit that included a black veil and white headpiece. We were clueless, although there were clues aplenty. For example, Sister Andrew Marie's method of punishment was to pull a green plastic shillelagh, a sort of Saint Patrick's Day prop, out of her desk drawer and sting the back of the offender's hands with it. As punishments went, it was fairly enlightened; the green shillelagh looked more imposing than it was. Sometimes, she would shake her head and, with a trace of a smile that made it seem a term of endearment, tell us, "You are a bunch of *amadans*," the Irish word for "fools." And indeed we were if we could not figure out that Sister Andrew Marie's ancestry was Irish.

When I looked into it while researching this book, I found that Sister Andrew Marie later became Sister Mary McLaughlin, returning to the name she grew up with. Census records show that her father, Andrew McLaughlin, was an immigrant from Ireland. After she died, on February 10, 2014, at the age of seventy-nine, her order posted an obituary that said her pleasures in life included dancing to Irish music. The sisters who lived with Sister Mary recalled her as a great wit who was proudly Irish. She knew the words of, it seemed, every Irish song. She never missed the Irish music programming on Fordham University's public radio station on Sunday afternoons. At her golden jubilee celebration, she suffered a broken hip when she fell while dancing the "Siege of Ennis."[30]

Even if my teachers were tactful enough not to reveal their ethnicity to their students, there was no mistaking the Irish Catholic nature of my schooling.

My wife, Maureen, on the other hand, grew up in the heavily Italian community of Elmont, just across the city line in Nassau County. As New York City's Irish and Italian Americans shifted to the suburbs and Staten Island, Elmont's proportion of Italians began to resemble that found in Brooklyn's most heavily Italian neighborhoods, such as Bensonhurst and Canarsie (where Maureen's family initially lived before going to Nassau County).[31] Much as many of my good friends were Irish American, many of hers were Italian American.

Our grandparents came of age in ethnically segregated communities—Maureen's ancestors lived for a time in the Irishtown on the Brooklyn waterfront, while mine arrived from Calabria and Basilicata to live in Manhattan's Little Italy. But when two tribes mingle in their houses of worship, in their schools, neighborhoods, and workplaces, the barriers of suspicion can eventually break down, replaced by cooperation and even love.

*   *   *

One question to ask at this point in the Irish-Italian history is whether ethnicity stopped mattering. Had intermarriage melted away the boundaries between these two former rivals to the point that ethnicity meant no more to their offspring than that they would wear green on Saint Patrick's Day or eat a great deal of seafood on Christmas Eve? Sociologists have debated this for decades. At the same time, contemporary historians of "whiteness" have shown ways racial identification drew together ethnic groups from various European nationalities as they sought to distinguish themselves from historically downtrodden blacks.[32]

There is no question that the ethnic attachments of the Italians, Irish, Jews, and many other onetime immigrant groups such as Germans and Scandinavians have weakened a great deal over time. But the work of scholars such as Monica McGoldrick, Joe Giordano, and other social scientists shows us that ethnicity does still matter in understanding Americans of European ancestry, if much less so than in their earliest generations in the United States.

The role of ethnicity is most pronounced within the family. To be sure, there are many other important factors in family life besides the influence of ethnic culture and tradition. And yet, as we have seen, ethnicity is not to be forgotten, even for groups as American-ized as the Italians and Irish.

Nowadays, ethnic differences between the Irish and Italians are often noted with humor. The television network Comedy Central's website served up some of those shopworn jokes. ("Proof that Jesus was Irish. He never got married." "Proof that Jesus was Italian. He talked with his hands." Or: an Irishman who eats Italian food has "Gaelic breath.")[33] These comments are a far cry from the days when supposedly scientific studies purported to identify ethnic differences based on skull shape and intelligence tests. But ethnic humor tells us, sometimes in a crude or stereotypical way, that we still sense distinctions based on ethnicity. Increasingly, these fad-ing differences between the Irish and Italians became the stuff of friendly humor, not violence or resentment.

That's not to say that Irish-Italian ethnic rivalry disappeared in New York even as the Baby Boom gave life to many an infant of dual Irish-Italian ancestry in the 1950s and 1960s. There were still issues to be worked out in such powerful institutions as the Roman Catholic Church and the Police Department, among others. But, as we will see, the divisive, turbulent politics of 1960s New York served to bring the Irish and Italians closer as they further united in the face of a perceived threat.

14

Sharing the Bastions of Power

On September 12, 1968, Francis J. Mugavero became the first Italian American to head a Roman Catholic diocese in New York State when he was ordained bishop of Brooklyn. A son of Sicilian immigrants who came of age upstairs from his father's barbershop on DeKalb Avenue in Brooklyn's Bedford-Stuyvesant section, he differed from his predecessors in many ways. The most obvious was his ethnicity; the four previous bishops of Brooklyn were all Irish, as were all but one of the leaders in the history of the New York archdiocese across the East River. Beyond that, he brought a new style to leadership of a diocese known nationally (especially through its newspaper, the *Tablet*) for a staunch Irish Catholic conservatism that had embraced such figures as Father Charles Coughlin and Senator Joseph McCarthy.

While previous bishops had been experts in canon law, Mugavero's field was social work. That meant that his expertise was helping the poor rather than interpreting and enforcing church law. When he issued the pastoral letter *Sexuality: God's Gift* in 1976, it circulated among Catholics far and wide because of its optimistic message that "we do not fear sexuality, we embrace it." He wrote that gay people had been subject to "unjust discrimination," and urged compassion for them. His diocese became known as a place where divorced Catholics seeking an annulment of their marriage would be treated mercifully.

The first Italian American bishop in New York State was a liberal. He was friends with liberal politicians such as Mario Cuomo, who affectionately called him "my bishop," and he didn't go along with the move to sanction Catholic elected officials who favored abortion rights. His personal style was also a sharp departure from the reserved approach of previous bishops: so friendly and informal that diocesan employees dubbed him "Mugsy." He refused to be called "Your Excellency." Partly because he was a born-and-bred Brooklyn priest—bishops are often plucked from some other diocese—there was an immediate rapport with his people.

Many of his traits reflected the times, an optimistic era after the Second Vatican Council when the Catholic Church sought to embrace the modern world. Bishops were chosen for their ability to connect with people. But Mugavero's warmly personal style was also connected intimately to his ethnic roots, even if people pronounced his name in a way that sounded almost like "McGovern" (muh-GUH-vero). There are surely dour Italian churchmen, but Mugavero's salt-of-the-earth manner, his appreciation for life's pleasures, and his rejection of clericalism were true to his heritage as the son of Sicilian immigrants.

"He was certainly very, very proud of his Italian background," recalled Frank DeRosa, who served as his spokesman. DeRosa, who became a reporter for the *Tablet* in 1958—he believes he was the first Italian American on the staff of the paper, which was founded in 1908—observed that while the new bishop's ethnicity was certainly noted, it didn't lead to tensions with Irish Catholics. Dating back to his seminary years, Mugavero had maintained friendships with Irish American priests. At the same time, DeRosa added, "I think the Italians were delighted to have an American-born Italian priest as their bishop." Mugavero had long served as chaplain for various Italian associations, and he always enjoyed talking about his love for Italian food: trips to off-the-beaten path restaurants in pre-gentrified Brooklyn, and his own cooking, especially his spaghetti with clam sauce.[1]

The result was a distinctly different style from that of the mother church across the East River, the Archdiocese of New York, which had an unbroken line of Irish prelates going back to John Hughes. For generations, the archbishop of New York had defined for the city what it meant to be Catholic. Archbishops of New York traditionally took a leading role in the conservative wing of the American Catholic bishops; Mugavero played an important role among liberals. He provided a new image to New Yorkers of what it meant to be a Catholic bishop, unlike any other in the city's history.

Just five years before Mugavero was appointed bishop, Nathan Glazer and Daniel Patrick Moynihan wrote in *Beyond the Melting Pot* that the peace between the Irish and Italians in the Catholic Church was not yet complete. They counted just one Italian auxiliary bishop among thirteen in the Archdiocese of New York, Joseph Pernicone, who was appointed in 1954. (An auxiliary bishop is a deputy to the bishop who leads a diocese.)[2]

In the early 1970s, more than half the U.S. Catholic bishops were of Irish ancestry; nine bishops had Italian ancestry. One reason for the paucity of Italian bishops was that there still weren't many Italian priests, a result of the anticlerical attitude many Italian immigrants held. Although Italian Americans had come to support parochial schools, an Italian family might well have discouraged a teenaged boy with an interest in the priesthood from pursuing a path that would produce no children. One Italian American priest from the Bronx, the Reverend Mario Zicarelli, observed in 1970 that when he became a priest, an uncle accused him of destroying the family's good name.

It was said that in the New York archdiocese, it seemed as likely that there would be an Italian cardinal as an Irish pope.[3] Perhaps it still hasn't been erased entirely, but the Irish-Italian divide in the church eventually became more the stuff of church humor, a far cry from the angry division in earlier generations.

We see that transition in the tale of one book in the library of Cathedral Preparatory Seminary, the Diocese of Brooklyn high school for boys with an interest in the priesthood. *Why God Loves the Irish* was written in 1918 by the Milwaukee journalist Humphrey J. Desmond. He wrote this book as a defense of the "Celtic race" at a time when Anglo-Saxon scholars and anti-Catholic nativists were smearing the Irish reputation. Among its gems is the story of a twelve-year-old Italian schoolboy who came to his Irish American teacher to ask for an "American" name: Patrick Dennis McCarthy. Eventually, the book was remaindered from the school library and fell into the hands of Patrick McNamara, a 1986 graduate and former diocesan archivist. He noticed when he opened up *Why God Loves the Irish* that someone had written inside, "And everyone else. Except the Italians!"[4] The Italian-Irish battle in the church survived in the form of schoolboys ribbing each other.

When the Vatican appointed the tenth Irish American archbishop of New York in a row in 2009—every leader of the New York archdiocese had been of Irish ancestry since 1842—no one questioned whether an Italian American candidate was available. A *New York Times* reporter did seek to raise the question of why yet another Irish American, Timothy Dolan, had been chosen to lead an archdiocese that was now nearly half Latino. Wasn't it time for a Latino archbishop? The Latino priests and scholars he spoke to mostly shrugged it off. One of the Latino scholars, himself a former Catholic priest, said half in jest, "We're all Irish Catholics."[5]

* * *

By the 1960s, Italians were taking leadership roles in the bastions of Irish power in New York: the church, the police and fire departments, and political parties. But even as Irish-Italian differences were being laid to rest in the years after World War II, a new rivalry was emerging that would change the city's politics, pitting the interests of white ethnic groups against those of growing new minority communities. From the American South and Puerto Rico came a wave of poor farm people, searching for decent jobs and housing. Like the Italian and Irish immigrants of the nineteenth century, these African American and Latino newcomers hoped to escape rural poverty. But they arrived at a difficult time, since New

York's mighty manufacturing sector had begun to diminish, caus-
ing thousands of jobs to vanish. The result is well known. Poverty
intensified. Crime rose. Welfare increased. Tempers flared, and
riots ensued.

The middle-class interests of the Irish and Italians often col-
lided with those of the new black and Puerto Rican minorities. In
the face of this perceived threat, they united politically. Campaign
operatives no longer talked as much about an "Irish vote" or an
"Italian vote." For political polling purposes, the Irish and Italians
became the bulk of a "white Catholic" vote.

The black vote had grown increasingly important in 1940s
New York, but the citywide tickets still were carefully weighted
to appeal to Italian, Irish, and Jewish voters. When Tammany-
backed William O'Dwyer was elected mayor in 1945, the man from
Mayo won 72 percent of the vote in heavily Italian neighborhoods.
That even beat the 63 percent he won in heavily Irish neighborhoods. O'Dwyer won again in 1949, the fourteenth time in a row
the Democratic candidate for mayor was of Irish descent, dating
back forty years. But O'Dwyer resigned in 1950 at a time when he
faced a police corruption scandal and suffered with poor health.
Sicilian-born Vincent Impellitteri, elected City Council president
on O'Dwyer's ethnically balanced ticket, became acting mayor.[6]

"Impy," as the *Daily News* christened him in headline short-
hand, was married to Eileen Agnes McLaughlin, a blonde, blue-
eyed Irish American he met at a fraternity dance while studying at
Fordham Law. With the mayoral election looming, he made sure
she got press (and credited her with cooking a good plate of spaghetti). Impellitteri defeated two other Italian-born mayoral candidates while running on a third-party slate in a special election
held in 1950. The Tammany boss Carmine De Sapio had granted
the Democratic line to Ferdinand Pecora, a respected judge. Edward Corsi was the Republican candidate. All in all, it was a show
of Italian political power unlike any the city had seen. When City
Hall reporters held their annual Inner Circle show in 1951, they
joked about that in their satirical song-and-dance production. "It's

the same old story all over town," they sang. "Italians are up, the Irish are down."[7]

But actually, the 1950s were a time when the Irish and Italians began to weld into a single political force in the city. One reason was the influence of the Catholic Church. The years after World War II happened to be a time when traditional religion peaked in America. This is seen in high rates of church attendance, especially among young adults in Catholic and mainline Protestant churches. This was particularly true among men of age to have served in World War II combat. Religion was not just a private matter: Polls showed that Americans often invited one another to church. Simply put, churchgoing became the American Way. In 1954 the Pledge of Allegiance was amended to declare that the United States is one nation "under God."[8]

This trend led many more Italian Americans into the church, as for others in American society. In particular, the growing Italian American middle class was attracted to Catholic parochial schools.[9] In New York's Catholic church, that meant participating in a Catholicism that fused God and country. Cardinal Francis Spellman, archbishop of New York and vicar for the U.S. military services, mobilized opinion against communism and built support for warfare in Korea and Vietnam. The underlying influence of the Catholic Church contributed to Irish-Italian political unity.

As the historian Joshua Zeitz writes, the Italians and Irish found a political worldview in Catholic morality and theology—differing from New York's Jews, who tended to view issues through social science. For Catholics, communism was a threat to religion and morality, not just a political or economic enemy. They prayed for the conversion of Russia. Marian devotion, so important to Italian Catholicism, surged in the 1950s, and Mary was implored to defeat the communists. The celebrated Monsignor Fulton J. Sheen, an Irish American televangelist with an audience of many millions, looked to Our Lady of Fatima for help in the fight against communism. He made ten pilgrimages to Fatima and thirty to the Marian shrine in Lourdes.[10] The politics of Italian unification had once divided Irish and Italian Catholics. Now, piety and politics mixed in a way that drew them closer.

Racial tension was an important factor as well. African Americans, of course, had lived in the city from its earliest days; a massive migration of the Irish drove them out of jobs and neighborhoods such as Greenwich Village in the nineteenth century. Later, the Italians did the same to the Irish. Now, it was the blacks and Puerto Ricans who flooded into the city. They were the ones who had trouble getting union jobs, who lacked political clout in proportion to their numbers, who were considered prone to crime, who had sour relations with the police. Inspired by the civil rights movement, they organized politically to seek government jobs, better pay, housing, social programs, and an end to racial discrimination. A new progressive political power emerged: a combine of liberal Jews, blacks, and Puerto Ricans.[11]

By the 1960s, New York's Irish and Italians were political bedfellows. A conservative Catholic worldview had helped to join them, with their unity also strengthened in opposition to rising crime, riots, and black power. Democratic candidates began to feel the sting of their move from the party. In the 1965 mayoral race, about 10 percent of the Irish Catholic vote went to the commentator William F. Buckley, the Conservative Party candidate, as did as much as 20 percent of the Italian vote. That defection from the Democratic ranks helped the liberal Republican John V. Lindsay defeat Abe Beame.

Once in office, Lindsay followed through on a campaign pledge to appoint a majority of non-police members to the board that investigated charges of police misconduct. Black and Puerto Rican leaders and their white liberal allies had been calling for such a board, saying it was needed to curb police brutality. Lindsay's announcement set off a donnybrook, with most of the city's Irish and Italians opposing the new board and blacks and Puerto Ricans heavily in favor. The fight came to a head when the Patrolmen's Benevolent Association put a referendum on the 1966 ballot to defeat Lindsay's plan. The PBA's ranks were heavily Irish, but the union's leader, fifty-three-year-old John Cassese, was the son of immigrants from Naples, thus highlighting the sense that the Irish and Italians were in this fight together. The political war over Lindsay's Civilian Complaint Review Board was extremely divisive. Cassese charged that civilian control would empower criminals and drug addicts. One ad for his campaign showed a white woman cowering in fear near a subway station at night and warned that her life may depend on stopping the civilian review board. Meanwhile, advocates for civilian review tried to link the PBA to neo-Nazis. Lindsay charged that the referendum would lead to "totalitarianism," and said that "the forces of fear and hatred" supported it.

Voters approved the PBA's referendum by a margin of nearly two to one; Lindsay's civilian review was defeated. Nearly nine of every ten Italian and Irish voters (and about eight in ten other non-Hispanic Catholics) opposed the board. Blacks and Puerto Ricans favored it overwhelmingly, while Jewish support was weak because of opposition among working-class Jews. In the end, it was a hugely divisive battle fought over an administrative change that meant relatively little. Even though Lindsay's review board had a civilian majority, it had no power to discipline officers. That authority remained with the police commissioner.[12]

Some five decades earlier, Francis L. Corrao had raged at the city's law enforcement community over its treatment of his people. Italians saw themselves as a minority group the Irish-controlled Police Department at best misunderstood. That was no longer the case. A detailed survey of Brooklyn voters conducted by experts at Harvard University and MIT found that Italians actually outpaced the Irish in their opposition to the Civilian Complaint Review Board. Significantly, a majority of white Catholics had a close friend or relative in the Police Department. During the 1960s and for years later, there could still be an "us versus them" attitude between the Irish and the Italians within the police and fire departments. But they were united in opposition to the political goals of liberal, black, and Hispanic activists. The Harvard-MIT study concluded, "Irish and Italian Catholics, apparently because of their close group identification with the police force and their larger representation in the working and lower middle class, opposed the board by a tremendous majority."[13]

*   *   *

On the day of New York's second-worst blizzard of the century, January 8, 1996, Deputy Mayor Peter Powers took some time out to make pizzas. He had worked in an Italian-owned pizzeria as a teenager growing up in an Irish American home in Middle Village, Queens. He knew how to flip the dough in the air. One time, it slipped off his hands and splashed into a pot of sauce when he was showing off for some neighborhood girls.

With the city trying to dig out from more than two feet of snow, Powers had stopped off in a pizzeria near City Hall on Chambers Street to get pizzas for city 911 operators working long hours at police headquarters. Forty pies were cooked; he made fifteen of them himself. They were turned over to Powers's high school classmate, Mayor Rudy Giuliani, who handled the delivery.[14]

By the time Giuliani was elected mayor in 1993, the Irish-Italian union in city politics was as casual as that. Powers's grandparents came from Ireland, and Giuliani's from Tuscany and near Naples. The two became best friends at Bishop Loughlin Memorial High School in Brooklyn, with Powers even agreeing to Giuliani's request to join the opera club he formed. They went on double dates, and then were godfathers to each other's children. Their differing temperaments were reflected in the routes they took after law school: Powers was a tax lawyer, and Giuliani a federal prosecutor who rose to fame by imprisoning mobsters. Powers was the more diplomatic of the two; Giuliani had the fire. When Giuliani ran for office, he turned to Powers to be his campaign manager and then deputy mayor.

The foundation of Giuliani's mayoral campaigns was the white Catholic vote—essentially an Irish-Italian alliance, along with other Catholic voters of European ancestry. Giuliani spoke their language, often in a moralistic way. Going back to his days as a star federal prosecutor, he reveled in his image as a crusader against evil. As the U.S. attorney in Manhattan in the 1980s, Giuliani didn't want to just put wrongdoers in prison. He consciously set out to transform the ethical climate in politics and on Wall Street through his prosecutions of political corruption and insider trading. His investigations of organized crime were showcased as a battle against evil, with the tabloid newspapers presenting him as a modern-day Eliot Ness. While he had a good sense of humor in private, his crime-busting public image was stern and severe. He dismayed some Italians who thought he hyped the threat of the Mafia, but Giuliani reveled in his organized crime cases. He imitated the gravelly voice of Don Corleone in *The Godfather*, even for campaign audiences, and after he announced a massive Sicilian heroin-trafficking case, he willingly dubbed it the "Pizza Connection" at the behest of a *Daily News* reporter. All in all, Giuliani struck a chord with white Catholic voters, especially those of Italian ancestry. His themes of discipline, order, and personal responsibility resonated with them.[15] But his critics accused him of running divisive campaigns that played on white resentment against minorities.

Giuliani lost his first race for mayor, in 1989, when Manhattan Borough President David Dinkins was elected New York's first black mayor. But he won in 1993, in part because of gains in the Jewish vote. In the second race, Giuliani hammered on Dinkins's failure to promptly quell anti-Hasidic rioting in Brooklyn's Crown Heights section in 1991, and won enough of the Jewish vote to edge out the incumbent.

The Irish-influenced Catholicism of 1950s New York left a strong imprint on Giuliani. It came primarily through his schooling; he attended Catholic schools right through his bachelor's degree at Manhattan College. There were other sources of this influence as well. His family was immersed in the Irish American world of the police and fire departments, with four of his uncles serving as police officers and one as a fire captain. And the tough federal judge who became his professional mentor was a devout Catholic with Irish ancestry. While Irish political clout in New York had weakened by the time Giuliani ran for mayor, Irish influence lived on in the culture of such institutions as the Catholic Church and the police and fire departments. Giuliani, the Italian American who dominated New York City politics in the 1990s, came of age in a world suffused with that influence.

The starting point was his schooling. "The first time I attended a class in which a prayer wasn't said at the beginning of class was my first day at NYU Law School," Giuliani said while campaigning for president in 2007.

In 1957 he enrolled as a freshman at Bishop Loughlin, a diocesan high school. His teachers were the black-robed De La Salle Christian Brothers. Although the order's origins were in France, it manifested a strong Irish influence that dated to the nineteenth century. The De La Salle Christian Brothers (not to be confused with the Irish Christian Brothers) educated many of New York's priests in their schools.[16]

Under the Christian Brothers' instruction, young Rudy seriously considered entering the priesthood. By his senior year, he was a member of the school's Catechism Club, offering religious instruction to children in poor neighborhoods. He visited Jesuit, Franciscan, and diocesan seminaries to see whether one might be right for him.

Giuliani and Peter Powers became close friends, going on to Manhattan College together after graduating from Bishop Loughlin in 1961 and from there to New York University Law School. Powers was the Republican, even though his father had been an organizer and delegate for the American Federation of Labor. Giuliani was the Democrat; he gave a speech in support of John F. Kennedy for president at a school assembly in 1960. While Powers lived in the city, Giuliani was a suburbanite. When he was a boy, his parents moved from Brooklyn to Garden City and then to North Bellmore, both on Long Island. He commuted to school on the Long Island Rail Road. The discipline of the education he received is seen in a story that the journalist Wayne Barrett relates in his biography of Giuliani: Brother Jack O'Leary smacked young Rudy in the head for wisecracking in class. O'Leary, Giuliani, and his family later became close, with Giuliani's father seeking the brother's advice and help.[17]

After law school, Giuliani found an important mentor in U.S. District Court Judge Lloyd F. MacMahon, who gave him a prestigious position as a law clerk. MacMahon, who had successfully prosecuted the gangster Frank Costello on income tax charges in 1955, was a devout Catholic with Irish ancestry.[18] Giuliani credited him as a mentor; they remained close. From many directions—his schooling, his family connection to the police and fire departments, his friends, and his professional mentor—Giuliani was exposed to an Irish Catholic ethic that emphasized morality, discipline, and service.

As Powers recalled, it was easy for the Irish and Italian kids to get along when he was young. In 1950s and 1960s New York, the Irish-Italian rivalry from days of yore wasn't entirely gone. At times, differences remained. But, Powers said, "I didn't sense that growing up." He paused. "Obviously we had different cuisines. You certainly wanted to eat over your Italian friend's house."

Powers said the Catholic Church had drawn together young people of Irish and Italian ancestry. "They went to grammar school together, then you have the high schools," he said. "When you put kids together as kids, they grow up together. . . . You liked a girl, you liked her. You didn't ask if she was Irish or Italian."[19]

Giuliani's political success showed that as the twentieth century came to a close, the Italian-Irish alliance still had some life. But at the same time, Giuliani's divisive dealings with minorities badly alienated black voters; he had frosty relations with most of New York's African American leaders. Critics said his 1993 campaign slogan, "One City, One Standard," had a racial undertone.

Notably, Giuliani hardly allowed Catholic prelates to dictate his political positions or even his personal life. He vigorously supported abortion rights and, during his second term, publicly announced his divorce from his second wife, Donna Hanover. But he spoke Catholic, and his 1950s Catholic upbringing in a family closely tied to the police and fire departments was readily reflected in many of his mayoral decisions. That was the case when he tried to evict the Brooklyn Museum from its city-owned building in 1999 because of his outrage over the exhibit of a painting of the Virgin Mary with components that included elephant dung and tiny images of genitalia cut out from magazines. (A federal judge ruled that Giuliani's plan violated the museum's First Amendment rights.) It was also seen in his steady and sometimes emotional defense of the Police Department against its critics, which further alienated the black community.

During his second term, New Yorkers tired of the judgmental nature of this worldview, which was on display even as Giuliani's family life broke down in public. But the Catholic ethic instilled in him in his youth—of discipline, service, and faith—flowered on what he later called the worst day of his life, September 11, 2001. While the terrorist attack that crumbled the World Trade Center brought together New Yorkers of many races, religions, and nationalities, the Catholic sensibility played an important role in the city's brave response. Perhaps that is to be expected in a city where about two in every five residents were Catholics. But it is more so the case because of the traditionally Irish Catholic culture of the police and fire departments, which bore the brunt of the city's response to the attack.

Giuliani's description of the early moments after the attack is a good indication of the Irish-Italian role on that day. As he told it, the first person he spoke with upon reaching the burning trade center was Father Mychal Judge, the Fire Department chaplain. Judge was proudly Irish American, the son of immigrants from County Leitrim. Giuliani asked the priest to pray for him, as he always did. Judge normally responded, "It would be better if you prayed for yourself. It would be more unusual." But on that day—on which Judge would die—the priest tensely answered, "Yes." After stopping to observe a man hurl himself down from the 102nd floor of a burning tower, a shocked Giuliani sought out Peter Ganci, chief of the Fire Department, who had set up a command center at one of the towers. Ganci was an Italian American who grew up in the Irish-Italian world of the suburbs, attending St. Kilian's School in Farmingdale. "My guys can save everybody below the fire," Giuliani recalled hearing from Ganci, who died when the second of the towers collapsed.

One scholar estimated that at least 69 of the 343 firefighters who died had Italian origins, and the number with Irish surnames is even larger.[20] Most of the firefighters and Port Authority and city police officers laid to rest were Catholic, and the mournful bagpipes and solemn homilies, very often from Irish American churchmen, gave the funerals a distinctly Irish Catholic feel, over and over in the weeks after the attack. The Catholic imagery that emerged also reflected the Catholic sensibility that resonated in the city's response. There was Father Mychal Judge's lifeless body, set on the safe ground of the altar at St. Peter's Church, New York's oldest Catholic parish, after he was killed. There was also the reaction to the cross-shaped pair of steel beams that the construction worker Frank Silecchia, a born-again Christian, spotted in the trade center's wreckage. It became the World Trade Center cross, blessed by a Franciscan friar, Father Brian Jordan. Many viewed it as a sacred relic.[21]

In remarks he made at Manhattan College a decade after the attack, Giuliani summarized his own sense of that when he spoke of the sacrifice that the firefighters and police officers had made:

That's an awesome bravery. That's also incredible love, a tremendous demonstration of love that you would stand your ground knowing that you could die because you could save other people. And many of them, not all of them, were taught that love in Catholic education. Because the overwhelming number of those firefighters and police officers were Catholics. I know that from the many services that I went to. . . . And faith was a very, very large part of why they were able to do what they did: their belief in human life is important, in individual human life, even of a stranger, is enormously important, that you have duties and obligations, that if it is your job to be a firefighter, it's your job to lay down your life if you have to save someone else. And without that background, training, value system, I don't know that this country would have been able to get through September 11th as well as it did.[22]

This is the same ethic of service and sacrifice that Donegal-born police commissioner William McAdoo had described in his 1906 book *Guarding a Great City*: how "the Irish spirit permeates all ranks of the police," including the officers who were not Irish, mainly Germans and some Italians at that time. Nearly a century later, it was still part of the life of a great city.[23]

By 2001, the old hatreds between New York's Irish and Italians were a mostly forgotten story, except to those with very long memories. Italians had leadership roles in the old Irish bastions of power: the church, the police and fire departments, City Hall. For political purposes, the Irish and Italians were fused into one entity, constituting much of the white Catholic vote in the city and well beyond on Long Island and in New Jersey and Connecticut.

In some ways, it is a happy ending, a story that started with rumbles and ended in romance. But in other ways, it is not. There are still distinct racial and ethnic boundaries in New York, where schools and neighborhoods are heavily segregated by race, and ethnic niches continue to be a prominent feature of the job market. The Irish and Italians overcame their rivalry with each other, but were now at odds with blacks and Latinos, certainly in politics at least. Can the rumbles-to-romance story of New York's Irish and Italians suggest some ways to overcome the ethnic and racial divisions that have been so much a part of the city's history? Perhaps there are lessons to be learned.

Conclusion

The saga of the Irish and the Italians in New York holds many shades of meaning, as all good stories do. For me, researching this book was a steady reminder of my own humble origins: that supposed authorities in government and academia had judged the blood my Italian ancestors bequeathed to me to be inferior. The same can be said for the Irish, who bore the brunt of anti-Catholic sentiment that remained powerful at least until the election of President John F. Kennedy in 1960. It's a simple fact that both were immigrant peoples, but it's easy to forget.

U.S. Catholic bishops are strong supporters of immigrant rights, much as they were in the days when the Irish and Italians were arriving in large numbers. But their campaign has not won very strong support among white Catholics, whom polls show to be only slightly more pro-immigrant than the public as a whole. Pew Research Center polling has found white Catholics evenly divided on the question of whether immigrants are a strength or a burden for the country, while Latino Catholics overwhelmingly saw immigrants as a boon.[1]

Still, there may be ways that the peace New York's Italians and Irish reached after decades of discord can be instructive for easing conflicts. As we have seen, New York's Italians and Irish at first fought it out in the church, the workplace, unions, and eventually in politics before finding common ground. The church was an important engine for this rapprochement, helping to lead many an

Italian-Irish couple to the altar. A national surge in religious devotion in the 1950s brought more of the Italians through the church doors and into the growing parochial school system. But other venues mattered as well. As the Italians advanced economically, they mingled more frequently with the Irish as equals in the workplace. A strong economy after World War II meant plenty of jobs, and less rivalry for them.[2] They served together in the military, and were welcomed home together on the docks of New York Harbor to a thunderous acclaim that overrode old ethnic boundaries. Then they joined the same veterans' associations and fraternal organizations. New highways and bridges brought them to the suburbs and the city's residential areas, far from their onetime Manhattan enclaves. They settled in as neighbors in new homes built with the help of federal loan insurance. Then their children befriended each other through the schools. So did the parents. These are among the reasons that New York's Irish and Italians were able to set aside their rivalry and become family.

Attitudes changed when the Irish and Italians really got to know each other as equals in schools, churches, and on the job, at least among young people. That led to a wave of intermarriage. We can see the same phenomenon, especially in the American West, where a growing number of couples have one Hispanic partner, according to the 2010 U.S. census. In Arizona, a state known for anti-immigration laws, 9 percent of the married couples had one Hispanic partner, as did 18 percent of the unmarried heterosexual couples living together. The percentages were higher still in California and Nevada. Nationally, couples classified as interracial or interethnic grew 28 percent between 2000 and 2010, the Census Bureau found.[3]

These numbers show that even in the midst of a divisive national debate over immigration, we can see some accord in the West between non-Hispanic whites and Hispanics, despite a history of conflict. This is also true for Asian Americans, who historically have suffered from venomous discrimination. More than half of Asian American marriages are with partners who are not Asian in origin. This doesn't mean an end to anti-Asian discrimination, but it does show that barriers are softening. As sociologists tell us, when the social boundaries blur between once-antagonistic groups, intermarriage can follow. That is what happened to New York's Irish and Italians, and it is happening again. The term "Irican" is used in New York and elsewhere for the children of Irish-Puerto Rican marriages, and in general for those of Irish-Hispanic origin.[4]

But it is uncertain whether intermarriage could occur for white-black relationships on a large scale, given how embedded racial discrimination has been in the American story. Even so, the sociologist Richard Alba has suggested that it is at least possible that the conditions that brought white ethnic groups such as the Irish and Italians together could apply to whites and blacks.

As we've seen for the Irish and Italians, larger social forces are behind their accord. One of the factors Alba points to is that there must be enough jobs so that the up-and-coming group doesn't have to take work away from the established group. That was the case for the Irish and Italians after World War II, he writes. We've seen that when the economy soured in the 1890s and yielded fewer jobs, violent confrontations between Italian and Irish workers were frequent. "Can't they be separated?" the *Brooklyn Eagle* asked. In the growing post–World War II economy, it was much easier to be friends in the workplace.

Another factor is social proximity: that the groups have an opportunity to mingle. Catholic parishes and schools helped to provide that common ground for the Irish and Italians. Also, new modes of transportation, starting with the subway and continuing with a slew of highways, bridges, and tunnels, broke up the old ethnic enclaves and created new neighborhoods where the Irish and the Italians could mingle in city and suburb. A third condition Alba sees is that the minority comes to be seen as having the same moral worth as the majority—which Italians seemed to have accomplished in part through their wartime role and through the successes of people like Joe DiMaggio, Frank Sinatra, and Fiorello La Guardia.

Alba cautiously writes of the possible opportunity for the same to occur in black-white relations. He envisions the exit of Baby Boomers from the job market as a significant moment when many better-paid jobs will be vacated, easing some of the competition for jobs and opening the way for minorities.[5]

If demographic forecasts are correct, interracial and interethnic marriage would have to increase. The Pew Research Center predicted that by 2060, the nation will be just 43 percent white. Its researchers noted that while Baby Boomers view interracial marriage as healthy for the nation, their children see it as simply a normal part of life.[6]

In the end, even when complex social forces are accounted for, we are still dealing with the stories of individuals who decide to cross boundaries. Among the Irish and Italians, some did it out of cunning, like Paul Vaccarelli and Big Tim Sullivan. Others did it for love, as in the stories of the Burke, Cronin, Bradley, and Macchiarola families. There was the passionately shared idealism of Elizabeth Gurley Flynn and Carlo Tresca. There is the sense that some of the Irish who resented the Italian "invasion," such as Father Thomas Lynch and Terence Powderly, saw the Italians in a better light later in life. Mother Cabrini may have turned Archbishop Corrigan's face red with anger in their first meeting, but the two worked well together after that. Bing Crosby and Frank Sinatra played their supposed rivalry for laughs. Fiorello La Guardia ended up on friendly terms with Jimmy Walker. Marie Bradley got even with the Irish by marrying one. And for so many young couples of Irish and Italian origin, there were songs of love, giddy processions from the altar, and babies.

The more individuals overcome social boundaries, the more likely it is that ethnic and racial resentments—which are so ruinous to American life—will diminish. Coming as it did after decades of contention and bitterness, the postwar peace of New York's Irish and Italians tells us that it is at least a possibility to hope for.

NOTES

ABBREVIATIONS

CMS: Center for Migration Studies.

AANY: Archives of the Archdiocese of New York.

All census, passport, Social Security death index, and draft registration records were accessed at www.ancestry.com unless otherwise noted.

INTRODUCTION

1 Jimmy Breslin, *The Gang That Couldn't Shoot Straight* (New York: Viking, 1969), 85.

2 Eliot Lord, John J. D. Trevor, and Samuel J. Barrows, *The Italian in America* (New York: Benjamin F. Buck, 1905), 68–69; *Oxford English Dictionary Online*, s.v. "Dago," accessed March 2014.

3 John Talbot Smith, *The Catholic Church in New York: A History of the New York Diocese from Its Establishment in 1808 to the Present* (New York: Hall and Locke, 1905), 2:471.

4 "F. P. A. Vaccarelli, Union Leader, Dies," *New York Times*, April 5, 1936, N10.

5 "Reasons for Rejecting Grace," *New York Times*, November 2, 1880, 4.

CHAPTER 1. "GARIBALDI AND HIS HORDES"

1 For Garibaldi in New York throughout this chapter, see *New York Herald*, June 30, July 13, July 25, 1850; *New York Tribune*, July 1, July 30, and August 5, 1850, March 7, 1851; George Macaulay Trevelyan, *Garibaldi the Thousand* (London: Longmans, Green, 1912), 14; Jasper Ridley, *Garibaldi* (New York: Viking, 1976), 356–64; H. Nelson Gay, "Garibaldi's American Contacts and His Claims to American Citizenship," *American Historical Review* 38 (October 1932): 5; Anne O'Connor, "'That Dangerous Serpent': Garibaldi and Ireland in the Nineteenth Century," *Modern Italy* 15 (2010): 401–15; Henry Tyrrell, "Garibaldi in New York," *Century*, June 1907, 174–84; Howard Marraro, *American Opinion on the Unification of Italy* (New York: Columbia University Press, 1932).

2 Patrick J. Blessing, "Irish," in *Harvard Encyclopedia of American Ethnic Groups*, ed. Stephan Thernstrom (Cambridge: Harvard University Press, 1980), 524–45, 525, 529; Hasia R. Diner, "'The Most Irish City in the Union': The Era of the Great Migration, 1844–1877," in *The New York Irish*, ed. Ronald H. Bayor and Timothy J. Meagher (Baltimore: Johns Hopkins University Press, 1996), 87–105, 89–91; David Noel Doyle, "The Remaking of Irish America, 1845–1880," in *Making the Irish*

American: History and Heritage of the Irish in the United States, ed. J. J. Lee and Marion R. Casey (New York: New York University Press, 2006), 213–52.

3 Lawrence Kehoe, ed., *Complete Works of the Most Reverend John Hughes, D.D.* (New York: Lawrence Kehoe, 1866), 2:791.

4 "Circular to the Clergy of New-York," June 20, 1849, in Kehoe, *Complete Works of the Most Reverend John Hughes,* 2:21.

5 Ibid., 2:23, 27–28.

6 Harold J. Abramson, *Ethnic Diversity in Catholic America* (New York: Wiley, 1973), 130–33, 136–39, summarizes the scholarly literature on this.

7 Frederick M. Binder and David M. Reimers, *All the Nations under Heaven: An Ethnic and Racial History of New York City* (New York: Columbia University Press, 1995), 135.

8 "Father Gavazzi in New-York," *New York Times,* March 24, 1853, 1; "Father Gavazzi's First Free Lecture," *New York Times,* April 27, 1853, 8; *Father Gavazzi's Lectures in New York, reported in full by T. C. Leland, phonographer; also, The Life of Father Gavazzi, corrected and authorized by himself; together with reports of his addresses in Italian, to his countrymen in New York, translated and revised by Madame Julie de Marguerittes* (New York: Dewitt and Davenport, 1858), 76, 78; Patrick Lynch letters: *New York Times,* March 25, March 31, April 28, 1853; Richard Shaw, *Dagger John: The Unquiet Life and Times of Archbishop John Hughes of New York* (New York: Paulist, 1977), 277. The Irish in London took part in anti-Garibaldi riots in 1862. See "Garibaldian Riots in Hyde Park," *New York Times,* October 22, 1862, 8.

9 "Excitement at Montreal," *New York Times,* June 11, 1853, 1; "The Gavazzi Riot at Montreal," *New York Times,* June 14, 1853, 3; "The Canada Rule," *New York Times,* June 16, 1853, 4.

10 Ridley, *Garibaldi,* 357; "Sicily and Italy," *New York Times,* June 19, 1860, 4; C. T. McIntire, *England against the Papacy, 1858–1861* (Cambridge: Cambridge University Press, 1983), 24, 201–2.

11 Naughten letter: reprinted in *New York Times,* June 20, 1860, 2. See also "The Papal States—Irish Recruits against Liberty," *New York Times,* June 20, 1860, 2; "The Pope's Irish Recruits," *New York Times,* July 9, 1860, 4; "The Irish at Home and Abroad," *Harper's,* July 7, 1860, 418.

12 Elizabeth Barrett Browning, *The Letters of Elizabeth Barrett Browning,* ed. Frederic G. Kenyon (New York: Macmillan, 1899), 398.

13 John R. G. Hassard, *Life of the Most Reverend John Hughes, D.D., First Archbishop of New York* (New York: Appleton, 1866), 431.

14 G. F.-H. Berkeley, *The Irish Battalion in the Papal Army of 1860* (Dublin: Talbot, 1929), 217. A monument located near the Rocca in Spoleto lists the names of fifteen Italians killed in the fighting.

15 "The Defeat of the Papal Levies," *New York Times,* October 5, 1860, 2; October 13, 1860, 2; November 6, 1860, 2.

16 Michael J. A. McCaffery, *The Siege of Spoleto: A Camp-Tale of Arlington Heights* (New York: P. O'Shea, 1864).

17 Thomas J. Shelley, *The Bicentennial History of the Archdiocese of New York, 1808–2008* (Strasbourg, France: Éditions du Signe, 2007), 107.

18 Smith, *The Catholic Church in New York,* 2:382. Recruiting in United States: Howard R. Marraro, "Canadian and American Zouaves in the Papal Army, 1868–1870,"

CCHA Report 12 (1944–45): 83–102, http://www.umanitoba.ca/colleges/st_pauls/ccha/ Back%20Issues/CCHA1944–45/Marraro.html, accessed June 10, 2010.

19 "Religious: Sermons in the Churches of New York Yesterday," *New York Times*, November 28, 1870, 5.

20 "Diocese of Many Tongues and Races," *New York Tribune*, April 19, 1908, 5.

21 Rudolph J. Vecoli, "Prelates and Peasants: Italian Immigrants and the Catholic Church," *Journal of Social History* 2 (Spring 1969): 222.

22 "La chiesa italiana in Nuova York," *L'Eco d'Italia*, August 19, 1874, 1. See also Howard Ralph Weisz, *Irish-American and Italian-American Educational Views and Activities, 1870–1900: A Comparison* (New York: Arno, 1976), 376; Joseph M. White, *"Peace and Good" in America: A History of the Holy Name Province Order of Friars Minor, 1850 to the Present* (New York: Holy Name Province, 2004).

23 Emmet Larkin, "The Devotional Revolution in Ireland, 1850–1875," *American Historical Review* 77 (June 1972): 649.

24 Giuseppe Garibaldi, *The Life of General Garibaldi, Written by Himself*, trans. Theodore Dwight (New York: Barnes and Burr, 1859), 233.

CHAPTER 2. "THE ITALIAN PROBLEM"

1 Thomas J. Shelley, *Greenwich Village Catholics: St. Joseph's Church and the Evolution of an Urban Faith Community, 1829–2002* (Washington, DC: Catholic University of America Press, 2003), 71; John Gilmary Shea, *Catholic Churches of New York City: Sketches of Their History and Lives of the Present Pastors* (New York: Lawrence G. Goulding, 1878), 158–60; "Close of St. Ann's Church Fair," *New York Times*, May 8, 1881, 5.

2 Tyler Anbinder, *Five Points: The 19th-Century New York City Neighborhood That Invented Tap Dance, Stole Elections and Became the World's Most Notorious Slum* (New York: Free Press, 2001), 1.

3 "In the Italian Quarter," *New York Sun*, August 22, 1880, 6.

4 Robert D. Putnam and David E. Campbell, *American Grace: How Religion Divides and Unites Us* (New York: Simon and Schuster, 2010), 260–319; Will Herberg, *Protestant—Catholic—Jew: An Essay in American Religious Sociology* (Garden City, NY: Doubleday, 1955), 40.

5 Ira Rosenwaike, *Population History of New York City* (Syracuse: Syracuse University Press, 1972), 73; Jay P. Dolan, *The Irish Americans: A History* (New York: Bloomsbury, 2008), 141. On the Irish struggle for urban power, see William V. Shannon, *The American Irish* (London: Macmillan, 1966), 27–46.

6 Anbinder, *Five Points*, 51.

7 "Italians Flocking Home," *New York Sun*, August 25, 1884, 1. Irish Americans were on their way to becoming highly urbanized, a remarkable transition from rural life. See Doyle, "The Remaking of Irish America," 225.

8 "Battle in Mulberry Street," *New York Sun*, March 24, 1884, 1; "None of the Irishmen Arrested," *New York Times*, March 25, 1884, 8.

9 Irene Whelan, "The Stigma of Souperism," in *The Great Irish Famine*, ed. Cathal Poirteir (Cork: Mercier, 1995), 135–54.

10 See James R. Barrett, *The Irish Way: Becoming American in the Multiethnic City* (New York: Penguin, 2012), 75–85; Irene Whelan, "Religious Rivalry and the Making of

Irish-American Identity," in Lee and Casey, *Making the Irish American*, 279–80; Anbinder, *Five Points*, 380, 497.

11 James R. Barrett and David R. Roediger, "The Irish and the 'Americanization' of the 'New Immigrants' in the Streets and in the Churches of the Urban United States, 1900–1930," *Journal of American Ethnic History* 24 (Summer 2005): 23.

12 "Report on the Italian Population and on the Church of the Transfiguration on Mott Street, by the Reverend Thomas Lynch, Rector of the Same Church," 1885, and Corrigan to Jacobini, November 18, 1885, in *For the Love of Immigrants: Migration Writings and Letters of Bishop John Baptist Scalabrini, 1839–1905*, ed. Silvano Tomasi (New York: Center for Migration Studies, 2000), 164–65, 171.

13 Lynch to Preston, September 20, 1886, CMS, Italians and Religion Box 1, Transfiguration file.

14 Sacred Congregation for the Propagation of the Faith, "Report on Italian Immigration" (November 1887), in Tomasi, *For the Love of Immigrants*, 146.

15 Bernard J. Lynch, "The Italians in New York," *Catholic World* 47 (April 1888): 71–72; *The College of St. Francis of Xavier: A Memorial and a Retrospect, 1847–1897* (New York: Meany, 1897), 248. The college was closed in 1913, but Xavier High School remains. See "Fordham College at Lincoln Center: A Brief History," www.fordham.edu/academics/colleges__graduate_s/undergraduate_colleg/fordham_college_at_l/a_brief/history/22305.asp, accessed December 4, 2010. Thomas J. Shelley, the historian of the Archdiocese of New York, has argued that Father Lynch authored the article under Bernard's name. See Shelley, *Greenwich Village Catholics*, 134. See also Anbinder, *Five Points*, 380–82; Mary Elizabeth Brown, *Churches, Communities, and Children: Italian Immigrants in the Archdiocese of New York, 1880–1945* (New York: Center for Migration Studies, 1995), 36–40.

16 Vecoli, "Prelates and Peasants," 244. De Concilio's pamphlet is contained in Raffaele Bellerini, "Delle condizioni religiose degli emigrati italiani negli Stati Uniti d'America," *Civilta Cattolica* 11 (1888): 641–53, CMS.

17 Stephen Michael DiGiovanni, *Archbishop Corrigan and the Italian Immigrants* (Huntington, IN: Our Sunday Visitor, 1994), 99–101, 241; Silvano M. Tomasi, *Piety and Power: The Role of Italian Parishes in the New York Metropolitan Area, 1880–1930* (New York: Center for Migration Studies, 1975), 222; Brown, *Churches, Communities, and Children*, 65.

18 De Concilio, in Bellerini, "Delle condizioni religiose."

19 Historical Census Browser, University of Virginia, Geospatial and Statistical Data Center, http://mapserver.lib.virginia.edu/collections/stats/histcensus/index.html, accessed January 3, 2014. New York County included the Bronx, where relatively few Italians lived at the time.

20 *Memorial of the Most Reverend Michael Augustine Corrigan, D.D.* (New York: Cathedral Library Association, 1902), 2–3, 70; "Archbishop Is Dead," *New York Tribune*, May 6, 1902, 1; Shelley, *Bicentennial History of the Archdiocese of New York*, 391–93. Description: National Archives and Records Administration, U.S. passport applications for Michael A. Corrigan, dated August 26, 1857, and January 25, 1887.

21 Frederick J. Zwierlein, *The Life and Letters of Bishop McQuaid* (Rochester, NY: Art Print Shop, 1926), 2:333–35.

22 Gibbons Correspondence relating to Italians, 1879–1916, copy, CMS, Saint Raphael Society Records, Box 1; Gibbons and Becker to Simeoni, January 13, 1885, Archives,

Archdiocese of Baltimore, copy in CMS, St. Raphael Society, Box 1, trans. from Latin by Silvano M. Tomasi and Edward C. Stibili.

23 Tomasi, *For the Love of Immigrants*, 3, 5.

24 Scalabrini to Corrigan, August 18, 1887, CMS, St. Raphael Society Records, Box 1, copy; Corrigan to Scalabrini, April 13, 1888, CMS, St. Raphael Society Records, Box 1, copy; Tomasi, *For the Love of Immigrants*, 236, 243.

25 Pope Leo XIII, *Quam Aerumnosa*, December 10, 1888, www.vatican.va/holy_father/leo_xiii/encyclicals/documents/hf_l-xiii_enc_10121888_quam-aerumnosa_en.html, accessed January 5, 2011; Lice Maria Signor, *John Baptist Scalabrini and Italian Migration: A Socio-Pastoral Project* (New York: Center for Migration Studies, 1994), 180.

26 "The Pope to American Bishops," *New York Times*, December 13, 1888, 1; "Italian Emigrants," *New York Sun*, December 13, 1888, 2; "The Papal Letter," *New York Times*, January 3, 1889, 5; Thomas S. Preston, "The Italians of New York City," *New York Sun*, January 15, 1889, 5.

27 Corrigan to Scalabrini, February 5, 1889, in Tomasi, *For the Love of Immigrants*, 254–55; Stephen Michael DiGiovanni, "Mother Cabrini: Early Years in New York," *Catholic Historical Review* 77 (January 1991): 60–69; *Cabrini Sisters, MSC, Celebrate a Centennial of Loving Service in the USA* (Missionary Sisters of the Sacred Heart of Jesus, 1989), in CMS.

28 Mary Louise Sullivan, *Mother Cabrini: "Italian Immigrant of the Century"* (New York: Center for Migration Studies, 1992), 79, citing the daughter of Mary di Cesnola, a wealthy New Yorker who planned the orphanage and assisted Cabrini. Her daughter, Gabriella, spoke in the proceedings leading to Mother Cabrini's canonization. She was recounting what her mother had told her.

29 Ibid., 78.

30 Ibid., 73, citing letter of April 11, 1889.

31 David R. Roediger, *Working toward Whiteness: How America's Immigrants Became White* (New York: Basic, 2006), 37–40.

32 Sullivan, *Mother Cabrini*, 78, citing "Memorie Stati Uniti," 44, 66, 59.

33 Corrigan to Scalabrini, May 8, 1889, in Tomasi, *For the Love of Immigrants*, 258.

34 Sullivan, *Mother Cabrini*, 80, citing "Memorie Stati Uniti," 62–63; DiGiovanni, *Archbishop Corrigan*, 187.

35 DiGiovanni, *Archbishop Corrigan*, 193, citing Mother Cabrini to Cardinal Ledóchowski, December 20, 1894.

CHAPTER 3. TIPPING POINT

1 "Old St. Patrick's Church," *New York Times*, May 5, 1890, 8.

2 Thernstrom, *Harvard Encyclopedia of American Ethnic Groups*, 413.

3 "Catholics in America," *New York Times*, July 1, 1891, 1.

4 Background on Kearney: "Old St. Patrick's Boys Dine," *New York Times*, May 11, 1909; Smith, *The Catholic Church in New York*, 2:599; *Souvenir of the Centennial Celebration of St. Patrick's Old Cathedral, 1809–1909* (New York, 1909), 16. AANY, St. Patrick's Cathedral (Old) file.

5 "A Street Fight," *New York Times*, March 29, 1880, 5. See also "A Wounded Italian Boy's Story," *New York Times*, August 16, 1881, 8; "A Boy Shot without Provocation," *New York Tribune*, August 16, 1881, 8; "Stabbed by Unknown Men," *New York Tribune*, December 26, 1881, 8.

6 Thomas Kessner, *The Golden Door: Italian and Jewish Immigrant Mobility in New York City, 1880–1915* (New York: Oxford University Press, 1977), 16.

7 "Assimilation of the Italian," *New York Sun*, April 2, 1899, 7; National Archives and Records Administration, U.S. passport application for Raffaele Asselta, October 20, 1893.

8 Kearney's report, "Old St. Patrick's Parish," is undated but the context indicates it was written in the first half of January 1889. CMS. John R. McKivigan and Thomas R. Robertson, "The Irish American Worker in Transition, 1877–1914," in Bayor and Meagher, *The New York Irish*, 302.

9 Edwin G. Burrows and Mike Wallace, *Gotham: A History of New York City to 1898* (New York: Oxford University Press, 1999), 1111–12.

10 See Mary Elizabeth Brown, "The Making of Italian-American Catholics: Jesuit Work on the Lower East Side, New York, 1890's–1950's," *Catholic Historical Review* 73 (April 1987): 195–201.

11 David Dunford, "Incardination and Excardination," in *Catholic Encyclopedia*, oce. catholic.com, accessed January 21, 2011; Brown, *Churches, Communities, and Children*, 68.

12 "The Rev. Philip Cardella Dead," *New York Sun*, June 19, 1901, 4; *Sadliers' Catholic Directory* (New York: Sadlier, 1891), 46; *Annual Report of the Regents, University of the State of New York* (Albany: James B. Lyon, 1890), 2:103, 363; "The Catholic Conference," *New York Times*, February 8, 1891, 9.

13 Russo to Corrigan, undated in 1891, CMS, IAR Box 1.

14 Nicholas Russo, "The Origin and Progress of Our Italian Mission in New York," *Woodstock Letters* 25 (1896): 135–43.

15 Smith, *The Catholic Church in New York*, 2:471; "Rev. John Talbot Smith, Sacred Heart Pastor Dies," *Dobbs Ferry (NY) Register*, September 28, 1923, 1, accessed at www.findagrave.com; 1880 U.S. Census for John Smith, Cohoes, NY.

16 Russo to Corrigan, May 3, 1891, CMS, IAR Box 1; "A New Italian Church," *New York Times*, September 18, 1892, 17.

17 Russo to Corrigan, October 24, 1891, CMS, IAR Box 1.

18 "For Italians to Worship In," *New York Times*, September 26, 1892, 9.

19 Russo to Corrigan, February 22, 1898, CMS, IAR Box 1.

20 Smith, *The Catholic Church in New York*, 2:421, 462.

21 *Souvenir of the Centennial Celebration*, 20.

22 1920 U.S. Census for Henry P. Tracy, Bronx, Assembly District 6.

23 *Souvenir of the Centennial Celebration*.

24 1900 U.S. Census for Ellen L. McInerney, Manhattan, Assembly District 2; 1920 U.S. Census for Monica Maria McInerney, Manhattan, Assembly District 2.

25 Binder and Reimers, *All the Nations under Heaven*, 102; Sister Marie de Lourdes Walsh, *The Sisters of Charity of New York, 1809–1959* (New York: Fordham University Press, 1960), 2:4–6.

26 "Old St. Patrick's Church," January 1889, CMS.

27 "Mgr. John F. Kearney Dies at 85 Years," *New York Times*, April 12, 1923, 19; "10,000 at Last Rites for Mgr. J. J. Kearney," *New York Times*, April 15, 1923, S4; "Father Russo Dead," *New York Times*, April 2, 1902, 9.

CHAPTER 4. "RACE WAR"

1 According to tradition, Donatus was an Irish monk who became bishop of Fiesole.

2 Lynch to Corrigan, October 12, 1891, CMS, IAR Box 1, Transfiguration, copy.

3 "Noisy Italians," *New York Times*, August 18, 1889, 6; "Child Killed by a Bomb," *New York Times*, August 18, 1897, 1; "The Newark Bomb Explosion," *New York Times*, October 9, 1891, 9; Jacob Riis, "Feast-Days in Little Italy," *Century*, August 1899, 491–93. Roosevelt was president of the Police Board from May 6, 1895, to April 19, 1897, www.theodoreroosevelt.org/life/timeline.htm, accessed January 25, 2011.

4 Lynch, "Italians in New York," 70; Dominic A. Aquila, "The View from the Outside," in *The Saints in the Lives of Italian-Americans: An Interdisciplinary Investigation*, ed. Joseph A. Varacalli et al. (Stony Brook, NY: Forum Italicum), 156–57; Mary Elizabeth Brown, "Italian-Americans and Their Saints: Historical Considerations," in Varacalli et al., *Saints*, 44; Whelan, "Religious Rivalry and the Making of Irish-American Identity," 279; Robert A. Orsi, *The Madonna of 115th Street* (New Haven: Yale University Press, 1985), 219; Domenico Pistella, *The Crowning of a Queen*, trans. Peter J. Rofrano (New York: Shrine of Our Lady of Mount Carmel, 1954), 38–40; Pietro di Donato, *Christ in Concrete* (1939; New York: Signet Classic, 1993).

5 DiGiovanni, *Archbishop Corrigan*, 144, citing AANY, Lynch to Corrigan, January 23, 1894; Corrigan to Scalabrini, September 29, 1893, in Tomasi, *For the Love of Immigrants*, 285–86; "Judgments against Father Morelli," *New York Sun*, August 29, 1893, 3; *New York Tribune*, February 21, 1894, 21; *New York Times*, February 21, 1894, 12; Vicentini to Scalabrini, November 4, 1893, CMS, copy.

6 Scalabrini to Corrigan, February 5, 1894, in Tomasi, *For the Love of Immigrants*, 289; Corrigan to Scalabrini, February 22, 1894, in Tomasi, *For the Love of Immigrants*, 291–92.

7 Francesco Cordasco and Rocco G. Galatioto, "Ethnic Displacement in the Interstitial Community: The East Harlem Experience," *Phylon* 31 (3rd Quarter, 1970): 304–6.

8 "Race War in a Church," *New York World*, August 26, 1892; "A Race War in the Church," *New York Sun*, August 27, 1892, 7; "Politics in It, Now," *New York World*, August 29, 1892, 2; DiGiovanni, *Archbishop Corrigan*, 121; Corrigan to Carmody, August 25, 1891, CMS; "Dr. Depew Off for Europe," *New York Sun*, July 28, 1892, 7. Ethnicity: Roediger, *Working toward Whiteness*, 24–25; Gary Potter, "Miracle on 115th Street," April 1, 2009, accessed at http://catholicism.org/miracle-on-115th-street.html.

9 Orsi, *The Madonna of 115th Street*; Pistella, *Crowning*, 79, 118; "Statue Crowned by Archbishop Farley in Jefferson Park," *New York Post*, July 12, 1904, 4.

10 John T. McNicholas, "The Need of American Priests for the Italian Missions," *American Ecclesiastical Review* 39 (December 1908): 680–81; 1910 U.S. Census for John T. McNicholas, Manhattan, Ward 19. See also Humphrey J. Desmond, "For Six American Cardinals," *North American Review* (April 1909): 554–60; John Talbot Smith, "The Irish in the United States," *Irish Ecclesiastical Record* 9 (January–June 1902): 532–44.

11 Edward C. Stibili, "Palmieri, Aurelio (1870–1926)," in *The Italian American Experience: An Encyclopedia*, ed. Salvatore J. Gumina (New York: Garland, 2000), 442; Aurelio Palmieri, *Il grave problema religioso italiano negli Stati Uniti* (Florence:

Libreria Editrice Fiorentina, 1921), 30, 37, 40; Aurelio Palmieri, "Il clero italiano negli Stati Uniti," *Vita Italiana* 15 (1920): 115, 120. The Palmieri publications were available at CMS.
12 Reilly to Farley, March 3, 1917, CMS, IAR; Collins to Hayes, January 25, 1925, AANY, Holy Rosary Manhattan folder.
13 "Ten Dead in Tunnel Cave-In," *New York Sun*, October 26, 1903, 1; *New York Herald*, October 26, 1903, 3; "Death List Now 10," *New York Tribune*, October 26, 1903, 1.

CHAPTER 5. "CAN'T THEY BE SEPARATED?"
 1 "Mr. Powderly Testifies," *New York World*, August 20, 1888, 1; "Imported Labor," *New York Post*, August 20, 1888, 7; U.S. House of Representatives, *Testimony Taken by the Select Committee of the House of Representatives to Inquire into the Alleged Violation of the Laws Prohibiting the Importation of Contract Laborers, Paupers, Convicts, and Other Classes* (Washington, DC: GPO, 1888), 496–506.
 2 Henri Le Caron, *Twenty-Five Years in the Secret Service: The Recollections of a Spy* (London: Heinemann, 1892), 201. The boycott tactics of the Land League movement that Davitt led influenced Powderly and other Irish American labor leaders. Barrett, *The Irish Way*, 111–13; McKivigan and Robertson, "The Irish American Worker in Transition," 305.
 3 Terence V. Powderly, *The Path I Trod* (New York: Columbia University Press, 1940), 4–5, 185–87.
 4 Frank W. Alduino and David J. Coles, *Sons of Garibaldi in Blue and Gray: Italians in the American Civil War* (Youngstown, NY: Cambria, 2007), 179–82; "Spinola Loved Poker," *Brooklyn Eagle*, May 24, 1891, 17.
 5 "After Spinola's Scalp," *New York Times*, July 25, 1886, 3.
 6 "Appealing to Irishmen's Sons," *New York Times*, February 6, 1886, 2; *New York Tribune*, November 1, 1886, 4; "Moral Support for Bayard," *New York Tribune*, November 10, 1886, 4; "Killed by Defeat," *New York Times*, September 15, 1887, 5; Stanley B. Parsons, Michael J. Dubin, and Karen Toombs Parsons, *United States Congressional Districts, 1883–1913* (New York: Greenwood, 1990), 92.
 7 U.S. House of Representatives, *Testimony Taken*, 163.
 8 *New York Sun*, January 22, 1889, 4. The *Sun* insisted that the legislator was wrong.
 9 "A New Immigration Policy," *New York Times*, January 21, 1889, 4.
10 Kenneth T. Jackson, ed., *The Encyclopedia of New York City* (New Haven: Yale University Press, 1995), 599; Bruce Nelson, *Divided We Stand: American Workers and the Struggle for Black Equality* (Princeton: Princeton University Press, 2001), 13–19.
11 "Italian Workmen," *New York Times*, June 25, 1874, 4; "Italian Labor," *New York Times*, June 29, 1874, 4.
12 Blessing, "Irish," 538.
13 "Under Labor's Banners," *New York Sun*, September 6, 1882, 3; "Working Men on Parade," *New York Times*, September 6, 1882, 8. See also Kevin Kenny, "Labor and Organization," in Lee and Casey, *Making the Irish American*, 358–60.
14 U.S. Senate, *Report of the Committee of the Senate upon the Relations between Capital and Labor* (Washington, DC: GPO, 1885), 1:810–11.
15 Burrows and Wallace, *Gotham*, 1047–51.
16 Jacob A. Riis, *How the Other Half Lives: Studies among the Tenements of New York* (New York: Scribner's, 1890), 24.

17 Edward Fenton, "Immigrants and Unions: A Case Study; Italians and American Labor, 1870–1920" (Ph.D. diss., Harvard University, 1957; reprint, New York: Arno, 1975).

18 Kessner, *Golden Door*, 50.

19 "Rival Races," *Brooklyn Eagle*, September 25, 1893, 4; "A Small Army of Prisoners," *Brooklyn Eagle*, September 25, 1893, 10; "Irish and Italians Fight," *New York Sun*, September 25, 1893, 2; "Riot in Brooklyn Streets," *New York Times*, September 25, 1893, 8.

20 "The Recent Riot," *Brooklyn Eagle*, September 28, 1893, 2; 1900 U.S. Census for Gerard Antonini, Brooklyn, Ward 8.

21 "Can't They Be Separated?," *Brooklyn Eagle*, October 5, 1894, 6.

22 "Irish Fight Italians," *New York Sun*, July 14, 1896, 7; "Riot among Workmen," *New York Tribune*, July 14, 1896, 5.

23 Barrett, *The Irish Way*, 152.

24 E. Lyell Earle, "Character Studies in New York's Foreign Quarters," *Catholic World* 68 (March 1899): 786.

25 *Reports of the Industrial Commission* 15 (Washington, DC: GPO, 1901), 41; *Papers Relating to the Foreign Relations of the United States* (Washington, DC: GPO, 1901), 411–33; "Baron Fava Forced to Act," *New York Times*, July 13, 1895, 4; "For Libeling Baron Fava," *New York Times*, July 12, 1895, 5; "Convicted of Criminal Libel," *New York Times*, October 30, 1895, 9; "Moreno Goes to Jail for Ninety Days," *New York Times*, November 12, 1895, 9; "His Dream Not Realized; Celso Caesar Moreno Dies Disappointed and Poor," *Washington Times*, March 13, 1901, 2.

26 1910 U.S. Census; Humbert S. Nelli, *From Immigrants to Ethnics: The Italian Americans* (New York: Oxford University Press, 1983), 44.

27 "Rapid Transit Contract," *New York Times*, January 20, 1900; 1900 U.S. Census for Edward McSweeney, Manhattan, District 635.

28 "To Bar Out Imported Labor," *New York Tribune*, January 23, 1900, 4.

29 Henry to Clancy, October 31, 1900, CMS, IAR Box 1, Mission of Our Lady of the Rosary file.

30 "Small Houses in Demand," *Brooklyn Eagle*, July 31, 1900, 3; "Our Italians," *Brooklyn Eagle*, July 1, 1900, 23.

31 Patrick F. McGowan, ed., *Journal of the American-Irish Historical Society* 10 (1911): 392; Mitchell C. Harrison, ed., *New York State's Prominent and Progressive Men: An Encyclopedia of Contemporaneous Biography* (New York: Tribune, 1902), 3:197–99.

32 "Strike at Jerome Park," *New York Sun*, May 9, 1899, 2; "Clubs Ending the Strike," *New York Sun*, May 10, 1899, 5; "Jerome Park Reservoir Strike," *New York Sun*, May 12, 1899, 5.

33 "Negro Laborers on the Subway," *New York Times*, September 1, 1901, SM14.

34 "Laborers Beat Inspector," *New York Tribune*, March 25, 1902, 9; "Gangs of Laborers Fight," *Tribune*, July 24, 1902, 5.

35 Fenton, "Immigrants and Unions," 197, 257.

36 "The Subway Builder," *New York Times*, March 18, 1911, 12; "Big Fund for Tammany," *New York Times*, October 28, 1903.

37 John Horace Mariano, *The Italian Contribution to American Democracy* (New York: Christopher, 1921), 129; "James E. March Dead," *New York Times*, August 31, 1918; "James E. March, Overlord of Third District, Ends Campaign," *New York Tribune*, August 31, 1918, 7.

38 "Row over Italian Subway Strikers," *New York Times*, May 4, 1903, 12; *New York Tribune*, May 4, 1903, 2; "La Federated Union e gli italiani," *L'Araldo Italiano*, May 7, 1903, 1.

39 "Lo sciopero degli italiani," *Il Progresso Italiano*, May 12, 1903, 1.

40 "Subway Strikers Are Angry," *New York Herald*, May 14, 1903, 4; "Subway Laborers Refuse to Return," *New York Times*, May 14, 1903, 3; "Women in Subway Fight," *New York Post*, May 18, 1903, 1; "Strikers Fighting Police," *New York Post*, May 19, 1903, 2; "Senseless Strike Riot," *New York Post*, May 22, 1903, 1; "Subway Strike Breaking," *New York Times*, May 17, 1903, 12.

41 "The Man Who Dug the Tunnel," *New York World*, October 27, 1904; Fenton, "Immigrants and Unions," 215–18.

42 Roediger, *Working toward Whiteness*, 15.

43 Terence Vincent Powderly Papers, City University of New York Graduate Center, microfilm of manuscript collection of the Catholic University of America.

CHAPTER 6. "THE OTHER HALF OF ME!"

1 Elizabeth Gurley Flynn, *The Rebel Girl: An Autobiography, My First Life, 1906–1926* (1955; reprint, New York: International Publishers, 1979), 26, 40, 23, 39.

2 "Safety in the People," *New York Times*, August 26, 1906, 8; "Girl Socialist, 16 and Pretty, Freed in Court," *New York World*, August 23, 1906, 3; "Life's Big Things Alone Interest Girl Socialist," *New York World*, August 24, 1906, 3.

3 Theodore Dreiser, "An East Side Joan of Arc," *Broadway* 16 (September 1906): 513; Flynn, *Rebel Girl*, 65.

4 Flynn, *Rebel Girl*, 73–74.

5 Ibid., 147.

6 For biographical information on Tresca, see Dorothy Gallagher, *All the Right Enemies: The Life and Murder of Carlo Tresca* (New Brunswick: Rutgers University Press, 1988); Nunzio Pernicone, *Carlo Tresca: Portrait of a Rebel* (Oakland: AK Press, 2010), 74. For Flynn, see Rosalyn Fraad Baxandall, *Words on Fire: The Life and Writings of Elizabeth Gurley Flynn* (New Brunswick: Rutgers University Press, 1987); Helen C. Camp, *Iron in Her Soul: Elizabeth Gurley Flynn and the American Left* (Pullman: Washington State University Press, 1995).

7 Tamiment Library, Elizabeth Gurley Flynn Papers, Box 1, Folder 23, Reel 2.

8 Jean-Albert Bédé and William B. Edgerton, eds., *Columbia Dictionary of Modern European Literature*, 2nd ed. (New York: Columbia University Press, 1980), 192.

9 Tamiment Library, Flynn Papers, Box 1, Folder 23, Reel 2. Dated November 24, 1912, Lawrence, Massachusetts, this is inscribed on the book *The Empire of Silence*. Also see Gallagher, *All the Right Enemies*, 39.

10 Aaron Brenner, Benjamin Day, and Immanuel Ness, eds., *The Encyclopedia of Strikes in American History* (Armonk, NY: M. E. Sharpe, 2009), 330–32.

11 "Young Woman Leads the Waiters' Strike," *New York Times*, January 14, 1913, 7.

12 "Waiters Attack the Ritz-Carlton," *New York Times*, January 25, 1913, 1; "Shots Are Fired in Strike Riot at Ritz-Carlton," *New York Herald*, January 25, 1913, 1.

13 "Waiters in Many Night Riots," *New York American*, January 25, 1913, 1.

14 Flynn, *Rebel Girl*, 220.

15 Pernicone, *Carlo Tresca*, 74.

16 "Italian Libel Suit Is Started," *Connellsville (PA) Daily Courier*, December 17, 1908, 1; "All Acquitted except Tresca," *Connellsville (PA) Weekly Courier*, December 24, 1908,

5; Camp, *Iron in Her Soul*, 41; "Mrs. Tresca Names Elizabeth Flynn," *New York Tribune*, September 20, 1914, 10. Ages of Helga and Beatrice and Helga's ethnicity: 1930 U.S. Census for Beatrice Tresca and Helga Belotti, Queens, NY, Assembly District 3.

17 Pernicone, *Carlo Tresca*, 74, 81; Flynn, *Rebel Girl*, 272.

18 Author interview with Nunzio Pernicone, April 25, 2011.

19 Flynn, *Rebel Girl*, 271–72.

20 Ibid., 227–28.

21 Ibid., 333.

22 Baxandall, *Words on Fire*, 102.

23 Pernicone, *Carlo Tresca*, 83.

24 Jennifer Guglielmo, *Living the Revolution: Italian Women's Resistance and Radicalism in New York City, 1880–1945* (Chapel Hill: University of North Carolina Press, 2010), 3, 134.

25 Max Eastman, "Troublemaker," *New Yorker*, September 22, 1934, 26–27.

26 Flynn, *Rebel Girl*, 335.

27 Gallagher, *All the Right Enemies*, 95–96, 110; Camp, *Iron in Her Soul*, 112–14.

28 Flynn, *Rebel Girl*, 335.

29 Dorothy Gallagher interview with Peter Martin, Tamiment Library, Carlo Tresca: Dorothy Gallagher Research Files, Box 2, Folder 27.

30 "To Carlo South Beach (after 14 years) 1925," Tamiment Library, Carlo Tresca: Dorothy Gallagher Research Files, Box 2, Folder 6.

31 "To Carlo—Murdered Jan. 11, 1943 (After an IWO meeting at 77–5 Ave)," Ibid.

32 Tamiment Library, Carlo Tresca: Dorothy Gallagher collection, Box 2, Folder 37, New York County District Attorney's Office file.

33 "To Carlo—Murdered Jan. 11, 1943."

CHAPTER 7. BLACK HAND

1 "Mafia or Vendetta Follows Cocchiara: A Study of the Latest Mysterious Italian Tragedy," *Brooklyn Eagle*, June 7, 1896, 5; *Brooklyn Daily Eagle Almanac 1897* (Brooklyn: Brooklyn Daily Eagle, 1897), 331.

2 William McAdoo, *Guarding a Great City* (New York: Harper, 1906), 262–66.

3 "A Captain Taken to Task," *Brooklyn Eagle*, June 10, 1896, 12.

4 "Organized for Mutual Improvement," *Brooklyn Eagle*, February 15, 1889, 1; "A Well Attended Ball Given by the Corrao Association," *Brooklyn Eagle*, February 7, 1890, 3.

5 "Fought in a Law Office," *Brooklyn Eagle*, February 8, 1891, 1. The Arbuckle Building, located on the site of the State Supreme Court, was destroyed by fire in 1954.

6 "The First Italian Lawyer," *Brooklyn Eagle*, May 15, 1892, 20.

7 "Shot Down at His Door," *New York Times*, October 17, 1890, 1.

8 "Lynch Law and the Mafia," *New York Times*, March 17, 1891, 4; Theodore Roosevelt to Anna Roosevelt, March 21, 1891, Theodore Roosevelt Collection, MS Am 1834 (307), Houghton Library, Harvard University, available at http://www.theodorerooseveltcenter.org/Research/Digital-Library/Record.aspx?libID=0280928, Theodore Roosevelt Digital Library, Dickinson State University.

9 T. J. English, *Paddy Whacked: The Untold Story of the Irish American Gangster* (New York: Regan Books, 2005), 43–47.

10 "Asking Justice," *Brooklyn Eagle*, March 23, 1891, 1.
11 *New York Tribune*, March 26, 1917, 9; "Williams, 'Ex-Czar' of Tenderloin, Dies," *New York Times*, March 26, 1917; "Williams the Clubber," *New York World*, May 25, 1895, 2
12 F. M. White, "Joe Petrosino: Scourge of the Black Hand," *Scrap Book* 4 (July 1907): 20.
13 A. R. Parkhurst Jr., "The Perils of Petrosino," *Washington Post*, June 28, 1914, 5.
14 "Italians Flocking Home," *New York Sun*, August 25, 1884, 1.
15 "Hogan on Police Brutality," *New York Sun*, August 17, 1903, 10; "Police 'Graft' Charges," *New York Times*, August 27, 1903, 14; "Appointments by the Mayor," *New York Times*, July 2, 1899, 10; 1900 U.S. Census for Edward Hogan, Bronx, District 1047.
16 Frank Moss, *The American Metropolis: From Knickerbocker Days to the Present Time, New York City Life in All Its Various Phases* (London: Authors' Syndicate, 1897), 130.
17 "Policeman Fatally Shot," *New York Times*, September 4, 1899, 1.
18 Burrows and Wallace, *Gotham*, 1200–1201; *New York Tribune*, July 20, 1895; "Detectives in New Jobs," *New York Times*, July 20, 1895, 1; *New York Tribune*, August 5, 1896, 8.
19 Transcript, *People v. Carbone*, New York State Supreme Court, Lloyd Sealy Library, John Jay College of Criminal Justice.
20 "Carbone Guilty of Murder," *New York Times*, December 16, 1897, 12; "The Brogno Murder Case," *New York Times*, December 29, 1897, 4; "Five Prisoners Sentenced," *New York Times*, December 18, 1897, 12; "Carbone May Be Saved," *New York Times*, January 27, 1898, 2; "Saved Just on the Brink," *New York Sun*, January 27, 1898, 1; "Ciaramello's Own Story," *New York Times*, January 28, 1898, 13; "Ciaramello Gets Life Sentence," *New York Times*, April 22, 1898, 12; "Angelo Carbone Insane," *New York Times*, November 18, 1898, 5; "Justice Smyth Is Dead," *New York Times*, August 19, 1900, 1.
21 "Mafia Murder Victim," *New York Tribune*, April 15, 1903, 1; "Man in Barrel Was Tortured, Then Murdered," *New York World*, April 14, 1903, 1.
22 *New York Sun*, April 13, 1903, 2; "Inspector McCafferty," *New York Times*, September 3, 1907, 8; "Inspector McCafferty Dead," *New York Sun*, January 28, 1911, 4; "Inspector McCafferty Dead," *New York Times*, January 28, 1911, 11; 1900 U.S. Census for James McCafferty, Manhattan, District 786.
23 Arthur A. Carey, *Memoirs of a Murder Man* (Garden City, NY: Doubleday, 1930), 2–4.
24 William J. Flynn, *The Barrel Mystery* (New York: McCann, 1919), 14.
25 James Lardner and Thomas Reppetto, *NYPD: A City and Its Police* (New York: Henry Holt, 2000), 130.
26 "Held for Passing Bad Money," *New York Times*, June 2, 1900, 2; Mike Dash, *The First Family: Terror, Extortion and the Birth of the American Mafia* (London: Simon and Schuster, 2009), 96.
27 "Black Hand Baffles Police," *New York Sun*, July 29, 1904, 10; "Asked Lives or $4,000," *New York Tribune*, August 12, 1904, 1; "Two 'Black Hand' Arrests," *New York Times*, August 12, 1904, 12; "Counterfeit 'Black Hands,'" *New York Sun*, August 12, 1904, 5.
28 For the Morello gang as the first organized crime family, see Dash, *The First Family*.
29 McAdoo, *Guarding a Great City*, 148.
30 Ibid., 151.

31 "Italian Merchants Act," *New York Tribune*, August 17, 1904, 1; "Italian Crime and Police Incompetence," *New York Tribune*, August 21, 1904, 1; *New York Times*, August 25, 1904, 6; *New York Tribune*, August 26, 1904, 8.

32 Arrigo Petacco, *Joe Petrosino* (New York: Macmillan, 1974), 32.

33 McAdoo, *Guarding a Great City*, 6–13.

34 "M'Adoo Aroused by Police Conditions," *New York Times*, September 14, 1904, 1.

35 "Plea from Detectives," *New York Times*, April 30, 1905, 12.

36 "Blames Immigration for the Black Hand," *New York Times*, January 6, 1908, 14; A. R. Parkhurst Jr., "The Perils of Petrosino," *Washington Post*, August 9, 1914, 6.

37 Parkhurst, "Perils of Petrosino"; "Raid on Petrosino," *New York Times*, August 9, 1914; *New York Times*, October 4, 1905, 9; "Why Petrosino Gets a New Office," *New York Tribune*, October 4, 1905, 3.

38 "New York Is Full of Italian Brigands," *New York Times*, October 15, 1905, 28.

39 1900 U.S. Census for John Murtha, Manhattan, District 45.

40 "Police Knew, but Let Black Hand Use Bomb," *New York Sun*, October 17, 1905, 1; "Petrosino Asks Aid to Catch Brigands," *New York Times*, October 18, 1905, 20; "Wreck by Blackmailers," *New York Tribune*, October 18, 1905, 11.

41 *New York Sun*, October 15, 1901, 9.

42 1900 U.S. Census for Laura Corrao, Brooklyn, Ward 22; 1910 U.S. Census for Laura M. Green, Brooklyn, Ward 22; "Correspondence Submitted," *Brooklyn Eagle*, February 5, 1902, 6.

43 "Fireworks and Religion," *Brooklyn Eagle*, August 21, 1902, 8.

44 Francis L. Corrao, *Shall Brooklyn Have Four Years More of Injustice, and Unchecked Crime? Part of the Record of the District Attorney's Office of Kings County* (Brooklyn: n.p., 1911).

45 "Murder 'Prosecution' Astounding and Unique," *Brooklyn Eagle*, January 30, 1908, 1; "A Matter That Grows Worse under Probing," *Brooklyn Eagle*, January 30, 1908, 4.

46 "Will Honor Corrao," *Brooklyn Eagle*, September 7, 1907, 6.

47 "Guests of Celtic Club Get Real Shamrocks," *Brooklyn Eagle*, March 18, 1909, 6; McGuirl: http://saintsmaryandgertrude.org/history8.htm, accessed December 27, 2011.

48 "Robert Emmet's Memory," *New York Times*, March 5, 1900, 2; "Clan-Na-Gael Sympathy with Boers," *New York Tribune*, March 5, 1900, 8.

49 Emma Dullet, "Many Brooklynites Are Now in Paris," *Brooklyn Eagle*, August 9, 1908, 6.

50 "Clarke Is Home Again, Silent on Black Hand," *Brooklyn Eagle*, September 2, 1908, 3; "Clarke, Minus Beard, Is Back at Work Again" *Brooklyn Eagle*, September 3, 1908, 3; "Studied Black Hand in Italy," *New York Tribune*, September 3, 1908.

51 Parkhurst, "Perils of Petrosino," August 9, 1914.

52 Petacco, *Joe Petrosino*, 67.

53 "Gen. Bingham Dies at Summer Home," *New York Times*, September 7, 1934, 21; Theodore A. Bingham, *Genealogy of the Bingham Family in the United States Especially of the State of Connecticut, Including Notes on the Binghams of Philadelphia and of Irish Descent, with Partial Genealogies of Allied Families* (Harrisburg, PA: Harrisburg Publishing Company, 1898).

54 "Petrosino Makes Another Haul," *New York Tribune*, January 17, 1907, 16; "Lieut. C. S. Corrao Is Dead," *New York Times*, October 10, 1934, 23.

55 Author interview with Susan Burke, September 16, 2013; Petacco, *Joe Petrosino*, 70–71; "Petrosini Married to Adelina Saulino," *New York World*, January 2, 1908, 21; *Il Progresso Italo Americano*, March 14, 1909, 2; 1900 U.S. Census for Vincent Saulino, Manhattan, District 119.

56 "Italians Open War on the Black Hand," *New York Times*, February 7, 1908, 3; "Must Stop Outrages by the Black Hand," *New York Times*, January 26, 1908, 1; "Bomb Shakes Up Bingham's Office," *New York Times*, March 2, 1908, 1; "Dynamite Shatters a Bank near Pati's," *New York Times*, March 27, 1908, 1; *New York World*, May 26, 1908, 16; "Foreign Criminals of New York," *North American Review* 187 (1908): 393.

57 "Little Tim Sullivan Is Dead at Forty," *New York Times*, December 23, 1909, 1.

58 *New York Sun*, March 16, 1909, 3; "Mission That Took Petrosino to Italy," *New York Times*, March 16, 1909, 1.

59 "Petrosino Buried with High Honors," *New York Times*, April 13, 1909, 1; *New York Sun*, April 13, 1909, 1.

60 Petacco, *Joe Petrosino*, 118; *New York Sun*, February 20, 1909, 3; "Spies on Petrosino at Naples," *New York Times*, March 14, 1909, 2; *New York Post*, March 13, 1909, 1.

61 "Italians to Help Petrosino's Widow," *New York Times*, March 15, 1909, 2; *New York World*, March 13, 1909, 2; *New York Sun*, March 14, 1909, 2; Gino C. Speranza, "Petrosino and the Black Hand," *Survey*, April 3, 1909, 13.

62 "Mrs. Petrosino Collapses over News of Death," *New York World*, March 13, 1909, 1.

63 Ibid.

64 "Petrosino's Body Arrives," *New York Sun*, April 10, 1909, 3.

65 *New York Sun*, March 16, 1909, 3; *New York Post*, April 12, 1901, 1; "Mrs. Petrosino Suffers," *New York Tribune*, March 19, 1909, 5; "Topics of the Times," *New York Times*, April 12, 1909, 6; "Mgr. John F. Kearney Dies at 85 Years," *New York Times*, April 12, 1923, 19.

66 "Mgr. Lavelle Dies; Rector for 52 Years," *New York Times*, October 18, 1939, 1; "Mgr. Lavelle Gets Italian Decoration," *New York Times*, June 18, 1929, 20. He served as grand marshal of the St. Patrick's Day Parade in 1939.

67 "Petrosino Buried with High Honors," *New York Times*, April 13, 1909, 1; "The Funeral of Petrosino," *New York Sun*, April 13, 1909, 3; "Chief Croker, Enemy of Fires," *Market World and Chronicle*, April 8, 1911, 29.

68 1910 U.S. Census for John Crowley, Brooklyn, Ward 6.

69 Michael Fiaschetti, with Prosper Buranelli, *You Gotta Be Rough: The Adventures of Detective Fiaschetti of the Italian Squad* (New York: Doubleday, Doran, 1930), 85; "Clew to Assassins of Lieut. Petrosino," *New York Times*, August 20, 1909, 4; "Italian Squad Needed, Says Italian Editor," *New York Tribune*, February 22, 1913, 5; "Why Police Take Graft," *New York Times*, February 22, 1913, 20.

70 "Petrosino's List Found Too Late," *New York Times*, September 12, 1913, 9.

71 See Leonard Levitt, "Secret Cop Squad: Pair Offers Rare Glimpse into Unit That Targets Blacks," *Newsday*, April 18, 1999, 5; Al Baker and Joseph Goldstein, "Working under Cover, and under Strain," *New York Times*, May 7, 2012, 16.

72 Franklin Marshall White, "The Black Hand in Control in Italian New York," *New Outlook*, August 16, 1913, 859; "7,700 Police Parade to Music and Cheers," *New York Times*, May 19, 1912, 7.

73 "Blame Italian Police," *New York Tribune*, March 14, 1909, 3.

74 "Assails Prosecutor Clarke," *New York Times*, April 27, 1910, 4.

75 Corrao, *Shall Brooklyn Have Four Years More of Injustice*; "James C. Cropsey, Jurist, Dies at 64," *New York Times*, June 17, 1937. Cropsey, who became district attorney, was a former police commissioner.

CHAPTER 8. ON THE WATERFRONT

1 Brenner, Day, and Ness, *Encyclopedia of Strikes in American History*, 547–53.

2 Nelson, *Divided We Stand*, 23.

3 Burrows and Wallace, *Gotham*, 744; James T. Fisher, *On the Irish Waterfront: The Crusader, the Movie, and the Soul of the Port of New York* (Ithaca: Cornell University Press, 2009), 2–13; Howard Kimeldorf, *Reds or Rackets? The Making of Radical and Conservative Unions on the Waterfront* (Berkeley: University of California Press, 1988), 45; Charles B. Barnes, *The Longshoremen* (New York: Survey Associates, 1915), 5.

4 Nelson, *Divided We Stand*, 45.

5 "Per lo sciopero della gente di mare," *Bollettino della Sera*, October 20, 1919, 3; "Strikers Meet Twice," *New York Times*, October 22, 1919, 1; *New York World*, October 21, 1919, 2; "T. V. O'Conner Dies; Shipping Leader," *New York Times*, October 18, 1935, 23; http://www.jonesgenealogy.net/getperson.php?personID=I6606&tree=Jones, accessed January 30, 2012.

6 "Thus Does a Gang Grow Up: A Study of East Side Badness as Shown in the Paul Kellys," *New York Sun*, October 11, 1903, 20.

7 Herbert Asbury, *The Gangs of New York: An Informal History of the Underworld* (New York: Knopf, 1927), 252–53.

8 Richard F. Welch, *King of the Bowery: Big Tim Sullivan, Tammany Hall, and New York City from the Gilded Age to the Progressive Era* (Madison, NJ: Fairleigh Dickinson University Press, 2008), 128; Daniel Czitrom, "Underworlds and Underdogs: Big Tim Sullivan and Metropolitan Politics in New York," *Journal of American History* 78 (September 1991): 536–58.

9 Oliver Simmons, "Passing of the Sullivan Dynasty," *Munsey's Magazine*, December 1913, 412.

10 "Foley Outgenerals and Defeats Divver," *New York Times*, September 18, 1901, 1; "A Den, a Gang and a Murder," *New York World*, November 24, 1905, 20.

11 Charles Henry Parkhurst, *Our Fight with Tammany* (New York: Scribner's, 1895), 249; 1910 U.S. Census for John Goff, Manhattan, Ward 12; "Failure of 'Pulls,'" *New York Tribune*, December 7, 1901, 6; "Recorder Censures Police," *New York Times*, December 7, 1901, 16; "New York City in Congress," *New York Times*, October 4, 1902, 8.

12 Transcript, *People v. William Delaney, alias Monk Eastman*, New York State Supreme Court, April 12, 1904, Lloyd Sealey Library Archive, Trial 421, Transcript 260.

13 "Paul Kelly's Men Cheered," *New York Times*, April 6, 1905, 6; 1900 U.S. Census for William Hogan, Bronx, District 1058; 1930 U.S. Census for Edward Bourke, Manhattan, District 550.

14 "Thus Does a Gang Grow Up," *New York Sun*, October 11, 1903, 8.

15 "Tammany Nominees for the Judiciary," *New York Times*, October 11, 1900, 5; "Delehanty to Be Judge by Grace of Murphy," *New York World*, October 8, 1900, reprinted, *New York Times*, November 5, 1900, 3. National Archives and Records Administration, U.S. passport application for Francis B. Delehanty, May 31, 1923.

16 "Death after Battle with Paul Kelley Gang," *New York Times*, November 27, 1905, 1; "Paul Kelly under Arrest," *New York Sun*, December 2, 1905, 5; "Paul Kelley Found in Cousin's House," *New York Times*, December 2, 1905, 16.
17 Alfred Henry Lewis, *The Apaches of New York* (New York: Dillingham, 1912), 253–54.
18 *New York World*, June 30, 1911, 11.
19 "Gangs Which Terrorize New York," *Public Opinion*, December 9, 1905, 753.
20 "How One Bowery Boy Rose from Pugilist to Power in Labor," *New York Times*, February 25, 1923, xx9.
21 Robert F. Foerster, *The Italian Emigration of Our Times* (Cambridge: Harvard University Press, 1919), 356.
22 "Paul Kelly Now Vaccarelli," *New York Times*, September 15, 1910, 20.
23 "Paul Kelly to Tell His Woes to Mayor," *New York Times*, May 8, 1912, 9; "Paul Kelly Arrested," *New York Tribune*, November 30, 1912, 4; "'Gun Men' of Two Rival Bands of the Underworld Using Bullet, Knife, and Dynamite on Each Other," *New York Times*, June 9, 1912.
24 "Body of 'Big Tim' Found in Morgue," *New York Call*, September 14, 1913, 2; English, *Paddy Whacked*, 108.
25 Shannon, *The American Irish*, 138–40; Frances Perkins, *The Roosevelt I Knew* (New York: Viking, 1946), 12–14; Terry Golway, *Machine Made: Tammany Hall and the Creation of Modern American Politics* (New York: Liveright, 2014), 244–46.
26 "Enormous Crowds at Big Tim's Funeral," *New York Sun*, September 16, 1913, 4.
27 Eric Ferrara, *Manhattan Mafia Guide: Hits, Homes and Headquarters* (Charleston, SC: History Press, 2011), 76.
28 *New York Tribune* and *New York Sun*, September 16, 1913; "Class Lines Vanish at Sullivan Burial," *New York Times*, September 16, 1913, 5.
29 Richard J. Butler and Joseph Driscoll, *Dock Walloper: The Story of "Big Dick" Butler* (New York: Putnam's, 1933), 93, 201, 220.
30 "Foiled German Plot to Tie Up Docks," *New York Times*, September 14, 1915, 3; "German Plot for Ship Strike Foiled," *New York Sun*, September 13, 1915, 4; "Matthew Cummings, Boston Contractor," *New York Times*, February 10, 1939, 28; "O'Connor Tells of Offer," *New York Times*, September 14, 1915, 3.
31 "Paul Kelly Strike Causes Embargo and Ties Up Piers," *New York Times*, May 17, 1916, 1; *New York Times*, May 18, 1916, 6.
32 Barnes, *The Longshoremen*, 8.
33 *Bollettino della Sera*, October 23, 1919, 2.
34 Brenner, Day, and Ness, *Encyclopedia of Strikes in American History*, 553–57; "Pier Strike Ends; Men Work Today," *New York Times*, November 6, 1919, 1.
35 Butler and Driscoll, *Dock Walloper*, 215; Fisher, *On the Irish Waterfront*, 17–21.
36 "F. P. A. Vaccarelli, Union Leader, Dies," *New York Times*, April 5, 1936, N10.

CHAPTER 9. WHITE HAND

1 Meyer Berger, "Lady in Crepe," pt. 1, *New Yorker*, October 5, 1935, 28; Fred Pasley, *Not Guilty: The Story of Samuel S. Leibowitz* (New York: Putnam's, 1933), 95, 97.
2 "'Foreign Gangsters' Staged Lonergan Murder, Women Folk Say; Hard Hit by New Tragedy," *Brooklyn Eagle*, December 27, 1925, 4A.
3 Berger, "Lady in Crepe," pt. 1, 28.

4 Jerry Capeci and Tom Robbins, *Mob Boss: The Life of Little Al D'Arco, the Man Who Brought Down the Mafia* (New York: Thomas Dunne Books, 2013), 22.

5 Berger, "Lady in Crepe," pt. 1, 28; English, *Paddy Whacked*, 158, attributes more than a hundred murders on the Brooklyn waterfront from 1915 to 1925 to clashes between Irish and Italian criminals.

6 "Gunman Murdered Asleep with Wife," *New York Times*, April 1, 1920, 15.

7 Robert J. Schoenberg, *Mr. Capone: The Real—and Complete—Story of Al Capone* (New York: HarperCollins, 1993), 31.

8 Jack McPhaul, *Johnny Torrio: First of the Gang Lords* (New Rochelle, NY: Arlington, 1970), 164, 204; 1910 U.S. Census for Frank Iola, Brooklyn, Ward 30; World War I Draft Registration Card for Frank Uale, Kings County, NY.

9 Bill Bell, "Big Shot Burying Frankie Yale," *New York Daily News*, May 1, 1998; "2,500 at Uale Burial," *Brooklyn Standard Union*, July 5, 1928, 1.

10 "Detectives in Crowd Seek Clew to Slayers of Gang Leader," *New York Tribune*, April 5, 1920, 6; "Gangster Rival Slew Lovett, Pal Says," *Brooklyn Eagle*, November 4, 1923, 8A; William Balsamo and John Balsamo, *Young Al Capone: The Untold Story of Scarface in New York, 1899–1925* (New York: Skyhorse, 2011), 174–77.

11 "How Fate Double-Crossed the Girl-Wife and the Gangster," Newspaper Feature Service, in *Salt Lake Tribune*, December 9, 1923.

12 "Bill Lovett Leaves Prison to Welcome 'Life Sentence,'" *New York Telegram*, July 27, 1923, 4; Berger, "Lady in Crepe," pt. 1, 32.

13 Balsamo and Balsamo, *Young Al Capone*, 204–11; "Bill Lovett Slain; Ex-Gang Mate Held," *New York Times*, November 2, 1923, 3.

14 Berger, "Lady in Crepe," pt. 1, 30, 32; World War I Draft Registration Card for Richard Joseph Lonergan, Kings County, NY, September 12, 1918; 1920 U.S. Census for Richard Lonergan, Brooklyn, Assembly District 1; Meyer Berger, "Lady in Crepe," pt. 2, *New Yorker*, October 12, 1935, 24; Frank Emery, "Only Stupid Gangs Get Caught," *Brooklyn Eagle*, January 10, 1926, F1.

15 "How They Killed 'Peg Leg' Lonergan, Gang Leader, at His Christmas Party," *Syracuse (NY) Journal*, "American Weekly," January 31, 1926, 6; Balsamo and Balsamo, *Young Al Capone*, 249; John Kobler, *Capone* (New York: Putnam, 1971), 163–64.

16 McPhaul, *Johnny Torrio*, 49–50; Laurence Bergreen, *Capone: The Man and the Era* (New York: Simon and Schuster, 1994), 155.

17 1900 U.S. Census for Mike Coughlin, Brooklyn, Ward 6; 1910 U.S. Census for Michael Coughlin, Brooklyn, Ward 12; World War I Draft Registration Card for Alphonse Capone, Kings County, NY.

18 Kobler, *Capone*, 36; 1935 Florida State Census for May Coughlin, Dade County.

19 1920 U.S. Census for James J. Delaney, Brooklyn, Assembly District 8; U.S. Social Security Death Index for Albert Francis. Albert Capone changed his last name to Francis. His Social Security death record lists his date of birth as December 4, 1915.

20 Deirdre Marie Capone, *Uncle Al Capone: The Untold Story from inside His Family* (New York: Recap, 2012), 24.

21 "Chicago's Al Capone Likes to Wear Apron, Cook Spaghetti," *Bismarck (ND) Tribune* via Newspaper Enterprise Association, June 4, 1929.

22 "Three Gangsters Slain in Dance Hall as Xmas Party Ends," *Brooklyn Eagle*, December 26, 1925, 1.

23 Pasley, *Not Guilty*, 114–17; "Arrest Three More in Connection with Lonergan Slaying," *Brooklyn Standard Union*, December 28, 1925, 1.

24 English, *Paddy Whacked*, 155.

25 "'Doublecross' Charge Led to Gang Shooting," *Brooklyn Eagle*, December 15, 1931, 1; "Gang Chief Dying, Jeers at Police," *Brooklyn Eagle*, December 15, 1931, 6.

26 "Anna Lonergan Knifed in Feud but Upholds 'Silent' Tradition," *Brooklyn Eagle*, May 17, 1932, 17.

27 "Bullet-Widowed Twice but Cupid Strikes Again," *Brooklyn Eagle*, November 26, 1932, 22.

28 Berger, "Lady in Crepe," pt. 2, 28.

29 Ibid., 24.

30 Asenath Nicholson, *Lights and Shades of Ireland* (London: Houlston and Stoneman, 1850), 259.

31 House of Commons, *Report from the Select Committee on Destitution (Gweedore and Cloughaneely) Together with the Proceedings of the Committee, Minutes of Evidence, Appendix, and Index* (1858), 44–45, 49–56.

32 "Two Monsignors Die on the Same Day," *New York Times*, December 2, 1920. Taafe Playground at Park and Myrtle Avenues is named for Taafe, as is Taafe Place in Bedford-Stuyvesant.

33 The name of the one-block street was changed to Martin Luther King Jr. Place in 1974. The street is between the Marcy and Tompkins housing projects.

34 Certificate of Marriage, Brooklyn, Henry Collins and Margaret Gallagher, February 27, 1884; Certificate of Death, Brooklyn, Henry Collins, May 7, 1891; Certificate of Marriage, Brooklyn, Owen Boyle and Margaret Gallagher, January 20, 1892; 1900 U.S. Census for Maggie Boyle, Brooklyn, Ward 12.

35 "Officer Jepson May Die as Result of Assault," *Brooklyn Eagle*, December 6, 1900, 18; "Owen Boyle Discharged," *Brooklyn Eagle*, April 19, 1901, 20.

36 Doyle, "The Remaking of Irish America," 231. The Italian death rate may have been lower, in part, because of the younger age of Italian immigrants.

37 "Two Men Arrested in Connection with Raid," *Dansville (NY) Breeze*, February 22, 1928, 1.

38 Author interview with Marie Bradley, December 15, 2009.

39 Wilfred Rauber, "Ossian Area Murder Victim Never Identified," *Danville (NY) Breeze–Genesee Country Express*, November 25, 1969, 1; "Ossian Murder Case Remains a Mystery Two Years Having Passed," *Picket Line Post and Mount Morris (NY) Union*, October 1, 1931, 7.

40 Roediger, *Working toward Whiteness*, 79.

41 Barrett, *The Irish Way*, 275–77.

CHAPTER 10. THE POLS

1 Fiorello H. La Guardia, *The Making of an Insurgent: An Autobiography, 1882–1919* (Philadelphia: Lippincott, 1947), 112–13.

2 Peter Quinn, *Looking for Jimmy: A Search for Irish America* (New York: Overlook, 2007).

3 *Angels with Dirty Faces*, DVD, directed by Michael Curtiz (1938; Burbank, CA: Warner Home Video, 2005).

4 La Guardia, *The Making of an Insurgent*, 69.

5 Henry F. Pringle, "Italian Table D'Hote," *New Yorker*, August 31, 1929, 26, 28; "Below the Belt," *New York Times*, October 27, 1933, 18.
6 Shannon, *The American Irish*, 68–85.
7 William L. Riordon, *Plunkitt of Tammany Hall* (New York: McClure, 1905), 58.
8 Arthur A. Goren, "Jews," in Thernstrom, *Harvard Encyclopedia of American Ethnic Groups*, 581.
9 Burton J. Hendrick, "The Twilight of Tammany Hall," *World's Work* 27 (February 1914): 432–33.
10 Oliver Simmons, "Passing of the Sullivan Dynasty," *Munsey's Magazine* 50 (December 1913): 412.
11 Ronald H. Bayor, *Neighbors in Conflict: The Irish, Germans, Jews and Italians of New York City, 1929–1941* (Urbana: University of Illinois Press, 1988), 30, citing *World's Work* 54 (1927).
12 "Italian Alliance to Ask Walker Aid," *Brooklyn Eagle*, March 31, 1926, 2; "Anti-McCooey Magazine," *Brooklyn Eagle*, September 10, 1926, 5; Charles LaCerra, "Irish Politics, the Madison Club of Brooklyn, and John H. McCooey," in *Italians and Irish in America: Proceedings of the Sixteenth Annual Conference of the American Italian Historical Association*, ed. Francis X. Femminella (Staten Island, NY: American Italian Historical Association, 1985), 235–39.
13 Riordon, *Plunkitt*, 177–79.
14 George Kibbe Turner, "Tammany's Control of New York," *McClure's* 33 (June 1909): 124, 133.
15 John Levi Martin, *Social Structures* (Princeton: Princeton University Press, 2009), 288–89; Gustav Meyers, *History of Tammany Hall* (New York: Boni and Liveright, 1917), 228; Nathan Glazer and Daniel Patrick Moynihan, *Beyond the Melting Pot: The Negroes, Puerto Ricans, Jews, Italians and Irish of New York City* (Cambridge: MIT Press, 1963), 223–26.
16 Laurence Franklin, "The Italian in America: What He Has Been, What He Shall Be," *Catholic World* 71 (April 1900): 72–73.
17 "Most Merciless of Vendetta's Waged with Law's Aid," *New York Sun*, October 22, 1916, section 5, 4.
18 Deaths Registered in Town of Williamsburg, MA, July 13, 1964, accessed at www.ancestry.com.
19 "Lie Passed at Civil Service Quiz," *New York Tribune*, September 30, 1914, 7; "Church of St. James," New York City Chapter of the American Guild of Organists, http://www.nycago.org/Organs/NYC/html/StJamesRC.html, accessed February 14, 2014; Joseph Marc Di Leo, "Governor Alfred Emanuel Smith: Multi-ethnic Politician; The Italian Connection," in Femminella, *Italians and Irish in America*, 250–51; Robert A. Slayton, *Empire Statesman* (New York: Free Press, 2001), 11–15; 1910 U.S. Census for Michael Rofrano, Manhattan, Ward 4; Emily Smith Warner with Hawthorne Daniel, *The Happy Warrior: A Biography of My Father Alfred E. Smith* (Garden City, NY: Doubleday, 1956), 14–20.
20 "M. A. Rofrano Dead; Ex-City Official," *New York Times*, July 4, 1932, 11; "Most Merciless of Vendettas," *New York Sun*, October 22, 1916; "Killed for Politics in Foley's District," *New York Times*, March 26, 1915, 22.
21 Transcript, *People v. Montimagno*, New York Supreme Court, Lloyd Sealy Library, 387–89, 504, 1031–33.

22 "Police Alarm for Rofrano," *New York Sun*, September 15, 1915, 5; "Rofrano Indicted as Plot Is Bared to Slay Tom Foley and Congressman," *New York World*, September 14, 1915, 1; "Rofrano Gives Up; Taken by Swann," *New York Times*, May 16, 1916, 1.

23 "'Rofrano Asked Me to Kill Gaimari,' Slayer Swears," *New York World*, October 17, 1916, 1; "Mrs. Rofrano Eager to Aid Husband," *New York Times*, November 2, 1916, 10; "Rofrano's Case Aided by Cornell," *New York Tribune*, November 3, 1916, 5.

24 "Rofrano's Jury Sets Him Free after 22 Hours," *New York Sun*, November 13, 1916, 1; "Rofrano Free; Hailed as Idol by His Friends," *New York Tribune*, November 13, 1916, 1; "Italian Colony Pleased," *New York Times*, November 13, 1916, 1.

25 *The Chicago Daily News Almanac and Year-Book for 1916* (Chicago: Chicago Daily News, 1915), 512.

26 George Britt, "The Real La Guardia," *New York World-Telegram*, October 3, 1933; La Guardia, *The Making of an Insurgent*, 122–27; Thomas Kessner, *Fiorello H. La Guardia and the Making of Modern New York* (New York: McGraw-Hill, 1989), 35, 38–39.

27 Ronald H. Bayor, *Fiorello La Guardia: Ethnicity and Reform* (Arlington Heights, IL: Harlan Davidson, 1993), 45; Arthur Mann, *La Guardia Comes to Power: 1933* (Philadelphia: Lippincott, 1965), 18; Kessner, *Fiorello H. La Guardia*, 76–78.

28 Louis J. Gribetz and Joseph Kaye, *Jimmy Walker: Story of a Personality* (New York: Dial Press, 1932), 47–48; Herbert Mitgang, *Once upon a Time in New York: Jimmy Walker, Franklin Roosevelt and the Last Great Battle of the Jazz Age* (New York: Free Press, 2000), 59; Kessner, *Fiorello H. La Guardia*, 158.

29 "Likely to Railroad Clean Book Bill; Strife at Hearing," *New York Times*, April 19, 1923, 1; "'Clean Book' Bill Dies in Senate," *New York Times, May 3, 1923, 1;* "Ernest Ball," Songwriters Hall of Fame, www.songwritershalloffame.org/exhibits/bio/C206, accessed December 3, 2012; Frederick M. Davenport, "Salvatore A. Cotillo," *Outlook*, July 28, 1920, 562.

30 "Republicans Press Rothstein Issue," *New York Times*, September 25, 1929, 10; "La Guardia Wind-Up a Rothstein Charge," *New York Times*, November 5, 1929, 1.

31 1900 U.S. Census for Albert Vitale, Bronx, District 1039; "Says Mayor Flouts Citizens on Budget," *New York Times*, September 15, 1929, 18; "Proof in Gambler's Files," *New York Times*, September 28, 1929, 1; "Vitale Says Friend Arranged for Loan," *New York Times*, September 28, 1929, 1; "Mayor Says He Cannot Act in Magistrate Vitale Case," *New York Times*, September 30, 1929, 1; "McManus to Insist That Banton Give Facts," *New York Times*, October 1, 1929, 2, referring to *Bronx Home-News*.

32 Gene Fowler, *Beau James: The Life and Times of Jimmy Walker* (New York: Viking, 1949), 120, 230; Edward J. Flynn, *You're the Boss* (New York: Viking, 1947), 18; "Walker Reaffirms Tammany Fealty," *New York Times*, October 4, 1929, 4.

33 "Mayor Makes 'Talkies' for City Campaign," *New York Times*, September 21, 1929; "Walker Ridicules Charges of Graft," *New York Times*, October 23, 1929.

34 "Mayoral Clothes," *New Yorker*, July 24, 1937, 10.

35 Fowler, *Beau James*, 246, 214; "La Guardia Sees Workingman His Aid to City Hall," *Brooklyn Eagle*, October 28, 1929, 7; "Walker Hits Pleas Based on Prejudice," *New York Times*, October 25, 1929, 6; Slayton, *Empire Statesman*, 222–24.

36 J. A. Hagerty, "Republicans Hope to Hold Walker to 250,000 Margin as Omen of 1930 Victory," *New York Times*, October 29, 1929, 1; "Walker Elected by 497,165 Votes," *New York Post*, November 6, 1929, 2; "Big Vote Piled Up," *New York Times*,

November 6, 1929, 1; "Election Night Zest of Yore Sadly Missing," *Brooklyn Eagle*, November 6, 1929, 5.

37 Richard F. Warner, "La Guardia Seen Dispelling 'Who Could Say No?' Myth," *New York Post*, October 28, 1929, 3.

38 *New York Times*, December 8, 1929, 1; December 9, 1929, 14.

39 Jay Maeder, "Vice Squad Confidential," *New York Daily News*, April 27, 2000.

40 "Profit in a Stock Deal," *New York Times*, May 13, 1932, 1; "Parries Counsel All Day," *New York Times*, May 26, 1932, 1.

41 "Ask 'Tax for Prosperity,'" *New York Times*, May 15, 1932, 1; *Brooklyn Eagle*, May 15, 1932.

42 "Day before Big Battle No Different to Mayor," *Brooklyn Eagle*, May 25, 1932, 3.

43 "O'Brien Won Note in Hylan's Regime," *New York Times*, November 9, 1932, 7; "O'Brien Predicts 1,000,000 Majority," *New York Times*, October 21, 1932, 19.

44 "O'Brien Will Name Man from Force to Head the Police Department," *New York Times*, April 12, 1933, 1.

45 "Mayor McKee," *New York Times*, September 3, 1932, 12.

46 1910 U.S. Census for Joseph McKee, Bronx, Assembly District 34.

47 "M'Kee Wants City to Censor Movies," *New York Times*, October 12, 1927, 1; "The Callahans and the Murphys," http://movies.nytimes.com/movie/86485/The-Callahans-and-the-Murphys/overview, accessed February 14, 2014.

48 "Irish Look to M'Kee for Political Jobs," *New York Times*, October 7, 1933, 17.

49 Mann, *La Guardia*, 92; Chris McNickle, "When New York Was Irish, and After," in Bayor and Meagher, *The New York Irish*, 340–41.

50 Joe Giordano and Monica McGoldrick, "Families of European Origin: An Overview," in *Ethnicity and Family Therapy*, 3rd ed., ed. Monica McGoldrick, Joe Giordano, and Nydia Garcia-Preto (New York: Guilford, 2005), 505.

51 Ronald H. Bayor, "Italians, Jews and Ethnic Conflict," *International Migration Review* 6 (Winter 1972): 379–81, 390; Bayor, *Neighbors in Conflict*, 98–99.

52 James A. Hagerty, "Disavow Seabury, M'Kee Asks Rival," *New York Times*, October 15, 1933, 3; "M'Kee Defended by Judge Lehman," *New York Times*, October 18, 1933, 16.

53 Mann, *La Guardia*, 25, 140.

54 "La Guardia Scoffs at Racial Appeals," *New York Times*, October 23, 1933, 6.

55 Paul A. Tierney, "New York's Secret Senate," *New York Post*, March 7, 1933, 7. Luciano: Thomas Reppetto, *American Mafia: A History of Its Rise to Power* (New York: Holt, 2004), 146; Bayor, *Neighbors in Conflict*, 43; Thomas E. Dewey, October 24, 1937, http://www.speeches-usa.com/Transcripts/thomas_dewey-ally.html, accessed February 14, 2014; B. L. Livingstone, "Tammany Takes Worst Beating," *Lowell (MA) Sun*, November 8, 1933, 3; S .J. Woolf, "On the Stump with Three Contenders," *New York Times*, October 22, 1933, SM6; "LaGuardia Holds to Flynn Attack," *New York Times*, October 25, 1933, 15; "O'Brien Winds Up Campaign in Bronx," *New York Times*, November 7, 1933, 21; Paul Blanshard, "LaGuardia versus McKee," *Nation*, October 25, 1933, 474–77.

56 Mann, *La Guardia*, 110, 134.

57 "Italians Celebrate LaGuardia Victory," *New York Times*, November 8, 1933, 2; "Mr. Rogers Moved to Song by the New York Election," *New York Times*, November 9, 1933, 23; "LaGuardia Begins Selecting Cabinet," *New York Times*, November 10, 1933, 1; Bayor, *Neighbors in Conflict*, 34.

58 Catherine Mackenzie, "Life for the Mayor Is One Mad Whirl," *New York Times*, December 10, 1933, SM8; "O'Brien Gives Jobs to 3 on Last Day," *New York Times*, December 31, 1933, 8. Santangelo eventually became a judge.

59 Kessner, *Fiorello H. La Guardia*, 289, 399; Bayor, *Neighbors in Conflict*, 30–40, 35; McNickle, "When New York Was Irish," 337.

60 Theodore J. Lowi, *At the Pleasure of the Mayor: Patronage and Power in New York City, 1898–1951* (London: Macmillan, 1964), 41.

61 "Inner Circle Twits Mayor and Smith," *New York Times*, March 8, 1936, N1.

62 Ibid.; "Rid City of Gangs Is Order to Police," *New York Times*, January 2, 1934, 1; "Market Clean-Up Starts," *New York Times*, January 9, 1934, 1; 1920 U.S. Census for Lewis Valentine, Brooklyn, Assembly District 11.

63 La Guardia, *The Making of an Insurgent*, 27; Meyer Berger, "Drums and Banners for St. Patrick," *New York Times*, March 15, 1936, SM10.

64 Kessner, *Fiorello H. La Guardia*, 418.

65 Ibid., 394, 403; "Religious Center at Fair Proposed," *New York Times*, March 4, 1937, 25; 1910 U.S. Census for Jerry Mahoney, Manhattan, Ward 12; Bayor, *Fiorello La Guardia*, 143; "La Guardia Is Cool to Communist Aid," *New York Times*, August 28, 1937, 1; "Lehman Endorses Mahoney's Ticket," *New York Times*, October 17, 1937, 1; "Mahoney Booklet Makes 'Red Peril' the Major Issue," *New York Post*, October 23, 1937, 5; *New York Post*, October 16, 1937, 4.

66 "Dr. Fama Appointed," *New York Times*, May 12, 1934, 9; National Archives and Records Administration, U.S. passport application for Charles Fama, December 28, 1920; Bayor, *Neighbors in Conflict*, 37, citing *Gaelic American*, October 6, 1934, 1; November 3, 1934, 1.

67 Bayor, *Fiorello La Guardia*, 143–144.

68 Ibid., 174; "Skin of Big Tiger Presented to Mayor," *New York Times*, November 5, 1937, 14.

69 "'Battery Dan,' Magistrate, Is Dead," *New York Times*, March 24, 1910, 18.

70 Bayor, *Neighbors in Conflict*, 45; *New York Times*, September 20, September 23, September 26, October 18, 1939; Donald Tricarico, *The Italians of Greenwich Village* (New York: Center for Migration Studies, 1984), 58–59; Jonathan Kandell, "Carmine De Sapio, Last Tammany Hall Boss, Dies at 95," *New York Times*, July 28, 2004, C12.

71 "Virtual Black-Out at Tammany Hall," *New York Times*, November 5, 1941, 18.

72 Bayor, *Neighbors in Conflict*, 144.

73 "Walker Salutes Mayor LaGuardia," *New York Times*, October 5, 1939, 21; "Qualification," *New Yorker*, October 21, 1939, 13.

CHAPTER 11. COOL

1 Mick Moloney, "Irish-American Popular Music," in Lee and Casey, *Making the Irish American*, 391–99.

2 Larry McCarthy, "Irish Americans in Sports," in Lee and Casey, *Making the Irish American*, 459–61; Lawrence Baldassaro, *Beyond DiMaggio: Italian Americans in Baseball*, foreword by Dom DiMaggio (Lincoln: University of Nebraska Press, 2011), xvi, 20, 62–63.

3 Baldassaro, *Beyond DiMaggio*, 212.

4 Gay Talese, "Frank Sinatra Has a Cold," *Esquire*, April 1966, http://www.esquire.com/features/ESQ1003-OCT_SINATRA_rev, accessed February 23, 2014; James

Kaplan, *Frank* (New York: Doubleday, 2010), 8; Nancy Sinatra, *Frank Sinatra, My Father* (Garden City, NY: Doubleday, 1985), 38.

5 Pete Hamill, *Why Sinatra Matters* (Boston: Little, Brown, 1998), 58, 77; Nancy Sinatra, *Frank Sinatra: An American Legend* (Santa Monica, CA: General, 1995), 15.

6 Kaplan, *Frank*, 15, 21; E. J. Kahn Jr., "Just a Kid from Hoboken," pt. 3, *New Yorker*, November 9, 1946, 36; Gerald Meyer, "Frank Sinatra: The Popular Front and an American Icon," *Science and Society* 66 (Fall 2002): 314.

7 Kaplan, *Frank*, 50, 24, 724, 30; Sinatra, *Frank Sinatra: An American Legend*, 20, 24–25; Sinatra, *Frank Sinatra, My Father*, 43, 47.

8 Kaplan, *Frank*, 64, 99–101; Peter J. Levinson, *Tommy Dorsey: Livin' in a Great Big Way* (New York: Da Capo, 2005), 95; Sinatra, *Frank Sinatra, My Father*, 60, 62–64; Sinatra, *Frank Sinatra: An American Legend*, 50.

9 Kaplan, *Frank*, 139, quoting Sidney Zion interview with Frank Sinatra at Yale University, April 15, 1986.

10 Levinson, *Tommy Dorsey*, 152, 154; Hamill, *Why Sinatra Matters*, 111; Kaplan, *Frank*, 144, 146.

11 Sinatra, *Frank Sinatra: An American Legend*, 50.

12 Edward O'Gorman, "Sinatra Looks at Sinatra—and $25,000," *New York Post*, January 30, 1943, 17; "He Can't Read a Note but He's Dethroning Bing," *Newsweek*, March 22, 1943, 62.

13 Gary Giddins, *Bing Crosby, a Pocketful of Dreams: The Early Years, 1903–1940* (Boston: Little, Brown, 2001), 15–28; Bing Crosby, with Pete Martin, *Call Me Lucky: Bing Crosby's Own Story* (1953; reprint, New York: Da Capo, 1993), 52.

14 1910 U.S. Census for James Kennelly, Spokane, WA, Ward 5; Crosby, *Call Me Lucky*, 70.

15 Giddins, *Bing Crosby*, 48.

16 Ibid., 9.

17 Richard B. O'Brien, "Crooners in Spotlight as Year Nears an End," *New York Times*, December 6, 1931, XX29.

18 Giddins, *Bing Crosby*, 227.

19 Bing Crosby, "Bing Crosby Hit Success Because He Loves to Sing," *Troy (NY) Times*, September 28, 1933, 19. This article was disseminated to publicize the movie *Too Much Harmony*.

20 Richard Murray, "Rich Man's Folly," *Brooklyn Standard Union*, November 27, 1931, 10; Jo Ransom, "Radio Dial-Log," *Brooklyn Eagle*, February 13, 1932, 7.

21 "Russ Columbo Fatally Wounded as Friend Shows Him Old Pistol," Associated Press via *New York Times*, September 3, 1934, 1; "Family's Tender Deceit of Ten Years Ends as Late Russ Columbo's Mother Dies at 78," Associated Press via *New York Times*, September 1, 1944, 15.

22 "Billboard's Sinatra Chronicles," *Billboard*, May 30, 1998, 21, quoting *Billboard*, March 27, 1943.

23 John K. Hutchens, "Of Sudden Wealth, etc." *New York Times*, June 6, 1943, X7; *New York Times*, July 4, 1943, X7; 1930 U.S. Census for Marjorie Wohl, Brooklyn, Assembly District 2.

24 Harold C. Burr, "Sports Shorts," *Brooklyn Eagle*, April 14, 1944, 15; "First High-School Music Poll," *Billboard*, June 3, 1943, 3.

25 Earl Wilson, "It Happened Last Night," *New York Post*, May 14, 1943, 31.

26 Bing Crosby, "Here's to Sinatra," *Motion Picture-Hollywood Magazine*, December 1943, http://www.examiner.com/article/bing-crosby-gave-frank-sinatra-advice-1943, accessed June 18, 2013.

27 "Heard and Overheard," *PM Daily*, November 21, 1943, 16.

28 Associated Press in *Zanesville (OH) Signal*, February 1, 1944, 8.

29 Armed Forces Radio Network, *Command Performance* 98, https://archive.org/details/CommandPerformance, accessed April 15, 2014.

30 "Flood of Oratory Ends Willkie Drive," *New York Times*, November 5, 1940, 22; "Crosby, Sinatra Split on Politics," Associated Press via *San Antonio (TX) Light*, September 29, 1944, 5-A. See Meyer, "Frank Sinatra: The Popular Front and an American Icon," 311–35.

31 Cecelia Ager, "Frank Sinatra, a Solid Sending Guy for FDR," *PM Daily*, October 2, 1944, 17.

32 Giddins, *Bing Crosby*, 556; Crosby, *Call Me Lucky*, 186–87.

33 *The Frank Sinatra Timex Show*, video, 59:11, October 19, 1959, https://archive.org/details/theFrankSinatraTimexShow-19October1959, accessed June 20, 2013.

34 Stephen Holden, "Dean Martin, Pop Crooner and Comic Actor, Dies at 78," *New York Times*, December 26, 1995, D8.

35 Horatio Alger Jr., *Phil the Fiddler* (New York, 1872), www.gutenberg.org, accessed June 20, 2013. Alger credited G. F. Secchi de Casale, editor of the New York newspaper *L'Eco d'Italia*, with helping him to reveal the cruel mistreatment of young Italian street musicians.

36 "4-F for 1-A Sinatra Puts Swoon Crooner Back in High-C Gear," *Brooklyn Eagle*, December 9, 1943, 1.

37 Earl Wilson, "It Happened Last Night," *New York Post*, August 7, 1947; Westbrook Pegler, "As Pegler Sees It," King Features, in *Kingston (NY) Daily Freeman*, September 12, 1947, 4.

38 *From Here to Eternity*, directed by Fred Zinnemann (Hollywood, CA: Columbia Pictures Corporation, 1953).

39 *High Society*, directed by Charles Walters (Culver City, CA: Metro-Goldwyn-Mayer Studios, 1956); Martha Weinman, "High Jinks in High Society," *Collier's*, June 8, 1956, 32. For Barry as an Irish Catholic writer intrigued by the rich, see Shannon, *The American Irish*, 281–88.

40 Sinatra, *Frank Sinatra, My Father*, 170–71.

41 Hamill, *Why Sinatra Matters*, 24.

CHAPTER 12. LOVE STORIES

1 1915 New York State Census for Adelina Petrosino, Brooklyn, Assembly District 9.

2 Author interview with Susan Burke, September 16, 2013.

3 Deanna L. Pagnini and S. Philip Morgan, "Intermarriage and Social Distance among U.S. Immigrants at the Turn of the Century," *American Journal of Sociology* 96 (September 1990): 405–32.

4 "Assimilation of the Italian," *New York Sun*, April 2, 1899, 7; Thomas Jesse Jones, *The Sociology of a New York City Block* (New York: Columbia University Press, 1904), 27.

5 Franklin, "The Italian in America," 78–80.

6 Julius Drachsler, *Democracy and Assimilation: The Blending of Immigrant Heritages in America* (New York: Macmillan, 1920), 42, citing H. B. Woolston, "Rating the

Nations," *American Journal of Sociology* (July 1916–May 1917): 281–390; E. A. Ross, "Racial Consequences of Immigration," in *Selected Articles on Immigration*, ed. M. K. Reely (New York: H. W. Wilson, 1915), 72; "Edward Alsworth Ross," American Sociological Association, http://www.asanet.org/about/presidents/Edward_Ross. cfm, accessed February 23, 2014.

7 Elizabeth G. Messina, "Perversions of Knowledge," in *Anti-Italianism: Essays on a Prejudice*, ed. William J. Connell and Fred Gardaphé (New York: Palgrave Macmillan, 2010), 49–55.

8 Silvano M. Tomasi, "The Ethnic Church and the Integration of Italian Immigrants in the United States," in *The Italian Experience in the United States*, ed. Silvano M. Tomasi and Madeline H. Engel (New York: Center for Migration Studies, 1970), 163–64.

9 Julius Drachsler, *Intermarriage in New York City: A Statistical Study of the Amalgamation of the European Peoples* (1921; reprint, New York: AMS, 1968), 118–20. Drachsler died of tuberculosis at the age of thirty-seven in 1927, ill for the last five years of his life. "Julius Drachsler, Sociologist, Dead," *New York Times*, July 23, 1937, 13.

10 Israel Zangwill, *The Melting-Pot* (New York: American Jewish Book Company, 1921), http://www.gutenberg.org/files/23893/23893-h/23893-h.htm, accessed February 23, 2014.

11 1880 U.S. Census for William Cronin, Manhattan, Enumeration District 615; 1940 U.S. Census for Gerard Cronin, Brooklyn, Enumeration District 24–1214B.

12 Author interview with Linda Cronin-Gross, November 8, 2013.

13 Richard Gambino, *Blood of My Blood: The Dilemma of the Italian Americans* (Toronto: Guernica, 2003), 1–41; Andrew M. Greeley, *Why Can't They Be Like Us? America's White Ethnic Groups* (New York: Dutton, 1971), 31.

14 Lord, Trevor, and Barrows, *The Italian in America*, 68–69; "The Italo-American: A Protest against a Prevailing Prejudice," *New York Times*, April 22, 1905, BR259; *New York Tribune*, April 20, 1905, 6; "Italians for Southern States," *Richmond (VA) Times Dispatch*, October 31, 1905, 7.

15 Ruby Jo Reeves Kennedy, "Single or Triple Melting-Pot? Intermarriage in New Haven, 1870–1950," *American Journal of Sociology* 58 (July 1952): 56–59, http://www.jstor.org/stable/2771794, accessed July 20, 2013; Herberg, *Protestant—Catholic—Jew*; Milton L. Barron, "Intermediacy: Conceptualization of Irish Status in America," *Social Forces* 27 (March 1949): 256–63.

16 Glazer and Moynihan, *Beyond the Melting Pot*, 204.

17 Greeley, *Why Can't They Be Like Us?*, 63, 66, 73, 77–79, 135.

18 Abramson, *Ethnic Diversity in Catholic America*, 66, 206, 209.

19 Nicholas J. Russo, "The Religious Acculturation of Italians in New York City" (Ph.D. diss., St. John's University, 1968), 231–32.

20 Abramson, *Ethnic Diversity in Catholic America*, 97.

21 Russo, "Religious Acculturation," 295. See also Glazer and Moynihan, *Beyond the Melting Pot*, 203–4.

22 *United States v. Ghagat Singh Thind*, 261 U.S. 204 (1923). Ronald H. Bayor writes that ethnic identity persisted well into the postwar period, and that a white identity does not wash away ethnic characteristics and differences. He notes that Joshua M. Zeitz makes this argument also in *White Ethnic New York: Jews, Catholics and the Shaping of*

Postwar Politics (Chapel Hill: University of North Carolina Press, 2007), 5; Ronald H. Bayor, "Another Look at 'Whiteness': The Persistence of Ethnicity in American Life," *Journal of American Ethnic History* 29 (Fall 2009): 13–30. For the history of how the Irish and Italians came to be seen as "white," see Roediger, *Working toward Whiteness*; and Noel Ignatiev, *How the Irish Became White* (New York: Routledge, 1995).

23 Russo, "Religious Acculturation," 260–61, 281–82, 285; Zeitz, *White Ethnic New York*, 78; Mary C. Waters, *Ethnic Options: Choosing Identities in America* (Berkeley: University of California Press, 1990), 110–14.

24 Sewell Chan, "White Ethnic Politics: Irish and Italian Catholics and Jews, Oh, My!," *City Room* (blog), *New York Times*, October 25, 2007, http://cityroom.blogs.nytimes.com/2007/10/25/white-ethnic-politics-irish-and-italian-catholics-and-jews-oh-my/?_r=0, accessed December 6, 2013.

25 Author interview with Mary Macchiarola, September 16, 2014.

26 Stanley Lieberson and Mary C. Waters, *From Many Strands: Ethnic and Racial Groups in Contemporary America* (New York: Russell Sage, 1988), 173. Their study is significant because it accounts for the fact that there are many more Americans who claim Irish ancestry than Italian. The in-marriage rate for both Irish American and Italian American women is the same, 39.5 percent, but Lieberson and Waters factored in that nearly 18 percent of American men claimed Irish descent, while only 5 percent claimed Italian. This is why the overall percentage of Italians marrying an Irish partner does not equal the percentage of Irish marrying an Italian partner.

27 Ibid., 234–35.

28 *Newtown (CT) Bee*, May 12, 1905. The author thanks Jim Bradley for sharing his thorough research of the Bradley family's genealogy.

29 "Wards Island Park," New York City Department of Parks and Recreation, http://www.nycgovparks.org/parks/wardsislandpark/history, accessed February 28, 2014.

30 Cecil Johnson, "Around the Borough," *Brooklyn Eagle*, October 3, 1951, 23.

31 John O'Beirne Ranelagh, email to author, October 11, 2013. He is the couple's son and author of *A Short History of Ireland* (Cambridge: Cambridge University Press, 1994).

32 Anne O'Neill-Barna, *Himself and I* (New York: Citadel, 1957).

33 "Easter Rising: Rebel Songs," BBC, http://www.bbc.co.uk/history/british/easterrising/songs/rso4.shtml, accessed February 28, 2014; Raymond Daly and Derek Warfield, *Celtic and Ireland in Song and Story* (n.p.: Raymond Daly and Derek Warfield, 2008), 193–96. Warfield is a Dublin musician well known for both playing and expounding on traditional Irish music.

34 Author interview with Marie Bradley, December 15, 2009.

CHAPTER 13. FOOD AND FAMILY

1 *New York Tribune*, December 6, 1903, illustrated supplement, 5.

2 *New York Herald Tribune*, April 21, 1939, quoted in John F. Mariani, *How Italian Food Conquered the World* (New York: Palgrave Macmillan, 2012), 45.

3 "BBC Fools the Nation," BBC, http://news.bbc.co.uk/onthisday/hi/dates/stories/april/1/newsid_2819000/2819261.stm, accessed December 23, 2013.

4 *The Caddy*, directed by Norman Taurog (Hollywood, CA: Paramount Studios, 1953).

5 McGoldrick, Giordano, and Garcia-Preto, *Ethnicity and Family Therapy*; Kathryn P. Alessandria and Maria A. Kopacz, "Incorporating Culture in Mental Health

Treatment of Italian Americans," in *Benessere Psicologico: Contemporary Thought on Italian American Mental Health*, ed. Dominick Carielli and Joseph Grosso (New York: John D. Calandra Italian American Institute, 2013), 79–81.

6 McGoldrick, Giordano, and Garcia-Preto, *Ethnicity and Family Therapy*, 525, citing Monica McGoldrick and Michael Rohrbaugh, "Researching Ethnic Family Stereotypes," *Family Process* 26 (March 1987): 89–98.

7 Hasia R. Diner, *Hungering for America: Italian, Irish, and Jewish Foodways in the Age of Migration* (Cambridge: Harvard University Press, 2001), 84–85; Richard D. Alba, *Ethnic Identity: The Transformation of White America* (New Haven: Yale University Press, 1990), 86–87.

8 McAdoo, *Guarding a Great City*, 149.

9 Chan, "White Ethnic Politics."

10 Pete Hamill, *North River: A Novel* (New York: Little, Brown, 2007).

11 Diner, *Hungering for America*, 79; Alba, *Ethnic Identity*, 92.

12 Author interview with Mary Macchiarola, September 16, 2014.

13 Monica McGoldrick, "Irish Families," in McGoldrick, Giordano, and Garcia-Preto, *Ethnicity and Family Therapy*, 600–601; Jennifer Nugent Duffy, *Who's Your Paddy? Racial Expectations and the Struggle for Irish American Identity* (New York: New York University Press, 2014), 95–99, 109.

14 Greeley, *Ethnicity in the United States*, 99; Gambino, *Blood of My Blood*, 148–49.

15 See Bayor, "Another Look at 'Whiteness.'"

16 Alba, *Ethnic Identity*, 193–94.

17 Greeley, *Why Can't They Be Like Us?*, 77; Joe Giordano, Monica McGoldrick, and Joanne Guarino Klages, "Italian Families," in McGoldrick, Giordano, and Garcia-Preto, *Ethnicity and Family Therapy*, 620–23.

18 *Everybody Loves Raymond* (1996–2005), created by Philip Rosenthal (New York: HBO Home Video, 2007); *Encyclopædia Britannica Online*, s.v. "Ray Romano," http://www.britannica.com.ez-proxy.brooklyn.cuny.edu:2048/EBchecked/topic/914846/Ray-Romano, accessed March 2, 2014.

19 Zachary Pincus Roth, "Phil Rosenthal, Creator of *Everybody Loves Raymond*, on His Journey through the World of Food," *LA Weekly*, April 26, 2012, http://www.laweekly.com/2012-04-26/eat-drink/phil-rosenthal-everybody-loves-raymond/.

20 Molly Beth Martin, "More Than Luck," *American Jewish Life*, January–February 2007, http://www.ajlmagazine.com/content/012007/books-rosenthal.html.

21 McGoldrick, Giordano, and Garcia-Preto, *Ethnicity and Family Therapy*, 620–21.

22 Author interview with Susan Burke, September 16, 2013.

23 Foerster, *The Italian Emigration of Our Times*, 95.

24 Hasia R. Diner, *Erin's Daughters in America: Irish Immigrant Women in the Nineteenth Century* (Baltimore: Johns Hopkins University Press, 1983), 140–41.

25 Foerster, *The Italian Emigration of Our Times*, 96; Gambino, *Blood of My Blood*, 14.

26 McGoldrick, Giordano, and Garcia-Preto, *Ethnicity and Family Therapy*, 601–3.

27 Miriam G. Vosburgh and Richard N. Juliani, "Contrasts in Ethnic Family Patterns: The Irish and the Italians," *Journal of Comparative Family Studies* 21 (Summer 1990): 278–82. They use samples of Irish and Italian Catholics from the General Social Survey done between 1972 and 1984. See also Greeley, *Ethnicity in the United States*, 95; and Zeitz, *White Ethnic New York*, 78–84. Zeitz contrasts the Irish and Italians with Jewish parents' greater permission for intellectual and personal freedom.

28 Glenn Collins, "Relationships: Ethnic Nuances in Therapy," *New York Times*, February 28, 1983, B5; McGoldrick, Giordano, and Garcia-Preto, *Ethnicity and Family Therapy*, 27.

29 *Saturday Night Fever*, directed by John Badham (Hollywood, CA: Paramount, 1977).

30 1930 U.S. Census for Andrew McLaughlin, Bronx, Assembly District 2; "Sisters Obituaries 2014," Dominican Sisters of Sparkill, http://www.sparkill.org/Public/membership/2014obituaries.html, accessed March 3, 2014; "Sister Mary McLaughlin, OP," *Nyack (NY) Patch*, February 13, 2014, http://nyack.patch.com/groups/obituaries/p/sister-mary-mclaughlin-op, accessed March 3, 2014; Sr. Maureen E. Foye, O.P., email to author, March 6, 2014.

31 Richard D. Alba, John R. Logan, and Kyle Crowder, "White Ethnic Neighborhoods and Assimilation: The Greater New York Region, 1980–1990," *Social Forces* 75, no. 3 (March 1997): 896–97.

32 For a good overview of the sociological writings on this subject, see Vosburgh and Juliani, "Contrasts in Ethnic Family Patterns," 269–72. For a sociologist's views on historians' whiteness studies, see Richard Alba, "Whiteness Just Isn't Enough," *Sociological Forum* 22 (June 2007): 232–41.

33 "CC: Jokes," http://jokes.cc.com/funny-food-jokes/8678pp/irish-eats-italian and http://jokes.cc.com/funny-god-jokes/xeop70/jesus—multi-ethnicity, accessed June 10, 2014.

CHAPTER 14. SHARING THE BASTIONS OF POWER

1 Author interview with Frank DeRosa, March 7, 2014; George W. Cornell, "Brooklyn, Biggest U.S. Diocese, Gets Bishop Who Doesn't Dodge Change," *Utica (NY) Daily Press* via Associated Press, September 7, 1968, 7; "New Brooklyn Bishop: Francis John Mugavero," *New York Times*, July 18, 1968, 30.

2 Glazer and Moynihan, *Beyond the Melting Pot*, 204.

3 Nelli, *From Immigrants to Ethnics*; Richard Severo, "New York's Italians: A Question of Identity," *New York Times*, November 9, 1970, 43.

4 Patrick McNamara, email to author, March 9, 2011; Humphrey J. Desmond, *Why God Loves the Irish* (New York: Devin-Adair, 1918), 58.

5 Paul Vitello, "Hoping for a Latino Archbishop, in Due Course," *New York Times*, March 3, 2009, 19.

6 Zeitz, *White Ethnic New York*, 95–96; Chris McNickle, *To Be Mayor of New York* (New York: Columbia University Press, 1993), 55, 83.

7 Madeleine Loeb, "First Lady Is Deluged by Good Wishes from Every Side," *New York Times*, September 5, 1950, 9; "Inner Circle Show Depicts City 'Haul,'" *New York Times*, March 4, 1951, 77.

8 Putnam and Campbell, *American Grace*, 82–88.

9 Glazer and Moynihan, *Beyond the Melting Pot*, 202–3.

10 Zeitz, *White Ethnic New York*, 110; Thomas A. Kselman and Steven Avella, "Marian Piety and the Cold War in the United States," *Catholic Historical Review* 72, no. 3 (July 1986): 411–12.

11 McNickle, *To Be Mayor of New York*, 175, 208; Peter Kihss, "How Voter Swings Elected Lindsay," *New York Times*, November 4, 1965, 1; Zeitz, *White Ethnic New York*, 176.

12 Vincent J. Cannato, *The Ungovernable City: John Lindsay and His Struggle to Save New York* (New York: Basic Books, 2001), 165–88; Thomas R. Brooks, "25,000 Police against the Review Board," *New York Times*, October 16, 1966, 253; Bernard Weinraub, "Lindsay Attacks Board Opponents," *New York Times*, November 7, 1966, 51; Paul Hoffman, "Review Board Is a Central Issue and Candidates Court Minorities," *New York Times*, November 6, 1966, 80; McNickle, *To Be Mayor of New York*, 215.

13 David W. Abbott, Louis H. Gold, and Edward T. Rogowsky, *Police, Politics and Race: The New York City Referendum on Civilian Review* (New York: American Jewish Committee and Joint Center for Urban Studies of Massachusetts Institute of Technology and Harvard University, 1969), 14, 43.

14 Paul Moses, "Blizzard of '96," *Newsday*, January 9, 1996, 3.

15 Jerome Krase, "Giuliani's Italianness" (lecture presented at Hofstra University, November 27, 2012), https://www.youtube.com/watch?v=d7_E6Iq8HcE (Vito DeSimone TV Productions, 2013), accessed March 23, 2014.

16 Luke Salim, "Brothers of the Christian Schools," *Catholic Education*, December 2007, 190.

17 Wayne Barrett, assisted by Adam Fifield, *Rudy! An Investigative Biography of Rudy Giuliani* (New York: Basic Books, 2000), 17–19, 28–41; Andrew Kirtzman, *Rudy Giuliani: Emperor of the City* (New York: William Morrow, 2000), 18.

18 1920 U.S. Census for Frank MacMahon, Elmira, NY, District 3.

19 Author interview with Peter J. Powers, March 10, 2014.

20 Anthony Julian Tamburri, "Italian America and September 11, 2001," *i-italy*, September 18, 2011, http://www.i-italy.org/18145/ italian-america-and-september-11–2001.

21 Rod Dreher, "Ground Zero's Blessed Cross," *New York Post*, October 5, 2001, 20.

22 Rudy Giuliani at Manhattan College, Bronx, NY, September 9, 2011, available at http://www.youtube.com/watch?v=z05n24GgCOA, accessed March 23, 2014. Due to various communication failures, many firefighters inside the towers did not receive vital information. See Jim Dwyer and Michelle O'Donnell, "9/11 Firefighters Told of Isolation amid Disaster," *New York Times*, September 9, 2005, 1; and U.S. National Commission on Terrorist Attacks upon the United States, *9/11 Commission Report: The Official Report of the 9/11 Commission and Related Publications*, by Thomas H. Kean and Lee Hamilton (Washington, DC: GPO, 2004), 297.

23 McAdoo, *Guarding a Great City*, 262.

CONCLUSION

1 Michael Lipka and Jessica Martinez, "Catholic Leaders Urge Immigration Reform," Pew Research Center, September 6, 2013, http://www.pewresearch.org/fact-tank/2013/09/06/ demographics-play-role-in-catholic-leaders-push-for-immigration-bill/. The poll aggregated data from surveys taken in January 2012 and March 2013.

2 Richard Alba, *Blurring the Color Line: The New Chance for a More Integrated America* (Cambridge: Harvard University Press, 2009), 16.

3 U.S. Bureau of the Census, Daphne Lofquist, Terry Lugaila, Martin O'Connell and Sarah Feliz, *Households and Families: 2010, 2010 Census Briefs*, April 25, 2012, http://www.census.gov/newsroom/releases/archives/2010_census/cb12–68.html.

4 "Irican," Urban Dictionary, www.urbandictionary.com, accessed April 18, 2014.

5 Alba, *Blurring the Color Line*, 74–75, 204–5, 238–40. See also Richard D. Alba and Victor Nee, *Remaking the American Mainstream: Assimilation and Contemporary Immigration* (Cambridge: Harvard University Press, 2003), 287–92.

6 Alba, *Blurring the Color Line*, 74–75, 238–40. See Paul Taylor, *The Next America* (New York: PublicAffairs, 2014); and "The Next America," Pew Research Center, April 10, 2014, http://www.pewresearch.org/next-america/.

BIBLIOGRAPHY

Abramson, Harold J. *Ethnic Diversity in Catholic America*. New York: Wiley, 1973.

Alba, Richard D. *Blurring the Color Line: The New Chance for a More Integrated America*. Cambridge: Harvard University Press, 2009.

———. *Ethnic Identity: The Transformation of White America*. New Haven: Yale University Press, 1990.

———. *Italian Americans: Into the Twilight of Ethnicity*. Englewood Cliffs, NJ: Prentice Hall, 1985.

Alba, Richard D., John R. Logan, and Kyle Crowder. "White Ethnic Neighborhoods and Assimilation: The Greater New York Region, 1980–1990." *Social Forces* 75 (March 1997): 883–912. http://www.jstor.org/stable/2580523. Accessed July 20, 2013.

Alba, Richard D., and Victor Nee. *Remaking the American Mainstream: Assimilation and Contemporary Immigration*. Cambridge: Harvard University Press, 2003.

Alger, Horatio, Jr. *Phil the Fiddler*. New York, 1872.

Anbinder, Tyler. *Five Points: The 19th-Century New York City Neighborhood That Invented Tap Dance, Stole Elections and Became the World's Most Notorious Slum*. New York: Free Press, 2001.

Asbury, Herbert. *The Gangs of New York: An Informal History of the Underworld*. New York: Knopf, 1928.

Baldassaro, Lawrence. *Beyond DiMaggio: Italian Americans in Baseball*. With a foreword by Dom DiMaggio. Lincoln: University of Nebraska Press, 2011.

Barnes, Charles B. *The Longshoremen*. New York: Survey Associates, 1915.

Barrett, James R. *The Irish Way: Becoming American in the Multiethnic City*. New York: Penguin, 2012.

Barrett, James R., and David R. Roediger. "The Irish and the 'Americanization' of the 'New Immigrants' in the Streets and in the Churches of the Urban United States, 1900–1930." *Journal of American Ethnic History* 24 (Summer 2005): 3–33. http://www.jstor.org/stable/27501633. Accessed August 1, 2014.

Baxandall, Rosalyn Fraad. *Words on Fire: The Life and Writings of Elizabeth Gurley Flynn*. New Brunswick: Rutgers University Press, 1987.

Bayor, Ronald H. "Another Look at 'Whiteness': The Persistence of Ethnicity in American Life." *Journal of American Ethnic History* 29 (Fall 2009): 13–30.

———. *Fiorello La Guardia: Ethnicity and Reform*. Arlington Heights, IL: Harlan Davidson, 1993.

———. *Neighbors in Conflict: The Irish, Germans, Jews and Italians of New York City, 1929–1941.* Urbana: University of Illinois Press, 1988.

Bayor, Ronald H., and Timothy J. Meagher, eds. *The New York Irish.* Baltimore: Johns Hopkins University Press, 1996.

Bellerini, Raffaele. "Delle condizioni religiose degli emigrati italiani negli Stati Uniti d'America." *Civilta Cattolica* 11 (1888): 641–53.

Berger, Meyer. "Lady in Crepe." Pts. 1 and 2. *New Yorker,* October 5, 1935, 28–32; October 12, 1935, 25–29.

Berkeley, G. F.-H. *The Irish Battalion in the Papal Army of 1860.* Dublin: Talbot, 1929.

Binder, Frederick M., and David M. Reimers. *All the Nations under Heaven: An Ethnic and Racial History of New York City.* New York: Columbia University Press, 1995.

Brown, Mary Elizabeth. *Churches, Communities, and Children: Italian Immigrants in the Archdiocese of New York, 1880–1945.* New York: Center for Migration Studies, 1995.

———. "Italian and Italian-American Secular Clergy in the Archdiocese of New York, 1880–1950." *U.S. Catholic Historian* 6 (Fall 1987): 281–300.

———. "The Making of Italian-American Catholics: Jesuit Work on the Lower East Side, New York, 1890's–1950's." *Catholic Historical Review* 73 (April 1987): 195–210.

Burrows, Edwin G., and Mike Wallace. *Gotham: A History of New York City to 1898.* New York: Oxford University Press, 1999.

Butler, Richard J., and Joseph Driscoll. *Dock Walloper: The Story of "Big Dick" Butler.* New York: Putnam's, 1933.

Camp, Helen C. *Iron in Her Soul: Elizabeth Gurley Flynn and the American Left.* Pullman: Washington State University Press, 1995.

Cannato, Vincent J. *The Ungovernable City: John Lindsay and His Struggle to Save New York.* New York: Basic, 2001.

Carey, Arthur A. *Memoirs of a Murder Man.* Garden City, NY: Doubleday, 1930.

Carielli, Dominick, and Joseph Grosso, eds. *Benessere Psicologico: Contemporary Thought on Italian American Mental Health.* New York: John D. Calandra Italian American Institute, 2013.

Connell, William J., and Fred Gardaphé, eds. *Anti-Italianism: Essays on a Prejudice.* New York: Palgrave Macmillan, 2010.

Corrao, Francis L. *Shall Brooklyn Have Four Years More of Injustice, and Unchecked Crime? Part of the Record of the District Attorney's Office of Kings County.* Brooklyn: n.p., 1911.

Cuneo, Ernest. *Life with Fiorello: A Memoir by Ernest Cuneo.* New York: Macmillan, 1955.

Czitrom, Daniel. "Underworlds and Underdogs: Big Tim Sullivan and Metropolitan Politics in New York." *Journal of American History* 78 (September 1991): 536–58. http://www.jstor.org/stable/2079533. Accessed July 1, 2014.

Dash, Mike. *The First Family: Terror, Extortion and the Birth of the American Mafia.* London: Simon and Schuster, 2009.

DiGiovanni, Stephen Michael. *Archbishop Corrigan and the Italian Immigrants.* Huntington, IN: Our Sunday Visitor, 1994.

Diner, Hasia R. *Erin's Daughters in America: Irish Immigrant Women in the Nineteenth Century.* Baltimore: Johns Hopkins University Press, 1983.

———. *Hungering for America: Italian, Irish and Jewish Foodways in the Age of Migration.* Cambridge: Harvard University Press, 2001.

Dolan, Jay P. *The Irish Americans: A History.* New York: Bloomsbury, 2008.

Drachsler, Julius. *Democracy and Assimilation: The Blending of Immigrant Heritages in America.* New York: Macmillan, 1920.

———. *Intermarriage in New York City: A Statistical Study of the Amalgamation of the European Peoples.* 1921. Reprint, New York: AMS, 1968.

Duffy, Jennifer Nugent. *Who's Your Paddy? Racial Expectations and the Struggle for Irish American Identity.* New York: New York University Press, 2014.

Edwards, R. Dudley, ed. *Ireland and the Italian Risorgimento.* Dublin: Italian Institute, 1960.

English, T. J. *Paddy Whacked: The Untold Story of the Irish American Gangster.* New York: Regan Books, 2005.

Femminella, Francis X., ed. *Italians and Irish in America: Proceedings of the Sixteenth Annual Conference of the American Italian Historical Association.* Staten Island, NY: American Italian Historical Association, 1985.

Fenton, Edward. "Immigrants and Unions: A Case Study; Italians and American Labor, 1870–1920." Ph.D. diss., Harvard University, 1957; reprint, New York: Arno, 1975.

Fisher, James T. *On the Irish Waterfront: The Crusader, the Movie and the Soul of the Port of New York.* Ithaca: Cornell University Press, 2009.

Flynn, Edward J. *You're the Boss.* New York: Viking, 1947.

Flynn, Elizabeth Gurley. *The Rebel Girl: An Autobiography, My First Life, 1906–1926.* 1955. Reprint: New York: International Publishers, 1979.

Flynn, William J. *The Barrel Mystery.* New York: McCann, 1919.

Foerster, Robert F. *The Italian Emigration of Our Times.* Cambridge: Harvard University Press, 1919.

Fowler, Gene. *Beau James: The Life and Times of Jimmy Walker.* New York: Viking, 1949.

Gallagher, Dorothy. *All the Right Enemies: The Life and Murder of Carlo Tresca.* New Brunswick: Rutgers University Press, 1988.

Gambino, Richard. *Blood of My Blood: The Dilemma of the Italian Americans.* Toronto: Guernica, 2003.

Gavazzi, Alessandro. *Father Gavazzi's Lectures in New York, reported in full by T. C. Leland, phonographer; also, The Life of Father Gavazzi, corrected and authorized by himself; together with reports of his addresses in Italian, to his countrymen in New York, translated and revised by Madame Julie de Marguerittes.* New York: DeWitt and Davenport, 1858.

Giddins, Gary. *Bing Crosby, a Pocketful of Dreams: The Early Years, 1903–1940.* Boston: Little, Brown, 2001.

Glazer, Nathan, and Daniel Patrick Moynihan. *Beyond the Melting Pot: The Negroes, Puerto Ricans, Jews, Italians and Irish of New York City.* Cambridge: MIT Press, 1963.

Golway, Terry. *Machine Made: Tammany Hall and the Creation of Modern American Politics.* New York: Liveright, 2014.

Greeley, Andrew M. *Ethnicity in the United States: A Preliminary Reconnaissance.* New York: Wiley, 1974.

———. *Why Can't They Be Like Us? America's White Ethnic Groups.* New York: Dutton, 1971.

Gribetz, Louis J., and Joseph Kaye. *Jimmy Walker: Story of a Personality.* New York: Dial, 1932.

Guglielmo, Jennifer. *Living the Revolution: Italian Women's Resistance and Radicalism in New York City, 1880–1945.* Chapel Hill: University of North Carolina Press, 2010.

Hamill, Pete. *Why Sinatra Matters.* Boston: Little, Brown, 1998.

Hassard, John R. G. *Life of the Most Reverend John Hughes, D.D., First Archbishop of New York.* New York: Appleton, 1866.

Herberg, Will. *Protestant—Catholic—Jew: An Essay in American Religious Sociology.* Garden City, NY: Doubleday, 1955.

House of Commons. *Report from the Select Committee on Destitution (Gweedore and Clougha-neely) Together with the Proceedings of the Committee, Minutes of Evidence, Appendix, and Index.* 1858.

Ignatiev, Noel. *How the Irish Became White.* New York: Routledge, 1995.

Jacobson, Matthew Frye. *Whiteness of a Different Color: European Immigrants and the Alchemy of Race.* Cambridge: Harvard University Press, 1999.

Kaplan, James. *Frank.* New York: Doubleday, 2010.

Kehoe, Lawrence, ed. *Complete Works of the Most Reverend John Hughes, D.D.* New York: Lawrence Kehoe, 1866.

Kennedy, Ruby Jo Reeves, "Single or Triple Melting-Pot? Intermarriage in New Haven, 1870–1950." *American Journal of Sociology* 58 (July 1952): 56–59.

Kessner, Thomas. *Fiorello H. La Guardia and the Making of Modern New York.* New York: McGraw-Hill, 1989.

———. *The Golden Door: Italian and Jewish Immigrant Mobility in New York City, 1880–1915.* New York: Oxford University Press, 1977.

Kimeldorf, Howard. *Reds or Rackets? The Making of Radical and Conservative Unions on the Waterfront.* Berkeley: University of California Press, 1988.

Krase, Jerome, and Judith N. DeSena, eds. *Italian Americans in a Multicultural Society: Proceedings of the Symposium of the American Italian Historical Society.* Stony Brook, NY: Forum Italicum, 1993.

La Guardia, Fiorello H. *The Making of an Insurgent: An Autobiography, 1882–1919.* Philadelphia: Lippincott, 1947.

Lardner, James, and Thomas Reppetto. *NYPD: A City and Its Police.* New York: Henry Holt, 2000.

Lee, J. J., and Marion R. Casey, eds. *Making the Irish American: History and Heritage of the Irish in the United States.* New York: New York University Press, 2006.

Levinson, Peter J. *Tommy Dorsey: Livin' in a Great Big Way.* New York: Da Capo, 2005.

Lieberson, Stanley, and Mary C. Waters. *From Many Strands: Ethnic and Racial Groups in Contemporary America.* New York: Russell Sage, 1988.

Lord, Eliot, John J. D. Trevor, and Samuel June Barrows. *The Italian in America.* New York: Benjamin F. Buck, 1905.

Lowi, Theodore J. *At the Pleasure of the Mayor: Patronage and Power in New York City, 1898–1951.* London: Macmillan, 1964.

Lynch, Bernard J. "Italians in NY." *Catholic World* 45 (April 1888): 67–73.

Mann, Arthur. *La Guardia Comes to Power: 1933.* Philadelphia: Lippincott, 1965.

Mariani, John F. *How Italian Food Conquered the World.* With a foreword by Lidia Bastianich. New York: Palgrave Macmillan, 2012.

Marraro, Howard. *American Opinion on the Unification of Italy.* New York: Columbia University Press, 1932.

McAdoo, William. *Guarding a Great City.* New York: Harper, 1906.

McCaffery, Michael J. A. *The Siege of Spoleto: A Camp-Tale of Arlington Heights.* New York: P. O'Shea, 1864.

McGoldrick, Monica, Joe Giordano, and Nydia Garcia-Preto, eds. *Ethnicity and Family Therapy.* 3rd ed. New York: Guilford, 2005.

McNickle, Chris. *To Be Mayor of New York.* New York: Columbia University Press, 1993.

Memorial of the Most Reverend Michael Augustine Corrigan, D.D. New York: Cathedral Library Association, 1902.

Meyer, Gerald. "Frank Sinatra: The Popular Front and an American Icon." *Science and Society* 66 (Fall 2002): 311–35.

Nelli, Humbert S. *From Immigrants to Ethnics: The Italian Americans*. New York: Oxford University Press, 1983.

Nelson, Bruce. *Divided We Stand: American Workers and the Struggle for Black Equality.* Princeton: Princeton University Press, 2001.

O'Connor, Anne. "'That Dangerous Serpent': Garibaldi and Ireland in the Nineteenth Century." *Modern Italy* 15 (2010): 401–15.

Orsi, Robert A. *The Madonna of 115th Street*. New Haven: Yale University Press, 1985.

Palmieri, Aurelio. "Il clero italiano negli Stati Uniti." *Vita Italiana* 15 (1920): 113–27.

————. "The Contribution of the Italian Catholic Clergy to the United States." *Catholic Builders of the Nation*. Vol. 2, 128–49. Boston: Continental, 1923.

————. *Il grave problema religioso italiano negli Stati Uniti*. Florence: Libreria Editrice Fiorentina, 1921.

————. "Italian Protestantism in the United States." *Catholic World* 107 (May 1918): 179–89.

Parkhurst, A. R., Jr. "The Perils of Petrosino." *Washington Post*, June 28, 1914.

Pernicone, Nunzio. *Carlo Tresca: Portrait of a Rebel*. Oakland: AK Press, 2010.

Pesci, Frank B., Sr., and Frank Alduino, eds. *Italian Americans before Mass Migration: We've Always Been Here*. New York: American Italian Historical Association, 2004.

Petacco, Arrigo. *Joe Petrosino*. New York: Macmillan, 1974.

Pistella, Domenico. *The Crowning of a Queen*. Translated by Peter J. Rofrano. New York: Shrine of Our Lady of Mount Carmel, 1954.

Powderly, Terence V. *The Path I Trod*. New York: Columbia University Press, 1940.

Putnam, Robert D., and David E. Campbell. *American Grace: How Religion Divides and Unites Us*. New York: Simon and Schuster, 2010.

Quinn, Peter A. *Looking for Jimmy: A Search for Irish America*. New York: Overlook, 2007.

Ridley, Jasper. *Garibaldi*. New York: Viking, 1976.

Riis, Jacob. *The Children of the Poor*. New York: Scribner's, 1892.

Riordon, William L. *Plunkitt of Tammany Hall*. New York: McClure, 1905.

Russo, Nicholas J. "The Religious Acculturation of Italians in New York City." Ph.D. diss., St. John's University, 1968.

Shannon, William V. *The American Irish*. London: Macmillan, 1966.

Shaw, Richard. *Dagger John: The Unquiet Life and Times of Archbishop John Hughes of New York*. New York: Paulist, 1977.

Shea, John Gilmary. *Catholic Churches of New York City: Sketches of Their History and Lives of the Present Pastors*. New York: Lawrence G. Goulding, 1878.

Shelley, Thomas J. *The Bicentennial History of the Archdiocese of New York, 1808–2008*. Strasbourg, France: Éditions du Signe, 2007.

————. *Greenwich Village Catholics: St. Joseph's Church and the Evolution of an Urban Faith Community, 1829–2002*. Washington, DC: Catholic University of America Press, 2003.

Signor, Lice Maria. *John Baptist Scalabrini and Italian Migration: A Socio-Pastoral Project*. New York: Center for Migration Studies, 1994.

Sinatra, Nancy. *Frank Sinatra: An American Legend*. Santa Monica, CA: General, 1995.

————. *Frank Sinatra, My Father*. Garden City, NY: Doubleday, 1985.

Smith, John Talbot. *The Catholic Church in New York: A History of the New York Diocese from Its Establishment in 1808 to the Present*. New York: Hall and Locke, 1905.

Stella, Antonio. *Some Aspects of Italian Immigration to the United States.* New York: Putnam's, 1924.

Sullivan, Mary Louise. *Mother Cabrini: "Italian Immigrant of the Century."* New York: Center for Migration Studies, 1992.

Tomasi, Silvano M., ed. *For the Love of Immigrants: Migration Writings and Letters of Bishop John Baptist Scalabrini, 1839–1905,* edited by Silvano Tomasi. New York: Center for Migration Studies, 2000.

———. *Piety and Power: The Role of Italian Parishes in the New York Metropolitan Area, 1880–1930.* New York: Center for Migration Studies, 1975.

Tricarico, Donald. *The Italians of Greenwich Village.* New York: Center for Migration Studies, 1984.

Varacalli, Joseph A., et al., eds. *The Saints in the Lives of Italian-Americans: An Interdisciplinary Investigation.* Stony Brook, NY: Forum Italicum, 1999.

Vecoli, Rudolph J. "Prelates and Peasants: Italian Immigrants and the Catholic Church." *Journal of Social History* 2 (Spring 1969): 217–68. http://www.jstor.org/stable/3786488. Accessed August 1, 2014.

Vosburgh, Miriam G., and Richard N. Juliani. "Contrasts in Ethnic Family Patterns: The Irish and the Italians." *Journal of Comparative Family Studies* 21 (Summer 1990): 269–86.

Waters, Mary C. *Ethnic Options: Choosing Identities in America.* Berkeley: University of California Press, 1990.

Weisz, Howard Ralph. *Irish-American and Italian-American Educational Views and Activities, 1870–1900: A Comparison.* New York: Arno, 1976.

Welch, Richard F. *King of the Bowery: Big Tim Sullivan, Tammany Hall and New York City from the Gilded Age to the Progressive Era.* Madison, NJ: Fairleigh Dickinson University Press, 2008.

Zeitz, Joshua M. *White Ethnic New York: Jews, Catholics and the Shaping of Postwar Politics.* Chapel Hill: University of North Carolina Press, 2007.

Ziegelman, Jane. *97 Orchard: An Edible History of Five Immigrant Families in One New York Tenement.* New York: Harper, 2010.

Zwierlein, Frederick J. *The Life and Letters of Bishop McQuaid.* Rochester, NY: Art Print Shop, 1926.

WEBSITES

Brooklyn Daily Eagle Online, offered by the Brooklyn Public Library. http://eagle.brooklynpubliclibrary.org.

Chronicling America: Historic American Newspapers, presented by the Library of Congress. http://chroniclingamerica.loc.gov.

Historical Census Browser, from the University of Virginia, Geospatial and Statistical Data Center, providing historical U.S. census data. http://mapserver.lib.virginia.edu/.

Italian Genealogical Group, an index of many New York City records, including birth, death, and marriage certificates. http://www.italiangen.org.

Old Fulton NY Post Cards, a searchable database of many New York State newspaper articles. http://www.fultonhistory.com/fulton.html.

Unz.org, a website for periodicals, books, and videos. http://www.unz.org/.

INDEX

ABOUT THE AUTHOR

Paul Moses is Professor of Journalism at Brooklyn College/
CUNY and former city editor of *Newsday*, where he was the
lead writer for a team that won the Pulitzer Prize. His book *The
Saint and the Sultan* won the 2010 Catholic Press Association award
for best history book. He lives in Brooklyn with his wife, Maureen.